Roman Military Disasters

Roman Military Disasters: Dark Days and Lost Legions

By Paul Chrystal

Pen & Sword
MILITARY

First published in Great Britain in 2015 by
Pen & Sword Military
An imprint of
Pen & Sword Books Ltd
47 Church Street
Barnsley
South Yorkshire
S70 2AS

Copyright © Paul Chrystal, 2015

ISBN 978 1 47382 357 0

A CIP catalogue record for this book is
available from the British Library.

Typeset in Ehrhardt by
Replika Press Pvt Ltd, India
Printed and bound in England
By CPI Group (UK) Ltd, Croydon, CR0 4YY

Pen & Sword Books Ltd incorporates the Imprints of Pen & Sword Aviation,
Pen & Sword Family History, Pen & Sword Maritime, Pen & Sword Military,
Pen & Sword Discovery, Pen & Sword Politics, Pen & Sword Atlas, Pen &
Sword Archaeology, Wharncliffe Local History, Wharncliffe True Crime,
Wharncliffe Transport, Pen & Sword Select, Pen & Sword Military Classics,
Leo Cooper, The Praetorian Press, Claymore Press, Remember When,
Seaforth Publishing and Frontline Publishing.

For a complete list of Pen & Sword titles please contact
PEN & SWORD BOOKS LIMITED
47 Church Street, Barnsley, South Yorkshire, S70 2AS, England
E-mail: enquiries@pen-and-sword.co.uk
Website: www.pen-and-sword.co.uk

For the late Eric Wright Chrystal

Contents

Acknowledgements

Thanks to my teachers at school and university, firstly for inspiring me in things classical and then for having the patience and skill to nurture that inspiration. They are: John Hogg, of Hartlepool Grammar School, who started it all with *Path to Latin I* and *Civis Romanus*; Dick Jenkinson, Stan Ireland and Tim Ryder at Hull University, who kept it going with *Virgil's Epische Technik*, Roman Britain and purple patches in Cary's *A History of Rome*; their colleagues, the late Frank Norman for Thucydides, Chris Strachan for Thales and Plato, and the late Jeff Hilton for Aeschylus' *Frogs* and Plautus; finally, David Rankin at Southampton University, my MPhil tutor, who gave sound advice on Roman love poets and their women, and some very enjoyable lunches.

I must also thank the following for supplying images: Theresa Calver, Colchester & Ipswich Museum Service, for the magnificent Temple of Claudius artwork on the front cover; Geoff Cook at Cardiff City Hall, for the photograph of the Boudica statue; Professor Tod Bolen at Bibleplaces.com, Santa Clarita, California, for the photos of Jerusalem; Markus Krueger at Digital Park in Lage, Germany, for the Hermann photo; euskadiz.com for the Teutoburg swamp; and The Schiller Inc, Washington, DC, for the Thomas Cole 'Destruction' image: www.theathenaeum.org/art/list.php?m=a&s=du&aid=375

Plates

List of Plates

1. *Brennus and His Share of the Spoils* (1837) by Paul Jamin
2. Figurehead from the French battleship *Brennus*
3. Hannibal looting slaughtered Romans after Cannae
4. Manuscript miniature showing Eleazar killing an elephant
5. Persian scythe-wheeled chariots at Carrhae
6. Statue of the Parthian general Surena
7. Statue of the rebel slave Eunus
8. Statue of Lusitanian guerrilla fighter Viriathus
9. *The Crucified Slaves* (1878) by Fyodor Andreyevich Bronnikov
10. *The Death of Spartacus* (1882) by Herman Vogel
11. Statue of Boudica and her daughters
12. Relief showing Roman soldiers casting lots for Christ's robes
13. Reconstruction of a Roman siege tower, as used at Masada
14. The rampart walk on the East Wall, Jerusalem
15. Frieze fragment showing Roman soldiers in their armour
16. *Germanic Warriors Storm the Field in the Varusschlact* (1909) by Otto Albert Koch
17. *Hermannsdenkmal* (1875), a huge copper monument to Arminius
18. *Das Siegreich Vordringende Hermann* by Peter Janssen (1844–1908)
19. Alaric's river-bed burial after his reluctant sack of Rome
20. The end of the Roman Empire, as depicted by Thomas Cole

Diagrams

List of Diagrams

Maps

List of Maps

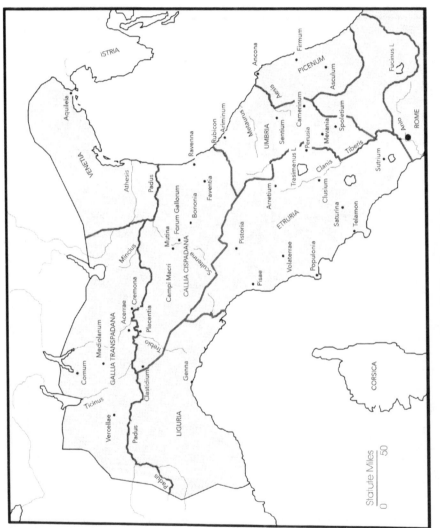

Map 1: Northern Italy

ISTRIA

Aquileia

VENETIA

Athesis

Padus

GALLIA TRANSPADANA

Mediolanum

Comum

Ticinus

Vercellae

Padus

Mincius

Cremona

Acerrae

Placentia

Trebio

Clastidium

Genna

LIGURIA

Padus

Campi Macri

Mutina

Forum Gallorum

Bononia

CALLIA CISPADANA

Scultenna

Faventia

Ravenna

Rubicon

Ariminum

Pistoria

Volaterrae

Pisae

Populonia

Saturnia

Telamon

ETRURIA

Arretium

Clusium

Trasimenus L.

Clanis

Sutrium

Metaurus

UMBRIA

Sentium

Sentium

Aesis

Camerinum

Perusia

Mevania

Spoletium

Tiberis

PICENUM

Firmum

Ancona

Asculum

Fucinus L.

Anio

ROME

CORSICA

Statute Miles

0   50

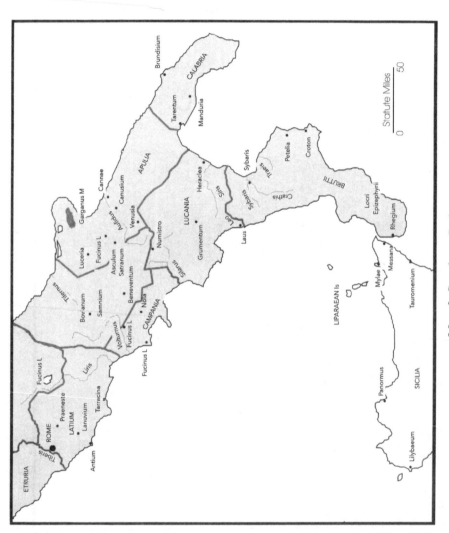

Map 2: Southern Italy

Map 3: North Africa

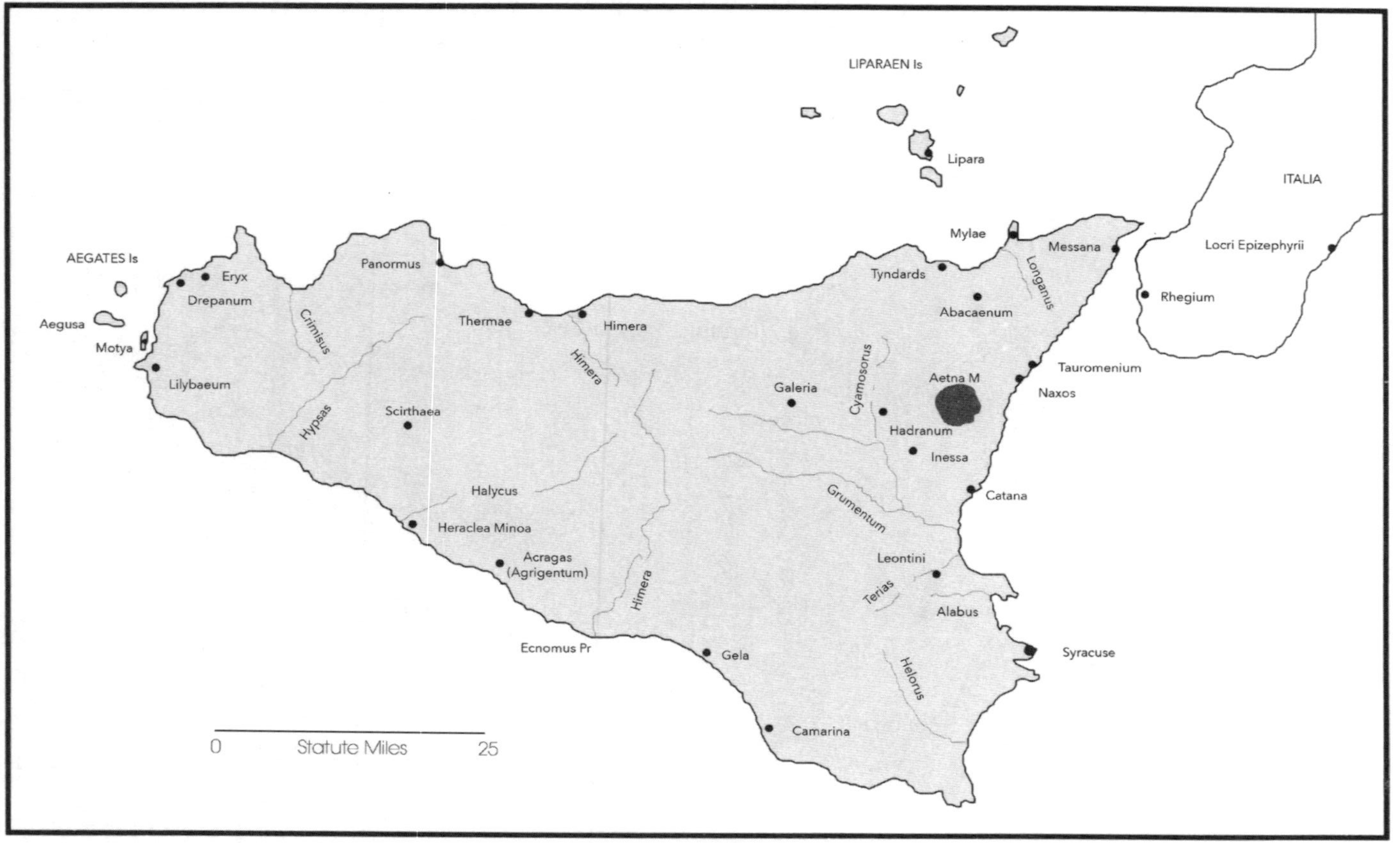

LIPARAEN Is
Lipara
ITALIA
Mylae
Messana
Locri Epizephyrii
AEGATES Is
Eryx
Panormus
Tyndards
Rhegium
Drepanum
Aegusa
Crimisus
Thermae
Himera
Abacaenum
Longanus
Motya
Himera
Tauromenium
Aetna M
Lilybaeum
Galeria
Cyamosorus
Naxos
Hypsas
Scirthaea
Hadranum
Inessa
Halycus
Catana
Grumentum
Heraclea Minoa
Acragas
(Agrigentum)
Leontini
Himera
Terias
Alabus
Ecnomus Pr
Gela
Syracuse
Helorus
Camarina
0
Statute Miles
25

Map 4: Sicily

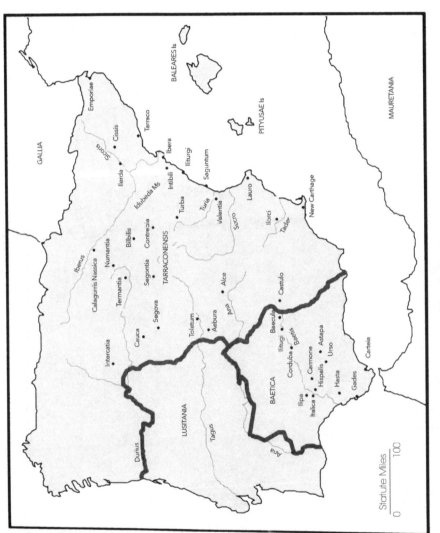

Map 5: Spain

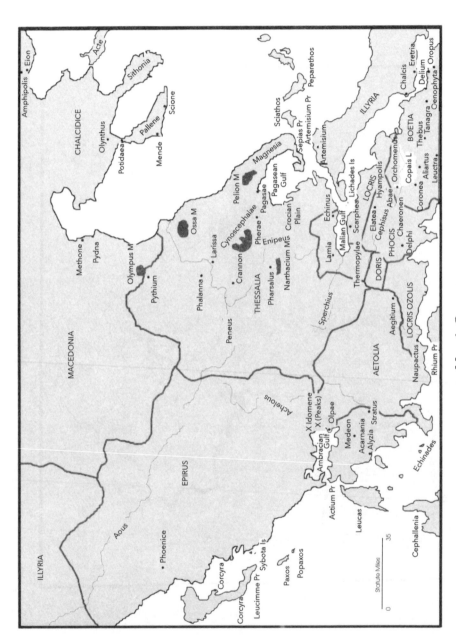

Map 6: Greece

The Near East at the time of the First Romano-Parthian War.

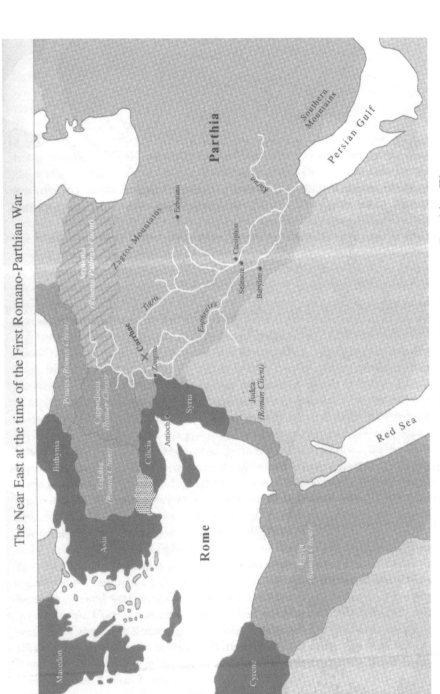

Map 7: The Near East at the Time of the First Romano-Parthian War

Timeline

BC

753 Traditional date for the founding of Rome by Romulus, as given by M. Terentius Varro.

578–535 Traditional dates for Servius Tullius, reputed to have introduced hoplite warfare to Rome (Servian Reform); built Servian Walls around Rome.

535–510 King Tarquinius Superbus – Rome's last king. Rome has control over all Latium.

496 Establishment of the Roman Republic.

496 Romans defeat the Latin League at Battle of Lake Regillus; Treaty of Cassius, *foedus Cassianum*.

494 First *secessio plebis*.

450 Romans defeat the Sabines.

430 Romans defeat the Volsci and Aequi.

400–396 Ten-year siege of Veii; Romans defeat the Etruscans.

390 Gauls sack Rome.

376 Consulship and military commands thrown open to plebeians.

370 Servian Walls rebuilt.

358 Second Treaty of Cassius.

343–341 First Samnite War.

341–338 Great Latin War; Antium taken.

326–304 Second Samnite War; Rome is victorious.

312 Work on Via Appia starts.

298–290 Third Samnite War; Rome wins.

295 Rome defeats the Gauls at Sentinum.

280–275 Pyrrhic War; Pyrrhic victories; Pyrrhus hired by the Tarentines to fight Rome.

264–241 First Punic War.

236 Gates of the Temple of Janus closed for a change; Birth of Scipio Africanus.

229–228 First Illyrian War; Rome wins.

224 Rome massacres Gauls at Battle of Telamon.

220–219 Second Illyrian War; Rome successful.

218–202 Second Punic War.

216 Disaster at Cannae.

215–205 First Macedonian War; Rome defeats Philip V.

213–211 Marcellus takes Syracuse; murder of Archimedes.

198 Second Macedonian War.

197 Philip V beaten at Cynoscephalae.

195 Rome defeats Sparta in Roman–Spartan War.

191–188 Rome defeats Antiochus III and the Aetolian League in Roman–Syrian War.

184 Death of Scipio Africanus.

181–179 First Celtiberian War.

171–168 Macedonian War.

155–139 Romans defeat Lusitanians under Viriathus.

154–151 First Numantine War.

150–146 Fourth Macedonian War.

149–146 Third Punic War; Carthage destroyed.

146–145 Achaean League defeated and Corinth razed in Achaean War.

143–133 Second Numantine War; Numantia destroyed.

135–132 First Servile War.

125–121 Rome victorious in Ligurian War.

121–120 Rome defeats Allobroges and Averni.

113–101 Rome defeats Cimbri and Teutones.

112–106 Jugurthine War.

104 Birth of Pompey.

104–103 Second Servile War; military reforms of Marius.

100 Birth of Julius Caesar.

91–88 Social War.

88–85 First Mithridatic War against Mithridates VI of Pontus.

83–82 First Roman civil war, between Sulla and the popular faction; Second Mithridatic War.

82 Sulla returns to Rome as *dictator.*

74–66 Third Mithridatic War, won by Pompey.

73–71 Servile War led by Spartacus.

67 Pompey drives out the pirates.

63 Fall of Jerusalem; consulship of Cicero; Catiline conspiracy.

60–54 First Triumvirate formed by Gaius Julius Caesar, Pompey and Marcus Licinius Crassus.

58–50 Caesar fights the Gallic Wars.

54–53 Crassus defeated by the Parthians and killed.

49 Caesar crosses the Rubicon and triggers the Second Roman Civil War against the *Optimates*, led by Pompey.

44 Caesar assassinated.

44–42 Third Roman Civil War, between the assassins of Caesar, led by Cassius and Brutus, and Octavian and Mark Antony.

43 Octavian, Antony and Lepidus form the Second Triumvirate.

31 Battle of Actium: Octavian defeats Antony and Cleopatra.

30 Antony and Cleopatra commit suicide; Egypt is now a Roman province.

27 End of the Republic, start of the Roman Empire; Octavian is now Augustus Caesar, the sole ruler of Rome.

AD

6 Judaea becomes a Roman province.

9 Three Roman legions are destroyed by the Germans in the battle of the Teutoburg Forest.

14 Death of Augustus; Tiberius emperor.

43 Claudius invades Britain.

60–61 Boudica, queen of the Iceni, leads a rebellion in Britain.

71–84 Pacification of Britain; conquest of modern Wales and Scotland.

238 Goths sack Roman Histria.

258 Goths invade Asia Minor.

260 Valerian taken captive by the Persians.

284 Diocletian splits the empire into two and appoints Maximian emperor of the West and Diocletian the East.

286 The Theban Legion massacre.

303 Diocletian presides over the persecution of Christians.

376 Greuthungi and Tervingi mass on the banks of the Danube seeking refuge within the Roman empire.

378 Battle of Adrianople; death of Valens.

395 Theodosius dies, leaving the Western Empire to his son Honorius and the Eastern Empire to his other son Arcadius.

397 Treaty between Alaric and Eutropius; Alaric is Roman commander in Illyricum.

405 Treaty between Alaric and Stilicho.

410 Alaric sacks Rome.

411 Alaric dies, succeeded by Athaulf.

412 Honorius informs British provincials that Rome can no longer support them.

Introduction

The natural tendency amongst historians and writers generally when analyzing world superpowers, and the reasons for their superpower status, is to focus on the successes achieved by those superpowers, politically, socially and militarily. After all, these are what made these powerful nations or civilizations superpowers in the first place. However, paradoxically perhaps, reverses and disasters that may have been suffered on the way to superpower status are equally pivotal and significant. The experience of ancient Rome is no different. This book is the first to examine the role military disasters played in the success of Rome – one of the world's greatest superpowers – as a Republic and as an Empire.

The Oxford Concise Dictionary defines 'disaster' as a 'great or sudden misfortune, a complete failure, a person or enterprise ending in failure'. Synonyms include failure, fiasco, catastrophe, calamity, mess, debacle. This book covers disasters in a military and a Roman context. It tells how and why the disasters occurred and how the Romans dealt with the consequences and aftermath of each calamity. It reveals how – apart from the final cataclysm that was the sack of Rome – they were able to rebound to achieve further military and political success. It is commonly believed that the Chinese ideogram for a crisis is the same as the character for opportunity. This has been exposed as a myth, but were it true, then the Romans would have recognized the connection: they frequently made an opportunity out of a military crisis.

History tells us that there are many causes for a military disaster – or put in other words, a devastating defeat or a battle of annihilation. They include blunders by generals (most famously described in Tennyson's *The Charge of the Light Brigade*); inadequate planning and preparation (as at the Somme); poor intelligence (as at Arnhem); confusion (Teutoburg Forest); mutiny (the Indian Mutiny); underestimation of the enemy (Adrianople); misjudgement (as at Cannae); arrogance or sloppy leadership on the part of the commander (as at Carrhae); complacency (Allia River); plain bad luck or, quite simply, a superior foe tactically or in terms of strength (Lake Trasimene). All of Rome's military disasters came as a result of one or other of these.

The ability to learn from military disasters and adapt accordingly is key to subsequent success and hegemony. The Romans, over some 1,200 years, were adept at learning the lessons of failure and adapting to new ways and methods, and it was this facility for flexibility and versatility which kept them in control of the Mediterranean and European worlds for much of that period. Arrian puts it well:

> [the Romans] are happy to pick out useful things all around and adapt them to their own use ... they have taken certain weapons from others and now call them Roman ... they also took military exercises from other peoples.[1]

Roman Military Disasters covers sixty or so decisive and significant defeats; it examines and analyzes the history, politics or strategies which led to each conflict, how and why the Romans were defeated, the tactics deployed, the generals and the casualties. However, the unique and crucial element of the book is its focus on the aftermath and consequences of defeat, and how the lessons learnt enabled the Romans, usually, to bounce back and win subsequent battles and wars. The Roman way of forming alliances and extending reliance on Rome had the absolutely crucial benefit of providing a fathomless source of new recruits; this enabled the Romans to replenish their armies even after crushing defeats like Cannae and Teutoburg Forest, the like of which brought other nations to their knees.

The Roman socio-political system also protected Rome against total annihilation. The dominance of the aristocracy, the senatorial and equestrian elite, provided a ready and self-perpetuating supply of generals and dictators, while the desire for military glory, triumphs and celebrity, and the increasing venality which accompanied the acquisition of more and more booty, kept the Roman war machine ticking over and, usually, in good order. Economics too played its part: as Roman territory expanded, so did the need to acquire more land on which to cultivate the crops needed to feed the growing number of citizens and inhabitants. The early insistence on a land qualification for the military, which, in turn, enabled the farmer or landowner-cum-soldier to pay for his essential weapons and armour, was central to the growth and development of the Roman army. Later, veterans had to be found somewhere to settle. Security too was an ever-present concern: as Rome's borders expanded, so did the need to secure and defend her borders to ensure the safety of the inhabitants, expanding trade and natural resources within. This manifested itself in further expansionism and the recruitment of more troops to man the borders or to invade beyond. Sometimes this caused a military disaster: when it did, it was all the more important to rebound with a vengeance.

The book also provides some useful context, with chapters on the military experience of early Rome and the evolving war machine. Primary sources are, of course, fundamental to any study of this kind: who and what they are and what they tell us, reliably or otherwise, is covered in a separate chapter. There are also helpful sections on various aspects of the Roman military experience, including war elephants, the chariot as an instrument of war, war rape and siegecraft.

Roman Military Disasters covers battles, sackings and sieges between 387 BC and AD 410, from the first real black-day disaster at the River Allia to the equally black sack of Rome by Alaric. Cleopatra was an ongoing disaster for the Romans militarily, politically and socially – for that reason, her intimate involvement with Rome and the fact that she was instrumental militarily in shaping Rome's future after Actium, ensures her inclusion.

Part One: The Republic

Chapter 1

Rome's Peninsular Wars

B efore they suffered their first disaster in 387 BC at the Battle of Allia, the Romans had enjoyed some 366 years of sustained and consistent military success, dating from the traditional founding of Rome in 753 BC.

Early reverses were suffered at Pometia in 502 BC and at Antium in 482 BC, but these were of little significance compared to what was to follow at the River Allia. The Romans' early record of success is a remarkable achievement in itself, particularly when we consider that war was a virtual constant, an inescapable way of life in the monarchy and the early Roman Republic. Of the 250 or so significant battles fought between 500 BC and 100 BC, 200 could be counted as victories. The doors of the Temple of Janus – that all too visible and tangible indicator of Rome's at-war status – stood open for the whole period. There were just three exceptions, when peace broke out for a significant amount of time: Numa Pompilius (Rome's second king after Romulus, 715–673 BC) founded the temple and established the tradition of the doors, and it was he who was first able to close those doors, for the duration of his reign[1]; after the First Punic War, during the consulship of Titus Manlius Torquatus, in 235 BC; and then after Augustus' victory at the battle of Actium.

The serial warmongering is well recorded. First, Josephus, writing in the first century AD, tells us that the Roman people were delivered from the womb bearing weapons. Centuries later, F.E. Adcock echoed these words in a round-about way when he said, 'A Roman was half a soldier from the start, and he would endure a discipline which soon produced the other half.'[2]

So what was the reason for – and the nature of – this constant warring? What was the cause and outcome of these three centuries of near continuous conflict?

The first Romans were an agricultural, pastoral community, living on defendable hilltops and grazing their sheep on the pastures in the valleys and plains below, around the River Tiber. Rome was the product of *synoikism* with other Latin settlements in the valley of the Tiber, a process that began in the seventh century BC. She was the largest of these settlements. Her first conflicts would have been little more than isolated cattle-stealing skirmishes involving hundreds of men at most; defence of the king and the livestock were the main causes of attrition. By the end of the monarchy, in roughly 509 BC, Roman territory would have comprised a small walled city within about 500 square miles of land. Defence was rudimentary, with alarms announcing the proximity of an Etruscan raiding party communicated to compatriots by hoisting a flag on the Janiculum. The army comprised no more than 8,000 men. Strategically, alliances were crucial, and it is with alliances involving one town or another that Rome fought most of her battles against enemy coalitions; from 486 the Hernici were the ally of choice for the Romans. Apart from battles at the Fucine Lake in 406 and against the Volsinii in 392, all of Rome's early wars were fought in the immediate vicinity of the city and on the Latin plain. Rome, then, was but one of many cities embroiled in fighting each other around the River Tiber. Many of her conflicts at this time were fought against the southern Etruscans, especially the Veii; also the Aequi, hill folk from the Aniene valley above Praeneste and Tibur; and the Volsci, who were originally from the Liri valley but had spilled onto the Latin plain to threaten Roman territory. As is often the case with mountain folk, the Volsci and the Aequi were covetous of lower lying, more yielding lands and were anxious to alleviate overcrowding back home and to banish famine and a dearth of cultivable land. They were to cause Rome much irritation with their raids and incursions in the fifth and fourth centuries BC. By now, though, Rome herself needed more land, and more fertile land at that; expansion and annexations continued apace to achieve this.

In the twenty-four years between 440 and 416, there were only ten years in which the Roman army was not fighting; in the next twenty-four years between 415 and 391, Rome was at peace only in 412 and 411. Warfare virtually every year was, therefore, a fact of Roman life which continued through to the end of the First Punic War, when overseas expansion began in earnest, and, inevitably, more war. Even when there was no critical reason for conflict – defending against attack, attacking to expand territory, for example – the consuls could always find a pretext for military action, if Livy's account of the year 303 BC is anything to go by.[3] This was a year in which no war was recorded, until, that is, the consuls mounted raids into Umbria, ostensibly to curtail the plundering activities of armed men there, *ne prorsus imbellem agerent annum* – 'lest they [the Romans] should have a war-free year.' Moreover, it was essential to keep the *socii* – the allies – on side, and one important way of cementing their alliances was to insist on their obligation to military support; interrupt or remove this and you remove one of the foundation stones of the alliance. Allies were acquired by enfranchisement: conquered enemies were subsumed into Rome and became *de facto* citizens, often enjoying many of the rights, privileges and obligations citizenship brought – paying taxes to Rome and fighting in her army, intermarriage and legal and political rights.

An invasion by Gauls in 390 BC wrecked the triple alliance between Rome, the Latins and the Hernici. For the next forty years, Rome was busy fighting former allies who then took advantage of her preoccupation with the Gallic marauders. It was not to be Rome's Italian neighbours who inflicted the first military disaster, but marauding Gauls at the battle of Allia around 387 BC.

The Romans, and others, had learnt much from the Etruscans, immigrants in the tenth and eighth centuries BC from Asia Minor. These newcomers brought with them sophisticated, urbanized skills in city building, metalworking and pottery. Much of what they made had, in turn, been influenced by contact with Phoenicia, Egypt and early Greece. The Etruscans capitalized on their skills by establishing Etruscan cities extending from the Po valley to Rome and trading with the Greek cities of Italy, opening up vital trade routes around Rome with strategic crossings over the Tiber at Fidenae and Lucus Feroniae. The Etruscans viewed Rome as a strategically important city because it was the last place before the sea where the Tiber could be crossed; the Tiber estuary was a major source of salt, a commodity much traded by Romans and Etruscans alike. Inevitably, the more cosmopolitan Etruscans, by now a loose confederation of twelve or so cities, overwhelmed the more agrarian Rome, introducing new ideas in architecture, town planning, commerce, science and medicine, and the arts. The Etruscans gave the Romans the Latin alphabet, the *fasces* (symbols of magisterial power), temple design and elements of their religion.[4]

So, by the end of the monarchy in 509 BC, Rome was developing from a settlement populated by former agricultural hill-dwellers to a more sophisticated, vibrant city, complete with a dedicated religion and a history. Rome had acquired a legendary past – with heroes like Aeneas, Romulus and Remus – a viable socio-political system, a thriving culture and a citizen army. The traditional heroes, of course, were warriors: Aeneas had to battle his way to the founding of Rome, while for Romulus the future involved slaying Remus, his brother – a victory for one, a disaster for the other. The latter-day hill people had come down from their hills and built a central market close to the Tiber, the forum, the crux of Roman life. Their kings wielded *imperium* – absolute power. They were also empowered to consult the gods (*auspicium*) on all manner of things, including declarations of war and most other military activity. The site of Rome was defensible, being backed by the Appenines and located at a crossing of the Tiber. It was also on the Italian trade routes, including the Via Salaria, by which commercially vital salt deposits were brought from the coast.

Between 700 and 500 BC, then, the Romans and the Etruscans were at odds with each other over land disputes in central Italy. The early conflicts have come down to us as legend, described by Livy in the opening books of his *Ab Urbe Condita*, and by Virgil in the second half of *The Aeneid* – both written some 700 years after the alleged events. In 509 BC, the monarchy, under Lucius Tarquinius Superbus, was replaced by a republic. Tarquinius, however, did not take this lying down and enlisted the support of the similarly disaffected cities of Veii and Tarquinii; they were all defeated by the Romans at the decisive Battle of Silva Arsia. The victorious consul, Publius Valerius Poplicola, returned to Rome weighed down with Etruscan booty; he celebrated a triumph from a four-horse chariot, thus providing a template and precedent for subsequent Roman triumphs.[5]

The Sabines were just as troublesome to the early Romans as the Etruscans. The first episode was the 'rape' – or abduction – of the Sabine women in 750 BC.[6] This essentially was an act of nation building; the Romans needed women to prolong their race, so they took what they found, married them and produced their offspring.

Later, Titus Tatius (d. 748 BC), the Sabine king of Cures, attacked Rome and captured the Capitol, helped by the duplicitous Tarpeia. The Sabine women, now Roman wives and mothers, bravely rallied to persuade Tatius and Romulus to bury their respective hatchets and cease hostilities; the outcome was joint rule by the Romans and Sabines.[7]

Later, during the reign of Rome's third king, Tullus Hostilius (r. 673–642 BC), the Sabines took a number of Roman merchants prisoner at a market near the Temple of Feronia. Tullus invaded and met the Sabines at the forest of Malitiosa. The Roman force was superior because the cavalry had been strengthened with ten new *turmae* of *equites* recruited from the Albans, now themselves citizens of Rome. The Romans won the battle with a successful cavalry charge, inflicting heavy losses on the Sabines.

The *Fasti Triumphales* record a triumph for a victory over the Sabines and the Veientes by Rome's fourth king, Ancus Marcius (r. 642–617 BC). Ancus it was who famously defeated the Latins before the Latin League had come to accept the leadership of Rome during the reign of Tarquinius Superbus (535–509 BC). The League was a confederation of about thirty or so towns and tribes in Latium who coalesced in the seventh century BC for mutual defence and protection. Rome made a treaty with Carthage, that other emerging Mediterranean power, in 507 BC, in which Rome arrogantly assumed Latin lands surrounding Rome to be Roman territory, an issue that would become a festering sore in Roman and Latin relations down the years.[8] The Latins had naively thought that Ancus was a man of peace like his grandfather, Numa

Pompilius, and so invaded Roman territory. When a Roman embassy sought reparations for war damage and received nothing more than an insult from the Latins, Ancus declared war. This is significant because it was the first time that the Romans had declared war through the rites of the *fetiales*. Ancus Marcius took the Latin town of Politorium and displaced its inhabitants to the Aventine Hill, where they were subsumed and granted Roman citizenship. The ghost town that Politorium now became was later occupied by other Latins; Ancus simply responded by taking the town again, sacked it and razed it. Much booty and many Latins were sent back to Rome, these new citizens being settled at the foot of the Aventine. Ancus fortified the city, annexing the Janiculum, strengthening it with a wall and connecting it with the city by the Pons Sublicis, with its crucial implications for trade. He built the Fossa Quiritium, a ditch fortification, and opened Rome's first prison, the Mamertine. He also developed lucrative salt mines at the mouth of the Tiber and snatched the Silva Maesia, a coastal forest north of the Tiber, from the Veientes.[9]

In 585 BC, during the reign of Rome's fifth king, Lucius Tarquinius Priscus (r. 616–579 BC), the Sabines resumed hostilities and attacked Rome. Tarquinius was busy strengthening Rome's defences with a stone wall around the city. The initial engagement led to heavy loss of life on both sides, but it was inconclusive. In the second battle, the Romans shipped rafts of burning logs down the River Anio in order to burn down the bridge over the river. The Roman cavalry outflanked the Sabine infantry, routed them, and blocked their flight from the battlefield, helped by the destruction of the bridge. Many Sabines drowned, their weapons drifting downstream into the Tiber, floating through Rome to give the citizens a palpable, very visible sign of victory. Tarquinius made a pyre and burnt the spoils in sacrifices to Vulcan, sending prisoners and booty back to Rome. He then invaded Sabine territory and destroyed their newly-formed army; the Sabines sued for peace. Tarquinius returned to Rome to celebrate a triumph on 13 September 585 BC.[10]

After he was deposed in 510, a disgruntled Lucius Tarquinius Superbus defected and persuaded the Sabines to help him restore the monarchy at Rome. After an initial defeat, Tarquinius, strengthened by the support of Fidenae and Cameria, was again defeated in 505 BC. The Sabines attacked again the following year, facing the two experienced Roman consuls, Publius Valerius Poplicola and Titus Lucretius Tricipitinus at the River Anio.

The Bloodless War followed in 501 BC, the result of a fracas which broke out with Sabine youths when they assaulted some prostitutes during games in Rome. The Sabine ambassadors sued for peace, but were rejected by the Romans who demanded that the Sabines pay Rome for the costs of a war. The Sabines refused, and war was declared, but it all evaporated and there was no battle. The war was significant because it marked the first appearance of a dictator. Dictators were appointed to deal specifically with the crisis in hand, to get the job done, *rei gerundae causa*, in place of the consuls. Their use died out in the Second Punic War, when Scipio Africanus and his successors assumed sole control of Roman armies, although it was revived by Sulla, who was appointed *dictator legibus faciendis et rei publicae constituendae causa* – 'dictator for the enacting of laws and for the setting of the constitution.'[11]

The One-day War of 495 BC was inconclusive too. A Sabine army invaded Roman territory as far as the river Anio, and devastated the land. Aulus Postumius Albus Regillensis and Publius Servilius Priscus Structus rounded up the Sabines. In 494 BC, the Volsci, Sabines and Aequi revolted. Manius Valerius Maximus was appointed dictator and an unprecedented ten legions were raised; four were assigned to Valerius to enable him to deal with the Sabines, who were duly routed.

The sixth century had ended badly for Rome. When in 502 BC the Latin colony of Pometia renounced its allegiance to Rome and sided with the Auruncians, an outraged Rome invaded and destroyed the Auruncians. At Pometia there was no quarter: over 300 hostages were slaughtered. The following year, the Romans laid siege to Pometia, but they badly underestimated the resolve and fury of the Pometians, who surged out of the town armed with firebrands. They inflicted serious casualties on the Romans, who were forced to withdraw.[12] The battle was a rare reverse and marked a first for the Romans, a baptism by fire in which they encountered men and women brandishing torches as their only weapons.

Nevertheless, the fifth century BC started well for the Romans. The victorious Battle of Lake Regillus in 496 BC became a cherished Roman memory, even embellished with divinity. According to legend, the Dioscuri, Castor and Pollux, gave assistance to the Romans during the battle; afterwards, they came back to Rome and watered their horses at the Fountain of Juturna in the Forum, announcing the victory to the nervously waiting inhabitants of the city. A temple was built in 484 BC, part of which can still be seen today.[13] The Roman commander was Aulus Postumius Albus Regillensis, the dictator appointed to quell the Latin threat. When he defiantly hurled a Roman standard into the midst of the enemy, in order for it to be retrieved by his fired-up soldiers, he set an important precedent which was repeated time and again over the years as a tactic to snatch victory out of likely defeat. The Latins fled with the loss of 30,000 men.

Raiding tribes from the Appenines intent on annexing more hospitable, more productive land continued to be a constant problem for Latin League towns. The Latins had to avoid hostilities on two fronts, so in around 493 BC, they signed the *foedus Cassianum* with the Romans to keep them on side. This is an early example of Roman 'divide and rule'. The treaty, according to Cicero, was inscribed on a bronze pillar and was on show in the Forum for 400 or so years.[14] The treaty was weighted heavily in favour of the Romans; its main points were the assurance of peace and mutual aid between the two signatories, providing a defence army with equal numbers of troops from both sides, a ban on free passage of or assistance to enemies and equal shares in any booty. This was Rome's first significant treaty, named after the consul Spurius Cassius Viscellinus, who was chief negotiator. Livy and Dionysius record that he would have preferred to have had the Latin cities destroyed.[15] The treaty effectively put Rome on an equal footing with the entire League and had the added benefit of removing a long-standing enemy. It also bolstered the Roman army, enabling it to pursue further its regional expansion. The treaty was renewed in 358 BC, but when the Romans reneged soon after, it led to the Second Latin War from 340 to 338 BC.

In 495 BC, the Romans soundly defeated the Aurunci at Aricia, after the Aurunci had given Rome an ultimatum to withdraw from Volscian territory.[16] The city then became a Roman *municipium* and an important town on the Via Appia. Duplicity and psychological warfare were evident in equal measure on both sides in the two battles of Antium (modern Anzio) fought by Rome against the Volsci in 482 and 468. They were important conflicts in the long-running war between Rome and the Volsci, the tribe to whom the exiled rebel Roman Caius Lucius Coriolanus defected. In 482 BC, the consul Lucius Aemilius went to Antium to deal with the Volsci. The ensuing battle was inconclusive, the Volsci cleverly feigning a retreat, which fooled the Romans into thinking that they were victorious. The Romans dropped their guard and plundered the Volsci dead, exposing themselves to attack. The Romans fled, suffering heavy casualties.[17] Although the Volsci were defeated at Longula later that year, the real revenge came for the Romans fourteen years later. The consul Titus Quinctius Capitolinus Barbatus was making heavy weather of a battle with the Volscians. He resorted to misinformation, telling one wing of his army that the other wing was winning; the balance was restored and the Romans triumphed. The Volsci launched a night attack soon after in which Quinctius posted a contingent of trumpeters on horseback outside the Volsci camp to create a mighty din. This had the obvious effect of keeping the Volsci awake. In the morning, the Romans, fresh from a good night's sleep, attacked, forcing the Volsci to retreat. Antium was taken despite heavy Roman casualties.[18]

In 480, the Roman army was riven by dissent and division. On one occasion some Roman soldiers had even gone so far as to walk off the battlefield. The Veians and their Etruscan allies saw their chance. Rome's two consuls, Marcus

Fabius and Gnaeus Manlius, faced their enemy with considerable anxiety, more afraid of what their own troops might do – or not do – than of any threat posed by the enemy. The Veians foolishly mocked the Romans, but the only effect was to incite them to frenzied action, swearing either to win or to die in the attempt. By the end of a long and bloody battle, Manlius and Quintus Fabius, a former consul, were both dead. Notwithstanding this blow, the Romans won through and the Veians withdrew.[19] The significance of the battle lies in its demonstration of how the Roman commanders reacted to potential mutiny in the ranks, and how the Roman soldiery reacted to derision from the enemy with an almost suicidal effort to win.

In the 470s, the Romans won modest victories against the Etruscans at the battles of the Temple of Hope on the Janiculum Hill and at the Colline Gate nearby. A raid by the Etruscans on the camp of Servilius, the consul, nearly ended in disaster for the Romans when Servilius foolishly attacked the Etruscans even though they commanded higher ground up on the Janiculum; the day was only saved when Servilius was reinforced by Verginius, his colleague, and the Etruscans were defeated. In 475, the Romans delivered a coup when they defeated the joint forces of the Sabines and the Veians at Veii, some 10 miles north of Rome; the inhabitants were massacred.

Mons Algidus, about 14 miles south-east of Rome, was the setting for a successful three-year campaign against the troublesome Aequi in 465. In 458 BC, a further conflict started with the Aequi when they broke a truce with Rome, which had been made only a year previously, and now threatened the city. The Aequi encamped on Mons Algidus. The Roman commander, Minucius, was indecisive and paid for his procrastination when the enemy walled him up in his own camp. Rome and the Romans panicked: they asked Lucius Quinctius Cincinnatus to come out of retirement and, as dictator, save them. Cincinnatus was commonly perceived as embodying the epitome of Roman *virtus*.

Typical of the man, Cincinnatus led from the front, while Lucius Tarquitius, his *magister equitum*, launched a cavalry attack, resulting in the death of many of the Aequi. Their surviving commanders begged Cincinnatus to spare them. Cincinnatus showed mercy, allowing them to live if they brought their leader, Gracchus Cloelius, and his officers to him bound in chains. The traditional yoke was set up, under which the humiliated Aequi passed, *sub iugum missi*. Warde Fowler aptly called this ritual 'a kind of dramatised form of degradation'. Job done, Cincinnatus, as a good dictator should, immediately disbanded his army, resigned his office promptly and returned to his farm – a mere sixteen days after assuming the dictatorship. Characteristically, he refused any share of the spoils. To Livy, Cincinnatus was *the* true Roman, *homo vere Romanus*, acting always with valour and dignity, displaying *pietas* for Rome.[20] The Aequi persisted, however, and in 455 BC attacked Tusculum, some 12 miles south-east of Rome, and a safe Roman ally. The resulting battle saw the Aequi lose 7,000 men, according to Livy. A further Roman victory at Mons Algidus followed in 449 BC.

In 431 BC, again at Mons Algidus, the Romans confronted the Volsci and the Aequi. They were spurred on when the consul, Vettius Messius, emulating Aulus Postumius Albus Regillensis, hurled his standard into the midst of the enemy for his troops to retrieve; the Romans won the day and sold the Volsci and Aequi survivors into slavery.[21] Two final battles on the mountain took place in 418 BC, against the Aequi and their new allies, the Labici. In the first, the Romans were forced to flee in disarray, but in the second they captured the enemy camp and sacked the city of Labici.

In 437 BC, the Romans at Fidenae were victorious under the dictator Mamercus Aemilius Mamercinus when the Fidenates, led by Lars Tolumnius, defected to Veii and murdered four Roman envoys, Tullus Cloelius, Gaius Fulcinius, Spurius Antius and Lucius Roscius; these unfortunates had been sent to Veii to demand the return of Fidenae. The feeble explanation for the outrage was that when Tolumnius' aides came and asked if they should execute the Roman ambassadors, Tolumnius, in the middle of history's most untimely game of dice, cried out 'Great stuff!', thus inadvertently ordering the execution of the Roman delegation. When the Romans duly sought revenge, Tolumnius died in close combat at the hands of the *tribunus militum* Aulus Cornelius Cossus, one of only three Roman generals to be awarded the *spolia opima*, a rare decoration bestowed on Romans for killing an enemy leader in single combat. After taking the cuirass from Tolumnius' body, Cossus hacked off his head and stuck it on a lance, parading it in front of the horrified Veians and Fidenates. Cossus donated Tolumnius' armour, shield and sword to the Temple of Jupiter Feretrius on the Capitoline, where it could still be seen during the reign of Augustus. The other two generals to win the *spolia opima* were Romulus when he slew King Acro, and Marcus Claudius Marcellus who killed King Viridomarus, an Insubrian chieftain at the Battle of Clastidium in 222 BC.

Two years after Cossus's heroics, Rome was nearly brought to its knees by a more insidious enemy: plague. Fidenae took advantage of this and sided with the Veians at Nomentum. The dictator Quintus Servilius raised an army to pursue them to Nomentum and then Fidenae, which Servilius captured. At Fidenae, in 426, the Fidenates and Veientes colluded again against the Romans, who were now led by Mamercus Aemilius Mamercinus in his second dictatorship. The Romans were terrified at the sight of the enemy column blazing with flaming torches, but, after recovering from their initial surprise and rallied by Mamercus, they seized the torches and attacked the enemy with their own brands; the Veians were then surrounded and the Fidenae forced back to their city where they surrendered.[22]

The Veian threat was finally extirpated in 396 BC. Rome had besieged Veii for a decade or so; it finally fell to the Roman dictator Marcus Furius Camillus. His victory was attended by startling prodigies, which included the rising of the level of the Alban Lake despite an absence of rain and the defection of the Veian goddess to the Romans. The Romans had no option but to consult the Delphic oracle. In his time, Camillus was awarded four triumphs, was dictator five times and lauded as the Second Founder of Rome.[23] Veii had been backed by Tarquinii, Capena and Falerii.

Camillus was far from the complete hero, though. He set a shocking precedent when he refused the Veians terms of surrender and resorted to looting on a grand scale and wrecking the city, butchering the men and enslaving the women and children, and no doubt raping the women. He committed iconoclasm when he stole the statue of Juno and established it in a temple on the Aventine; back in Rome his triumph went on for four long days as he paraded on a *quadriga*, a chariot pulled by four white horses, the like of which had never been seen before or after in a triumph. Polybius tells us that the Romans thought all of this somewhat arrogant and hubristic: the white horses and the *quadriga* were sacred, the preserve of Jupiter.

Policy was to repopulate Veii, with half of the new inhabitants made up of impoverished Romans, something Camillus and the patricians opposed. He made himself even more unpopular in both heaven and on earth when he broke his promise to donate a tenth of the booty to Apollo. Soothsayers muttered the gods' displeasure. In 395 BC, Camillus besieged Falerii, where a school teacher had given up local children as hostages to the Romans, thus forcing the Falerians to make peace with Rome. The Aequi, Volsci and Capena all followed suite, and Rome's territory increased by 70 per cent at a stroke. Camillus was later convicted of embezzling booty and was sent into exile near Ardea.[24] Rome was now the most powerful state in central Italy. Cary highlights the momentous significance of Rome's victory over Veii when he describes the success as 'the first definite step in Rome's career of world conquest ... a turning point in the military history of the city.'[25]

The key levers in Rome's endless belligerence and in her military and political success were by now very much in place and the machinery of war was well oiled and established: a shrewd network of alliances and the deployment of the military resources which accrued from them; the requirement to annex more and more land to feed land distribution and other economic and social needs; the sheer expectation of continuous warfare back at home; the pursuit of glory and kudos amongst individual commanders; the contagious cupidity for more and yet more booty; a need for legions of slaves and prisoners of war as cheap labour to work the expanding *ager Italicus* and to navvy on the public works programmes and civic buildings that were springing up in Rome as she became increasingly powerful; and an obligation to finance these public works.

Moreover, although the Romans had yet to suffer a military disaster of any magnitude, by the beginning of the third century BC they knew all too well what it meant to be on the wrong end of a battlefield calamity. After all, they had enjoyed the spoils and glory of enough victories and, by the same token, had handed out more than enough defeats or disasters to their Italian neighbours. One army's victory was the other army's disaster. When Rome was victorious, she celebrated in style, sometimes with a triumph with all its pomp, proudly and haughtily processing through an exultant Rome.

The triumph gave the Roman people what the Roman people wanted: a virtual re-run of the battlefield victory, an enactment of the superiority and efficiency of the Roman war engine before their eyes, humiliation for the impertinent vanquished. If it shamed a defeated enemy leader, who was paraded ignominiously before the jubilant crowds of Romans, then so much the better. On a more personal level, a triumph delivered slaves and copious amounts of often exotic booty. The *Fasti Triumphales* formally and dryly list these extravaganza. Stone tablets originally erected in the Forum around 12 BC during the reign of Augustus, they give the commander's name, the names of his father and grandfather, the place where the triumph was awarded and the date of the triumphal procession. They record over 200 triumphs, starting with the three mythical events celebrated by Romulus and ending with that awarded to Lucius Cornelius Balbus in 19 BC.[26] In the empire, the imperial family assumed a monopoly on military victory.

A defeated enemy was either murdered or enslaved, their women raped or enslaved or both, their children often orphaned, estranged and enslaved; their homes were ransacked and their cities sometimes razed to the ground. The Romans had little reason not to assume that a similar awful fate awaited Roman men, women and children should the unthinkable happen and Rome be heavily defeated. If the Roman soldier ever needed an incentive to keep on winning, then this was it; and this was another reason for Rome's series of successes, until, that is, the coming of the Gauls. Victory in battle suggested that the very gods were on the victors' side; defeat, the converse. To the Roman, defeat was literally for losers; the Roman way was to win and to win again – the Roman did not easily countenance defeat. Nevertheless, it is likely that there always was that natural, nagging feeling gnawing away in the background: enjoy it while you can, *memento mori* – a Roman version of 'there but for the grace of God go I.' Moreover, it is axiomatic that the point of most, if not all, wars is to visit disaster on the enemy. Why would the Romans be any different? Defeat meant loss of possessions, national identity, family and leadership – all things that Romans prized and that they would fight to the death to preserve.

The very number of triumphs awarded, and the images on triumphal arches and on the columns of Trajan and Marcus Aurelius provide evidence of this and of the dogged seriousness with which the Roman military took their wars, battles and imperialism. Only three of Rome's thirty-six triumphal arches survive – those built for Titus, Septimius Severus and Constantine – but we can assume that all of them were replete with images portraying aspects of Roman military prowess and supremacy. All of this is, of course, was propaganda for the people, providing an injection, a fix of celebrity for the emperor-commander. But it also clearly demonstrates how the victorious Roman perceived his downtrodden, defeated enemy, his own single-minded prosecution of his war and the absolute necessity that was success on all battlefields, in all arenas.

Trajan's Column graphically depicts Romans torching Dacian huts, stealing livestock and making off with booty. The deforestation of Dacian lands shown thereon is the ultimate in devastation and a vivid demonstration of Roman might. The Arch of Titus has that truly iconic image of Romans symbolically wiping out the religion of the Jews when they carry off the sacred *menorah* from the temple of Jerusalem. These monuments may not just reflect triumphalism on the part of the Romans; rather, they indelibly underscore the humiliation of the enemy. The confiscation or destruction of absolutely everything that meant anything to that enemy is executed with pragmatic solemnity, emphasizing the seriousness with which the Romans took their victories and how they themselves cooly accepted the inevitability of looting and destruction. All the certainties of life are erased; everything is destabilized. Next time it might be them on the receiving end.[27] The shame implicit in defeat can be seen on the column of Marcus Aurelius: the Romans methodically decapitate the captured enemy soldiers while they trample underfoot, abuse and rape their utterly distraught women – to the Roman, just so much inevitable collateral damage, just as odious as the murder of barbarian children which the column also displays. The defeated men were rendered impotent; they could do nothing to stop the extermination of their family, tribe or race – to the Romans, just manifestations of feebleness and failure that was anathema to them. On the other hand, Trajan's Column also clearly depicts the barbarity of Dacian women: they are shown torturing Roman prisoners of war. From the Roman point of view then, they deserve everything they get. A convenient attitude adopted by rampaging armies throughout history. As significantly, though, the scenes on the column paradoxically allow the Romans, officially at least, to illustrate the levels to which barbarians stoop; Roman victory with or without its attendant atrocities, not only saved Roman women and children from rape, enslavement and murder, it also obviated the need for their women to indulge in such unmatronly, un-Roman, barbaric atrocities. The column of Marcus Aurelius shows a German woman fleeing her home in panic; she is a symbol of barbarian disorder, displacement and mayhem – of physical and psychological trauma. Her clothes are ruffled, her hair is dishevelled – all in graphic contrast to the neatness of the victorious, tidy Romans. Defeated women were frequently dragged away by their hair, just as their nations were dragged into the civilization of Rome.[28]

War was viewed as an inevitable fact of life and has been called the ultimate man-made disaster. For the Romans, it is probably true to say that *defeat or disaster in war* was the ultimate man-made disaster, to be avoided at all costs because they, as inveterate victors, knew and feared the consequences of defeat only too well.[29] Dio Chrysostom describes the paradox of military disaster:

Again, whenever there comes a pestilence or an earthquake, we blame the gods, in the belief that they cause misery for mankind, and we claim they are not righteous or benevolent, not even if they are punishing us justly for most grievous sins; so great is our hatred of those evils which occur through chance. Yet war, which is no less destructive than an earthquake, we choose of our own volition; and we do not blame at all the human beings who are responsible for these evils, as we blame the gods for earthquake or pestilence, but we even think them patriotic and we listen to them with delight when they speak, we follow their advice, and in payment for the evils they occasion we give them every kind of – I won't say return, for return would mean evil for evil – but rather thanks and honours and words of praise; and so they would be very witless indeed if they spared those who are even grateful for their evils.[30]

We can now move on to examine how the Roman war machine worked.

Chapter 2

The Roman War Machine

At the end of the fifth century BC, Rome was still, like the towns around her, emerging from an agricultural society driven by an agrarian economy. Rome was different because she became increasingly larger than her enemies and she was extraordinarily receptive to outside influences – melding the best facets and successful practices from friend and foe alike. Militarily, Rome had a facility for adapting tactically and developing weaponry and armour based on extensive combat experience. Every battle fought, even those she lost, was a lesson in military science for the Romans.

In early summer each year, the army was summoned and trooped out to the latest theatre of war. Every autumn, the army, or what was left of it, was discharged until the call to arms the following year. The armies were usually led by two consuls, or by consular tribunes, or by dictators in times of *tumultus*, times of dire crisis. These consuls usually operated in concert with each other, not always harmoniously. They often brought no experience in leading an army or prosecuting a campaign. Time spent in the army or navy was simply another rung on the ladder of the *cursus honorum*, the political career path of the elite Roman. The army, and war, came with the career, and the successful execution of the military element went some way to contributing to long-term glory and success. This, in turn, fostered a belligerent attitude amongst Roman politicians-cum-commanders. Victory in war meant success in politics; success in politics was often dependent on victory on the battlefield.

The lower ranks of the army, the heavily armed infantrymen known as *classis*, were self-financing and recruited from farmers. Below the *classis* was the *infra classem*, skirmishers with less and lighter armour which required a smaller financial outlay. Above the *classes* were the *equites*, patricians with some wealth who made up the majority of the cavalry, officers and staff. Their money often came from land ownership. Soldiers were unpaid in the early days, providing their own rations, arms and armour.[1]

War was not kind to the *classes*. It usually meant that they were away from their lands, forced to neglect their very livelihood for increasingly long stretches of military service. Moreover, they suffered virtual ruin when their farms were depradated by enemy action. The longer they served, the greater the chance of being killed or badly wounded and disabled, rendering them unfit to work on their lands. A ready supply of slaves to work on the lands of the wealthy was fuelled by prisoners of war, reducing the Roman or Italian agricultural worker's value in the job market to little better than slaves themselves. Military duty plunged some *classes* into debt and led to virtual bondage to patricians – an ignominious semi-servile arrangement, *nexum*, which forced a farmer or farm worker to provide labour on the security of his person. Defaulting led to enslavement. Richer landowners could bear losses better as they were the beneficiaries of this bond–debt process, which allowed them to procure yet more land and cheap labour at the expense of the *classes* and *infra classes*.[2] In short, the rich just got richer, a process helped also by their favourable share of increasing amounts of booty. Once Rome had conquered the Italian peninsula, the poorer workers could not even be helped out by land distribution; after 170 BC, land distribution stopped altogether. This, of course, led to resentment, which was only assuaged by personal allocations from tribunes and generals. Land allocations overseas were not considered an option until the time of Julius Caesar.

Oakley has tabulated the number of prisoners of war captured and subsequently enslaved by Rome in the nineteen battles between 297 and 293 BC, and recorded in Livy: approximately 70,000. Even allowing for some exaggeration, this clearly illustrates the impact conquest had on the careers and employment prospects of many agricultural workers. It did not stop there, of course: when Agrigentum was captured in 262 BC, no less than 25,000 prisoners were reportedly taken, all swelling the already competitive job market.[3]

Roman warfare was then inseparable from Roman politics and from Roman economics; land questions and the Conflict of the Orders provided a constant soundtrack to the early wars. The soldier depended on the value of and income from his land for financial clout, the ability to qualify for service and pay for his armour and weapons. The Conflict of the Orders ran from 494 BC to 287 BC and was a 200-year battle fought by the plebeians to win political equality. The *secessio plebis* was the powerful bargaining tool with which the plebeians effectively brought Rome grinding to a halt and left the patricians and aristocrats to get on with running the city and the economy themselves – the Roman equivalent to a general strike. The first *secessio*, in 494 BC, saw the plebeians down weapons and withdraw military support during the wars with the Aequi, Sabines and Volsci.[4] That year marked the first real breakthrough between the people and the patricians, when some plebeian debts were cancelled. The patricians yielded more power when the office of Tribune of the Plebeians was created. This was the first government position to be held by the plebeians, and plebeian tribunes were sacrosanct during their time in office.

Servius Tullius, Rome's sixth king, may have gone some way to militarizing Rome when he divided the population into wealth groups – their rank in the army determined by what weapons and armour they could afford to buy, with the wealthiest serving in the cavalry due in part to the cost of horses. Servius was certainly responsible for changes in the organization of the Roman army: he shifted the emphasis from cavalry to infantry and with it the inevitable modification in battlefield tactics. Before Servius, the army comprised 600 or so horse reinforced by heavily-armed infantry and lightly-armed skirmishers; it was little more than a militia of landowning infantry wielding *pilum*, shield and sword (*gladius*), operating like Greek hoplites in phalanx formation. The rest were composed of eighteen centuries of *equites* and thirty-two centuries of slingers. (A century was made up of ten *conturbenia*, amounting to eighty or so men.) The Etruscans, and then the Romans, absorbed Greek influences when they adopted full body armour, the hoplite shield and a thrusting spear – essential for phalanx-style close combat warfare.

Men without property, assessed by headcount, *capite censi*, were not welcome in the army, in much the same way that debtors, convicted criminals, women and slaves were excluded. However, slaves were recruited in exceptional circumstances, notably after the calamitous battle of Cannae and the manpower shortage it caused. Servius also reorganized the army into centuries and formed the parallel political assemblies, reinforcing the inextricable connection between Roman politics and Roman military. His ground-breaking census established who was fit – physically and financially – to serve in the Roman army.[5] Recruitment extended from between age 17 and 46 (*iuniores*), and between 47 and 60 (*seniores*), the more elderly constituting a kind of home guard. The lower *classes* were not required to report with full body armour; this led to the use of the long body shield, the *scutum*, for protection, instead of the circular hoplite shield.

Sixty centuries made up a legion, known as a *legio* – literally a 'levying'. The original *legio* was split in two in the early Republic, each the responsibility of one of the two consuls for the year. Often this worked; sometimes it led to divisiveness, with predictable consequences. By 311 BC, there were four legions, reinforced by troops recruited from Rome's Italian allies and by mercenaries with special skills, such as archery. By the mid-Republic, the legions were generally divided into cavalry, light infantry and heavy infantry, the latter, in turn, subdivided into three further groups: the *hastati* – raw recruits; the *principes* – troops at their peak, in their twenties and thirties; and the *triarii* – veterans deployed in crises or in support of the *hastati* and *principes.* The *triarii* carried the long spear, the *hasta*, rather than the *pilum* and *gladius*. Each of these three units was subdivided into ten units or maniples, comprising two centuries and led by the senior of the two centurions. Each century of *hastati* and *principes* was made up of sixty men, while a century of *triarii* comprised thirty men. These 3,000 troops (twenty maniples of 120 men, and ten maniples of sixty men), along with 1,200 *velites* and 300 cavalry, formed a legion, which was about 4,500 men strong when at full strength.

Infantry soldiers signed on for six consecutive campaigns and were to be available for up to sixteen years; cavalrymen had to be on standby for ten years. When Marius dispensed with the property qualification in 107 BC, it was a one-off arrangement, and armies continued to be raised on an *ad hoc* basis,

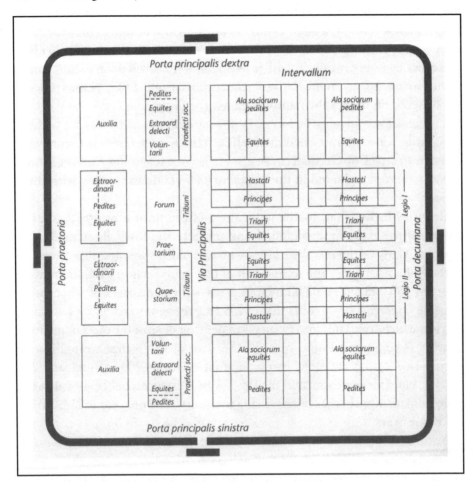

Diagram 1: A Roman marching camp, as described by Polybius. (Courtesy of Cambridge University Press; originally published in J.P. Roth, *Roman Warfare*, 2009.)

with the press gang becoming all the more influential. The legionary army, as we have seen, was reinforced by the *auxilia* – infantry and cavalry suppplied by the allies. These could offer local knowledge and intelligence, and provide special forces such as archers, slingers and 'marines' for amphibious assaults.

A Roman army marched encumbered by its baggage train, comprising merchants, prostitutes and soothsayers – all essential hangers-on. Some generals, for example Scipio Aemilianus, Metellus and Marius, saw the baggage train as the impediment it no doubt was and either banished it or restricted its numbers. Tacitus tells us that they were more unruly even than slaves and that they could be more rapacious than the soldiery, citing the second sack of Cremona as an example. Occasionally, the camp servants assumed a military role, either posing as soldiers to inflate the size of the army and making it appear bigger than it actually was, or riding on donkeys at a distance from the main force to give the impression that reinforcements were on the way. In 209 BC, these motley forces, while under fire in Spain, were called upon to hurl stones at the Carthaginians. At the Battle of Aquae Sextiae in 102 BC, Marius ordered the hangers-on to join the fighting against the Germans. Later, they helped Julius Caesar win against the Nervi. Following a Roman army was not without its hazards: those who attached themselves to the army of Quintus Cicero were killed in an attack by German cavalry; merchants and families with the armies of Varus were slaughtered in the Teutoburg Forest disaster along with three legions.[6]

Brunt estimates that, by the latter third of the third century BC, nearly a third of the Italian inhabitants living south of the River Po were Roman citizens. Many of the rest were allies who had obligations to military service in the Roman army. By the second half of the second century BC, there were between 380,000 and 480,000 men in arms – three-quarters of whom were valuable *iuniores*. Livy records that in 295 BC, there were six legions in active service, which translates into twenty-five per cent or so of the male population in arms. The Second Punic War saw the army at its greatest strength, with twenty-two legions available, comprising on average 4,200 infantry and 200 cavalry. Hopkins has estimated that by 225 BC seventeen per cent of all adult male Romans were in the legions, rising to twenty-nine per cent in 213, during the Punic Wars.[7]

Naturally, war took its toll on the Roman population – on men and women – especially when it took the form of a disaster. Men became casualties: some of those who survived would often live on with permanent physical and psychological disabilities. Women and girls may have had to suffer the stigma and shame of war rape, along with the pregnancies and disease that often attend this. Women were often left with the responsibility of running the farm and raising the family during the absence of their husband or sons. Casualties and disabilities amongst soldiers would often render a family fatherless, with no one to work the land. Women would have to care full- or part-time for disabled veterans. As in any war, bereavement caused by the death of husbands, fathers, sons and siblings was a heavy price for many women to pay.

Overseas expansion meant longer postings abroad in armies of occupation. One example would be after the Roman conquests in Sicily and Sardinia in 241 and 238 BC, following the First Punic War. The opening years of the Second Punic War racked up some 50,000 Roman casualties: seventeen per cent of all adult Roman males and five per cent of the total population. These figures are all the more horrible when compared with the casualty figures for the First World War: in the period 1914–1918, the seven nations fighting at the beginning of the conflict lost two per cent of their combined populations. As we have seen, the Second Punic War saw the Romans deploying more legions than ever before. In contravention of the standard *cursus honorum*, the Romans were forced to fill vacancies for commanders with *praetors*, deferring the retirement of magistrates beyond their term of office or appointing private citizens to commands – *privati cum imperio*. In the next century, wars in Spain, northern Italy and against Philip V, Antiochus III and Persius led to yet more overseas campaigns and the usual ramifications for the Romans.

It was not all bad news, however. For the Roman citizen, despite the serious problems it may cause with running the farm and cultivating the land, military service clearly demonstrated his patriotism, *pietas*, dutifulness and a visible discharge of responsibility. It also brought prestige, affording the soldier and his family opportunities for glory reflected in *dona militaria* (military decorations), citations, prizes and – the highlight of them all – a triumph processing through the streets of Rome. Military service showed that this Roman was a patriotic Roman, that he was brave and possessed *pietas*, *virtus* and *Romanitas*.

Triumphs were most frequent between 312 and 293 BC, for which the triumphal *Fasti* record no less than eighteen, with a further twenty-two between 282 and 264 BC. These apogees of pomp and ceremony not only reflect the continual military success of Roman consuls, they also galvanized warmongering amongst the elite; win a battle and you might win a triumph – the pinnacle of success.

Military service and combat were, as noted, indicative of *Romanitas*, which translates as 'Roman-ness' – the essence of being a Roman and of how, as a Roman, you conducted yourself in the increasingly Roman world. The Roman demonstrated 'virtue' and 'bravery' – both enshrined in the same word, *virtus*, which has its root in *vir*, meaning 'man'. Although it was possible for a woman to exhibit *virtus*, it was essentially a badge of masculinity. Indeed, *virtus* often denoted courage in war: Caesar, Sallust and Horace all use it in this context.[8]

Meanwhile, the enemies of Rome were viewed and described as weak, lazy and effeminate, deficient in *virtus*; both Greeks and Carthaginians suffer the worst of Roman verbal xenophobia.[9] Sexually, the Carthaginians were out of control, they were cowards and they ate dogs. Greeks, according to Tacitus, were all cowards; Lucan, through the voice Julius Caesar, believed that they were soft, lazy and frightened – even by their own shouting.[10] Conversely, Romans were masters of war: Rome's victories proved that. All the more disastrous, then, when Rome did lose a battle or when a Roman army was annihilated. Defeat sat uncomfortably in the Roman psyche and had dreadful ramifications, politically and socially.

Military glory and its attendant celebrity and kudos were, as we have seen, signified by the complex system of decorations – *dona militaria* – and rewards that reflected military success. The *spolia opima* was, of course, a highly prestigious and rare award,[11] but, as with the triumph, it was restricted to commanders. Discipline and loyalty too were nurtured by in-service benefits, which included promotion to the rank of centurion. After Marius, the pay for centurions was twice that of the common soldier and the share of booty bigger. Gratuities, pay rises, better rations and promotion all helped, in theory at least, to make the soldier a happier, prouder soldier. So did the prospect of social mobility for the common soldier and political success and recognition for a member of Rome's political elite as he progressed along the *cursus honorum*. That said, the average pay for the average soldier or sailor was still niggardly, as measured in 'asses' – the monetary currency of the time. He could earn three times more doing manual labour in the fields at twelve asses per day; it took until Julius Caesar's time for a soldier's remuneration to be raised to ten asses per day, in 49 BC. Pay (*stipendium*) probably came around 406 BC as a daily cash allowance after the wars with the Veii. It was never a living wage, more of a contribution to the cost of food, equipment and clothing. The introduction of pay probably came as a concession by the senate to the plebeians, and was usually payment in kind, as the minting of coinage only came on stream 100 years later. Increasingly, booty was the answer to financial hardship.

The *devotio* was the ultimate route to everlasting military glory, but with the disadvantage that you had to die to win one. The Mus family were the true champions of this extreme, suicidal dedication, with Decius Mus, his grandfather and father all 'devoting' themselves. The *devotio* involved a one-way charge into the enemy's midst after devoting oneself to the gods of the underworld. The effect on morale (for those around) must have been considerable.

Bellicosity is reflected in the increasing war statuary erected in Rome from the end of the third century BC. Victoria was predictably the most popular: she features in the prodigies of 296 BC, as described by Dio, in the vow of Fabius Rullianus for a temple of Jupiter Victor at Sentinum in 294, and in a temple of Victoria dedicated in the same year.[12]

If the Roman war machine was inseperable from Roman politics, so it also was from religion and the religious calendar. Important rituals accompanied the beginning and end of the Roman campaigning season. The Roman religious calendar was peppered with sacred preparations for warfare: in February and March, in races at the feast of *Equirria*, the Salii performed their sacred dances, banging their holy shields, purifying the equipment and horses; trumpets were blessed on the day of the *tubilustrium*, weapons on the *armilustrium* in the autumn; on 15 October, a race horse – the 'October horse' – was killed as a sacrifice to Mars, marking the end of the campaigning season. Before an army left for war, it was lustrated; the commander shook the Salian shields and held aloft the lance of Mars. The doors of the Temple of Janus were opened. During a campaign, omens were read at every critical juncture, sacrifices were made and auspices were taken.

It was necessary to perform a three-stage procedure before a war could be considered just: in the first place, the war had to be declared (*denuntio*); a formal warning to the potential enemy had to delivered (*indictio*); and reparations had to be sought (*rerum repetitio*) by a delegation of four *fetiales*, or *oratores*, who were responsible for formal declarations of war. They established the *fas*, the rightness of any conflict, and were Rome's ambassadors and diplomats in negotiations. The *fetiales* applied the fetial law (*ius fetiale*), ensuring that *fides*, treaties, *foedera* and oaths had been properly observed. Iuppiter Lapis was their deity. Three *fetiales* and the chief fetial (*pater patratus*) were despatched as envoys to the perpetrator of the crime committed against Rome; this might involve anything from cattle stealing to a full-scale incursion. Their job was to secure restitution (*ad res repetundas*); failure of the enemy to comply after thirty days would lead to action (*denuntiatio* or *rerum repetitio*): the *fetiales* returned to Rome and invoked the gods to witness that the Romans' case was legitimate (*fas*), the *testatio deorum*. The chief fetial could then declare war within thirty-three days. After ratification by the Senate and the people, the two adversaries would then officially be at war, all sanctioned by the gods. A sacred spear was then hurled into the enemy's territory, *indictio belli*. As Rome's reach extended further away from the city, some of these rituals became impractical: the *fetiales* often needed more than thirty days, and occasionally it was difficult to find a suitable place in which to hurl the spear. In 270 BC, a special location near the Temple of Bellona was given over to spear hurling. By the Second Punic War, the whole procedure was secularized when the *fetiales* were replaced with senatorial *legati* (envoys). The traditional three journeys were condensed into one, without recourse to Rome.

Once it had been set in motion, it was critical that the Roman war engine be constantly maintained with new recruits – in itself something of a vicious circle. As noted already, by the end of the third century BC, about one third of Italians around and south of Rome had been vanquished and were Roman citizens.[13] They were, therefore, already eligible for military service, bolstered by auxiliary troops supplied by allies. The allies, while they remained allies, were already on the books, so to speak. Casualties, fatal and otherwise, sustained in war after bloody war often meant that Rome had to go on conquering more tribes and towns if it was to fuel recruitment and maintain the strength of its forces.

There was another factor at play which helped to keep the Romans on the battlefield, widening its circle of power. The more conservative amongst the Romans felt that to stop fighting encouraged laxity and fostered moral decay amongst the men of Rome. As champion of the traditional *mos maiorum* and fervent hater of things Greek, Cato the Elder (234–149 BC) criticized what he saw around him as moral decline and the erosion of the rigorous principles on which Rome had been built. The defeat of Hannibal at Zama in 202 BC, the victory over the Macedonians at Pydna in 168 and the final erasing of the Carthaginian threat in 146 BC all allowed Rome to relax more and caused an unprecedented influx of Greek and eastern customs and luxuries into an increasingly porous Rome. The waging of war was an effective antidote to all of this and was seen as the panacea for Rome's growing feebleness.[14]

However that may be, military service as a pre-requisite and a pre-condition for political progress was on the decline. At the end of the first century BC, the requirement for ten campaigns to be endured before the start of public office was no longer enforced. Flair in oratory and conspicuous success at the bar were replacing the battlefield as entry points to a successful political career. Augustus encouraged senators to be *expers castrorum* – experienced in camp life – but even the statutory year as a military tribune was often dispensed with.[15]

It was not until the reforms of Augustus that the Roman army as a citizen militia was replaced by a professional standing army with troops mainly concentrated at the borders of the empire. By then the average length of service was twenty-five years; the provision of land in lieu of cash payments ended, to be replaced with salaries funded at first by Augustus himself and then by taxation. Augustus also introduced the law prohibiting soldiers from marrying in service, although we know that *ad hoc* unions were common and that families were raised with local women.[16] One of the fascinating Vindolanda Tablets from around AD 100 shows that wives of officers clearly did accompany their husbands abroad: Claudia Severa sends her sister Lepidina an invitation to her birthday on 11 September, asking her to make her day by attending. The body of the letter is written by a scribe, but the postscript is written by Claudia and is the oldest example in existence of a woman's handwriting in Latin.[17] The restriction officially lasted until the reign of Septimius Severus, when the ban was relaxed in AD 197. In AD 21, Aulus Caecina Severus had adopted an extreme view on wives and military service, exaggerated in his unsuccessful speech and reported by Tacitus; it nevertheless contains within it arguments which shaped the regulations relating to accompanied postings. Severus gets on with his wife – they have had six children together. However, he has left her at home for the forty years he has been away in the provinces. Why? Because women encourage extravagance in peace time and weakness during war; they are feeble and tire easily; left unrestrained, they get irascible, they scheme and boss the commanders about. He cites instances of women running patrols and exercises, of how they attract spivs and embrace extortion.

Tiberius took a similarly dim view, moaning that women were taking over the army and that his generals were now more or less redundant. On the other hand, Livia, wife of Augustus and mother of Tiberius, was praised on her death for her rejection of camp life; Livia obviously 'did not do camping.' Augustus, it seems, was never keen on women joining their men and made it his business to approve requests for visits on a case-by-case basis.

It was fully expected of Augustus that he continue the centuries of expansion and extend the empire. Initially, this is what he did, with successful campaigns in northern Iberia and the Alps, pushing his borders up to the Danube in the east and to the Elbe in Germany. However, the disaster which took place in the Teutoburg Forest in AD 9, when Varus lost three precious legions, stopped all that. Claudius went on to conquer Britannia – a campaign not without its own military disaster in the shape of Boudica – and Trajan subdued Dacia, but by and large, aggressive and compulsive expansionism was consigned to the past. The *pax Romana* (Roman peace) took over. Augustus was more or less happy to pursue a diplomatic foreign policy of containment. In any event, in terms of mineral resources or opportunity for booty, there was now little out there beyond the existing borders that the Romans considered worth the expense or the bother of conquering.

The Romans were generally ruthless and thorough in their pursuit of victory, and by the same token, their avoidance of defeat. Calgacus speaks for many in his *declamatio* at Mons Graupius (in modern Scotland) in AD 83 when he exhorts his army before the decisive conflict with Agricola's legions. The Romans, he asserts, are rapists on a global scale, *raptores orbis*; to plunder, butchery and rape they give the misnomer 'government'; they call the desolation they create 'peace'.[18] Earlier in the British campaign, Boudica's daughters had been raped and she had been flogged by the rapacious and venal Romans.

That rape was a characteristic of Roman conquest – and a particularly repellent postscript to many battles and sieges – seems inarguable. After all, it was an accepted, if repugnant, characteristic of warfare well before the Romans and has been a consequence of defeat in many a conflict ever since. The only way it is ever averted, it seems, is by the tightest control exerted by commanders over their troops. The odious notion that victorious soldiers win the right to rape, or even *should* rape to exact revenge or exert total dominance over a defeated foe and his women and children, only made and continues to make that control more difficult and unlikely. Despite the silence of the historians, who is to say that the many women subjugated by the Romans did not suffer rape, gang rape and its consequences – physical and psychological trauma, abortion, sexually transmitted infections, conjugal rejection, social rejection and ostracization – on a scale relative to, say, the two million or so German women and girls raped by the Red Army in 1944 and 1945 on the way to Berlin?

There is infrequent mention of war rape in by all of the historians of the period, particularly Livy, who describes rape in legend but infrequently in history. An illustration of the general ubiquity of Roman rape perhaps comes in Livy's description of the sack of Victumulae by Hannibal in 218 BC, when all manner of atrocity was visited upon the hapless inhabitants, including rape:

> Every form of debauchery, cruelty and inhuman arrogance was inflicted on the wretched.[19]

Because he considers it inevitable that rape will be inflicted, the Capuan Vibius Virrius defects to Hannibal in 216 BC during the Second Punic War. Virrius wants to see the rape of Capuan women, girls and boys no more than he does his own execution or the sacking of his city:

> I am not going to watch my city being wrecked and torched, or Campanian women, young girls and freeborn young men raped.[20]

In 204 BC, the Locrians complain about the behaviour of Roman soldiers garrisoned in their town: rape and plunder are rife and relentless:

They all rob, plunder, thrash, wound, murder. They rape women, young girls and free-born boys, dragged from the embrace of their parents. Every day our city is captured, every day it is plundered. Day and night every part of it re-echoes with the wailing of women and children who are being seized and carried off.[21]

There were, however, glimmers of humanity. Livy also reports the episode in which a beautiful Spanish girl is brought to Scipio Africanus during the siege of Carthago Nova, presumably to pleasure the commander. Scipio sends her away, knowing that she was betrothed to a local man. This civilized behaviour led to obvious gratitude from the girl's family, which in itself resulted in a welcome conscription of 1,400 local men to the Roman cause.[22]

Cicero, in his *In Verrem* of 70 BC, tells of the unbridled lust of Verres in Sicily:

To how many noble virgins, to how many matrons do you think he offered violence in that foul and obscene lieutenancy? In what town did he set his foot that he did not leave more traces of his rapes and atrocities than he did of his arrival?[23]

The observation is undoubtedly supported by Verres' lubricious but unsuccessful attempt to rape the virgin daughter of Philodamus in Lampsacus:

His daughter, who was living with her father because she had not yet got a husband, was a woman of extraordinary beauty, but was also considered exceedingly modest and virtuous. [Verres], when he heard this, was so inflamed with desire ... that he said he should like to go to Philodamus immediately.[24]

This behaviour was by no means out of character: Verres' rape of Syracuse was consistent with his soldiers' rape of the women there.

I won't mention the violence offered to the nobility or the rape of matrons, atrocities which then, when the city was taken, were just not done, either through hatred of enemies, through military licence, or through the customs of war or the rights of victory.[25]

There are examples of violent behaviour by the Roman military in the early Principate. Some of these may be untypical, belying a greater level of discipline than is actually recorded. However, Roman soldiers were free to sieze a captured woman and effectively enslave her at their own personal pleasure for life – the equivalent of the mass abduction of the Sabine women on a personal, individual level. We hear from Tacitus regarding the indiscriminate rape, violence, sacrilege and pillage inflicted on Italy by Vitellius' troops in AD 69:

> Italy was beset by something much worse and atrocious than war: dispersed through towns and colonies Vitellius' troops plundered, raped and polluted the land with their violence and lechery; greed and corruption made them go for the sacred and the profane, the good and the bad.[26]

Tacitus also describes the unrivalled, un-Roman, savage licentiousness and rapine of Vitellius' armies later in the year:

> Then Vitellius and his army exploded into savagery, rape and lust that knew no equal – the behaviour of foreigners.

He describes Vitellius' hugely corrupt recruitment campaign amongst the aggrieved Batavians, involving the systematic rape of adolescent boys. And the ferocious sack of Cremona by Antonius, in which women and the elderly were raped and butchered on a prodigious scale:

> Forty thousand soldiers burst into Cremona, with even more army suppliers and camp followers, who were even more corrupted by lust and savagery. Age and dignity provided no protection as they exchanged rape with slaughter and slaughter with rape. Old men and aging women – useless as booty – were dragged into the 'fun'; any grown up girl or fine-looking man who came along was torn apart at the violent hands of the rapists.

Public opinion viewed this particular episode as repellent; it turned the Roman public against the armies of Antonius. Slaves taken at Cremona remained unsold on the slave markets. Survivors were surreptitiously ransomed by their relatives.[27] The revulsion may have been exacerbated because the victims were Italians caught up in a civil war, rather than foreigners or barbarians.

Sieges, particularly their aftermath, seem to have generated some of the worst atrocities perpetrated by the Romans – and they also created exceptions to the general *iures belli* and rules of fair play. Retribution, reprisals and exacting reparations for the time, trouble and lives expended on a siege were judged good enough reasons to reject the rule book. Frontinus tells how Sulla broke the siege at Preaeneste in 82 BC by sticking the heads of the enemy generals on spears and displaying them to the remaining inhabitants to shatter their morale and break their resolve.[28]

Domitius Corbulo was especially brutal while besieging Tigranocerta in AD 60. Corbulo executed the noble Vadandus, whom he had captured, and shot his head from a balista into the enemy camp. This well-aimed human projectile landed in the middle of a meeting that the enemy was holding. The meeting ended immediately, persuading the Tigranocertans to seek terms for surrender.[29] Scenes 24, 72 and 57 of Trajan's Column depict Dacian heads on poles. Scene 147 shows the head of Decebalus, king of the Dacians.

Of course, such atrocities were not exlusive to the Romans; in the same piece, Frontinus tells how, in AD 9, the Germans under Arminiuson fixed the heads of the Roman dead on spears and had them brought up to the Roman camp.[30]

It seems that cities which elected to surrender rather than be taken by storm received a relative degree of clemency. Livy describes two such cases: Pometia in 502 BC and Phocaea in 190 BC.[31] At Cartagena, in 209 BC, Scipio stopped the wholesale slaughter (which included slicing dogs and other animals in half) once Mago had surrendered.[32] The clear message from the Romans was that resistance was just not worth the vicious reprisals that would inevitably follow; holding out in a siege was just as unacceptable as any other form of anti-Roman hostility. In 216 BC, savage retribution followed in Capua when the inhabitants locked up a number of Roman citizens in the steaming, airless bath house; they died a terrible suffocating death according to Livy.[33] Images of the Black Hole of Calcutta spring to mind. At Uxellodunum, in 51 BC, Julius Caesar had the hands of the enemy cut off as a terrible and tangible warning to anyone else contemplating resistance.[34] In AD 78, Agricola started as he meant to go on when he massacred the Ordovices. They had the temerity to attack one of his cavalry squadrons. He then took the island of Anglesey.[35]

The Roman army was always the senior service. Until the wars against Carthage, sea power was always something of an afterthought. Carthage, on the other hand, maintained a fleet because their extensive overseas trade demanded they do so. Egypt, Athens and Rhodes, at one time or another, all kept a standing navy for reasons of both trade and warfare. By comparison, early Rome's attitude towards overseas trade was decidedly casual, so their naval capability was similarly limited. Overseas expansion, the conquest of Sicily, and the inescapable, worrying fact that the Carthaginians had a viable and formidable fleet, a navy, dockyards and harbours, forced the Romans into naval warfare, paving the way for the eventual defeat of Carthage and Octavian's victory at Actium. But the Roman way was always to raise a navy on demand and as required.

The *tributum* was a war tax levied on all those eligible for military service, regardless of whether they were called up or not. Apart from a few years, such as 347 BC, when there was no war, the tax was paid every year until 167, when booty paid the defence budget.[36]

Chapter 3

The Sources

There was, of course, no shortage of advice to be had on strategy and tactics and the right and proper way to run a war, break a siege, lay an ambush or win a battle.[1] Polybius wrote his textbook on camps (*c.* 200 BC – *c.* 118 BC); Julius Caesar (100–44 BC) expatiated on the conflict in Gaul and the Civil Wars; Onasander (first century AD) wrote the *Strategikos*; Frontinus (*c.* AD 40–103) wrote the *Strategemata*; more camp building came from Pseudo-Hyginus in the third century with *De Munitionibus Castrorum*; Vegetius wrote the *De Re Militari* in the late fourth century; and Zosimus' *Historia Nova*, written sometime between 490 and 510, was a fertile source of military information.[2]

Taking siege warfare as an example, Onasander sensibly recommends restraint when it comes to looting and plunder, and not to threaten massacre. Both, he argues, just make for a more defiant and intractable enemy, while prisoners of war should be spared for the same reasons. Indeed, all prisoners should routinely be herded into the besieged city to exacerbate food shortages and hasten starvation. However, Onasander is not averse to brutality when it is necessary.[3] Zosimus records how Lydius, at the siege of Cremona in AD 278, evicted all the prisoners, young and old. The Romans sent them back to Lydius, only for Lydius to hurl them to their deaths down a ravine.[4] Frontinus advocated terrorising the besieged. Terror tactics generally were not lost on Agricola in his first year in command of Britannia.[5]

Some of this military education was based on personal combat experience. We know that Polybius, Julius Caesar, Josephus and Frontinus all saw military action. By the end of the Roman Empire, there was more than enough instruction to be had in the prosecution of war for those who cared to take it. Depending on when they lived, our principle historiographical sources would have had access to much of this. We might assume that other war manuals existed which have not survived.

For the first 500 years or so of Rome's history, there was little or no historiography. The *Fasti*, the official reports of the magistracies and triumphs, are the only extant factual records we have for the early years. The lost *Annales Maximi* would have been another vital primary source. It was only with

Quintus Fabius Pictor, writing in Greek around 200 BC, and the Latin *Origines* of Marcus Porcius Cato, the Censor, some forty years later, that the Romans started recording historical events. The detailed work only really began with Livy and Dionysius of Halicarnassus at the end of the Republic. In the absence of actual verifiable facts, then, much of the early history of Rome consisted of ideology and stereotypes exemplified by well-known legends and fables, much of which may have been handed down through oral traditions. Moreover, some of these legends smack of hagiography; they will have been refashioned and re-interpreted to fit a particular historian's agenda, or span to reinforce the messages about the present or the past he or his patron wanted to promulgate.

For the disasters which took place in the Republic, Livy is our principle source. He is guilty of a number of sins at various points – exaggeration, misinterpretation or confusion with his sources, bias and poor analysis. A good example of confusion is the description of the two battles of Toletum in 193 and 192, in which Marcus Fulvius routed the Vettones – on both occasions. Surely, these are one and the same conflict. To make matters worse, there is the vexed issue of transcription of manuscripts and the endless problems this brings.

Livy was a patriot, so it is to be expected that elements of his work are biased towards the Romans. Julius Caesar's works were partly political manifestos and freighted with personal propaganda. Livy was writing some 200 years after the events he described, so he no doubt struggled with the vagaries imposed by the passage of time – and with the credibility and accuracy of his own primary sources. Despite his shortcomings though, Livy's achievement is both admirable and outstanding. We have always to remember that he was researching and writing with few if any of the reference tools and indexes which we take for granted today.[6] He had no access, of course, to witnesses to any of the events.

Livy would nevertheless have been able to use many more primary sources than have survived today. Some of these may, however, have been of questionable reliability. Apart from the official *Fasti,* he would have been familiar with the pontifical annals, which were published in eighty books as the *Annales Maximi* by Pontifex Maximus Publius Mucius Scaevola. These books were a compilation of the daily pronouncements written up on a board publicly, announcing the latest news – a kind of extended newspaper headline board, or a rolling newscast, as seen today looping along brightly on public or office buildings. They would have featured the latest earthquakes, eclipses, famines and other natural events and disasters. The beginnings and ends of wars, and forthcoming triumphs would have been up there for all to see – meat and drink for the keen contemporary historian.

As we have noted, real history, and Livy's earliest written history primary source, began with Fabius Pictor and his contemporary Lucius Cincius Alimentus – a veteran of the wars against Hannibal who was taken prisoner and allegedly met and spoke with the Carthaginian leader. Cato was the first to write Roman history in Latin. Not long after, Lucius Coelius Antipater delivered the first historical monograph (on the Second Punic War) around 120 BC. The extensive works of Claudius Quadrigarius and Valerias Antias would have been valuable sources for Livy. Hannibal too provided some information from his inscription in Punic and Greek, set up at Cape Lacinium, listing his achievements.[7]

Unfortunately, though, that is all we have from the Carthaginian point of view. Livy, of course, was on the winning side and his accounts of the wars with Carthage are freighted with Roman propaganda, hostile and embroidered. The Romans, in victory, destroyed all the Carthaginian records, destroyed, in effect, their history and heritage in a kind of national *damnatio memoriae*, leaving us with an exclusively Roman view of events. Hannibal's qualities as a general were acknowledged because by 'bigging him up', Rome's eventual victory looked notably more impressive. That apart, Hannibal is portrayed by a xenophobic Livy as unscrupulous: godless, cruel, duplicitous, mendacious, without integrity. Carthaginians generally were derided and ridiculed: they wore earrings, they wore underclothes, they ate salt fish and chewed garlic.

The historian was expected to parade his skill at presenting certain *topoi* and rhetorical devices. He needed to entertain his audience and to keep them listening, so the exciting bits – the sieges and battles, for example – would naturally take precedence over the minutiae regarding weaponry, armour, uneventful patrols and the like. The need to entertain will have been at the expense of the full facts, or even the facts themselves.

Polybius was a key source for Livy. The *Histories* provide us with a unique point of comparison with much of Livy's version of events between 264 and 146 BC. His account is generally balanced and fair, it seems, to both Rome and to her enemies. He was uniquely qualified to write his history – as a former soldier and hostage of Rome, a member of Scipio Africanus' coterie and a witness to the siege of Carthage in 147 BC. He describes Roman equipment, organization and their camps, providing invaluable information for Livy and subsequent historians of the period. Appian and Plutarch complement some of this with details that have been usefully mined from other historians whose works have not survived.

For the disasters of the early Empire, Tacitus is our chief source; Josephus provides us with a contemporary account of the conflicts involving the Jews. Later writers include Ammianus Marcellinus – another first-hand witness with an eye for detail. In addition to the manual writers mentioned above, there are theoretical works by Arrian, *Battle Order Against the Alans* and *Ars Tactica*, and *On the Construction of a Camp* by Pseudo-Hyginus.

Archaeology, of course, provides ongoing evidence to support (or dispute) the literary evidence; digging at the site of the Teutoburg Forest disaster is a case in point. Papyri and writing tablets are similarly useful; although they may not specifically shed light on the military disasters described in this book, they adumbrate aspects of the Roman war machine, which helps us to understand better the causes and effects of some of these disasters. Epigraphy too is helpful with inscriptions that mark the completion of building work, or detailed dedications by a legion to a god or goddess, listing names and ranks. Art and sculpture are a very visible, tangible source of evidence, particularly statuary. Coins and the depictions on, for example, Trajan's Column and the *Tropaeum Traiani* at Adamklissi provide crucial images of the Roman armies and its commanders and soldiers. Tombstones too give us invaluable information about a soldier's lot – albeit often idealized and sterotyped – and his equipment and career progression.

Numbers, particularly casualty figures, present a particular problem. Bias can easily contort these, inflating, as propaganda, enemy losses and minimizing Roman deaths and injuries. The size of an army was regularly estimated in multiples of 5,000 even though we know – and Livy, Appian and Polybius surely knew too – that the strength of the legions was notoriously inconsistent. If bias or rounding down or up did not bedevil the number, then the copyist may well have done – that inadvertent missing zero could change the complexion and interpretation of many a battle.

Dates add to the confusion, with scholars inconsistent in their interpretation of the *Fasti* – our one reliable dateable source. The invasion of the Gauls – with which we begin our study – is a case in point: some, after Varro, say it happened in 390 BC, while others prefer 387. The canonical date for the foundation of Rome is largely agreed to be 753 BC, but even that has been open to some doubt down the years. So, extreme caution is required at every juncture to ensure a reasonably accurate and historical interpretation of the disasters discussed.

Chapter 4

The Fourth Century: the Gallic Invasion and the Samnite Wars

River Allia and the Sack of Rome c. 387 BC

The battle on 18 July was a disaster of some magnitude for the Romans; 18 July, *dies Alliensis*, was labelled a black day, *dies ater*, which darkened the memories of Romans for many years to come. The enemy was foreign, the first time Rome had been in conflict with non-Italians. The Gauls had a very different fighting style and they had very different objectives from the Italians. They were frightening: clamorous, colourful, they wielded strange weapons and wore unfamiliar armour. Alarmingly for the Romans, some of them even fought naked – to avoid their clothing snagging on hedgerows. The battle, and the run up to it, exposed complacency and arrogance on the part of the Romans: centuries of military success were to come to an abrupt and shocking end, which compromised the security of the very city of Rome and all the military achievements won so far.

Who were these Gauls and where did they come from? The Gauls in question were the Senones, a tribe which had crossed the Apennines in search of trade and new land to settle. They, and other Gauls, were massing in Cisalpine Gaul – that part of Italy immediately south of the Alps. They traded with towns such as Massilia and Etruria, which drew them in successive waves over the mountains from parts of what is now France, southern Germany, Switzerland, Austria and the Czech Republic into northern Italy and the Balkans via the rivers Rhône, Seine, Rhine and Danube, from about 500 BC. Conflict was inevitable: around 400 BC, the Insubres occupied Lombardy and took Mediolanum (near Milan) in 396 BC; next came the Boii who crossed the River Po and settled in Bononia (Bologna). The Senones audaciously penetrated further south; they drove out the Umbrians and established the *ager Gallicus* on the east coast of Italy between Ariminum and Ancona, then founded Sena Gallica (Sinigaglia), which became their capital. Etruscan towns further south, such as Marzabotto, were taken, probably by the Boii. Significantly for the Romans, Gauls were selling their services as mercenaries to southern Italian towns and tribes, and to various Hellenistic powers in the eastern Mediterranean. This entailed their transit down through the length of the Italian peninsula *en route* to rendezvous with their paymasters and warlords in their various theatres of war.

The Gauls, not surprisingly, usually received a bad press from Roman writers: Livy says that they came from the very ends of the world. Strabo describes them as 'war-mad', quick to fight but not malicious – a description at odds with his later report of their enthusiasm for head hunting and the use of other body parts hacked from the vanquished as battle trophies.[1] He emphasizes their naivety in strategy and tactics – something survivors of the sack of Rome may have found difficult to reconcile with their experience of events. Diodorus Siculus details the Gauls' military equipment or, in some cases, the absence of it amongst those relying on nature's protection alone; he also describes their skilful use of the chariot in battle – which their Celtic cousins in Britannia successfully deployed when facing Julius Caesar's invasion.[2]

In the early fourth century BC, the Senones finally reached Clusium (Chiusi) in the Etruscan province of Siena and made camp there. We can dismiss the story that the Senones were invited by Arruns of Clusium to assist him in taking revenge on his wife's lover, the powerful Lucomo. The Senones began to negotiate for land rights; understandably, the Clusians felt threatened by the terrifying sight of hordes of strange-looking, weird warriors at their gates and called for help from Rome. Rome, however, was somewhat weakened by recent wars; they had no obligations to Clusium and half-heartedly sent a delegation of three ambassadors, the Fabii brothers from the powerful patrician family, to negotiate.[3] The Fabii counselled peaceful negotiation, warning the Senones that Rome would be obliged to help Clusium should it be threatened. According to Livy, however, 'The envoys behaved more like savage Gauls than Romans.'[4]

The Gauls gave an ultimatum: a portion of the Clusium lands, or war. When the negotiations came to nothing, the Clusians attempted to force the Senones off their land. The ambassadors got involved and, in so doing, according to Livy, 'broke the law of nations' – *ius gentium* – when they disregarded their oath of neutrality as ambassadors 'and took up arms' against the Senones. Things got completely out of hand when Quintus Fabius killed one of the Gallic chieftains. When Quintus Fabius proceeded to strip the Gaul of his armour, the outraged Senones withdrew to take stock, only too aware that the sacred trust of the ambassador had been violated. The Romans had clearly not reckoned on the fact that the Gauls took their law and diplomacy very seriously. The issue was not now with the Clusians but with Rome.

The Senones despatched their own ambassadors to Rome, demanding that the Fabians be handed over to them so that justice might be done. Many Romans were sympathetic, and agreed that there had been a breach of the law of nations. Plutarch adds that the *fetiales* – that sacred body of military diplomats and envoys – were keen for Quintus Fabius to be punished. The Senate, although fully aware that surrendering the Fabii was the right way to go, were swayed by the people and refused to hand them over. Livy records the perversity of the situation and how Rome added insult to injury, or rather murder, in his report that two of the Fabii, far from being punished, were actually appointed for the coming year as military tribunes with consular powers. The Gauls were understandably incandescent and left, threatening war with Rome.[5]

The 130km march of the Senones from Clusium to Rome to take revenge was quite remarkable and further reinforced their claim that they desired to occupy land by agreement, and peacefully at that. According to Livy, the Senones left the peoples they passed *en route* unmolested and did not plunder their lands. It was with Rome, and with Rome alone, that they had an issue.

The Senones advanced with amazing rapidity and on 18 July confronted the Romans about 18km north of the city, at the River Allia, the Fosso della Bettina, a small tributary of the Tiber, north of Fidenae. Livy predicts the immense calamity that was about to unfold: 'When such a mass of evil was looming,'[6] incredulous that the Romans had not seen fit to appoint a dictator – so often their saviour in battles past – and oblivious to the fact that this was a new kind of enemy, prone to ferocious anger, with unpredictable ways and unfamiliar tactics, cacophonous and full of verve. The Gauls were obviously no Italians. Plutarch describes the naivety of the Roman army and, crucially, the fact that the hubristic Romans omitted to consult the gods or the augurs in advance of the battle.

The Roman forces under Q. Servilius Fidenas, Q. Sulpicius Lagus, and P. Cornelius Maluginensis numbered 15,000, made up of Romans and Italian allies; the Gauls, led by a chieftain called Brennus, were at least double that strength, anything up to 70,000 strong. Hopelessly unprepared and seriously outnumbered, the Romans kept their centre dangerously thin. They were cut down in their droves: the Roman reserves, positioned on higher ground, were routed without a Roman sword being drawn when Brennus attacked these first and slew them in flight; predictably, the centre then collapsed; the left wing was destroyed and those that could escape swam the river or drowned, dragged under the water by their cumbersome kit. Diodorus adds that the Gauls picked off the Romans with their javelins; the Romans were at the mercy of the long-reach Gallic swords. Survivors retreated to the town of Veii, a former enemy settlement laid waste by the Romans. The soldiers on the left fled back to Rome to take refuge on the Capitol, carelessly leaving the city gates open and undefended. Livy says that the Gauls were dumbstruck (*Gallos obstupefactos*) at the ease of their victory and feared a trap. There was no trap.

Diodorus melodramatically records that the Gauls spent the next day cutting off the heads of the Roman dead. Reassured that they had won the day, the Gauls heaped up the discarded Roman weapons and moved on Rome. Incredulously, scouts confronted a city with its gates ajar, no sentries on duty and with no soldiers manning the walls. The Roman citizens inside had no reason not to believe that those who had taken refuge in Veii were also dead, a misjudgement which served only to amplify their lamentations. They were also terrified, their fear heightened by the baying on the other side of the walls. Eventually, the Gauls entered the city by the Colline Gate. The surviving Romans, under the command of Marcus Manlius Capitolinus, had sensibly decided against defending the city and, as we have seen, ignominiously took refuge with women and children on the Capitol, where they hoped to make a final stand. The elderly were left down in the city so as not to be a burden to the fighters on the Capitol: Livy gives a wretched description of the older, non-combatant, men and the wailing women who were denied a place on the Capitol. Excavations have revealed contemporary burn marks in the Forum and on the Palatine which indicate extensive fires in Rome around this time.

The Roman state was in jeopardy. The Vestal Virgins and their essential flame, symbols of the sanctity, survival and well-being of Rome, were in peril, but they escaped to Caere with the *flamen Quirinalis* and other sacred objects. What they could not carry, the Vestals buried in earthen jars next to the Flamen's house; it was forbidden to spit on that sacred ground thereafter. Plutarch tells that it was imperative not to let the flame fall into enemy hands or to allow it to expire, such was the the awe in which it was held by the Romans. A plebeian, Lucius Albinus, was fleeing the city along with thousands of other refugees, his wagon laden with his family and everything he owned. Livy tells the tale:

> they were seen by L. Albinius, a Roman plebeian who with the rest of the crowd who were unfit for war was leaving the city. Even in that critical hour the distinction between sacred and profane was not forgotten. He had his wife and children with him in a wagon, and it seemed to him an act of impiety for him and his family to be seen in a vehicle whilst the national priests should be trudging along on foot, bearing the sacred vessels of Rome. He ordered his wife and children to get down, put the Virgins and their sacred burden in the wagon, and drove them to Caere, their destination.[7]

Indeed, Lucius Albinus as much as anyone could lay claim to being the saviour of Rome when he dutifully and selflessly brought the *sacra* to safety, preserving the very symbol of the security and sanctity of the city. Rome was surely doomed if the Vestal flame spluttered and went out.

Thousands of plebeians, refugees in their own city, likewise streamed out of Rome and headed for the relative safety of the Janiculum – a scenario repeated time and time again down the years throughout history to the present day, Syria being just the current example. Nearer home, the inhabitants of British cities echoed the fate of the Romans during the blitz, when they, the 'trekkers', left their homes each evening and took refuge in the countryside to escape that night's incendiaries and high explosive bombs.[8]

Elderly senators were prepared to die for Rome in a kind of *devotio*; they proudly took up positions outside their homes on ivory chairs, dignified, statue-like and stoic, to await their fate. The Gauls found them, a surreal sight, dressed in their finery and sporting their military medals: at first they were mesmerized, but astonishment soon turned into slaughter when one of the Gauls stroked the long beard of Marcus Papirius; Marcus Papirius responded by striking him with his staff, with predictable consequences.[9]

The Gauls then proceeded to sack the city, showing neither quarter nor mercy. According to Plutarch, 'the Gauls inflicted every outrage upon the city, and put to the sword all whom they captured, men and women, old and young alike.'[10] But Livy records that it was nowhere near as bad as it might have been; the Gauls seemed to have shown some restraint.[11] Neverthless, nothing was going to stop them preparing for an assault on the Capitol. The Romans, however, had gravity and momentum on their side: their first sally against the clambering Gauls effectively sent them hurtling back down the hill. The Gauls did not repeat the assault but prepared for a siege. The siege, however, was embarrassed somewhat by the fact that the Gauls had foolishly burnt all the grain when they torched the city, and were compelled to go out to forage for more.[12] This gave the Romans invaluable time.

Servius, in his commentary on the *Aeneid*, tells how during the siege women banded together and donated their gold and hair to make bowstrings for the Roman archers.

But Rome needed a saviour. As it happened, a disaffected Marcus Furius Camillus was in exile in nearby Ardea. Acting independently, during a night raid, he and a motley army slaughtered sleeping, inebriated Gauls who had been enjoying the spoils of victory. Similar butchery was visited on opportunistic Etruscans near Veii for failing to assist the Romans in their hour of need.

Camillus could not continue to act as a maverick commander and sought to make his position official. Once the necessary formalities with the Senate were concluded, he was free to rouse the Ardeans to assist the Romans bottled up on the Capitol.[13] As it happened, Camillus was always an obvious choice: a seasoned general, he had also commanded many of the Romans now in Veii and on the Capitol. Camillus himself had earned four triumphs, was dictator five times and became known as the Second Founder of Rome; in short, a highly successful, swashbuckling commander. He was, however, later convicted of embezzling booty and went back into exile.[14]

Camillus refused an impromptu generalship but accepted a one-year dictatorship *in absentia* with the task of ridding Rome of the Gauls. He recruited an army of 12,000 men from Veii to help him. In the meantime, the Gauls made a daring assault on the Capitol which took the Romans by surprise. The plan was hatched when the Gauls spotted the foot and handprints left by the brave Pontius Comitius who had acted as envoy between the Romans in the Senate, wending his way through the enemy lines to secure the approval of the Senate for Camillus to be made dictator. According to legend, the sacred geese of Juno heard the assailants (the guard dogs did not, it seems) and by their din alerted the consul Marcus Manlius.[15] Manlius promptly sent a Gaul toppling down the cliff, creating a kind of human avalanche, taking all his comrades tumbling down with him. Manlius was rewarded with gifts of food and drink – an exceptional gesture in view of the prevailing shortages and imminent famine on the Capitol – while one of the negligent guards was thrown over the cliff to his death, *more militare*, the way the army does.

The Gauls were now camped in a valley where conditions were less than salubrious: it was dry, hot and dusty – the complete antithesis to the climate and environment they were used to back in Gaul. They were soon plagued by an epidemic, exacerbated, no doubt, by the putrefying corpses of the unburied dead; the corpses were later burnt on mass pyres.[16] Seven months had now passed and famine was gripping the Romans on the Capitol, but still Camillus was nowhere to be seen, busy as he was recruiting and training an army capable of dealing with the Gauls. The Romans could either capitulate or negotiate terms. The Senate agreed to talks led by Brennus and Quintus Sulpicius.

Brennus negotiated an end to the siege whereby the Romans agreed to pay 1,000lb in gold. Brennus, however, acted duplicitously when he used heavier weights than standard when weighing out the gold. The Romans protested, only to have the Gaul angrily throw his sword and belt on the scales and shout insultingly in Latin, *'Vae victis!'* – 'Woe betide the vanquished!' Meaning, the winner takes it all. At this point, Camillus arrived back with his army; he entered the negotiations and placed his sword on the scale, exclaiming, *'Non auro, sed ferro, recuperanda est patria'* – 'You only win back this country with iron, not gold.' The deal was annulled and the gold was taken back. Just as significantly, this was a virtual declaration of war: two battles ensued, the second, decisive one on the road to Gabii. Camillus routed the Gauls and returned triumphant to Rome; it was at this point that he was hailed a second Romulus, a second founder of Rome.[17]

The battle at the Allio and the subsequent sack and siege of Rome saw the Romans displaying breathtaking military naivety, diplomatic arrogance and impiety; they were within an ace of losing everything they had gained since 753 BC and, had it not been for the Gauls sticking to their original, true objectives – simply to settle new lands – they might well have done. The Romans could be forgiven for their military ingenuousness: they had never endured a foreign invasion before and they, for the most part, had never before encountered a Gaul, a barbarian force. How could they know how best to repel such an extraordinary invader? Their tactics at the river were, admittedly, hopeless; perhaps another example of complacency and arrogance. Their own national pride and haughty feelings of military superiority cost them dearly.

The colourful episodes peppering the descriptions of the Battle of the River Allia and the sack of Rome are, of course, legends. They are embellishments, fictional anecdotes designed to conceal or mitigate the scale of the disaster and to restore Roman pride with *pietatis exempla et fortitudinis* – examples of dutifulness and bravery. The story of the Vestal Virgins and the handcart, and the tale of Roman women giving gold to help finance the Roman cause, the geese, brave, stalwart Marcus Papirius and his colleagues and the valour of Pontius Comitius were all invented to salvage Rome's reputation for military might in those times of extreme danger. Even Camillus' intervention has been called by Cornell 'the most artificially contrived of all Rome's heroes.'[18]

If the Romans were complacent before and during the battle, there was certainly no evidence of this in the immediate aftermath. Camillus effectively saved Rome a second time when he helped scotch a move to relocate the devastated capital to the ghost town that was Veii.[19] Rome would remain the capital city. Camillus took the initiative in a number of reforms. Unusually, Camillus did not resign the dictatorship at this point: he considered that there was still much work to done in saving Rome. His first move was to rebuild or restore each of the sacred buildings wrecked by the Gauls, aided by consultation of the august Sibylline Books – only ever consulted in times of dire emegency.[20] Caere, the ultimate destination of the Vestal flame and the Vestals on the cart that fateful day, was honoured, while the Capitoline Games were set up to celebrate Jupiter, saviour of the city. The women who gave the gold to pay off the Gauls were rewarded by having orations delivered at their funerals, hitherto an honour reserved for men – a small but important step forward for Roman women.[21]

Camillus proceeded to rebuild the city of Rome. Sadly, according to Livy, it was a bit of a botch, with crooked roads, errant sewers and unrestricted, indiscriminate plundering of timber and stone for haphazard housing developments. According to Plutarch, however, things were not all that bad: 'within a year's time, it is said, a new city had arisen, with walls to guard it and homes in which to dwell.'[22]

Defensively, the tufa Servian Wall – *murus Servii Tullii* – may well have been constructed around this time, up to 10m high in places, 3.6m wide at its base and 11km long, with sixteen gates. The wall served its purpose well during the Punic Wars. Surviving sections can be seen outside Termini Railway Station in Rome, including a small piece in the McDonald's at the station, and on the Aventine, where it incorporates an arch for a catapult from the late Republic.

In spite of their complacency, the Romans obviously observed the Gallic army closely, noting areas in which they excelled, weapons and tactics which could be adapted and incorporated into the Roman way of doing things. The Romans adopted the more agile, Gallic style of combat: the unwieldy phalanx was replaced by the more versatile maniple; the *pilum*, or javelin, superseded the thrusting spear; close-quarter weaponry was introduced, including heavier long swords and full-body shields (the *scutum*) which could be interlocked to enable tighter defense in the 'tortoise', or *testudo*. Support for the infantry came in the shape of fleet-footed troops (*velites*) armed with slings and javelins. The concentration of the cream of the patricians (*principes*) in the more vulnerable and exposed first line of infantry was abolished, and younger, highly trained soldiers replaced them.[23]

The introduction of a daily stipend around this time brought the benefit of relaxing the bond the Roman soldier had to the land. In effect, this eventually helped usher in a professional army which could fight and be garrisoned further and further from home without the need to return to farm the lands and raise money for weapons. Booty too was an increasingly important factor in the economic equation: as Rome extended its reach, so the opulent cities of the east fell under her sway and looted booty found its way back to Rome in the baggage trains of commanders.

The Gauls left Rome a poorer place militarily and economically. They also rendered her alarmingly vulnerable, which encouraged a number of conquered Italian cities to vacillate and rebel in an attempt to regain their independence. These included all the old suspects, enemies like the Etruscans, Volsci, Hernici, and Aequi. Rome, however, responded positively to this treachery by defeating them all systematically and completely until she had reasserted her dominance. Antium, the Volsci capital, was subdued in 338 BC; in 295 BC, the Samnite Wars ended when Rome vanquished a coalition of Samnites, Gauls,

Etruscans, and Umbrians. Stephen Oakley has estimated that, of the 130,000 square kilometres of land in the peninsula, the *ager Romanus* grew from 822 sq km (0.6 per cent) in 510 BC to 1,902 sq km in 340 BC and then to 23,226 sq km (17.9 per cent) in 264 BC. This expanse of contiguous territory made it increasingly difficult for enemies to threaten Rome. Her population was around 347,300 in 338 BC, rising to 900,000 in 264 BC.

Caudine Forks 321 BC

In the sixty-six years or so that followed the sack of Rome, the Romans enjoyed unbroken military success; that is until they walked into danger and disaster at the Caudine Forks. More of an ambush than a battle, it took place somewhere between Capua and Beneventum and was a source of much humiliation for the Romans. Successful battles had been fought against the Hernici, the Gauls, in the Samnite Wars, in the Great Latin Wars and in the Tarentine Wars. Caudine Forks was the second engagement in the Second Samnite War; it took place after a victory by Q. Fabius Maximus Rullianus at Imbrinium.

Rumours were put about by the Samnite chief, Gaius Pontius, that his army was besieging Luceria, a staunch ally of Rome. Pontius and his army were stealthily camped at Caudium (Montesarchio). The rumours were reinforced by *agents provocateurs* when Pontius had ten soldiers masquerading as shepherds peddle the same story. Rome's reaction was precipitate: they made their way to relieve friendly Luceria by way of a mountain combe accessible only through two defiles; at the end of one, their way was blocked off and when they had to retrace their steps they found the other exit similarly blockaded. The Romans were surrounded by the Samnites and were eventually forced to surrender.[24]

If the Romans were confounded by this reverse, the victorious Samnites were equally uncertain of what to do, in what was a unique situation for them. Pontius sent a letter to his father, Herennius Pontius, asking advice, but when the reply came back saying that the Romans should be allowed to go on their way, unharmed, Pontius was unimpressed, rejected it and wrote again to his father. This time the advice that came back was to kill all the Romans. Pontius was none the wiser, baffled by the ambiguity, thinking that his aging father had taken leave of his senses. He, therefore, asked Herennius to come to him in person: Herennius arrived, and set out the options. If they were to set the Romans free they would win the Romans' invaluable, enduring friendship. Alternatively, if they killed them, then Rome would be so weakened as not to pose a threat for many years. Pontius asked if there was a middle way, but Herennius advised that such a strategy would be stupid, leaving as it would the Romans hungry for revenge with no depletion in numbers. In the end, the Samnites took 600 *equites* as hostages and negotiated a treaty, the Caudine Peace, the terms of which obliged the entire Roman army, now close to starvation, to pass under the yoke: the ultimate humiliation for a Roman. The Samnites' action here was dictated by political rather than warlike considerations: with an eye to the future, perhaps, they saw that it may be better to release the Romans as insurance against future developments in which they may need to negotiate with the Roman aggressor on less secure grounds.

Caudine Forks, however, was not all bad news. It gave Rome time to breathe: they used that time well, increasing the army from two to four legions, each of approximatly 4,200 men. With the contingents supplied by the allies, this made the Roman army an impressive, and fearsome, force of 35,000–40,000 men.

When the Romans defeated an enemy army, they had three options: they could massacre the surviviors, but this was not always popular at home; they could sell the survivors as slaves, but this posed major logistical problems in transportation, feeding, security, and the fact that there were no viable slave markets anyway until the later Republic; or they could set the survivors free, but not before they had been demeaned and degraded by forcing them under the yoke. As we know, sometimes this ritual humiliation was turned on the Romans, much to the glee, no doubt, of their enemies. It had considerable effect on morale: the terrible suggestion being that the Roman soldier (and by extension Rome itself) had lost *virtus*, that he was emasculated. Here is Livy's vivid description of the Caudine Forks degradation:

> The consuls were the first to be sent, little more than half–clothed, under the yoke, then each in the order of his rank was exposed to the same disgrace, and finally, the legionaries one after another. Around them stood the enemy fully armed, reviling and jeering at them; swords were pointed at most of them, and when they offended their victors by showing their indignation and resentment too plainly some were wounded and even killed. Thus were they marched under the yoke. But what was still harder to bear was that after they had emerged from the pass under the eyes of the foe, though, like men dragged up from the jaws of hell, they seemed to behold the light for the first time, the very light itself, serving only to reveal such a hideous sight as they marched along, was more gloomy than any shape of death. They could have reached Capua before nightfall, but not knowing how their allies would receive them, and kept back by a feeling of shame, they all flung themselves, destitute of everything, on the sides of the road near Capua.[25]

Appian adds that this was a fate worse than death for a Roman. He gives us some detail of the procedure:

> When the oaths had been taken, Pontius opened a passage from the defile, and having fixed two spears in the ground and laid another across the top, caused the Romans to go under it as they passed out, one by one.[26]

Caesar describes in his *De Bello Gallico* the Roman army under Lucius Cassius being routed and 'sent under the yoke' by the Helvetii under Divico in 107 BC. Caesar had ordered Lucius Cassius, Piso and Publicus to drive the Helvetii from around Lake Geneva but Divico trapped the Romans.[27] The heads of the Roman commanders were impaled on stakes; the Roman soldiers were allowed to surrender and return home, but not before they were forced to pass beneath the yoke in humiliating enactment of their defeat. The famous painting by Charles Gleyre (1808–1874), *The Romans Passing Under the Yoke* (1858), is now an important and resonant part of the Swiss national iconography.

In 110 BC, the Romans under Aulus Albinus were defeated by the Numantian king Jugurtha and also forced to pass under the yoke. In effect, the yoke symbolized the relegation from heroic and brave free soldier to farm animal.[28] Our word 'subjugate' is derived from *subjugatus*: *sub*, meaning 'under', plus *jugum*, meaning 'yoke'.

Latulae 316 BC

In 316, the Romans reneged on the Caudine Peace. Under the appointed dictator, Quintus Fabius Rullianus, L. Papirius Cursor advanced into Apulia to lay siege to the Samnites at Luceria while Q. Publilius Philo attacked the Samnites at Saticula. At the same time, Rullianus assaulted Satricum and Volscian rebels in the Liris valley. All this amounted to an ill-conceived, muddled strategy which involved splitting the Roman forces: the Samnites defeated Philo and advanced on Latium; Rullianus confronted the Samnites at Fregellae. He could have gone on to Rome along the Trerus valley or confronted the Samnites. There was a disastrous battle at Latulae in which the Romans, attempting to regain the coast road to Campania under Rullianus, suffered great losses after panic in the ranks. Quintus Aulius Cerratanus alone, *magister equitum*, stood his ground and died a hero, but not before he had speared the Samnite general in a solo cavalry charge.

Capua joined the Samnites. The Samnites took Sora, which had also defected from Rome; the Roman colonists there were murdered. The territory south of Rome was then populated with non-Roman citizens who capitulated to the Samnites, while the land to the north, inhabited by Roman citizens (*Latium vetus*), was devastated.

Rome had paid the price for splitting her forces at Latulae. She bounced back, however, and drove the Samnites from Tarracina.[29] The Romans, ever ready to learn from their mistakes, took two very important lessons from Latulae. The first was the importance and necessity of maintaining lines of communication; this resulted in the construction of the super *autostrada* Via Appia. The second was confirmation, if needed, of the need to fight in maniples armed with *pila* (javelins) and *scuta* (shields). A series of victories between 315 and 305 BC brought the Second Samnite War to a successful conclusion for the Romans, involving defeats for the Etruscans, Umbrians and Apulians as well as the Samnites.

Chapter 5

The Third Century: the Wars with Pyrrhus, the Punic Wars and the Gallic Invasion

Camerinum 298 BC

The Third Samnite War began when the Romans invaded Samnite territory. The Samnites, meanwhile, penetrated Campania and Umbria and Sabine lands as far as the territory of the Senones under Gellius Ignatius. At the Battle of Camerinum in Umbria, Rome faced a formidable combined force of Gauls, Etruscans, Umbrians and Samnites under Gellius Egnatius; his objective was to crush Rome once and for all. The intelligence picked up by the Roman general, Lucius Cornelius Scipio Barbatus, left much to be desired: Scipio had led his men onto higher ground to compensate for his inferior numbers, only to find it already occupied by the enemy. The Romans were routed. The decisive Battle of Sentinum followed shortly after this devastating reverse. Only too aware of their vulnerability, the Romans strengthened their army by enlisting ex-slaves and conscripting somewhat older men to garrison the camps; this brought their field numbers up to 40,000. The victorious commanders were P. Decius Mus and Quintus Fabius Maximus Rullianus. Never before had such numbers been gathered together to do battle on Italian soil. The victory here marked Rome's unification of Italy.[1]

Arretium 284 BC

The Samnites were at last defeated. Their Etruscan allies had capitulated to the Romans in 294 BC and, by 290 BC, they were surrounded by towns and cities allied to Rome. The Samnites sued for peace in 290 BC, surrendering some of their land. The Gauls, however, continued to harry Rome.

The Senones laid siege to Arretium and defeated the Roman relief force. Lucius Caecilius Metellus Denter replaced the Roman praetor who had been killed, and sent envoys to the Gauls to negotiate over prisoners. The Gauls unceremoniously slew the envoys, prompting Denter to take revenge by defeating the Gauls and expelling the Senones. He then proceeded to devastate the Senonian lands, the *ager Gallicus*, which became little more than a desert for the next 50 years. A later uprising by the Boii at Lake Vadimonis was suppressed by P. Cornelius Dolabella.[2] The Romans had no doubts as to how to deal with such treachery; they responded with uncompromising savagery, hoping to send out a message to others who might contemplate dealing with them in such a dishonourable and despicable way.

Heraclea (280 BC)

The Pyrrhic War (280–275 BC) started after a minor naval battle in the Bay of Tarentum which violated the treaty obligations between the city of Tarentum and Epirus in Greece. When Roman ships sailed into Tarentine waters, Tarentum saw this as a breach of treaty. To help them against Rome they sought help from Pyrrhus as payback for the aid they had given him in his conflict with Korkyra. Pyrrhus saw this as an empire-building opportunity.

Tarentum was founded in 706 BC by Dorian Greek immigrants and was Sparta's only colony. Its founders were Partheniae, biological anomalies believed to be the sons of virgins. In reality, they were the sons of unmarried Spartan women and Perioeci, free men who were not officially citizens of Sparta and whose sole function in life was to increase the Spartan birthrate and thereby recruitment to the Spartan army during the Messenian wars. These spurious marriages were later annulled and the sons were exiled. Phalanthus, the Parthenian leader, consulted the oracle at Delphi as to how best to handle this and was told that Tarentum was to be the new home of the exiles. Tarentum grew, and by the time Roman power was spreading south, it had become a leading commercial and military force amongst the cities of Magna Graecia in southern Italy.

From the eighth and seventh centuries BC, famine, overcrowding and a need for new commercial opportunities, trade and ports, led the Greeks into a programme of extensive colonization which included such widespread places as the eastern coast of the Black Sea, Libya and Massalia, Sicily and the southern tip of the Italian peninsula – territories collectively known as Magna Graecia. With the Greeks came Greek culture: dialects of the Greek language, arts, religious rites, the *polis* – all subsumed into native Italic culture. The Chalcidean–Cumaean version of the Greek alphabet was adopted by the Etruscans and the resulting Old Italic alphabet subsequently evolved into the Latin alphabet. Major cities included Neapolis, Syracuse, Acragas and Sybaris, Tarentum, Rhegium, Nola, Ancona and Bari.

Sheep farming was a major factor in Tarentum's economic and commercial success; fleeces, dyed purple with the mussels from the harbour, were much in demand throughout Italy. Ceramics too were important to the economy, and trade generally soon spread into the lands bordering on the Aegean, beyond the Po and across the Alps. Commercial prowess was matched by political stability and the ability to raise an army of some 15,000 men, to complement the strongest navy in the Mediterranean. The Tarentine armed forces were strengthened further by bands of Greek mercenaries, giving them the power not only to snuff out incursions by the Oscans but also indulge in territorial expansion. During the First Samnite War, the Tarentines allied with King Archidamus of Sparta and then, in 334 BC, with his brother-in-law, King Alexander of Epirus. Alexander successfully quelled incursions by the Brutii, Samnites and Lucanians and concluded a non-aggression pact with the Romans on behalf of Tarentum. Tarentum, however, was increasingly suspicious of Alexander's motives and left him to hang out to dry, and to be murdered by the Lucanians. Rome's expansionism, too, was viewed with some anxiety in Tarentum; they rejected Rome's attempts at diplomacy. The Battle of Tarentum followed soon after.

Pyrrhus was King of Epirus (r. 306–302, 297–272 BC) and Macedon (r. 288–284, 273–272 BC). He was the son of Aeacides and Phthia, a Thessalian woman who was second cousin of Alexander the Great, through Alexander's mother, Olympias. In 298 BC, at the age of 21, King Pyrrhus was taken hostage to Alexandria, as one of the terms of a peace treaty between Demetrius, his brother-in-law, and Ptolemy I Soter. There, he married Ptolemy I's step-daughter Antigone and was restored to his kingdom in Epirus in 297 BC with aid from Ptolemy I. Neoptolemus II of Epirus was his co-ruler; Pyrrhus had him murdered. One of Greece's more flamboyant brigands, whose dubious services were freely available throughout the Mediterranean, Pyrrhus answered Tarentum's plea for support against Rome with undisguised alacrity.

The Roman victory over Tarentum, their defeat at Heraclea and the subjugation of Magna Graecia are not the only significant features in the wars with Pyrrhus. They give us the term every victorious general fears, the 'Pyhrric victory' – and the first deployments of that giant of all war machines, the elephant, against the Roman army.

We first meet the elephant as an instrument of war with the Indians, described in the Sanskrit epics, and in stories of the Mahabharata and the Ramayana in the fourth century BC. To some rulers, an army without elephants was nothing short of absurd: as objectionable as a forest without a lion, a kingdom without a king or courage unaided by weapons. Training an elephant for combat duty was no simple matter: first they had to be captured in the wild, because selective breeding took so long; and then there was the wait until the elephant was mature – only mature elephants were fit to fight. War elephants were males, not because males exhibited the right aggressive temperament, but rather because a female elephant will flee from a male in a battle situation. Female elephants were nevertheless still used for logistic duties.

Battle elephants spread westwards to the Persians in their wars with Alexander the Great. The first confrontation came at the Battle of Gaugamela in 331 BC, when the Persians deployed fifteen elephants. They made such a terrific and terrifying impact that Alexander sacrificed to the God of Fear on the eve of the battle. Next day, Alexander won and was so taken by this novel and fantastic war machine that he enlisted the fifteen he had captured into his own army, adding to the herd as he overran the rest of Persia. Alexander confronted up to 100 war elephants at the battle of the Hydaspes River against Porus, in the modern day Punjabi region of Pakistan. But this was insignificant compared to what the kings of the Nanda Empire (Maghada) and Gangaridai (present-day Bangladesh and the Indian state of West Bengal) could throw against him: no fewer than between 3,000 and 6,000 war elephants, which put an end to Alexander's invasion of India. Returning home, he formed a unit of elephants to guard his palace at Babylon, and established the office of *elephantarch* to take command of the beasts.

The successful military use of elephants spread further. Alexander's successors, the Diadochi, continued the practice, using many hundreds of Indian war elephants in their wars; the Seleucids likewise. In the Seleucid–Mauryan war of 305–303 BC, the Seleucids gave up extensive lands in the east in exchange for 500 Mauryan war elephants, a mere handful from the 9,000 elephants Pliny the Elder tells us they could draw on.[3] The Seleucids made good use of their 500 at the Battle of Ipsus in 301 BC against the Diadochi. Later the Seleucids deployed elephants in the Maccabean Revolt in Judea, 167–160 BC. Eleazar Maccabeus bravely slew an elephant in the Battle of Beth Zechariah by sticking a spear into its belly, wrongly thinking it to be carrying Antiochus V. Unfortunately, the dying elephant crushed Eleazar to death as it crashed to the ground.[4] Some elephants were fitted with leather or metal rings around their legs to protect against the enemy cutting their heel muscles.

War elephants made their European debut in 318 BC when Polyperchon, one of Alexander's generals, besieged Megalopolis with the help of sixty elephants brought from Asia along with their *mahouts*. The elephants saw a lot of action: another of Alexander's generals, Damis, defeated Polyperchon – the elephants were posted by Cassander to other battle theatres in Greece; part of the journey was by sea so we can take it that Cassander was responsible for building some of the first elephant sea transports. Some of his elephants starved to death in Pydna in 316 BC while under siege.

Elephants became popular for deployment in battle with the Ptolemies, Carthaginians, Numidians and Kushites, making use of the North African forest elephant (later to become extinct from over-exploitation). The North African species was smaller than the Asian elephants used in the east; the most famous was Hannibal's beast called *Surus*, 'the Syrian'. Debate has raged for some sixty years over whether the African elephants used by Numidian, Ptolemaic and Punic armies carried howdahs or turrets in battle, given the relative physical weakness of the species. Some depictions and descriptions of turrets are without doubt anachronistic or fictitious, but there is strong evidence, for example, that Juba I of Numidia used turreted elephants in 46 BC.[5] In addition, there is the image of a turreted African elephant on the coinage of Juba II.[6] Polybius records that in 217 BC the elephants of Ptolemy IV sported turrets at the Battle of Raphia.[7] In his Book 6, Pliny the Elder says that Sri Lankan elephants were bigger and fiercer, thus making Sri Lanka's elephants much in demand for military use.

Pyrrhus introduced the combat elephant to Italy at the Battle of Heraclea, in Lucania on the Gulf of Otranto. Here the elephants were of the Indian variety and were given the sobriquet 'Lucanian oxen' by the awe-struck Roman soldiers. We shall, of course, meet these formidable, temperamental and wholly unpredictable instruments of war again in the wars against Hannibal.

In 280 BC, Pyrrhus landed in Italy with 25,000 troops and twenty or so war-trained elephants. His army was made up of 3,000 cavalry, 2,000 archers, 500 slingers and 20,000 infantry. The elephants were on loan from Ptolemy II, who also promised 9,000 troops and fifty more elephants to defend Epirus while Pyrrhus was absent fighting in Italy. On his arrival at Tarentum, Pyrrhus found a city enjoying life and quite happy to allow him to fight their wars for them. He immediately put an end to this sybaritic lifestyle, banning banquets, drinking parties and festivals and organizing a mobilization of Tarentines. Displeased at having to give up their indulgent lives, many Tarentines left the city.

The Romans had never faced elephants in battle before. It is easy to imagine their consternation and terror when they saw what they were up against at Heraclea. Valerius Laevinus, with an inferior force of 20,000 men, crossed the River Siris, but his army crumbled in the face of a 3,000-strong cavalry charge followed by infantry. The Romans were finally defeated when Pyrrhus' elephants caused the Roman horses to panic and stampede. The Thessalian cavalry then routed the Roman troops. Pyrrhus lost 13,000 men to the Romans' 15,000, although the figures may be nearer 7,000 and 4,000. The Lucanians and the Samnites went over to Pyrrhus after this victory.[8]

Ausculum Satrianum 279 BC

The introduction of the elephant to the battlefield was quickly followed by the introduction of anti-elephant tactics and techniques to deter, deflect and destroy them. At Ausculum in Apulia, Pyrrhus brought elephants, nineteen of them, onto the front line again, but the Romans had learnt their lesson and responded. They came to the battle equipped with fire and anti-elephant devices and traps: ox-drawn wagons with long spikes to impale the beasts, buckets of fire to terrify them and a squad of troops whose role it was to fire off salvoes of javelins at the elephants. Roman infantrymen would frequently try to cut off their trunks, causing panic so that the animal hurtled back into its own lines. The flank was their Achilles heel, exploited by skirmishers armed with javelins which, when on target, could enrage an elephant. The cavalry sport of tent pegging comes from training exercises in which horsemen injured or repulsed war elephants. The war pig was a particularly popular weapon against the elephant. Pliny the Elder writes that 'elephants are scared by the smallest squeal of a pig.'[9] We know from Aelian that, at the siege of Megara during the Diadochi wars, the Megarians poured boiling oil on a herd of pigs, set them on fire, and drove them towards the enemy's elephants. The elephants ran amok, terrified by the burning, squealing pigs.[10]

The two armies at Ausculum were of similar size, with 40,000 men each. The Romans comprised four legions or so of infantry, plus allies made up of the Dauni. Pyrrhus' force was something of a motley army, comprising Epirotes, Greeks, allies from Magna Graecia, Etruscans and Umbrians, his own Macedonian infantry and cavalry, Greek mercenaries, war elephants, and Samnite infantry and cavalry. On the second day of the battle, the elephants were to prove decisive, as at Heraclea: the elephants, and light infantry, punctured the Roman line and, despite an attack by anti-elephant Roman chariots, the Romans were overrun by Greek *psiloi*, lightly armed skirmishers. The elephants charged again; the Romans broke ranks and Pyrrhus, deploying his cavalry, delivered a significant rout.

Roman casualties were in the region of 8,000, while Pyrrhus lost a considerable 3,000, including many officers. The costly victory here gives us the term 'Pyrrhic victory' – where casualties are so great in victory that the loss is greater than any gain. Plutarch describes it neatly:

> The armies separated; and, it is said, Pyrrhus replied to one that gave him joy of his victory that one more such victory would utterly undo him. For he had lost a great part of the forces he brought with him, and almost all his particular friends and principal commanders; there were no others there

to make recruits, and he found the confederates in Italy backward. On the other hand, as from a fountain continually flowing out of the city, the Roman camp was quickly and plentifully filled up with fresh men, not at all abating in courage for the loss they sustained, but even from their very anger gaining new force and resolution to go on with the war.[11]

Pyrrhus, recognizing his dilemma, is reputed to have commented: 'Another victory like that and I'll be going back to Epirus without a single soldier,' and, 'If we win one more battle with the Romans, we shall be utterly ruined.' Disaster was not just the preserve of the defeated. Accounts of the battle vary greatly between Plutarch and those of Dionysius, Zonaras, Orosius and Livy.[12] For Orosius it was an overwhelming victory for the Romans.

The advantages of the elephant on the battlfield are obvious: trampling weight, crushing bulk and swirling tusks were formidable weapons. An elephant charged at around 30km/h and, unlike horse cavalry, could be unstoppable; the terror they instilled in the enemy up against them was awesome. Horses panicked just at their smell. The elephant's thick hide was like armour; some elephants were fitted with armour. Where turrets were used they gave the rider or commander a unique view of the battlefield or else a platform from which to loose fusillades of arrows. But elephants had their disadvantages too.

'Friendly fire', as we euphemistically call it, would have been very frequent in the head-on, close-quarter combat fighting of the tightly-knit Roman fighting units. It would have been exacerbated by a number of factors: no distinctive or recognizable uniforms, similar languages yelled out by enemies and allies in the heat of battle, to name but two. The general mayhem and turmoil would only have increased the chances of fighting your own men or raining arrows, spears and sling-shot down on friends and allies. The consternation of the Athenian defeat at the night-time Battle of Epipolae in 413 BC is graphically described by Thucydides – a blueprint for 'blue-on-blue' battlefield confusion. He asks how anyone can possibly know what is really going on in the dark: 'many parts of the enemy ended by falling upon each other, friend against friend, citizen against citizen.'[13] This nightmare scenario must have been repeated endlessly down the years. Despite attempts to control and direct it effectively against the enemy, the elephant often can only have added to the 'friendly fire'. Despite its advantage as a psychological and physical instrument of war, the elephant was prone to panic, difficult to control and indiscriminately deadly when on the rampage. Time and time again, when a startled, frightened or injured elephant turned and fled, it trampled over its own soldiers in its blind rush to flee the field of battle.

The Battle of Heraclea was the first battle the Romans lost to a Greek enemy and to an army which deployed elephants as a weapon of war. Ausculum was the second. The Carthaginians observed the strategic advantage that could be gained by the successful deployment of elephants and recruited them for support in the First Punic War. Rome too was seduced and, after the Punic Wars, made significant use of them: the invasion of Macedonia in 199 BC, the battles of Cynoscephalae in 197 BC and Thermopylae and Magnesia in 190 BC when Antiochus III's fifty-four elephants faced the Romans' sixteen. The Romans sent out twenty-two elephants at Pydna in 168 BC. They also featured in the Roman campaigns against the Celtiberians in Hispania, against the Gauls and in the invasion of Britannia. Polyaenus tells of Caesar's use of an elephant to defeat Cassivellaunus's men at a river crossing:

Caesar had one large elephant, which was equipped with armour and carried archers and slingers in its tower. When this unknown creature entered the river, the Britons and their horses fled and the Roman army crossed over.[14]

However, the story is not true, the elephant being deployed in Claudius' later invasion. The Romans faced the elephant for the last time at the Battle of Thapsus, 46 BC, when Julius Caesar equipped his Vth legion (*Alaudae*) with axes for hacking the elephants' legs. The Romans hacked away and survived the charge; the Vth adopted the elephant as its symbol.

In the Empire, the Parthians used war elephants against Rome, as did the Sassanid Dynasty. Their more famous engagements were the Battle of Vartanantz in AD 451, at which the Sassanid elephants struck terror in the Armenians and the Battle of al-Qādisiyyah in AD 636, when thirty-three elephants were deployed against insurgent Arab armies.

Military execution by elephant was a terrible feature of the Roman, Carthaginian and Macedonian criminal justice systems. Deserters, prisoners of war and military criminals generally are known to have met their deaths squashed under the foot of an elephant. Perdiccas, regent of Macedon after the death of Alexander the Great in 323 BC, threw Meleager mutineers to the elephants in Babylon. Quintus Curtius Rufus in his *Historiae Alexandri Magni* vividly describes the scene:

Perdiccas saw that they [the mutineers] were paralyzed and at his mercy. He withdrew from the main body some 300 men who had followed Meleager at the time when he burst from the first meeting held after Alexander's death, and before the eyes of the entire army he threw them to the elephants. All were trampled to death beneath the feet of the beasts.[15]

A disciplinarian, Valerius Maximus, reports how the general Lucius Aemilius Paulus Macedonicus:

> after King Perseus was vanquished [in 167 BC], for the same fault [desertion] threw men under elephants to be trampled ... And indeed military discipline needs this kind of severe and abrupt punishment, because this is how strength of arms stands firm, which, when it falls away from the right course, will be subverted.

Lipari Islands 260 BC

The Gauls were Rome's first foreign enemy. Mighty Carthage was its second. The city was founded in 814 BC on the Gulf of Tunis, outside what is now Tunis, by Phoenicians from Tyre, at the junction of a number of Mediterranean trading routes. *Carthago* is a Latinization of *Kart-Hadasht*, which means 'new city'. From about 600 BC, Carthage began a 300-year process of eliminating Greek influence from the coasts of Spain and the islands of the western Mediterranean, leaving the Greeks with only a tenuous presence in eastern Sicily. The Carthaginians shrewdly established colonial cities along the Mediterranean coasts to provide safe harbours for their merchant fleets, from which to extract natural resources, and trade, free from outside interference. Carthage was somewhat unusual amongst ancient societies Rome came into contact with because of its focus and dependence on overseas trade.

Carthaginian Spain yielded silver, lead, copper and tin ore – essential for the manufacture of bronze objects, weapons and armour – notably at Tartessos (modern Andalusia, at the mouth of the Guadalquivir River). Carthage was the Mediterranean's largest silver producer, mined both in Spain and on the North-African coast; one mine alone in Iberia reputedly gave Hannibal 300 Roman pounds of silver every day. Other lucrative industries included Cornish tin from the Cassiterides – or Tin Islands – in Britannia, and gold and ivory from West Africa. Exports included wine, textiles and pottery; from the fourth century BC these were bolstered by agricultural produce from the fertile North-African hinterland.

The Carthaginian empire in the fourth century BC, when it came up against Rome, comprised southern Spain, north Africa, Malta, Sardinia, Corsica and western Sicily; colonies included cities on Cyprus, Sardinia, Corsica, the Balearics, Crete and Sicily, as well as at modern-day Genoa and Marseille. Polybius reports that alone amongst all nations the Carthaginians were most preoccupied with maritime affairs, that they ruled the waves and that their fleet numbered up to 350 vessels. The navy was a professional, permanently manned senior service while, on the other hand, the army was enlisted for a particular campaign and then demobilized. It was the complete opposite to the Roman system. If you believe Eratosthenes of Cyrene (*c.* 276 BC – *c.* 195 BC) the Carthaginians, in defence of their maritime supremacy, would seize every ship sailing towards the Straights of Gades or Sardinia and throw everyone on board into the sea to drown.

Carthage was naturally anxious to defend its commercial assets and monopolies; generally, she tried diplomacy before resorting to conflict. As the Romans spread inexorably down the Italian coast, so the Carthaginians maintained amicable relations through a string of treaties with Rome, the first of which, as we have seen, was in 509 BC, the year in which the Republic was established. Preserving each other's interests and co-existing commercially and militarily was the mutual objective, initially. When Carthage formed an alliance with Rome against Pyrrhus in 279 BC, Rome eyed Carthage's intentions with suspicion, believing that their aim, like their own, was to take control of the Italian coast. Accordingly, between 350 BC and 270 BC, the Romans established a chain of coastal colonies from Etruria to Campania. Rome was also careful to ensure that in each of its treaties it stipulated that Carthage must not settle on Italian soil. In 311 BC, Rome commissioned a flotilla to patrol the Italian coast; the small Roman navy was beefed up with the formation of the *classici* to supervise naval fortifications. From the Carthaginian viewpoint, Rome's annexation of lands on the Italian side of the Straits of Messina looked threatening and ominous, leaving the Carthaginian territories on Sicily exposed.

The Battle of the Lipari Islands was the opening shot between the fleets of Carthage and the Romans in the First Punic War. The Carthaginian victory was more of an ambush, rather than a fixed battle. By 260 BC, the Romans could deploy 140 warships under the command of Gnaeus Cornelius Scipio Asina; but things did not start well for the fledgling Roman navy. Scipio led an advance force of seventeen quinqueremes to Lipara (modern Lipari), which he had been tricked into believing was keen to side with the Romans. Intent on taking what he thought to be an easy prize and thereby covering himself in glory, Scipio rashly entered the port, only to find himself blocked in by the Carthaginian flotilla of twenty ships commanded by Boodes and Hannibal Gisco. Polybius says that the crews fled onto the island while Scipio was captured with the ships and taken to Hannibal. Zonaras has a version in which Scipio and his officers were taken aboard the Punic flagship, arrested and sent to Carthage.

Things improved for the Romans when the remainder of their fleet sailed for Sicily and engaged a Carthaginian scouting party of fifty ships; the Romans came out on top, destroying most of Hannibal's vessels.[16] If nothing else, Lipara underlined for the Romans the strategic importance of a fleet and forced them to realize the need to rule the waves if they were to defeat the Carthaginians. The experience of Lipara, despite Scipio's asinine behaviour, was well learnt and the Romans went on to defeat the Carthaginians in a naval engagement at Mylae in 260 BC. Scipio's folly earned him the insulting cognomen Asina, 'donkey'; all the more humiliating for a man because *asina* is the feminine form of *asinus*.

Tunis (Bagradas River) 255 BC

After the Roman victory at Adys on the Carthaginian mainland, the Carthaginians rejected what they saw as the Romans' unreasonable and extortionate terms, and responded by rebuilding, retraining and replenishing their army with the help of Xanthippus, a charismatic Spartan warlord and mercenary. He rekindled the old Carthaginian confidence and brought Regulus to battle at the Bagradas River. The Punic forces numbered 12,000 infantry, 4,000 cavalry and 100 elephants. The Roman centre was hemmed in by the Carthaginian infantry and elephants, and surrounded by their cavalry. The Romans were virtually wiped out, with only 2,000 survivors to the Punic loss of 800; Marcus Atilius Regulus was taken prisoner along with 500 of his men. Apparently, his eyelids were cut off and he was trampled to death by a rogue elephant, but accounts of his death vary widely and wildly.

Horace says that he was in captivity until 250 BC, when, after the Roman success at the Battle of Panormus, the Carthaginians sent him back to Rome on parole to negotiate a peace settlement or an exchange of prisoners. Once there, he did neither, urging instead the Senate to continue fighting; nevertheless, he honoured his parole and returned to Carthage, where he was executed for his troubles. Valerius Maximus says he was tortured with sleep deprivation until he died; Aulus Gellius believes that he was thrown into a dark dungeon, hauled out and forced to look straight into the sun after his eyelids had been cut off; Florus says he was crucified; Augustine would have us believe that he was entombed alive in a coffin lined with nails.[17] Another version has him being rolled down a hill in a barrel lined with spikes. Whatever the truth, the story and hyperbole surrounding it came to epitomize Roman *pietas*, honour and patriotism to the state; Regulus is seen as an examplar of the good Roman. Much of it may well have been construed by historians as propaganda to foster hatred towards Carthage, even to justify Rome's own atrocities towards Carthaginian prisoners.[18]

Legend has it that after the battle, Xanthippus visited Lilybaeum, which was under siege by the Romans. The city, jealous of his successes, gave him an unseaworthy, leaking ship in which to continue his journey, with inevitable consequences: Xanthippus drowned in the Adriatic Sea.

Drepana 249 BC

In 249, the Romans, under the consuls Publius Claudius Pulcher and Lucius Junius Pullus, laid siege to Lilybaeum – but with no success. Hannibal (son of Hamilcar) broke the siege by day and replenished the garrison by night with his flotilla. Indeed, the only real result of the humiliating Roman efforts was to encourage the Carthaginians to rebuild their fleet. Claudius attacked Drepana, the site of the Punic shipyards. Adherbal, the Carthaginian commander, sailed from the harbour; when Claudius saw this, he ordered his fleet to pursue him. The outcome was a huge and muddled Roman naval calamity, with multiple collisions and utter confusion. The Romans were now exposed along the shoreline, allowing Adherbal to take ninety-three of Claudius' vessels and their crews. The remaining thirty Roman ships, under Junius Pullus, were attacked by the Carthaginian admiral Carthalo and driven onto rocks off Cape Passaro, where they were wrecked in a strengthening gale. However, Pullus did not give up: he attacked and took the lofty, strategically important fortress of Eryx (Erice) by land. Lucius Iunius Pullus committed suicide rather than return to Rome in disgrace. The war-weary Romans had, for the time being, gone as far as they could – militarily and financially.

If geese were reputedly involved in the sack of Rome in 390 BC, then chickens are said to have played a leading role in the outcome of the Battle of Drepana. In his *De Natura Deorum*, Cicero tells us that the defeat was due to Claudius' hubristic disrespect for the pre-battle auspices. The sacred chickens would not eat the corn— traditionally a terrible omen, clearly indicating that the gods were not in favour of a battle. In an ill-advised bid to calm his quaking crew, Claudius unceremoniously threw the chickens overboard, pronouncing: 'If they won't eat, let them drink.' Claudius survived the battle but not the aftermath; he returned to Rome in disgrace on charges of treason – occasioned not by his ineptitude, but for his sacrilege in the chickens incident. He was exiled.

Clusium (Faesulae) 225 BC

In 225 BC, the Gauls were back. A combined force comprising mainly of Transalpine mercenaries, Insubres and Boii numbering 50,000 infantry and

25,000 horse, marched into Etruria. The Romans summoned help from their Italian allies and put together some 130,000 infantry, with many more troops available in reserve: 70,000 Samnites, Etruscans, Umbrians, Campanians and Romans came together to face the Gauls. Gaius Atilius Regulus was ordered to return immediately from Sardinia, while the other consul, Lucius Aemilius Papus, marched to Ariminum to protect the east coast. Sabines and Etruscans advanced into Etruria, where the two armies met at Clusium (Chiusi) – three days from Rome – the Gauls devastating and plundering the land *en route*. On the eve of the battle, the Gallic infantry withdrew to Faesulae (Fiesoli) and lay in ambush, leaving the cavalry behind in reserve. In the morning, the Romans attacked the cavalry, who were themselves now retreating towards Faesulae; 6,000 Romans fell in the ensuing ambush, the remainder finding refuge on a nearby hilltop. Meanwhile, the other Roman army, under the consul Lucius Aemilius Papus, made a timely arrival at the scene, saving the Romans from total destruction. Judging discretion to be the better part of valour, the Gauls withdrew without further Roman loss. Forty thousand Gauls reputedly died. Papus then marched into Liguria to inflict punitive actions against the Boii; he was awarded a triumph.[19] The Romans had their revenge at Telamon later that year.

Ticinus River 218 BC

Hannibal started the Second Punic War in 219 BC when he assaulted the city of Saguntum (in Valencia), firm allies of the Romans. To Rome, this amounted to a *casus belli*; she demanded the extradition of Hannibal through the envoys Publius Valerius Flaccus and Quintus Baebius Tamphilus. Carthage refused. Rome read the writing on the wall and raised six legions: 24,000 infantry, with 1,800 cavalry, reinforced with the recruitment of 40,000 allied infantry and 1,800 cavalry. The Romans voted for war. A further delegation was then sent to Carthage, with the authority to declare war if necessary. Quintus Fabius offered peace or war; the Carthaginians – according to Livy – affected indifference. Fabius responded, 'Here we bring you war and peace, take which you please.' He was met by a defiant shout bidding him give whichever he preferred, and when, letting the folds of his toga fall, he said that he gave them war, they replied that they accepted war and would carry it on in the same spirit in which they accepted it. The Second Punic War had begun.

Hannibal now proceeded to march on Italy, by way of the Alps. His army originally compromised approximately 102,000 men and a number of war elephants. The epic two-week crossing of the unforgiving mountains, however, cost him dearly: his force was reduced to 26,000 exhausted men. Against the odds, though, he defeated the Ligurians, outraging the Romans. He was now able to consolidate his army with Gallic and other allies to bring it up to 90,000 men: 80,000 infantry and 10,000 cavalry.

The first battle of the war fought on Italian soil was at Ticinus – the first battle to entail armies up to legion strength. Publius Scipio faced the Carthaginians at the River Ticinus near Victimulae (Vigerano) and built a bridge at Piacenza to enable him to cross the river and leave his camp. Scipio led with his javelin throwers in front of his cavalry, while the Carthaginians deployed their nimble Numidians on the flanks. The Carthaginian charge using these highly trained, speedy Numidian horsemen was so furious that it forced the Roman javelin throwers to retreat in confusion through the ranks where they were trampled by the Numidian cavalry. The Romans' ineffective cavalry was also destroyed and Scipio was badly injured. The Numidians were to prove themselves time and time again.[20]

The Illergetes, the Bargusii, the Aeronosii, and the Andosini were soon subdued by the Carthaginians and a number of cities were taken – all with considerable losses, though, to Hannibal. His brother Hanno remained behind in command of what is now roughly Catalonia, with 10,000 infantry and 1,000 cavalry. From 220 BC, Hannibal had been preparing for such an awesome journey by sending envoys to the Gallic tribes in the Po valley, from whom he secured promises of money, food, and guides. It was an easy sell for Hannibal: Rome's clumsy treatment of the conquered Gauls and the cavalier disposal of their lands made supporting the Carthaginians a simple choice, particularly for the Insubres and the Boii. Polybius describes the diplomacy as follows:

> [Hannibal] conducted his enterprise with consummate judgement; for he had accurately ascertained the excellent nature of the country in which he was to arrive, and the hostile disposition of its inhabitants towards the Romans; and he had for guides and conductors through the difficult passes which lay in the way of natives of the country, men who were to partake of the same hopes with himself.

Hannibal brought to the battlefield military skill and vision the like of which the Romans had not hitherto found in her enemies. He also brought a deep-rooted and long-standing hatred of Rome which can only have honed his tactical brilliance and sharpened his determination to defeat Rome. For the Carthaginian commanders, defeat was not an option – a quality which the Romans will have recognized in themselves; the only difference being that a defeated Carthaginian was rewarded with crucifixion. They would also have recognized the self-discipline drummed into the Carthaginian; for example, they were much more stringent regarding the use of alcohol than the Romans. Magistrates, lawyers, slaves, ships' captains and marching soldiers were all banned from drinking while on duty. Alcohol was prohibited during the day, and before having sex if conception was the aim.

Trebia River 218 BC

Things got worse for the Romans when 2,200 Gallic allies defected and attacked the Romans as they slept; they decapitated the slain before they crossed to the Carthaginian camp. That night Scipio crossed the Trebia River and headed south along its left bank, keeping the river between him and Hannibal. The Numidian cavalry gave chase but made the error of stopping to torch the Roman camp first, giving Scipio time to complete his crossing of the river. A day's march later, Scipio made camp and waited for the the second consul, Tiberius Sempronius Longus, to arrive. Hannibal camped on the plain below, supported by the Gauls.

Longus duly arrived with his army from Sicily and took over the command from the still-wounded Scipio. The Carthaginians used the Numidians as bait; the impetuous Longus fell for it and, against Scipio's orders and oblivious to the trap he was walking into, foolishly sent his 4,000 cavalry, 6,000 javelin throwers, 16,000 infantry and 20,000 allies across the icy river in pursuit. Hannibal now had the cold and drenched Romans just where he wanted them and faced with 20,000 fresh and dry infantrymen supported by 10,000 cavalry on the wings. The Romans were soundly defeated when a 1,000 strong force led by Mago, Hannibal's brother, suddenly emerged from the rear leaving them cut off at the river. A combination of light-armed troops and elephants sealed the fate of the Romans. The surviving 10,000 men in the Roman centre were surrounded and could only hack their way out of the disaster, fleeing back to Placentia. The Romans then withdrew south from northern Italy, leaving garrisons at Cremona and Placentia. Things deteriorated when their Gallic allies, content to sit on the fence until now, defected to the Carthaginians.[21]

It is interesting to read Sir Walter Raleigh's assessment of the Battle of the Trebia River:

Three great errors Sempronius committed, of which every one deserved to be recompensed with the loss that followed. The first was, that he fought with Hannibal in a champain, being by far inferior in horse, and withal thereby subject to the African elephants, which in enclosed or uneven grounds, and woodlands, would have been of no use. His second error was, that he made no discovery of the place upon which he fought, whereby he was grossly overreached, and ensnared, by the ambush which Hannibal had laid for him. The third was, that he drenched his footmen with empty stomachs, in the river of Trebia, even in a most cold and frosty day, whereby in effect they lost the use of their limbs.[22]

Lake Trasimene 217 BC

The Romans were now very much on the defensive and took up positions at Ariminum to defend the Via Flaminia. Four new legions had to be raised to reinforce the Roman army after the losses at Ticinus and Trebia. Hannibal proceeded south towards Rome under the watchful eye of Gaius Flaminius Nepos, a notoriously conceited and impetuous man, who was camped at Arretium, guarding Etruria. He had already caused serious concern in Rome by leaving the city before he had discharged all the religious formalites required when a consul takes up his post. Hannibal cunningly played on Flaminius' weaknesses, attempting to draw him into an ambush by marching through an undefended Apennine pass straight past Arretium and devastating the land as he went. Rome was within reach. Unable to entice Flaminius into battle, Hannibal outflanked him and effectively cut him off from Rome; in so doing he executed the earliest recorded turning movement in military history. Flaminius still remained obstinately in his camp.[23]

Livy tells us what happened next:

> Though every one else in the council advised cautious rather than extravagant action, urging that he should wait for his colleague, so that, combining their armies, they might carry on the war with combined courage and strategy ... Flaminius, in a fury ... gave out the signal for marching for battle .

When Hannibal passed Lake Trasimene, he spotted a place that would be ideal for an ambush. To the north were heavily wooded hills; Hannibal camped in full view of anyone entering the northern defile, spending the night setting his troops up for battle. He placed his heavy infantry comprising Iberians, Celts and Africans below the camp on a slight elevation. From here, they could charge down on the Roman column on the left flank. He concealed his cavalry and the Gallic infantry in the the wooded valley where the Romans would first enter, blocking the Roman route of retreat, stationing his light troops at intervals along the heights overlooking the plain. The night before the battle Hannibal ordered his men to light camp fires on the hills of Tuoro some distance away, so as to give the impression that his forces were further away than they actually were.

Juvenal, who later cited these apocryphal fictions as rhetorical exercises, tells us that Hannibal himself travelled on his one surviving elephant and, despite the marshy terrain and having lost an eye through exposure, managed to draw his foe onto the shore of Lake Trasimene. The morning of the battle dawned misty as the battle-hungry Flaminius led his men into the defile on the banks of the lake. Crucially, the general had omitted to reconnoitre the area, with devastating consequences. He and 15,000 of his men were slaughtered when the Carthaginians suddenly emerged from the mist, pouring down from the hills, blocking off the road, attacking the astonished Romans from three sides and forcing them into desperate hand-to-hand combat. The Romans were split into three: the Carthaginian cavalry forced one group into the lake, leaving the other two groups cut off. The centre, led by Flaminius, stood its ground, but was eventually routed by Hannibal's Gauls after three hours. Many Romans drowned as they attempted to swim for their lives encumbered by full armour; 15,000 were taken prisoner. A mere 10,000 made it back to Rome, while Hannibal lost 1,500 men.

Flaminius was killed by the Insubres leader, Ducarius. A further 6,000 Romans escaped in the fog, but were captured by Maharbal next day. Livy and Polybius tell us that Maharbal promised safe passage, allowing each soldier to go, wearing one item of clothing, if the Romans surrendered their weapons and armour; but Hannibal had them sold into slavery anyway. A few days later, half of a 4,000-strong reinforcement unit under the pro-praetor Gaius Centenius was destroyed; the destroyer was the capable general Maharbal.

The Battle of Lake Trasimene has gone down as one of the biggest and most successful ambushes in military history. Livy says that so great was the din caused by the carnage, and so preoccupied were the combatants, that no one at Lake Trasimene noticed an earthquake which struck during the battle. The earthquake flattened many nearby cities, diverted rivers, flooded river estuaries with tidal surges and triggered avalanches. According to tradition, the volume of blood which filled the lake for three days after the battle created a stream leading into the lake which was renamed *Sanguineto*, the Blood River. Other evidence of the carnage, apparently, survives locally in place names which include *Ossaia* (Charnel House), *Sepoltaglia* (Sepulchre), *Caporosso* (Cape Red) and *Pian di Marte* (Field of Mars).

The way to Rome was now wide open to Hannibal, but he chose instead to devastate the lands on the Adriatic side of the peninsula, as far south of Apulia. Hannibal obviously appreciated what a stronghold Rome now was, and the futility of laying siege to such a city without access to a ready and fertile source of re-supply. His cause was not helped when, contrary to expectation, none of the towns or cities either to the north or to the south and east of Rome defected to him. After ten days, he reached Herita and rested his army; many of the soldiers were suffering from scurvy. He retrained the African troops with captured Roman equipment, and restored the health of his horses by using cheap local wine (*acetum*) as an ointment.

There was widespread panic in Rome. Rumours about Trasimene were tactlessly confirmed when the praetor Marcus Pomponius bluntly announced in the Forum that, 'We have been defeated in a great battle.' He unhelpfully left it at that, plunging the citizens into further anxiety, reliant on a notoriously unreliable rash of rumours infecting them as a disease. The result was a social and public relations disaster as bad as the military calamity at the lake. News of the reverse by Maharbal followed. For the first time since 249 BC, the Senate and the people elected a dictator to steady and fix the deteriorating situation.

The dictator appointed was Quintus Fabius Verrucosus Maximus; he was nicknamed *Cunctator*, 'the Delayer'. His unfortunate cognomen, Verrucosus, came about from the wart on his upper lip. Fabius was a master of patience and followed Hannibal's progress move by move with astonishing restraint. Fabius too was a master at raiding enemy supply lines to replenish his own reserves, a skill which earned him the honour of being called the father of guerilla warfare. Viewing, no doubt, the negligence and fatal hubris of some of his predecessors, he was at pains to appease the patently displeased gods. Plutarch believes that Fabius ascribed the disaster at Lake Trasimene in part to Flaminius' impiety: not only had he demonstrated a cavalier attitude to the gods before leaving Rome, he had ignored a flurry of portentous lightning bolts. Characteristically leaving nothing to chance, Fabius organized a huge sacrifice – allegedly the equivalent to Italy's whole harvest, including cattle, goats, pigs and sheep. Music festivals were arranged and everyone was instructed to go out and spend precisely 333 *sestertia* and 333 *denari*.[24]

To be doubly sure of his ground with the gods, Fabius recommended the Senate consult the *Sibylline Books*, the *libri Sibyllini* – a collection of oracular responses in three books which were brought to Rome by Tarquinius Priscus, after some haggling about what they were worth with the Sibyl at Cumae. Virgil guarantees their eternal fame by featuring them in the list of religious initiatives Aeneas will take when he establishes Rome:

A great sanctuary awaits you too in our kingdom; for this is where I will put your oracles and the mysterious prophecies told to my people; here I will ordain chosen men, propitious Sibyl.[25]

Ten men guarded the *Books*, which were stored underground in a stone chest, beneath the temple of Jupiter Optimus Maximus on the Capitoline; access was exclusive to fifteen specially appointed augurs, *quindecimviri sacris faciundis*. Consultation of the *Books* was by Senatorial decree at a propitiatory ceremony when Rome felt threatened by civil strife, external threat, military disaster or on the appearance of strange prodigies or phenomena.

Yet more prudent Fabian preparations followed. The city walls were strengthened; the *magister equitum*, Marcus Minucius Rufus, raised two Roman and two allied legions with cavalry units to defend the city at Tibur. Unfortified towns in Latium were abandoned and their inhabitants relocated into fortified settlements. Bridges at strategic points were destroyed. Publius Servilius Geminus took command of the fleet at Ostia as proconsul. Fabius was leaving nothing to chance.

Wherever Hannibal went, Fabius followed. Indeed, it is apt that as a child Fabius had earned another nickname: *ovicula*, 'Little Sheep', denoting his docility and the tendency he had to follow others about. Such childlike behaviour served him well in his strategy against Hannibal, ever resisting the temptation to engage in battle. He exercised restraint even when Hannibal devastated the rich and fertile lands of the Falernian Plain around Capua. He painstakingly and deliberately declined to do battle, opting instead to shadow the Carthaginians at a safe distance. He routinely took the high ground wherever he could and positioned his army in between Rome and Hannibal whenever possible. He ensured that his army camped where they were unlikely to attract a Punic attack; and while Roman forage parties were always protected by light infantry and cavalry, Carthaginian foragers were cut down at every opportunity. The strategy, though, had its serious disadvantages. While Fabius was busy delaying, Hannibal was busy depradating prime agricultural land on the Falernian Plain, wreaking economic havoc and compromising the food supply to Rome. There was also the increasing frustration felt by Fabius' colleagues and the anxious Roman people, all looking for victory, and to avoid, at all costs, another disaster.

Callicula (or Ager Falernus) 217 BC

The second Roman consular army under Gnaeus Servilius Geminus was out of position in northern Italy, on the wrong side of the Apennines near Ariminum. To make matters worse, Geminus had lost his reconnaissance capability when his 4,000 cavalry were destroyed in an ambush by Maharbal near Assisi.

Hannibal's scorching of the Falernian plain was a strategic success. Not only did it unnerve and aggravate the Roman Senate and people, it demonstrated that he could operate on Rome's doorstep with virtual impunity and damage the Romans economically. Hannibal had to get out, though, at some point; he could not winter in the exposed *Ager Falernum*. There were eight possible routes out, but because he was north of the Volturnus River, and all the bridges were in Roman hands, there were only three ways that Hannibal could exit the Falernian plain. Fabius seized the day and laid plans to trap the Carthaginian army; he blocked off two of the available escape routes, Casilinum and Cales, and posted a unit of 4,000 troops at Callicula. Fabius began his characteristic waiting game, content to force Hannibal into desperate measures when his provisions started to run out. Rome, nevertheless, demanded decisive action now: the Carthaginians were trapped and all the time more and more precious lands were being devastated. Fabius returned to Rome apparently to discharge some religious duties but more likely to sell his strategy. His case was helped by another defeat after L. Hostilius Mancinus made a foray to reconnoitre the Numidians with 400 horsemen and engaged the Carthaginians. He was killed with all his troops by the Carthaginian cavalry under Carthalo.

Fabius first reinforced the Roman garrison at Casilinum, and Cales on the south of the Ager Falernus. Minucius guarded the *via Latina* and *via Appia*; Taenum was also garrisoned. The main Roman army camped near Mount Massicus, north of the plain to the west of Minucius, ready in support. The Romans now had the Carthaginians trapped in the plain, evidently leaving Hannibal no choice but to battle his way out and attack the Romans.

Fabius could be forgiven for thinking he was in the best possible position. He sensibly refused a night battle on rough terrain. However, with his usual resourcefulness and perspicacity, Hannibal saw the predicament he faced in exiting the plain and, in a stroke of genius, enlisted the help of 2,000 cows. The disaster that was to follow at Callicula was, perversely, due as much to these 2,000 oxen as anything or anyone else. Hannibal tied burning bundles of wood to their horns. The cattle were herded by 2,000 camp followers while the whole force was protected by 2,000 spearmen. Appian records how Hannibal had 5,000 Roman prisoners executed to prevent them escaping and rejoining the Romans.

The Romans guarding the pass left their posts at the head of the pass to attack what they believed was the main Carthaginian army trying to outflank their position and escape. The minute the Romans left their posts, Hannibal's army moved, with the African infantry leading, the cavalry, the baggage train and the cattle behind, with Celts and Iberian infantry guarding the rear. The kindling on the cattle was set alight and the terrified cows stampeded over the hills towards the Roman camp; the Romans were nonplussed and terrified. Hannibal, meanwhile, marched back unmolested through the pass with his army, having pulled off one of the most audacious decoys in military history. To make matters worse for the Romans, Hannibal sent a detachment of Spanish troops experienced in mountain warfare back to defend the Carthaginians who had herded the cattle; the Romans subsequently lost 1,000 men in the ensuing battle.

After Lake Trasimene and Callicula, Rome was in urgent need of time in which to recruit and restore her shattered armies. Fabius' ongoing delaying tactics gave them some of that time. The last thing he needed was more casualties in his seriously depleted forces. Despite the apparent wisdom in his strategy, though, the *Cunctator* was criticized for his caution and his lack of aggression; he was vilified as Hannibal's lap-dog, his *paedagogus*, a slur which cruelly compared him with the slaves whose job it was to follow Roman children to school carrying their books. The frustrated and hostile Marcus Minucius Rufus, Fabius' second-in-command, foisted on him by the Senate as *magister equitum*, was one of Fabius' most vitriolic critics. Petulantly, he moaned: 'Rome grew great through audacity and action, not through the lazy plans the timid describe as caution.' The poet Ennius, writing in the 170s BC, though, was more perceptive when he described Fabius as, *'unus homo nobis cunctando restituit rem,'* – 'the one man who gave us back our Rome by showing restraint.' Calm and rational hindsight approved the Fabian way.

Indeed, all the while Fabius was shadowing and pestering him, Hannibal failed to take one Roman town as he skirted around Rome. Fabius' close attentions actually began to raise morale and inspired confidence in the nervous Italian and Roman populations. *Cunctando* became a byword for military wisdom and a symbol of the Roman way of doing things, taken up later by Livy, Sallust, Cicero, Virgil and others.[26] Fabius' name, as in Fabian strategy, became synonymous with delaying tactics: a war of attrition waged by avoiding conventional, predictable pitched battles and grinding the enemy down by continually keeping him at arm's length, always keeping him guessing. As an indication of the reverence with which he came to be held, when Fabius died in 203 BC it is alleged that every Roman citizen contributed to the cost of his funeral: they were burying the father of their country.

Fabius' tactics are understandable when we remember that after recent conflicts at least half of the Roman army comprised inexperienced conscripts and the rest had survived three consecutive Hannibal victories over Roman armies. On the other hand, the Carthaginian army was made up of battle-hardened veterans. In avoiding battle, Fabius denied Hannibal the opportunity to win yet another victory over yet another Roman army, thus crucially preventing Hannibal from winning over disaffected Roman allies. Fabius kept Hannibal on the move, extending his already vulnerable lines of supply. At the same time, Fabius was all the while tying up elements of the Carthaginian army deputed to forage parties and the protection of those parties.[27]

A more recent example of Fabian strategy is George Washington's campaigns during the American War of Independence, as advocated by his subordinate, General Nathaniel Greene. Washington was at first reluctant, but in the wake of major defeats in 1776 and 1777, he changed his strategy and sought to wear down the British militarily and politically. Despite criticism by Congressional leaders, the strategy was successful, causing the British to lose the will to continue the war. Other examples include: the Russians in response to Napoleon's invasion in 1812; the Russians in response to Germany's invasion in 1941; North Vietnam's tactics during most of the Vietnam War (1965–1973); Iraqi insurgents' approach to the American invasion of Iraq (2003).

Gerunium 216

Hannibal was not idle. His army headed for Molise, busy foraging and building up supplies for the coming winter, which he stored in Gerunium, the first town he was able to take when the inhabitants fled. The town became a temporary granary store and livestock compound with the camp outside defended by a trench and palisade. The sick and wounded recuperated in the camp; two-thirds of the army foraged in the vicinity while the rest guarded the camp.

Fabius' colleague, Marcus Minucius, was a constant thorn in his side. After a skillful victory over 2,000 Numidian spearmen in which he captured a strategic hilltop, he went on to win a minor skirmish over bands of foragers. Minucius was elevated to a status equal to the dictator by the Senate, delighted by and desperate for the least crumb of success. Rome could now rely on the services of two dictators at the same time – reducing their powers, in effect, to those of a consul, thus nullifying the benefit of having one man in charge. Minucius' impetuousity, nevertheless, forced the cautious one to offer Minucius a stark choice: take full command every other day or else take control of half the army. The first option was obviously unworkable so Minucius chose the latter. It was not long before Hannibal's intelligence apprised him of the schism, allowing him to lay an ambush by posting 500 cavalry and 5,000 infantry on a nearby hill. Minucius was drawn into the trap and overwhelmed by Hannibal's army. Fabius, however, came to the rescue and saved the day.[28]

Cannae 216 BC

The following spring, Hannibal left Gerunium and headed south for Apulia and the town of Cannae. This he promptly took, along with the Roman supplies warehoused there. Back in Rome, some factions were still impatient to challenge Hannibal and, in true Minucius style, threw caution to the wind. The Senate voted an unprecedented army of eight legions, 40,000 men, to deal with the invaders, making a total force of 80,000 infantry plus cavalry. Hannibal's army was half the size. The Romans were led by the consuls of that year: L. Aemilius Paullus and Gaius Terentius Varro. The former was safe and prudent, the latter precipitate and impatient, but both ominously inexperienced in the Punic brand of warfare. Hannibal encamped on the south bank of the River Aufidus with the wind and the mountains to his back. Despite advice to the contrary from Paullus, the impetuous Varro drew the army up against the Carthaginian force. His legionaries were concentrated in the centre, his cavalry on the wings. Hannibal craftily deployed his men in a crescent, with his less battle-hardened troops, the Spaniards and the Celts, in the prominent centre.

The Romans attacked and, predictably, soon found themselves penetrating the weak Punic centre. However, just as predictably, they were quickly surrounded by the Numidians closing in from the wings and cut down. On the far left, Hasdrubal's cavalry destroyed the opposing Roman horse then moved behind to the right flank to support the Numidians. More carnage followed, enabling Hasdrubal then to take the Roman infantry from behind. The annihilation was almost total: the Romans lost between 50,000 and 70,000 men – the flower of their generation – to the Carthaginians' 6,000. Ironically, Paullus was killed, while Varro escaped. Various tales circulated regarding the treachery of some Numidians: Livy says that they allegedly pretended to defect to the Romans but attacked with concealed daggers; Appian and Zonaras accredit the perfidy to the Celtiberians – all feeble attempts at mitigating the Romans' responsibility for a disaster of breathtaking proportions.

Cannae was especially expensive in terms of its toll on the Roman military top brass, and on the elite classes generally. Apart from the consul Paullus, Livy tells that among the dead were two quaestors, twenty-nine of the forty-eight military tribunes – some of whom were of consular rank, including the previous year's consul, Gnaeus Servilius Geminus – the former *magister equitum*, Marcus Minucius Rufus, and eighty senators. Appian says 50,000 Romans died and many were taken prisoner. Plutarch likewise: 50,000 Romans dead, 4,000 taken alive; Quintilian says 60,000 dead. According to Eutropius, 'twenty officers of consular and praetorian rank, thirty senators, and 300 others of noble descent, were taken or slain, as well as 40,000 foot-soldiers, and 3,500 horse.'

The toll from the Second Punic War so far was unprecedented: Hannibal had crushed the equivalent of eight consular armies within just three campaign seasons; Rome had lost one-fifth – 150,000 – of the entire population of male citizens over 17 years of age.

It is interesting to compare the casualty figures with more recent slaughters. The British army on the first day of the Somme in 1916 suffered 57,740 casualties in total, of whom 19,240 were killed or died later of their wounds. More Romans died at Cannae than US servicemen perished in the entire Vietnam War: 58,178 – of whom 48,386 died in action, 5,242 died of their wounds, and 3,523 are missing. Cannae has become synonymous with carnage. In a sinister forecast, Goebbels, during the Second World War, chillingly predicted that 'the Jews at the end of this war are going to experience their Cannae.'

The evening of Cannae, according to Polybius (though Livy says it was the next day), Hannibal mopped up the survivors in the Roman camps and took 2,000 or so prisoners who had taken refuge in Cannae itself. They were allowed to retain one garment while surrendering all other clothes and equipment. They also had to agree to a ransom, fixed according to their rank or status. The largest group of survivors was holed up in Canusium, assembled there by Publius Sempronius Tuditanus from 600 disorientated survivors from the camps whom he managed to persuade to flee along with part of the garrison of the main camp. These had played little part in the main conflict and were, presumably, still organized to some extent. Numbers at Canusium would have been in the region of 4,000 infantry and 200 cavalry. Varro had mustered 4,500 stragglers at Venusia. On hearing of the Canusium survivors, he joined them there to form a rag-bag army numbering 10,000 men, still far too weak to pose a credible threat to a tergiversating Hannibal. Command of the remnants of the Roman army devolved to four military tribunes: Quintus Fabius Maximus (son of the *Cunctator*), Lucius Bibulus, Publius Cornelius Scipio (later Africanus) and Appius Claudius.

The social and political ramifications of Cannae to Rome and to the Romans were enormous and far-reaching. To keep public order and to maintain what little morale that remained, Fabius Maximus persuaded a much reduced Senate to censure and prohibit public mourning and post guards on the gates of Rome to prevent wholesale panic and flight from the city. Scouts were sent out frantically to try and gather intelligence about Hannibal's movements. The absence of intelligence about his plans and intentions – would he come, or not – must have been excruciating for the Romans, heaping yet more anxiety on an already terrified and desparate population. Depressingly for the populace, rumours spread that the required holy rites had once again been neglected before the battle. Extreme attempts were made to mitigate the hubris: a delegation was despatched to the shrine of Apollo at Delphi to appease the gods and obtain the highest level of divine advice as to what to do next. The Romans were led by Fabius Pictor, soon to become Rome's first prose historian.

The august *Sibylline Books* were consulted. They demanded that a Greek man and woman, and a Gallic man and woman should be buried alive under the venerable Forum Boarium in Rome. The manner of death – immuration – associates it with that reserved for a promiscuous Vestal Virgin. The disaster at Cannae was as bad as it gets – equal to an unchaste Vestal – an affront to the very essence of Rome and its security.

The women of Rome were the forgotten victims of the battle: bereaved, uncertain of the fate of prisoners of war (their husbands, fathers, sons and brothers) or left with disabled husbands, sons or siblings for whom they would have to care for the rest of the invalids' lives. Those women who could get there may have trawled the stinking, bloody battlefield in the ensuing days, searching for surviving loved ones, desperately hoping against hope to discover a body which would give them some measure of closure. What they would have witnessed – wholesale mutilation and putrefaction – would have been truly awful.

On the other hand, women may, in other ways, have benefitted from their war widowhood. Welcome or not, the need to take greater control of the family and household may have brought increased independence, while some women would have inherited property and cash in their bereavement. Ovid prescribes how, in normal circumstances, a widow should allow a reasonable period of ten months for mourning her late husband before starting a new relationship. The ten-month rule was occasionally relaxed for religious and political expediency. Cannae provides an example of this, with celebration of the annual rites of Ceres being cancelled because those tainted with death were excluded from the ceremonies, and every bereaved Roman *matrona* had been tainted by the battle.[29]

The aftermath of the battle also allowed women to exert rare political power and to voice political rights usually unheard. The *Lex Oppia*, enacted in 215 BC, limited the amount of gold women could own and required that all the assets of wards, single women, and widows be handed over to the State; the wearing of dresses with purple trim and riding in carriages within Rome or nearby towns was also prohibited, except during religious festivals. Support for its repeal in 195 BC by women of Rome evoked disgust and misogynistic condemnation when those women came out from their homes and demonstrated in the Forum. The feeling amongst these uncharacteristically obtrusive women was that the law had served its purpose and had run its course. In the event, the law was repealed.

The enhanced power and independence of women also manifested itself in a collective lobby of the Senate. To avoid further bloodshed and to win back some of their captured sons and husbands, the *matronae* banded together to persuade the Senate to accept Hannibal's ransom demand in exchange for

8,000 Roman prisoners of war – their husbands, brothers, fathers and sons. The demonstration was unsuccessful, but the fact that women were able to rise up and make such an impact is significant. Vestal Virgins sometimes took the blame and were officially scapegoated when catastrophe struck in Rome: alleged *incestum*, sexual impropiety amongst Vestals, was held directly responsible for the slaughter at Cannae. Two Vestals, Opimia and Floronia, were duly convicted: one was entombed alive and allowed to starve slowly to death, in keeping with the traditional punishment; the other committed suicide, thus avoiding that atrocious punishment. Lucius Cantilius, the secretary of the Pontiffs who had allegedly deflowered Floronia, was beaten to death.

On the other hand, the calamity brought out the best in some. In her efforts to support and rehabilitate survivors, Busa is a shining example of generosity and patriotism. After the catastrophe, the stragglers from battle who made their way to Canusium were the beneficiaries of a rare and uplifting example of charity. Here the wealthy Busa provided them with food, clothing and money. Eventually, a force of some 10,000 men was assembled, which Publius Scipio was able to turn into a fighting unit to face Hannibal again. Indeed, Busa's loyalty and beneficence was looked upon by some with envy, to the extent that the neighbouring town of Venusia, not to be outdone, did much good work when they recruited a force of cavalry and infantry as their contribution to the war effort, rebuilding Rome's depleted forces. Busa was rightly honoured by the Senate for her unique act of charity and patriotism. Varro too emerged from the holocaust well, thanked by the Senate for his exemplary behaviour in rallying the survivors, rather than being condemned for his rash behaviour.

Comparable only to the catastrophic Battle of Allia and the subsequent sacking of Rome, it seems this latest *dies ater* (dark day) had the unexpected effect of bringing the Roman people together and, in the words of Polybius, made them a yet more intractable opponent.[30] The Senate was left to get on with its job in an unprecedented outbreak of political harmony between the elite classes and the common people. In addition to the *Lex Oppia*, the Romans accepted a doubling of the property tax; they donated slaves for military or naval service; they gave money and supplies on the mere promise of repayment. Soldiers, for once, did not agitate for their arrears and peace seems never to have been mentioned. Rome's coin, the *as*, was devalued.

Scapegoated Vestal Virgins apart, the only instance of harsh recrimination was reserved for the soldiers who had fled the field of battle. These were punished with twelve years of service in Sicily, in what amounts to a penal regiment. Not surprisingly, morale in the army generally was exceptionally low, so low that Lucius Caecilius Metellus, a military tribune from a distinguished

Roman family, and Publius Furius Philus became desparate; believing all was lost, they urged the other tribunes to emigrate and enlist as mercenaries in foreign armies. Metellus' punishment could have been far more severe than it actually was: he was compelled to swear – at the business end of a sword – an everlasting oath of allegiance to Rome, to cure his lack of moral fibre.

The extent of the human loss at Cannae was brought vividly into focus with the awful report that Hannibal and his men gathered up more than 200 gold signet rings from the Roman corpses strewn on the battlefield. This macabre horde was triumphantly poured out onto the floor in front of the Punic Senate. The rings have a poignant symbolism: a gold ring was a badge of the elite classes of Roman society and the harvest from Cannae left no doubt about the damage done to that Roman elite. A statue by Sébastien Slodtz from 1704, depicting Hannibal with the signet rings of the Roman *equites* killed during the battle, stands in the Louvre.

After the battle, Maharbal, frustrated by Hannibal's procrastination, suggested they march on Rome without further ado. Within five days, according to Maharbal, Hannibal could be taking dinner on the Capitol. Hannibal answered, 'I admire your passion but need time to think about your plan.'

Disappointed and deflated, Maharbal replied, 'No one man has got all of God's gifts. You, Hannibal, know how to win a victory, but you have no idea how to use it.' Livy, for one, is in no doubt about how critical Hannibal's hesitation was in saving Rome and its possessions from annihilation:

Never before, while Rome itself was still safe, had there been such tumult and panic within its walls. I won't try to describe it, nor will I dilute the reality by going into details ... it was not wound upon wound but disaster after disaster that was now announced. For according to the reports two consular armies and two consuls were lost; there was no longer any Roman camp, any general, any single soldier left; Apulia, Samnium, almost the whole of Italy lay at Hannibal's feet. Certainly there is no other nation that would not have gone under in such a weighty calamity.[31]

Hannibal's brilliance on the field at Cannae has never been in doubt. Nevertheless, debate and discord rages to this day over how he well he acted in the aftermath. Should he have marched on Rome, or was he right to desist? On balance, it seems that his decision not to take the city was the right one, despite the insistent urgings of Maharbal, and no doubt others. Hannibal's army was exhausted and it would have taken much longer to reach the city, which lay 400km away, than Maharbal's expeditious five days. Rome would have been busy shoring up her defences. In reality, sieges were notoriously drawn out over months, even years (Saguntum, for example, took eight months to break). They were also sapping in terms of casualties and *matériel*. If the Carthaginians had managed to breach the walls, they would have been hard-pressed to exact a victory in 'house-to-house' fighting. In reality, Hannibal would have had difficulty in organizing logistics and effective lines of supply. It may always have been Hannibal's strategy to subdue Rome on the battlefield, destroying her network of alliances through opportunistic defections while wiping out her aspirations for Mediterranean hegemony. Taking Rome appeared an unattractive option.

Hannibal buried his dead, took care of his wounded and arranged an honourable burial for Paullus. He then attempted to negotiate a dignified settlement with the Romans on the repatriation of prisoners of war and peace terms. Given the recent battles, in which Rome had been virtually annihilated and humiliated, Hannibal must have felt hopeful.

A defiant Rome, however, was in no mood for compromise. It had begun the slow and painful process of rebuilding its armies. The battle-experienced Marcus Claudius Marcellus took over Varro's ramshackle army; Marcus Junius Pictor was appointed dictator to get the job done expediently; his *magister equitum* was the skillful Tiberius Sempronius Gracchus. Boys as young as 17 were pressed into service, while 8,000 slaves were emancipated and enlisted. Six thousand prisoners were released from jail – and given their freedom in exchange for military service. Weapons and armour last used by invading Gauls were 'looted' from temples where they had been displayed as war trophies from the victories of Roman history. Significantly though, only 1,000 cavalry could be mustered, indicative of the extensive losses suffered by the equestrian order. The whole scenario is somewhat reminiscent of the desperate measures the Nazi Party was forced to take at the end of the Second World War when they established the *Volkssturm*, recruiting boys from age 13 to men as old as 60, poorly armed, to defend Berlin from the Russians.

As a measure of their proud defiance, the Romans unequivocally refused to negotiate with the Carthaginian delegation; Carthalo was rebuffed. There was to be no ransom. Rome, perhaps buoyed up by its own determination to rise again Phoenix-like from the hell of virtual annihilation, was determined to fight another day.

Militarily, Cannae was as indecisive as it was apocalyptic. Hannibal's victory gave him dominance in the south but he still remained cut off from the north (and a potential source of Gallic manpower) by the Roman allies in central Italy. Even his power in the south did not deliver the allied recruits he needed to redress his deficiency in military strength.

The day after the battle dawned cold. Livy describes the atrocious and horrific scene on the battlefield in Lucanesque technicolour:

> The morning after, as soon as it was light, [the Carthaginians] pressed forward to collect the spoil and to gaze on a carnage ghastly even to enemies. There lay thousands upon thousands of Romans, infantry and cavalry indiscriminately mingled, as chance had brought them together in the battle or the ensuing rout. Here and there amidst the slain a blood soaked figure started up, whose wounds had begun to throb with the chill of dawn, and was cut down again by his enemies; some were found lying there alive, with thighs and tendons slashed, baring their necks and throats and begging their conquerors to drain what was left of their blood. Others were found with their heads buried in holes they had dug in the ground. They had apparently made these pits for themselves, heaping the dirt over their faces to suffocate themselves. But what was most astonishing was a Numidian with mutilated nose and ears who was dragged out alive from under a dead Roman; the Roman, unable to hold a weapon in his hands, had died in a frenzy of rage, while tearing at the Numidian with his teeth.[32]

It is reasonable to assume that the Romans would never again fall foul of encirclement, or double envelopment. To that end, the unmanoevrable infantry phalanx was dropped. Paret describes this major change:

> [The Romans] articulated the phalanx, then divided it into columns, and finally split it up into a great number of small tactical bodies that were capable, now of closing together in a compact impenetrable union, now of changing the pattern with consummate flexibility, of separating one from the other and turning in this or that direction.[33]

The days of the potentially divisive two consular armies were numbered. A unified command was imperative to ensure unity, morale and strength in numbers as required. Scipio Africanus was promoted to commander in-chief of the Roman armies in Africa, as a permanent appointment for the duration of the war.

Cannae is *the* battle of annihilation. It remains today a case study in military academies. To illustrate its enduring impact over the centuries, and its place in recent and contemporary military thinking, here are a number of endorsements: Eisenhower, Supreme Commander of the Allied Expeditionary Force in the Second World War, offered the following: 'Every ground commander seeks the battle of annihilation; so far as conditions permit, he tries to duplicate in modern war the classic example of Cannae.' Frederick the Great and Helmuth von Moltke, commander of German forces in the First World War, craved to re-create their own Cannaes; the Chief of the German General Staff, Alfred von Schlieffen, was inspired by Hannibal's manoeuvre in his eponymous Schlieffen Plan, predicting that Cannae would remain relevant in manoeuvre warfare throughout the twentieth century. General Norman Schwartzkopf admits he 'learned many things from the Battle of Cannae which [he] applied to Desert Storm.'

Herdonia 212 BC

There was more trouble at Nola that year, which the Romans had to deal with. The following year, in Spain, Gnaeus Scipio relieved the blockaded garrison at Iliturgi and defeated a Punic force, slaying 12,000. Scipio was later wounded at Munda, where the Romans killed 12,000 more of the enemy; a further 8,000 fell at Aurinx in Rome's third successive victory. In Italy, in 212 BC, the Romans under Appius Claudius and Gnaeus Quintus Fulvius Flaccus were defeated at Capua. It was rumoured that Fulvius' forces had turned undisciplined and careless; moreover, they were burdened with booty. Hannibal exploited this sloppiness by posting 3,000 light infantry under cover in the vicinity, supported by 2,000 cavalry under Mago, covering all escape routes. Hannibal also despatched 2,000 Numidians to control the roads to the rear of Fulvius' army. At Herdonia, Hannibal offered battle and was accepted by a hasty and incautious Fulvius. Hannibal duly ambushed the Romans and butchered 16,000 of Fulvius' troops, although not Fulvius. The general, it seems, had made an early exit from the field of battle.[34] Astonishingly, Fulvius did not spot the Carthaginian strategy; either a tribute to the skill of Hannibal's commanders or a staggering example of Roman incompetence.

Upper Baetis River 211 BC

A double battle, comprising Castulo and Ilorca (Lorca), was fought between Hannibal's brother, Hasdrubal Barca, Publius Cornelius Scipio and his brother Gnaeus. Between 218 BC and 211 BC, the Roman campaigns in Hispania, by detaining Punic forces there, had the effect of restricting the resources available to Hannibal, who was preoccupied with fighting the Romans in Italy.

Upper Baetis River was the only Carthaginian land victory during the Second Punic War in which Hannibal was not in command of the Carthaginian armies.

The Scipios hired 20,000 Celtiberian mercenaries to reinforce their army of 30,000 infantry and 3,000 horse. Observing that the Carthaginian armies were deployed separately from each other, Hasdrubal Barca held his 15,000 troops near Amtorgis, while Mago Barca and Hasdrubal Gisco, each with 10,000 troops, were positioned some miles to the west. The Scipios divided their forces: Publius Scipio with 20,000 Romans attacked Mago Barca near Castulo, while Gnaeus Scipio took 10,000 troops and the mercenaries to attack Hasdrubal Barca at Ilorca. Barca had already ordered the allies Indibilis and Mandonius to join Mago near Castulo. He held his ground against Gnaeus Scipio, staying within his fortified camp, then bribed the Celtiberian mercenaries to desert Scipio, who was consequently outnumbered. Hasdrubal took a leaf out of the Fabian book, avoiding any conflict with the Romans.

Publius Scipio approached Castulo, harassed constantly by the Numidian light cavalry commanded by the precocious Masinissa. Publius Scipio decided not to face Mago when he learned that Indibilis, with 7,500 Iberians, was about to cut him off. Leaving 2,000 soldiers behind in his camp under Tiberius Fonteus, he attacked the Iberians by night and caught Indibilis by surprise. However, the Iberians managed to hold the Romans off until Masinissa arrived; the Romans yielded under the Numidians. When Mago and Hasdrubal Gisco arrived, the Romans finally broke and fled, leaving Publius Scipio and most of their comrades dead. Mago allowed the Numidians to loot the corpses before rushing them towards Hasdrubal Barca. A few Roman survivors managed to reach the safety of their camp.

The Carthaginians had not quite finished yet, though. Gnaeus was forced to flee because the Celtiberian mercenaries deserted, leaving him badly under strength. This was made worse when the armies of the two Hasdrubals joined forces with Mago. The Numidian cavalry caught up with the Romans at Ilorca and hacked them to death. With pathetic desperation, the Romans had scrambled to create an impromptu defensive wall with baggage and saddles, as the ground was too rocky for digging. Most of his army was destroyed: Gnaeus Scipio was among the dead, the second Scipio to die in as many years.[35]

The two Scipios made a significant contribution to the Roman victory in the Second Punic War. Their Iberian operations had, for a long period, prevented reinforcements reaching Hannibal from Spain; and they had, by their presence, detained the crack Numidian horsemen in Spain, keeping them away from their overstretched comrades and compatriots in Italy.

Sapriportis 210 BC

Tarentum was betrayed to the Carthaginians in 210 BC but, despite his best efforts, Hannibal was unable to take the citadel where the Roman garrison dug in for a two-year siege. Decimus Quinctius was shipping supplies to relieve the Romans in a fleet of twenty ships when they were attacked by the Carthaginians in Tarentine vessels under the command of Democrates off Sapriportis, some fifteen miles from Tarentum. Quinctius was speared by a Tarentine; the Romans dispersed and fled. The valuable supplies never reached Tarentum.[36]

Herdonia 210 BC

That same year Hannibal was back at Herdonia facing Gnaeus Fulvius Centumalus. The other Roman army stationed nearby was under the command of the consul Marcus Claudius Marcellus, making a combined force of four legions plus an equal number of allies. Hannibal, therefore, declined to engage. Marcellus was able to capture Salapia, betrayed to him by a small faction of its citizens, and to destroy the Carthaginian garrison.

Hannibal retreated back to Bruttium; Marcellus advanced on Samnium and took two more Carthaginian garrisons. Hannibal then returned to northern Apulia, catching Centumalus by surprise during his siege of Herdonia. Despite being outnumbered, Centumalus accepted the offer to do battle. Shrewdly, Hannibal waited until the Romans and their allies were fully engaged before he sent his Numidian cavalry to surround them. Other Numidians attacked the lightly defended Roman camp, which was insufficiently protected; yet others fell upon the Roman rear, scattering it. Centumalus, eleven out of twelve military tribunes, and thousands of troops were slain. Some escaped to Marcellus in Samnium.

The Romans came out of Herdonia II badly – not just militarily but politically too. The Senate persisted with its belligerence when it meted out severe punishment to the remnants of the shattered and, no doubt, shocked Roman army. More than 4,000 men were rounded up and sent to Sicily, where they joined the long-suffering deserters of Cannae to serve in the penal colony on the island until the end of the war. A particularly clumsy move, given that many of the deportees were Latins. It roused bitter discontent among the Latin colonies, already exasperated by ten years of non-stop warfare in Italy fighting for the Romans. At a time of Rome's great need for substantial additional manpower and financial support, twelve out of thirty colonies declined to send any more troops or money to Rome. This avoidable crisis endured for five years and put a debilitating and severe strain on the Roman war effort.

In Spain the twenty-five-year-old Publius Cornelius Scipio Africanus took command after the deaths of his father and uncle; his first success was the capture of Cartagena in 209, which he assaulted by land and sea. In doing so he took control of the Carthaginian arsenal and deprived them of the revenues from the nearby mines. Polybius' description of Scipio's capture of the city shows it to have been particularly brutal; the butchery was not confined to the men and women of Cartagena:

> [Scipio] directed [his soldiers], according to the Roman custom, against the people in the city, telling them to kill everyone they met and to spare no one, and not to start looting until they received the order. The purpose of this custom is to strike terror. Accordingly, one can see in cities captured by the Romans not only humans who have been slaughtered, but even dogs sliced in two and the limbs of other animals cut off. On this occasion the amount of such slaughter was very great.

The potential of the precocious and gifted Scipio Africanus was clear for anyone in them to see if they were looking for a charismatic and competent leader to rid them of the Carthaginian scourge. He had been fast-tracked along his *cursus honorum*, missing out the usual service as praetor and consul to be invested with proconsular *imperium*. Scipio's greatest quality was his ability to inspire those around him and to adapt Hannibal's own battle tactics and recycle them against him. Scipio was, of course, no young hot-head. Tellingly, he spent time and trouble training his troops in Hannibal's tactics and perfecting the use of the superior Spanish sword, which had become regular issue. A born diplomat too, he perfected his father's practice of winning the support of local tribes, thus seriously weakening the Carthaginians. The training was to pay off in 208 BC in his victory at Baecula (Bailen), where his troops employed a new flexibility of movement unheard of in the strict three-line formation characteristic of the legions as annhilated at Cannae. The local Spaniards in Scipio's army celebrated him as king – an honour which he modestly declined. At the same time he was probably hailed as *imperator* by his own men, an honour that was later to become commonplace for victorious commanders.[37]

Canusium 209 BC

The years 209 and 208 BC brought yet more disaster for Rome. Back in Italy there were battles against Hannibal at Canusium, a bloody conflict in which the Carthaginian elephants turned on their own forces again. Roman losses were, nevertheless, considerable. Canusium was a three-day battle, part of a wider

Roman campaign, the aim of which was to subdue and punish cities that had deserted and abandoned Rome after the Battle of Cannae. Intent on defeating Hannibal at his Tarentum stronghold, Marcus Claudius Marcellus confronted the Carthaginians at Canusium; Hannibal avoided battle but Marcellus caught up with him. The outcome was indecisive for some time until Fabius attempted to bring in reinforcements, the result of which was confusion in the Roman ranks, allowing Hannibal to rout them with the loss of 2,700 men.[38]

Petelia, Venusia and Locri Epizephrii 208 BC

Petelia was a classic ambush sprung by the Carthaginians on a Roman force which was *en route* to attack Locri Epizephrii in the extreme toe of Italy. Hannibal's intelligence did not let him down; he set an ambush at Petelia and proceeded to massacre 2,000 or so Romans.

Marcus Claudius Marcellus and Quinctius Crispinus planned to attack Hannibal at Venusia and, with astonishing carelessness, set out to reconnoitre with just 220 cavalry as escort, some of which were Romans from Fregellae, while others were Etruscans. Unknown to Marcellus, Hannibal had posted a detachment of Numidians in the woods on the way. The Numidians attacked the Romans, who were deserted by the Etruscans. Marcellus was killed by a spear, while Crispinus escaped injured but died from his wounds some time later.[39] Back at Locri, the Romans under Lucius Cincius were still laying siege to the town from the sea. Hannibal, with his Numidian cavalry, advanced to break the siege. His commander, Mago, marched out to face the Romans, taking them by surprise. Once again, it was the Numidians who made all the difference: when they attacked, the Romans fled.[40]

Chapter 6

The Second Century: the Spanish Wars, Viriathus, the Invasion of the Northmen

Callinicus 171 BC

Rome resumed hostilities against the Macedonians in 171 BC in what was known as the Third Macdonian War. For the previous seventeen years or so, Philip V had been at peace, strengthening his country economically and politically, reinforcing his borders, exploiting mineral resources, introducing new taxation and settling Thracians in Macedonia in response to a manpower problem. Philip had two sons, Perseus and Demetrias; Demetrias was close to Rome, so all augured well for the future between the two states. However, Perseus saw this as a complication to his own aspirations to succeed his father, and had his brother executed on spurious charges of treason. Philip was racked with a father's guilt, and planned to disinherit Perseus, but Perseus acceded to the throne on Philip's death in 179 BC.

Initially cautious, Perseus carried on his father's prudent work – but Rome viewed him with suspicion. His marriage to Laodice, daughter of Seleucus IV of Syria (successor to Antiochus III), and his sister Apame's marriage to Prusias II of Bythinia, only served to muddy the waters. Furthermore, his pro-Roman neighbours were spying on him, spinning everything he did with an anti-Perseus twist. Most active was Eumenes III, of ever-hostile Pergamum, who turned up at Rome to deliver a character assassination of Perseus in person. This led to a declaration of war, in which the Macedonians – thanks to the prudent war preparations of Philip and Perseus – fielded an army of some 40,000 men and 4,000 cavalry.

Perseus antagonized the Romans by invading Thessaly and setting up a garrison at Mount Othrys, from which his forces foraged. P. Licinius Crassus marched to meet him from Epirus, and camped at Larissa with 30,000 men. After several days' delay, in which the Macedonians showed up twice ready for battle, the Macedonians turned up a third time, surprising the Romans and finally clashing in what was to be a disaster of the first magnitude for the Romans. They lost 3,000 men to the Macedonians' sixty. Perseus offered peace, which the Romans flatly rejected.

Uscana 170 BC

Another disaster awaited the Romans at Uscana. Appius Claudius Cento opposed a force led by Gentius, King of the Illyrians, who was now an ally of Macedonia. Claudius fell for a trap in which the inhabitants of Uscana pretended to be willing to betray their city to him. As Claudius approached what he believed to be an empty city, his army was overcome by the inhabitants charging out to fight him. Only half of Claudius' 4,000 men escaped with their lives.[1]

Numantia 153 BC

Spain continued to be a thorn in Rome's side. The peace treaty signed by the Celtiberians and Gracchus had lasted over twenty years, but ongoing clumsy and insensitive governing by the Romans and a new generation of Celtiberians and Lusitanians rendered it redundant by 153 BC. The Lusitanians invaded Hispania Ulterior in 154 BC, while the Celtiberians rose up the following year.

The consul for 153 BC, Fulvius Nobilior, marched to Numantia, the principal Celtiberian city on the Douro, to oppose the Celtiberians with 30,000 infantry, later supplemented with 300 cavalry and ten elephants provided by Masinissa. The elephants were concealed (believe it or not) at the back of the Roman lines and only revealed to the Celtiberians when they were engaged in close quarter combat. Never having seen an elephant before, they were naturally terrified and fled in panic. Unfortunately for the Romans, however, one of the beasts got close to the city walls and was struck by falling masonry, causing it to panic the rest of the herd. The elephants turned on the Romans who, not surprisingly, fled. The Numantines had an easy job picking off the Romans, killing 4,000 men and three elephants in this most unlikely of all Roman military disasters. Against the wishes of the Senate, M. Claudius Marcellus, Nobilior's successor, concluded a new treaty with the Celtiberians which held until 141 BC. This enabled the Romans to focus on the Lusitanians.

The Lusitanians had defeated Servius Sulpicius Galba in 151 BC at the battle of Cauca. The same year, L. Licinius Lucullus, notorious for his brutality, arrived in Spain as consul. With no provocation and without senatorial authority he attacked the Vaccaei, even though they had no quarrel with Rome. On a spurious excuse for war, Lucullus attacked Cauca and slew 3,000 of the Vaccaei; the following day they requested peace and compliantly agreed to all of the Romans' terms. This did not, however, stop Lucullus entering the town and butchering the surviving adult males.

At Intercatia the townsfolk, understandably cautious in the light of the atrocity perpetrated at Cauca, refused a treaty with Lucullus. Lucullus was outraged and began to besiege the town. The Intercatians refused Lucullus' angry demands for battle; however, one of them, a giant of a man, rode out, resplendent in his armour, offering single combat. Scipio Aemilianus accepted and slew the Spaniard. The Romans then battered their way into the city but were unable to defeat the Intercatians – both sides were weakened by malnutrition. Scipio made a treaty and gave his word that it would not be violated.[2]

In 150 BC, Lucullus joined up with Servius Sulpicius (cos 144) Galba and attacked with such ferocity that the Lusitanians surrendered. In the subsequent negotiations, however, Galba showed himself to be just as duplicitous as Lucullus. The Lusitanians were persuaded to leave their homes on the promise of a life in better lands in other regions. However, a trench was dug around them to prevent their escape and they were massacred. The only thing this atrocious act of ethnic cleansing actually achieved was a stronger resolve among the Lusitanians to resist the Romans. Their time was to come in 147 BC, when Viriathus, a natural guerrilla fighter, burst onto the scene.

Tribola 147 BC

Viriathus rose from lowly shepherd stock to a military career which saw him defeat five Roman generals, including Gaius Plautius, Claudius Unimanus and Gaius Negidius. So successful was he that the Celtiberians were tempted back onto the battlefield in 143 BC to join him. In 147 BC, 10,000 Lusitanians who had survived the atrocities committed by Lucullus and Galba rose up, only to find themselves ensnared in a trap by Marcus Vetilius with a similar number of men. The Lusitanians had no option but to surrender, that is until Viriathus reminded them of the perfidious, murderous Galba and Lucullus. Taking 1,000 men, Viriathus distracted the Romans, allowing the rest of the Lusitanians to escape with orders to rendezvous at Tribola. He then ambushed Vetilius, killing 4,000 of the Romans.

Erisana 141 BC

Quintus Fabius Maximus Aemilianus was sent out with 15,000 infantry and 2,000 cavalry to reinforce Gaius Laelius Sapiens; most of the force was lost at Ossuma. Quintus Fabius was defeated again at Beja (modern day Alentejo). Rome then sent one of its best generals, Quintus Fabius Maximus Servilianus, to Iberia. Years of harrying later, a frustrated Fabius Maximus besieged Erisana; he was attacked by the irrepressible Viriathus, who forced the Romans up against a cliff with no prospect of escape. Viriathus took this opportunity to negotiate peace terms, emerging, or so he thought, as a friend of the Romans, *amicus populi Romani*, with the freedom of the Lusitanian people assured. However, Viriathus had gone against his own advice: never trust the word of a compatriot of Galba. The treaty was soon revoked by Quintus Servilius Caepio and the Senate, allowing the Romans to resume hostilities. In the ensuing battle, Viriathus had the upper hand but was left marooned when his army deserted. In 139 BC, Servilius bribed three Lusitanians to assassinate Viriathus; he was killed in his sleep by Audax, Ditalcus and Minurus – three former friends who had been sent as envoys to the Romans. Unfortunately for the treacherous trio, the Romans had them executed, on the grounds that 'Rome does not pay traitors who kill their chief.' According to Appian, Servilius had paid them and sent them to Rome to collect the rest of their fee.[3]

Theodor Mommsen summed up the romantic warrior image of Viriathus when he said of him, 'It seemed as if, in that thoroughly prosaic age, one of the Homeric heroes had reappeared.'[4] He was of the Lusitanian warrior class; to the Romans he was the *dux* (leader) of the Lusitanian army, the *adsertor* (protector) of Hispania or *imperator* (general) of the Lusitanian and Celtiberian tribes.[5] Appian and Valerius Maximus say Viriathus was one of the few survivors of the atrocities committed by Galba when he massacred the *flos iuventutis* ('the flower of the Lusitanian youth') in 150 BC. It was only two years after the massacre that Viriathus became the leader of the Lusitanian army. Various sources describe him as physically strong, highly intelligent, a great strategist, honest and fair. He was a guerrilla fighter and a bandit – *latrocinium*. Livy calls him *vir duxque magnus* – 'a great man and leader'. To Polybius, the war with Viriathus was the 'War of Fire'. He fought for glory, not for booty like the common soldier. According to Dio:

> he carried on the war not for the sake of personal gain or power nor through anger, but for the sake of warlike deeds in themselves; hence he was accounted at once a lover of war and a master of war.

The life of Viriathus has been embellished with legend, as befits Portugal's earliest national hero. He goes down in history not only as the most successful leader in Iberia who fought against the Romans, but also as one of the most successful generals ever to have defied Rome. He was defeated in battle by the Romans only once.

Henna 135 BC

When we think of slave revolts, we tend to think of Spartacus, and indeed, his has gone down as the greatest of them all in the classical era. There is, however, a long tradition of servile rebellion in Greece and Rome, before and after Spartacus. Indeed, it seems, wherever a large number of slaves are gathered together, there will be a dash for freedom. Chios in Greece was one of the first places where slaves often took sanctuary in the mountains to form bandit groups and raid farms. In the fourth century BC, there was a king of the slaves, Drimachos. In 413 BC, 20,000 Attican slaves deserted to the Spartans during the Peloponnesian War, mainly miners. In the third century BC the 'red' King Nablis abolished debts, taxed the rich and freed the slaves. In 134 BC, there was an insurrection of slaves at the Laurium silver mines in Attica. Attalus, the heirless king of Pergamum, bequeathed his state to Rome to prevent a simmering slave revolt. An illegitimate member of the royal household, Aristonicus, led an unsuccessful revolt against the Romans. His chief advisor was an egalitarian Stoic who promised that all slaves who followed him would be granted their freedom. In Lydia, in AD 399, during the time of the Roman Empire, hordes of slaves joined the Ostrogoth army. Slaves plundered Thrace in AD 401. In the siege of Rome by the Goths in AD 408–9, most of Rome's slaves, 40,000 in all, went over to the Goths.

Spartacus knew that Sicily had a reputation for slave revolts and attempted to reach there at the end of his uprising. The extensive *latifundia* on the island meant high populations of slave workers from the mid-third century BC. Sometimes they were prisoners of war; some had been bought on the slave markets of the eastern Mediterranean such as Rhodes and Delos. The huge tracts of land had come onto the market after the Romans expelled the Carthaginians and opened the door to speculators. Not unusually, the new owners, mainly *equites*, treated their slaves badly, according to Diodorus, which fomented rebellion and banditry.

The revolt (the First Servile War 135–132 BC) began on a large farm owned by a Greek from Henna, called Damophilius. In 136 BC, Eunus, a slave from Apamea in Syria (his followers were called the 'Syrians') occupied the town of Henna in central Sicily with 400 other runaways. Our principal source is the *Epitome* written by Publius Annius Florus in the early second century AD. This text is excerpted from the *Periochae* of Livy, who in turn probably used earlier historians to describe the exploits of Eunus, such as Polybius, a contemporary of Eunus. We also get information from the writings of pro-Roman Diodorus Siculus, who in turn used Posidonius as his primary source. Eunus quickly gathered a large following, bolstered by his claim that he was related to the Syrian mother goddess Atargatis, the equivalent to the Greek goddess Demeter, who had a shrine at Henna. Feigning divine possession and frenzy, he incited the slaves to arms and freedom, pretending that it was all divinely sanctioned. Something of a prophet too, he happened to predict role-reversal revolution in which rebellious slaves would capture the city of Henna. Apparently, one of his party tricks was fire-eating, which he brought off by secreting in his mouth a nut filled with sulphur, and exhaling a flame every time he spoke. This 'miracle' brought in 2,000 recruits. A tip at the performance guaranteed the donor protection come the revolution.

The revolt spread, and Eunus' army (now up to 200,000 men strong, if Diodorus is to be believed; 70,000 according to Livy and Orosius) defeated the army led by the praetor of Sicily. Eunus and another leader called Cleon then moved south to capture Agrigentum, and Tauromenium and Catana in the east. Eunus was declared king of Sicily and renamed himself Antiochus, a common regal name in Seleucid Syria and other states in the region. Interestingly, with Orwellian irony, the dynastic implications of the name are diametrically opposed to the personal liberty Eunus was trying to achieve for his fellow slaves. Archaeological evidence includes a bronze coin, minted at Henna and featuring the name 'King Antiochus'.

Rome, meanwhile, was heavily preoccupied with its campaign in Celtiberia, but when Scipio Aemilianus broke the siege at the Celtiberian capital, Numantia, Rome could turn its attention to Eunus. The consul Lucius Calpurnius Piso Frugi had already arrived in Sicily and blockaded Henna; contemporary sling-bullets bearing the legend 'Piso' have been discovered there. Henna, built on a mountain as it is, was not an easy siege: the Saracens took thirty-one years to break the stronghold, and the Normans needed twenty-one years to take it. Piso, with only one mere consular year at his disposal, failed, while back in Rome, the reform bills of Tiberius Sempronius Gracchus were proving somewhat diverting.

In 132, Publius Rutilius took over the prosecution of the war, his army bolstered with homecoming troops from Hispania. The slaves took Henna, Tauromenium and Morgantina, reducing the Romans' occupation of the island to little more than a tenuous foothold. Rome had to act if she was to contain this ongoing disaster, perpetrated by Eunus, a hysterical magician, and a slave at that. The armies sent to crush the revolt in 134 and 133 BC were both defected, and it was not until 132 BC, when occupied Messina fell to the Romans, that the slave army was defeated and the survivors crucified. The praetor, Perperna, was directly responsible for the victory and the aftermath, as Florus records:

At last punishment was inflicted upon them under the leadership of Perperna, who, after defeating them and finally besieging them at Henna reduced them by famine as effectually as by a plague and requited the surviving marauders with fetters, chains and the cross.[6]

As Crassus was to find out to his chagrin after defeating Spartacus, triumphs were not awarded for victory over mere slaves, regardless of the threat they posed or the military disaster they may have visited on highly-trained, disciplined and experienced Roman armies. Paperna had to make do with the watered down version, the *ovatio*. He may have found some consolation in the following year when he became the first of his family to be elected consul.

Eunus and his retinue took refuge in a cave but they were captured and brought to Rome, where Eunus died. Eccentricity apart, Eunus was obviously a charismatic leader with considerable military skills. He left a proud legacy that no doubt inspired slave revolts in 104 to 101 BC when Salvius Trypho and Athenio rebelled on Sicily in what is known as the Second Servile War, and in 73–71 BC with the insurrection led by Spartacus, the Third Servile War. Within thirty years of his death, the slaves were up in arms again in Sicily. Slaves belonging to Publius Clonius rebelled and elected a 'king', one Salvius, who assumed the name Trypho; his army numbered 30,000 slaves. Separately, another rebellion erupted when Athenio led a 10,000-strong army of slaves. Soon the two armies joined forces. Trypho established his capital at impregnable Triocala in the south-west of the island, building further fortifications against the inevitable attack. Athenio, however, advised against a siege, preferring open battle. The 40,000-strong slave army encountered Lucinius Licinius Lucullus at Scirthaea; the slaves initially took the upper-hand but lost impetus when Athenio was badly injured. Licinius eventually won the day, and Tryphone fled, leaving behind 20,000 dead slaves. Survivors fled to Triocola, which Lucullus failed to take. According to Diodorus, he returned to Rome in shame and was punished – such was the price of failing against a rabble of slaves.[7] So, from 104 to 101 BC, slaves were in control of Sicily. In 100 BC, the consul Aquilus took Triocala and finally quashed the slave rebellion.

Noreia 113 BC

The Northmen, or more precisely, the Cimbri and Teutones, left Frisia and Jutland in the second century BC when the sea began to encroach, possibly through climate change. After years of wandering along the Danube and the Rhine, they found themselves on the borders of Italy near Noricum (modern

Austria and part of Slovenia), where they defeated the Taurisci in 113 BC. The Taurisci were allies of Rome and appealed for help. The Cimbri and Teutones made a conciliatory offer to retreat, but were attacked by a Roman army under Gnaeus Papirius Carbo at Noreia (modern Ljubljana). The Northmen won convincingly but stopped short of advancing into Italy.[8] The Romans were saved from total annihilation by a storm. Carbo committed suicide by drinking vitriol (*atramentum sutorium*, or sulphuric acid).

In 109 BC, reinforced by the Helvetian Tigurini under Divico, the Cimbri and Teutones invaded eastern France, on the borders of Gallia Narbonensis. M. Junius Silanus attacked when the Senate refused an offer of mercenaries in exchange for land within Italy. The Northmen defeated the Romans again, and again they wisely refrained from invading Italy. The Tigurini, however, raided Roman territory on the Rhone and caused a revolt in Languedoc amongst the Volcae Tectosages. In 107 BC, Lucius Cassius Longinus was killed in an ambush by the Tigurini at the Battle of Burdigala (Bordeaux). His second in command, Gaius Popillius Laenas, was released, but only after he and his men were forced to surrender half of their baggage and ignominiously pass under the yoke. The Tigurini retreated, allowing the consul Q. Servilius Caepio to sack the Tectosage headquarters at Tolosa. The fantastic booty found there was estimated at 100,000lb of gold and 110,000lb of silver. The gold, according to Strabo, the famous *aurum Tolosanum* (allegedly the 'cursed gold' looted by the Gauls during the sack of Delphi in 279 BC) never made it back to Rome; Caepio was the prime suspect.[9] This is Strabo's account:

> and it was on account of having laid hands on them that Caepio ended his life in misfortunes – for he was cast out by his native land as a temple-robber, and he left behind as his heirs female children only, who, as it turned out, became prostitutes ... and therefore perished in disgrace.

Caepio did have a son, the maternal grandfather of Marcus Junius Brutus, the assassin of Julius Caesar. Caepio ended his life in exile in Smyrna.[10]

Arausio 105 BC

For the first time since the Second Punic War, Rome was under serious threat from a foreign power. In 105 BC, the Cimbri and the Teutones were back with reinforcements and a less accomodating attitude towards Roman territory. An army was levied, led by Cnaeus Mallius Maximus, to join forces with Caepio. The diplomacy attempted by the Northmen was rejected, while Mallius' army became increasingly ill-disciplined and disputatious. Caepio, meanwhile, was not obeying orders and failed to support Mallius: a disturbing example of class rivalry, in which the *novus homo*, Mallius, was snubbed by the aristocratic Caepio. A skirmish opened the hostilities in which Marcus Aurelius Scaurus and his cavalry were attacked in their camp. Scaurus was captured and brought before the king of the Cimbri, Boiorix, whom he advised to withdraw before inevitable destruction by the Romans. Boiorix responded by having Scaurus roasted alive slowly in a wicker cage – a horrible death, which he endured with consummate dignity. The Romans, though in disarray, attacked at Arausio (Orange) and were routed in what was the worst disaster since Cannae. Typically, Orosius exaggerates when he claims that only ten Romans survived, a nod to the fact that the camp followers and slaves were also butchered. Plutarch graphically records that the soil from the battlefield was made so fertile by corpses and body parts that they produced *magna copia*, high yields, for years to come. Still somewhat in awe of Roman might, the Northmen threw up this new chance to invade Italy: the Cimbri headed for Spain while the Teutones moved back into Gaul.

Chapter 7

The First Century: the Social War, Spartacus, Mithridates, Crassus, the Parthians and the Gauls

The Social War Disaster 90–88 BC

The name the 'Social Wars' derives from the Latin for 'allies', *socii*. The wars are also known as the Allied War, the Italian War or the Marsic War – a war waged from 90 to 88 BC between the Romans and a number of the other Italian cities, which had been Roman allies, often for centuries, and had paid tribute and routinely supplied troops to sustain Rome's conquest of the Italian peninsula and beyond. The war has received comparatively little attention down the years, despite its crucial impact on Roman politics and social history.

By the time of the Punic Wars, there were more than 150 allied treaties in force up and down the peninsula. The military importance of the allies cannot be understated: by the second century BC, between half and two-thirds of the troops in Roman armies were sourced from allies. Military obligations were stipulated in the *formula togatorum*, the list of those who wear the toga, establishing precisely the number of troops which could be called upon from each ally. Rome dictated their foreign policies to the advantage of Rome and, generally speaking, the allies were happy to coexist with Rome as client states in exchange for local autonomy. Loyalty to Rome was amply demonstrated during the wars with Hannibal. Other benefits included security, a share of booty and tax receipts where appropriate, and the right to participate in the assignment of land and colonies.

The age-old vexed question of land distribution was central to the Roman relationship with her Italian allies. By the time of Marius, the system had become exploitative and unfair, heavily biased as it was to the Romans. Appian gives a bleak assessment of the situation when he tells us that the Romans' policy of land distribution was prejudiced and caused inequality of land-ownership and wealth, leading to the 'Italic people declining little by little into pauperism and paucity of numbers without any hope of remedy.' Smallholders tended to farm wheat and barley, on which the return was far lower than on the cash crops like figs, olives and wine – the preserve of the wealthy owners of the larger estates. The lower prices meant smaller harvests and a fragile food supply. Lucilius, a contemporary poet, pithily sums it up with: 'the nourishing grain runs out and there is no bread for the common people.' Such agricultural arrangements and the resulting hunger caused growing disaffection; add to this the ritual exploitation by the rich, and we have the perfect recipe for rebellion.

It was a hopeless situation. Some tried to avert the inevitable but discretion was ever the better part of valour: Scipio Aemilianus – heroic victor over Carthage – was one, but he pulled out when he saw the hostility he was attracting. Likewise Gaius Laelius, who, in the 140s BC, withdrew his agrarian bill for the same reason, according to Plutarch in his *Life of Tiberius Gracchus*.[1] The brothers Gracchi died for their troubles. So-called Committees of Action were convened in a number of Italian towns and one armed force 10,000 strong under Q. Poppaedius Silo, leader of the Marsi, even set off to march on Rome, intent on surrounding the Senate house and demanding citizenship for his people. Discretion was again the winner when Silo soon turned back. In 91 BC, the tribune Marcus Livius Drusus attempted to ease the problem by offering to extend Roman citizenship to the allies, thus giving them a bigger say in national affairs and control of their own lands. In return, the allies agreed to join Drusus' clientele, boosting his power considerably. Crassus, originally a powerful backer in the senate, deserted him. The proposals were universally unpopular, particularly among the landowning elite, and were dismissed out of hand by the senate. Drusus was left with nothing except sky and mud – *caelum et caenum*. He was then assassinated on suspicion of having been complicit with Silo. Romans of all classes were urged to pull together against what was seen as the most dangerous threat since Carthage. The allies were outraged, and the Social War started.

Velleius Paterculus encapsulates the situation:

> The [rebels] were totally within their rights. All they wanted was to be citizens in an empire whose lands their weapons defended. Every year and in every war they contributed twice as many infantry and cavalry ... the state treated with scorn the people of its own race and kin, rejecting them as strangers and foreigners.[2]

The rebellion was largely confined to territories in the central and southern Apennines and the central part of the Adriatic coastland. However, these lands could offer some of Italy's best soldiers – including veterans from Marius' battle-hardened armies. The aim of the allies was to secede from Rome and to create their own independent confederation, to be called *Italia*, with its own capital at Corfinium (modern Abruzzo), to be renamed *Italica*. A federal senate was formed from 500 delegates sent from the rebel towns. As for economics, they minted their own coinage to pay for the army. Some coins depict eight warriors taking an oath, presumably representing the former allies involved: Marsi, Picentines, Paeligni, Marrucini, Vestini, Frentani, Samnites and Hirpini. The other four rebel allies were the Pompeiani, Venusini, Iapygii and Lucani. Other coins graphically depict the Italian bull goring the Roman wolf. Militarily, the Allies mimicked Roman organization by having two consuls leading two separate armies. Naturally, there were differences in aspirations: the Latin-speaking northern allies wanted an extension of the franchise; the Oscan-speaking Samnites wanted nothing less than total independence.

Rome's strategy was to deal with the immediate military threat and to prevent any further defections. One of the two separate theatres of war was assigned to each of the consuls of 90 BC. In the north, the consul Publius Rutilius Lupus was joined by Gaius Marius and Pompeius Strabo; in the south, the consul Lucius Julius Caesar (Sextus Julius) commanded with Lucius Cornelius Sulla and Titus Didius. Politics had intervened in the choice of generals: Caesar and Rutilius were both relatively inexperienced compared with the commanders Marius and Didius. Levies of citizens in loyal areas were bolstered by auxiliary units made of Gauls, Spaniards and Numidians; ex-slaves were recruited to carry out naval patrols. Fifteen legions, or 150,000 men, were signed in all.

Hostilities opened when the Samnite general Vettius Scaton heavily defeated the army of Lucius Julius Caesar, killing 2,000 of his men. Scaton then laid siege to Aesernia, which fell in 90 BC. Sulla relieved the town with twenty-four cohorts, inflicting great losses on the allies. The relief was short-lived, however, as the town was back in allied hands later that year.[3] The Romans suffered a further defeat when Marcus Lamponius killed 800 soldiers led by Publius Licinius Crassus and drove the survivors into the town of Grumentum. Meanwhile, in the south, the Samnite commander, Gaius Papius Mutilus, was wreaking havoc in Campania. To bolster his army, he pressed 10,000 infantry and 1,000 cavalry into his service, using them to good effect in his siege of Acerrae (near modern Naples). Pompeii and Nola fell, but Capua with its arsenal was successfully defended. A battle then ensued with Sextus Julius and his 10,000 foot and African cavalry; Sextus Julius slew 6,000 allies and withdrew.[4] The following year, Vettius Scaton laid a deadly ambush for the Romans, killing 8,000 at the Battle of Tolenus River. The Romans had built two bridges over the river out of sight of each other – one constructed by Rutilius, the other by Marius. When Rutilius crossed the bridge with his army, Vettius Scaton attacked with deadly consequences. Rutilius died from wounds after the battle. With hindsight, Ovid, and the Magna Mater, saw it coming in AD 8:

> They say she asked you Rutilius, 'Where are you dashing off to? As consul you'll die at the hands of the Marsi on the Materalia, my feast day'. Her words came true: the Tolenus flowed crimson: blood mixed in the water.[5]

Marius saw it too, in the shape of the bodies of his compatriots floating down the river. He feared the worst and attacked the allies; according to Orosius, he slew 8,000 of the Marsi. The allies retreated.

More disaster came for the Romans when Sextus Julius marched into a ravine near Teanum Sidicinum with a huge army: 30,000 infantry and 5,000 cavalry. He was attacked by the Samnite general, Marius Egnatius, and routed. Sextus Julius fell ill here and was carried out of the gorge on a litter.[6] In the north, Gnaeus Pompeius suffered defeat near Mount Falernus when he was attacked by Vidacilius, Lafrenius and Vettius. He was chased to Firmum and besieged by Lafrenius. Pompeius learnt that another allied army was on its way and sent out Publius Sulpicius Rufus to attack Lafrenius' force from behind while he mounted a frontal attack. Sulpicius torched the allies' camp; Lafrenius died in the battle.

Enough was enough. The defiant Romans finally climbed down and offered concessions to the allies in the form of the *Lex Iulia de Civitate Latinis Danda* brought by L. Julius Caesar. The law gave full citizenship to all Latin and Italian communities who had not taken part in the rebellion. Citizenship might also be granted in recognition of distinguished military service in combat.[7] But the war went on.

In 89 BC, the allied army fled to Asculum, home town of the Picentes, which was promptly besieged by Pompeius.[8] Allegedly, 60,000 Italians faced 75,000 Romans here. The Marsi lost 18,000 men when they attacked; they were later joined by the Picentes led by Vidacilius with eight cohorts. He barged his way into the town through the Roman ranks but realized that all was lost. He built a huge pyre, had a good meal and committed suicide by taking poison. The pyre was lit and the town fell to the Romans.[9] Archaeology has revealed graffiti-marked sling stones intended for Pompeius: *feri Pompeium* – 'hit Pompeius.' Some even stipulate where: *ventri* – 'in the stomach'.

Marius saved the day for Rome when he managed to divert the rebels from marching on Rome down the Via Valeria after the battle of the Fucine Lake; Rutilius Lupus was killed here. The battle is also notable for the death of Lucius Porcius Cato. He insulted Marius by comparing and equating their achievements and was surreptitiously murdered during the battle by Marius' son.[10]

Later that year, Sulla camped in the Pompaean Hills and was confronted by Lucius Cluentius. An impetuous Sulla attacked the allied army even though he was under strength due to the absence of foraging parties. Sulla was defeated but made good in a second attack. Cluentius took reinforcements and challenged Sulla for a third time. Proceedings began with a giant of a Gaul on the allied side offering single combat to a Roman. A diminutive Roman stepped forward and slew the Goliath; the rest of the Gauls turned and fled. Taking advantage of this, Sulla attacked and killed 3,000 allies in their flight to Nola. The allies, however, suffered much greater losses outside the gates of the city when the inhabitants cautiously only opened one of the gates: 20,000 allies died there, including Lucius. At Canusium later that year, the Romans suffered another reverse when Gaius Cosconius laid siege to the town and was routed by the Samnites; he retreated to Cannae. The Social War came to an end at the Battle of the Teanus River, when the allied leaders Poppaedius Silo and Obsidius were killed in a furious battle against the pro-Roman Apulians.[11]

Matyszak sums up the contradictions and paradoxes inherent in the Social War:

> Nations so desperate to give up their independence that they fought a war against the state that refused to take it; of the Roman Republic losing that war – itself a rarity – then winning by giving their enemies what they wanted. So the only instance in history of the opposite of a war of independence, was also one of the few cases where surrrender brought victory to the losing side.[12]

Arguably, the Romans had a lucky escape. The allies pursued a policy of wearing down their quarry by sporadic incursions and attacks on the Roman centres of communication. Had they pressed home their notable victories with more direct, aggressive action – particularly with an assault on Rome – then the outcome might have been very different. Rome's eventual, tortuously won victory had the accidental benefit of consolidating Rome with Italy, thus making Rome a stronger power generally, inheriting as she did a fecund supply of able officials and administrators, making her better equipped to deal with the destructive civil wars and the demanding empire which were on the horizon. However, politically and military, the Social War was a disaster. Losses of manpower and money apart, it widened further the schism between army and state, facilitating the ruinous rise of the triumvirates, expediting the end of the Republic.

The Spartacus Revolt 73–71 BC

The youths who polluted with blood the Punic Sea
Those who slew Pyrrhus
And hit almighty Antiochus,
And harrowing Hannibal –
They were a masculine mob of country soldiers
Who knew how to dig the fields with a Sabine spade,
Dragging in the cut down firewood
When ordered by their stern mothers to do so.

Horace, *Odes* 3, 6, 34-40

We have already noted how pivotal the land and agriculture were to the development of the Roman army, to the life of the Roman soldier-cum-farmer, and to the Roman economy. As Rome's power spread throughout the Italian peninsula and then into overseas countries, so the traditional landowner was compelled to spend more time away, to the detriment of his livelihood and farms. Many went bankrupt; many sold up, no doubt at depressed prices, to increasingly wealthy patrician landowners who transformed the Italian farm lands into sprawling estates – the *latifundia*. Many farm labourers were made redundant, replaced by the surge of free labour slaves who were increasingly available in the wake of Rome's conquests. The Romans sought work in the towns and cities when the slaves took over their farm jobs. Appian summarizes this economic and social revolution:

> The rich ... used persuasion or force to buy or seize property which adjoined their own, or any other smallholdings belonging to poor men, and came to operate great ranches instead of single farms. They employed slave hands and shepherds on these estates to avoid having free men dragged off the land to serve in the army, and they derived great profit from this form of ownership too, as the slaves had many children and no liability to military service and their numbers increased freely. For these reasons the powerful were becoming extremely rich, and the number of slaves in the country was reaching large proportions, while the Italian people were suffering from depopulation and a shortage of men, worn down as they were by poverty and taxes and military service. And if they had any respite from these tribulations, they had no employment, because the land was owned by the rich who used slave farm workers instead of free men.[13]

A farm of 1,000 acres would be on the small side. To give an idea of the potential magnitude of the landowning, we can cite one owner who died in 8 BC leaving

4,000 slaves, 3,000 yoke of oxen and 257,000 other farm animals. The lands of Marcus Licinius Crassus (115–53 BC) were valued at 50 million denarii. In 49 BC, Lucius Domitius Ahenobarbus owned 270,000 acres.

Italy was thronged with slaves, mainly prisoners of war but many also from the burgeoning slave markets, some of which were enthusiastically supplied by pirates. Estimates suggest two million slaves in the early first century BC against an Italian–Roman population of six million. One of the lucrative sidelines and benefits of owning slaves was their potential role as gladiators – or as wild-animal fodder in gladiatorial contests. Money could be made here, particularly with the rise in celebrity amongst the more successful survivors of the arena. One such celebrity was a slave by the name of Spartacus.

Gladiatorial contests were serious business. The gladiators had to be good if the baying crowds which flocked to the shows all around the empire were to be satisfied. Gladiators, then, underwent training in gladiatorial schools. In 73 BC, seventy-eight of them escaped from the fighting school of Gnaeus Lentulus Batiatus at Capua. Initially, the breakout was inspired more by the hope of freedom than anything else: according to Plutarch, the gladiators were only armed with meat cleavers and spits, stolen from the kitchen. As luck had it, they came upon a wagon filled with gladiatorial weaponry; now heavily armed, they occupied a slope on Mount Vesuvius. Their nominated leaders were Spartacus, Oenomaus and Crixus: a Thracian, a Greek and a German.

Plutarch gives us some detail:

> Spartacus was a Thracian from the nomadic tribes and not only had a great spirit and great physical strength, but was, much more than one would expect from his condition, most intelligent and cultured, being more like a Greek than a Thracian.[14]

His physical and military prowess were no doubt honed by his experience fighting for Rome as an auxiliary. His small band was soon bolstered by other runaway slaves and disaffected farm workers who successfully cut their combat teeth on a militia despatched from Capua to deal with them. Rome could not now ignore Spartacus, even though she was preoccupied with two other wars: Pompey was fighting against Sertorius in Hispania, and Lucullus was at war with Mithridates VI of Pontus in the east. At home, there was mounting unrest at the resulting grain shortages. Florus picks up the story, showing revenge as an additional element:

> When, by summoning the slaves to their standard, they had quickly collected more than 10,000 adherents, these men, who had been originally

content merely to have escaped, soon began to wish to take their revenge also.[15]

The propraetor Gaius Claudius Glaber hastily raised an army of 3,000 untrained men to bring the revolt to an end. Things started well for Claudius: he quickly isolated the gladiators on a hill high up on Vesuvius and looked to be in control. However, this did not account for the tactical ingenuity of the slaves when they made ladders from the branches of the vines, enabling them to get down from the hill by night and penetrate behind Claudius' lines. The armies of Lucius Cossinus, Lucius Furius and Caius Toranius were all soundly defeated. Varinius managed to surround the slave army, but they escaped, leaving dead sentries lashed to stakes guarding an empty camp.[16] The Romans panicked and fled, deserting their camp and allowing it to be looted by the gladiators, who were able to arm themselves from the weapons they found there. The Romans regrouped and attacked a second time, now under the command of the praetor Publius Varinius. Oddly, Varenus split his forces, enabling the rebels to defeat them comfortably. Varinius' humiliation and shame were complete when he lost not only the horse from beneath him but both his lictors (who were taken prisoner), and their *fasces*, which Spartacus triumphantly paraded through his camp. Florus again:

> The first position which attracted them (a suitable one for such ravening monsters) was Mt. Vesuvius. Being besieged here by Clodius Glabrus, they slid by means of ropes made of vine-twigs through a passage in the hollow of the mountain down into its very depths, and issuing forth by a hidden exit, seized the camp of the general by a sudden attack which he never expected. They then attacked other camps, that of Varenius and afterwards that of Thoranus; and they ranged over the whole of Campania. Not content with the plundering of country houses and villages, they laid waste Nola, Nuceria, Thurii and Metapontum with terrible destruction.

The rebels became more like a regular army every day, reinforced as they were by more and more malcontents.[17] Nothing if not industrious, Spartacus and his slave army spent the winter of 73–72 BC productively, making crude shields of wicker-work and animal skins, and swords and other weapons by melting down the iron in the slave jails. A cavalry unit was formed with the horses they rounded up. The plan was to cross the Apennines and head north so that his army could exit Italy and head back home to Germania or the Balkans. The logistic difficulties of moving 70,000 men over mountainous terrain were not lost on Spartacus, and he was forced to split his forces.

The Romans saw their chance. In the spring of 72 BC, the consul Lucius Gellius Publicola launched a surprise attack on a unit Plutarch called 'the German contingent' and Appian 'the force of Crixus'. Appian records that Crixus was killed and lost two-thirds of his 30,000 Germans and Gauls in the battle, which took place at Mount Garganus near modern Foggia. Crixus and Spartacus had fallen out over whether to leave Italy or engage the Romans as Crixus wanted.[18] Simultaneously, the consul Gnaeus Cornelius Lentulus Clodianus intercepted Spartacus' main force in the Apennines. The strategy was to wait for Gellius before engaging, so as to attack Spartacus from both sides. Spartacus scuppered this when he defeated both armies separately, looted their equipment and pressed on to the Adriatic Sea. Here is Plutarch's account:

> The consul Gellius, falling suddenly upon a party of Germans, who through contempt, and confidence had straggled from Spartacus, cut them all to pieces. But when Lentulus with a large army besieged Spartacus, he sallied out upon him, and, joining battle, defeated his chief officers, and captured all his baggage. As he made toward the Alps, Cassius, who was praetor of that part of Gaul that lies about the Po, met him with ten thousand men, but being overcome in the battle, he had much ado to escape himself, with the loss of a great many of his men.

Our sources differ here, with Appian recording:

> In the aftermath the consuls retreated in confusion, while Spartacus, first sacrificing 300 Roman prisoners to Crixus, made for Rome with 120,000 foot soldiers after burning the useless equipment and putting all the prisoners to death and slaughtering the draught animals to free himself of all encumbrances.[19]

Plutarch omits the atrocity. Perhaps it did not chime well enough with his description of Spartacus as 'intelligent and cultured, more like a Greek than a Thracian.' Florus and Orosius differ again:

> He also celebrated the obsequies of his officers who had fallen in battle with funerals like those of Roman generals, and ordered his captives to fight at their pyres, just as though he wished to wipe out all his past dishonour by having become, instead of a gladiator, a giver of gladiatorial shows.[20]

Spartacus rubbed salt in the Romans' wounds when he mocked the Romans and turned the tables on them by making *them* perform in gladiatorial contests and imitating their funeral rites in honour of Crixus.

Cato the Younger volunteered for service in this battle and, unlike the bungling Gellius, acquitted himself well. The Romans retreated back to Rome, pursued for a while by Spartacus, who then turned and headed for the Alps along the Adriatic coastline. This time the Romans followed Spartacus and reached Ancona first, where the slave army was victorious again.

The way to the Alps was almost clear; they only had to defeat the army of the governor Gaius Cassius Longinus at Modena in Gallia Cisalpina. Spartacus won yet again. He had convincingly achieved his objective, but it did not go quite to plan:

> Spartacus' view was that they should cross the mountains and then disperse to their own homes ... His men, however, would not listen to him. They were strong in numbers and full of confidence, and they went about Italy ravaging everything in their way.[21]

Plutarch tells us that some at least of the slaves chose not to leave and proceeded to lay waste the northern cities of Roman Italy. No doubt they were seduced by the promise of booty and rapine, only too happy to prolong the camaraderie which had built up between the slaves.

For Rome, this was all an embarrassing and humiliating disaster. The eyes of the Roman world would be on Spartacus and his victories. Rumour spread that slaves could defeat the Roman military; slaves everywhere would be taking note. Highly trained and battle-hardened Roman armies were being beaten by little more than a rabble of enthusiastic and headstrong amateurs. The demonstration of slave power had gone on too long; Roman military prestige had to be restored at all costs.

Marcus Licinius Crassus, praetor in 72 BC, was sent to deal with Spartacus. He defeated him at Camalatrum with ten legions, six of which were newly recruited. He ordered the commander of the remnants of the army, Mummius, to head south but to avoid contact with the enemy at all costs. Mummius thought he knew better and attacked Spartacus; he was defeated. Crassus proceeded to decimate the legion as an example to anyone else considering insubordination. He picked out the 500 men who were the first to run away and divided them into fifty groups of ten; one man from of each was doomed to die by lot, 'with a variety of appalling and terrible circumstances, presented before the eyes of the whole army, assembled as spectators,' according to Plutarch.[22]

After the dilemma in the north, Spartacus had headed south at the end of 72 BC and took Thurii – the only town to be captured by the slaves in the whole campaign. He made camp at Rhegium. The intention was to escape to Sicily, which, as we have seen, had a good reputation for slave rebellion. Not surprisingly, there were no ships available to the rebels. In desperation, they tried to make rafts from beams and barrels bound together. Spartacus collaborated with the notorious Cilician pirates; the prospect of what would have been a coalition from hell must have enraged, and terrified, the Romans. A base on Sicily would benefit the pirates enormously, allowing them to pillage the Italian coast with virtual impunity. Money changed hands, a meeting was arranged – but the pirates, being pirates, did not show. Instead, Crassus turned up, and ordered that a 60km trench be dug right across Bruttium, from the Tyrrhenian to the Ionian Sea. Crassus' legions made short work of it. Plutarch explains this great feat of civil engineering and the strategy behind it:

> This great and difficult work he perfected in a space of time short beyond all expectation, making a ditch from one sea to the other, over the neck of land, three hundred furlongs long, fifteen feet broad, and as much in depth, and above it built a wonderfully high and strong wall.[23]

Not only did the wall give the Roman soldiers something constructive to do, it prevented Spartacus from foraging for food. Spartacus was perilously boxed in, but he was up to the challenge: during a stormy, snowy night, he filled in part of the ditch with earth and branches and with the corpses of dead soldiers, horses and cattle to create a bridge over which he crossed with one third of his army. Spartacus now attacked first but lost 6,000 men to the Romans' (incredible) three. Spartacus resorted to guerrilla tactics. Desperate to maintain discipline, he crucified a Roman prisoner in no-man's land to show his troops what awaited them if they were defeated.[24]

Crassus now had Spartacus just where he wanted him over the winter. Spartacus' provisions would be exhausted come the spring, when he would have just a starving and undernourished army to attack. However, the Senate was having none of it and summoned the recently victorious Pompey from Hispania to get involved. Nothing could be guaranteed to galvanize Crassus more than the propect of his arch-enemy raining on his parade. According to Plutarch:

> News was already brought that Pompey was at hand; and people began to talk openly that the honour of this war was reserved to him, who would come and at once oblige the enemy to fight and put an end to the war. Crassus,

therefore, eager to fight a decisive battle, encamped very near the enemy, and began to make lines of circumvallation; but the slaves made a sally and attacked the pioneers.[25]

As it happened, Spartacus attacked first at the Battle of Cantenna on the Lucanian Lake, and punctured Crassus' lines, but with only one third of his army; serious divisions and mutiny had split his forces. The remaining two-thirds were then picked off by the legions under Quintus Marcius Rufus and Lucius Pomptinus. Even worse, the slave force which had punched through the Roman lines was split, and one of these groups too was subjected to serious casualties. Luckily, Spartacus appeared just in time to prevent the annihilation of his whole army, but he reputedly lost 35,000 men that day, including the generals Castus and Cannicus.[26]

The Romans now had a significant numerical superiority. Crassus boldly attacked Spartacus and won the day. Around 12,300 slaves were killed. Apparently, only two were wounded in the back; the rest all died holding their ground, according to Livy in his *Periochae*. The casualties were massive, but exaggerated, at 60,000. Spartacus made a futile attempt to negotiate a peace with Crassus but he was snubbed. He then retreated further south, to Petelia, where he defiantly defeated both Quintus Marcius Rufus and Gnaeus Tremellius Scrofa. These victories were to be the death of the slaves, according to Plutarch:

> ... since it filled [Spartacus'] slaves with over-confidence. They refused any longer to avoid battle and would not even obey their officers. Instead, they surrounded them with arms in their hands as soon as they began to march and forced them to lead them back through Lucania against the Romans.[27]

In March 71 BC, Spartacus attempted to seize Brundisium, perhaps with a view to sailing to Sicily or Epirus. However, the Governor of Macedonia, Marcus Teretius Varro Lucullus, had been recalled by the Senate and was already there lying in wait. Spartacus knew that all was up. His horse was brought to him, Spartacus drew out his sword and killed it in front of the army, saying: 'If we win the day I shall have a great many better horses from the enemy, and if we lose, I shall have no need of one.' In a word: win or die. The rebels paid for their incaution and over-enthusiasm at the conclusive Battle of the River Silarus: the 35,000 rebels remaining were heavily defeated. Crassus recovered five legionary eagle-standards, twenty-six other standards, and five *fasces*. Spartacus died in the battle; his body was never recovered.[28] Appian has the last word:

Spartacus was wounded in the thigh with a spear and sank upon his knee, holding his shield in front of him and contending in this way against his assailants until he and the great mass of those with him were surrounded and slain.

The scattered remnants of Spartacus' army took refuge in the mountains of Bruttium where, led by one Publipor, they organized themselves into four groups on the banks of the River Silarus and conducted a guerilla war against the Romans until they were finally wiped out by Pompey and Crassus.

The Romans captured 6,000 unfortunate slaves alive. As a stark, rotting reminder of the fate which awaits the rebellious slave, they were all crucified on crosses placed every 40m or so along the 150 miles of the Via Appia between Rome and Capua. The corpses were gradually eaten away by wild dogs and carrion. Pompey butchered a further 5,000 'survivors'. By contrast, 3,000 Roman prisoners of war were found at Spartacus' camp at Rhegium, alive and well.

A duplicitous Pompey claimed credit for ending the war. He was awarded a triumph for defeating Sertorius in Spain; a disappointed and angry Crassus had to make do with an *ovatio*, a low-rent triumph.[29] This lesser decoration reflected the official embarrassment and shame felt in Rome at the humiliating runaround a bunch of slaves had given them over the last two years. The Romans needed an expensive seventy-one legions to quell the rebellion. It was inconceivable that a victory, essential as it was, over a slave army could merit a glorious triumph. Members of the establishment like Cicero naturally thought Spartacus was comparable to the worst of Romans, fit only to be despised, deserving of everything he got. To Horace he was a devastator and fierce, *acer*.[30] Down the years, he was dragged out as a bogeyman by Roman mothers to frighten naughty children into obedience. Spartacus had threatened everything Roman and everything that the Romans stood for and cherished. The disaster that was the revolt of Spartacus was quietly consigned to history.

We suggested earlier that the rebellion was born more from a desperate bid for freedom than anything else. It was never going to succeed in overthrowing the system of slavery in Rome, even if it was intended to achieve that end. If a number of the slaves were repatriated after the quandary in northern Italy, then that was a limited success, but the fact remains that the tens of thousands of slaves toiling away in Roman towns and cities did not flock to Spartacus' cause as he and his army strutted and pillaged up and down the peninsula. The Roman army, as we have observed, had a seemingly endless source of recruits: when one army was routed, it was immediately replaced by another. Spartacus was not the first and he would not be the last to suffer from this relentless regeneration of armies. Indeed, Varinia, Spartacus' perceptive wife in the famous twentieth century film, shows a resigned appreciation of this: 'No matter how many times we beat them, they always seem to have another army to send against us. And another.'

The Romans seemed to have learnt their lesson. Mile after mile of putrefying roadside crucifixions would have kept memories fresh for many years – a salutary reminder of the folly of running away and of rebellion. During the Catiline conspiracy crisis in 63 BC, gangs of gladiators were removed to Campania from Rome for security reasons. In 49, Julius Caesar relocated 5,000 gladiators to Capua; Lucius Cornelius Lentulus wanted to recruit them into his army, but Pompey, according to Cicero, 'very sensibly distributed [them] ... among the population, two per household.'[31]

The word 'crucifixion' comes from the Latin for 'cross' and 'fix' – *crux* and *figere* – and that is exactly what this excruciatingly slow and painful torture-to-the-death amounts to. It is a number-one deterrent; the sight of someone hanging on the cross, slowly dying, must have deterred many a speculative criminal or rebel – just what Crassus intended. Hanging on a cross, spread-eagled and at least half-naked was humiliating in the extreme. We tend to think of Jesus Christ when we think of crucifixion, but the way Jesus, and the slaves of Spartacus before him, were tortured is but one of a number of methods. Seneca the Younger was something of an authority, as he describes in his dialogue *To Marcia on Consolation*:

> I see crosses there, not just of one kind but made in many different ways: some have their victims with head facing down to the ground; some impale their genitals; others stretch out their arms on the gibbet.[32]

Tacitus tells us that there was a special place in Rome outside the Esquiline Gate for crucifixions, with an area reserved for the execution of slaves.[33] Sometime the victim was attached to the cross with rope, but often the more traumatic option of painful nails was used, as decribed by Josephus in writing about the aftermath of the siege of Jerusalem in his *Jewish War*: 'the soldiers out of rage and hatred, nailed those they caught, one after one way, and another after another, to the crosses, as a bit of a joke.'[34]

Nails and other paraphernalia used in crucifixions were much sought after as amulets with alleged medicinal qualities. Some Romans found crucifixion repellent, not least Cicero, who protested that it was 'a most cruel and disgusting punishment', recommending that 'the very mention of the cross should be far removed not only from a Roman citizen's body, but from his mind, his eyes, his ears.'[35] To expedite the death of the victim, their legs were smashed with an iron club, a procedure called *crurifragium*. The cross itself could be of one of three shapes: either simply a vertical stake (*crux simplex*); a stake with a cross-piece attached at the top to form a T (*crux commissa*), or just below the top (*crux immissa*); there were also crosses in the shape of the letters X and Y. The oldest surviving image of a Roman crucifixion is a graffito discovered in a taverna in Puteoli from the time of Trajan or Hadrian. The cross is T-shaped; the inscription identifies the woman victim as Alkimila.

The only surviving skeleton of a Roman-era crucifixion was found in 1968 at Giv'at ha-Mivtar in Jerusalem, from the first century AD. These remains of one Jehohanan include a heel bone with a nail driven through it from the side, suggesting that his heels were nailed to opposite sides of the upright.

The intended outcome was, of course, death – but not before hours of intensifying pain. Death occurred in a range from hours to days depending on the method of crucifixion, the victim's health, co-exisiting deseases or injuries, and the environment. Medical experts reporting research in the *Journal of the Royal Society of Medicine* (Maslen *et al*) and in the *South African Medical Journal* have indicated the following as possible causes of death: cardiac rupture; heart failure; hypovolemic shock; acidosis asphyxia; arrhythmia; and pulmonary embolism.[36]

Sepsis, too, was common from wound infection caused by the nails or lashings. And there was always dehydration or being eaten alive as carrion by wild animals. Survival was possible – Josephus successfully appealed to Titus to take down three victims, and one lived – but it must have been very rare.[37]

Crucifixion was very popular. It was used in one form or another by Persians, Carthaginians, Macedonians and, of course, Romans. In Roman times, we know that it was common for death to be expedited for very mundane reasons: the *South African Medical Journal* (Retief *et al*) report that 'the attending Roman guards could only leave the site after the victim had died, and were known to precipitate death by means of deliberate fracturing of the tibia and/or fibula, spear stab wounds into the heart, sharp blows to the front of the chest, or a smoking fire built at the foot of the cross to asphyxiate the victim.'[38]

The Greeks were never keen, although Herodotus describes the crucifixion of a Persian general, Artaces, around 479 BC: 'They nailed him to a plank and hung him up ... who suffered death by crucifixion.' Alexander the Great reputedly crucified 2,000 survivors from his siege of Tyre, as well as the hapless doctor who unsuccessfully treated Alexander's friend Hephaestion.

Nearer home, Plautus in his *Miles Gloriosus* describes the laborious task of carrying one's cross, or at least a good part of it: 'The *patibulum* was a crossbar which the convicted criminal carried on his shoulders, with his arms fastened to it, to the place for [execution] ... Hoisted up on an upright post, the patibulum became the crossbar of the cross.'[39]

In 337, Constantine abolished crucifixion in deference to Jesus Christ.

It comes as no surprise that Spartacus and his revolt against Rome has become a symbol down the years of freedom and emancipation. Rome's disaster showed the rest of the world that repression could be resisted, for a while at least. Bernard-Joseph Saurin's 1760 tragedy *Spartacus* is responsible for the modern image we have, showing him as a noble hero in the mould of Viriathus and Boudica.[40] Susanna Strickland wrote her *Spartacus – a Roman Tale* for children in 1822. Just twenty years before the revolution in his own country, Voltaire believed that 'The war of Spartacus and the slaves was perhaps the most just war in history; perhaps the only just war in history.'[41] Francois Dominique Toussaint L'Ouverture (1744–1803) became known as the 'black Spartacus' when in 1791, inspired by the liberty, equality and brotherhood espoused by the French Revolution, he led his enslaved compatriots on the French colony of Saint Domingue in Caribbean Hispaniola to freedom, establishing Haiti, the first black state outside Africa that was independent of European control.[42] L'Ouverture defeated first the Spanish and then the British, relying on the military expertise he picked up from Julius Caesar's *Commentarii*. In 1793, concerned that L'Ouverture's revolt would spread to the British slave colony of Jamaica next door, and hoping to make the island a British possession, King George III sent 27,000 troops to Haiti. It was one of the greatest military catastrophes in British imperial history. Tropical disease killed thousands of Redcoats before they surrendered to L'Ouverture. This was the first time in history that a European army had surrendered to a black general. The defeat inspired William Blake's 1793 *America: A Prophecy*:

Let the slave grinding at the mill run out into the field;
Let him look up into the heavens and laugh in the bright air.

During the First World War, Rosa Luxemburg and Karl Liebknecht paid homage to Spartacus when they launched the Spartakist League (*Spartakusbund*), a forerunner of the German Communist Party that made use of the gladiator's name. To Karl Marx, Spartacus was the 'finest fellow antiquity had to offer.' In a letter to Engels in 1861 (in which Pompey incidentally gets his comeuppance), Marx says that he was reading about Spartacus in Appian's *Civil Wars of Rome*, and he concludes: 'Spartacus emerges as the most capital fellow in the whole history of antiquity. A great general ... of noble character, a "real representative" of the proletariat of ancient times.' Pompey, according to Marx, was 'a real shit'.[43]

Spartacus became a talisman for the repressed poor in countries like Bulgaria, and for the working class in the Communist countries during the Cold War. In 1960, he was adopted as a gay icon after Kirk Douglas' performance in Stanley Kubrick's *Spartacus*, based on Howard Fast's novel.[44] Fast had been inspired by Rosa Luxemburg and her Spartakists when reading about them in the library of Mount Point prison, where he was serving time during the anti-Communist hysteria. Significantly, Fast's novel was adapted by Dalton Trumbo, a blacklisted Communist American screen-writer; Douglas insisted on listing Trumbo's name in the credits, the first example of open defiance of the Communist blacklist, leading to its obsolescence. Hitherto Hollywood had steered clear of 'political angles'.

Amnias River and Protopachium, or the Asian Vespers 88 BC

In AD 1282, a rebellion broke out on Sicily against Charles I of France, ruler of Sicily since 1266, which became known as the Sicilian Vespers. Within six weeks, 3,000 French men and women were butchered by the rebels, and Charles was ousted. This was the War of the Sicilian Vespers. Steven Runciman describes the carnage:

> To the sound of the bells, messengers ran through the city calling on the men of Palermo to rise against the oppressor. At once the streets were filled with angry armed men, crying, 'Death to the French' ('*Moranu li francisi*' in the Sicilian language). Every Frenchman they met was struck down. They poured into the inns frequented by the French and the houses where they dwelt, sparing neither man, woman nor child. Sicilian girls who had married Frenchmen perished with their husbands. The rioters broke into the Dominican and Franciscan convents, and all the foreign friars were dragged out and told to pronounce the word '*ciciri*', whose sound the French tongue could never accurately reproduce. Anyone who failed the test was slain ... By the next morning some two thousand French men and women lay dead; and the rebels were in complete control of the city.[45]

The battles of Amnias River and Protopachium, fought in 88 BC during the First Mithridatic War, are two of the battles often known as the Asian or Asiatic Vespers, by analogy with the Sicilian Vespers. Mithridates VI, the king of Pontus, fomented opposition to the Romans, predicated on their onerous taxes. This reached its climax in the brutal execution of 80,000 Roman and Italian citizens and other immigrants in Asia Minor. The massacre was planned scrupulously and coordinated clinically to occur on the same day in several towns throughout the region. The outraged Roman Senate responded by sending a huge invasion force to cripple Mithridates and annex his territory. This was the Mithridatic Wars.

Mithridates was born in Sinope. His mother, Laodice VI, was a Seleucid princess and the daughter of the Seleucid monarchs Antiochus IV Epiphanes and his wife-sister Laodice IV. His father, Mithridates V, was assassinated in about 120 BC at a banquet. In his will, he left the Pontic kingdom to the joint rule of Laodice VI, Mithridates and his younger brother, Mithridates Chrestus. Both sons were still minors, so their mother reigned all-powerful as regent. Her regency lasted from 120 BC to 116 BC, during which Chrestus was the favourite; Mithridates went into hiding to escape from his mother's plots against him.

Mithridates came back around 115 BC as king, removing his mother and brother from the throne and throwing them into prison where Laodice died. Chrestus either died in prison or was tried for treason and executed. Whatever the case, Mithridates gave both a royal funeral. He married his 16-year-old sister Laodice, to preserve the integrity of the bloodline, to co-rule over Pontus with him, guarantee the succession of his legitimate children and reinforce his hold on the throne.

At the beginning of the century, Mithridates, in expansionist mood, overran Cappadocia, but, much to his irritation, he was ordered by the Romans to withdraw. He aimed to carve up Paphlagonia and Galatia with Nicomedes III of Bithynia. Mithridates realized that Nicomedes was nothing more than a Roman puppet intent on an anti-Pontic alliance with the Roman Republic. Mithridates duly clashed with Nicomedes over Cappadocia, and defeated him in a series of battles. Nicomedes had no option but to enlist the assistance of Rome. The Romans twice acted on behalf of Nicomedes (95–92 BC). Mithridates inclined towards war with Rome. His sister Laodice became Queen of Cappadocia after Mithridates had his brother-in-law, Ariarathes VI, assassinated by Gordius, a Cappadocian nobleman and ally of Mithridates. Laodice ruled as regent for her son Ariarathes VII. Things got very complicated when Laodice married Nicomedes III of Bithynia, arch enemies of Pontus. Nicomedes took Cappadocia; Mithridates removed him. Unfortunately for the king, he was now virtually surrounded by Roman client states, so empire-building inevitably brought him into conflict with Rome. While Rome was preoccupied with the Social Wars, he tried again, expelling Nicomedes from Bithynia and Ariobarzanes from Cappadocia. The Romans sent Manius Aquillius to restore the leaders. Diplomacy, in the shape of the Aquillian Delegation, came to nothing, so Mithridates attacked Cappadocia again, all the while amassing a huge army of some 250,000 infantry and 40,000 cavalry. Neoptomelus and Archelaus were his generals. Aquilius could only muster 120,000 soldiers, which he divided into three divisions. Nicomedes struck first at the Amnias River in Paphlagonia with 50,000 infantry and 6,000 cavalry against the smaller force of Neoptomelus and Archelaus; they, however, were equipped with highly effective scythe-wheeled chariots, literally scything down the Bithynians. The Bithynians were routed by the twin forces of Neoptomelus and Archelaus, but the prisoners that were taken were treated by Mithridates with notable humanity. This defeat by an inferior force gave the Romans pause for thought. Aquilius was captured, with terrible consequences recorded by Appian:

> [Mithridates] captured Manius Aquilius, one of the ambassadors and the one who was most to blame for this war. Mithridates led him around, bound on an ass, and compelled him to introduce himself to the public as 'maniac'. Finally, at Pergamon, Mithridates poured molten gold down his throat, thus rebuking the Romans for their bribe-taking.[46]

Neoptomelus later slew 10,000 of Manlius Maltinus' army of 40,000 at Protopachium, where, incidentally, more prisoners were taken, treated decently and released; Manlius fled to Pergamum. Mithridates had won and was free to move around the region without impediment. For Rome it was disaster, but worse was to follow. It was at this time that Mithridates ordered the extermination of all Romans and Italians in the Asiatic Vespers.[47] In 88 BC, Mithridates had received some sinister and mischievous advice from a leading Greek philosopher at his court, Metrodoros of Skepsis, *ho misoromaios* – the Roman-hater. Metrodoros convinced the king that, if he wanted to bring more communities on side against the Romans, he should exterminate all Romans in the province, regardless of age or sex; this was the only way to be rid of Roman rule forever. As noted, the massacre was clinically executed and timed to take the victims by surprise, in every community and simultaneously. In a letter to all the civic authorities, Mithridates stipulated that the atrocity was to happen one month after the date of his letter. Appian takes up the gruesome story, its precision and insidious planning:

> [Mithridates] wrote secretly to all his satraps and magistrates that on the thirtieth day thereafter they should set upon all Romans and Italians in their towns, and upon their wives and children and their domestics of Italian birth, kill them and throw their bodies out unburied, and share their goods with himself. He threatened to punish any who should bury the dead or conceal the living, and offered rewards to informers and to those who should

kill persons in hiding, and freedom to slaves for betraying their masters. To debtors for killing money-lenders he offered release from one half of their obligations.[48]

This is what happened in the atrocity:

The Ephesians tore fugitives, who had taken refuge in the temple of Artemis, from the very images of the goddess and slew them. The Pergameans shot with arrows those who had fled to the temple of Aesculapius, while they were still clinging to his statues. The Adramytteans followed those who sought to escape by swimming, into the sea, and killed them and drowned their children. The Caunii, who had been made subject to Rhodes after the war against [the Seleucid king Antiochus III] and had been lately liberated by the Romans, pursued the Italians who had taken refuge about the Vesta statue of the senate house, tore them from the shrine, killed children before their mothers' eyes, and then killed the mothers themselves and their husbands after them. The citizens of Tralles, in order to avoid the appearance of blood-guiltiness, hired a savage monster named Theophilus, of Paphlagonia, to do the work. He conducted the victims to the temple of Concord, and there murdered them, chopping off the hands of some who were embracing the sacred images.[49]

Mithridates now eyed Europe. His crony Aristion stirred up unrest in Athens and was made tyrant there; the city, Piraeus and other parts of southern and central Greece were taken. Sulla came in pursuit and won over most of the Greek states; he laid siege to Athens, which fell to him in March 86 BC. He re-captured Piraeus, looted and ransacked the area, most of which was destroyed by fire, including Philon's famous Arsenal. Sulla recaptured the city, assisted by famine amongst the occupants:

Knowing that the defenders of Athens were severely pressed by hunger, that they had devoured all their cattle, boiled the hides and skins, and licked what they could get therefrom, and that some had even partaken of human flesh, Sulla directed his soldiers to encircle the city with a ditch so that the inhabitants might not escape secretly, even one by one. This done, he brought up his ladders and at the same time began to break through the wall. The feeble defenders were soon put to flight, and the Romans rushed into the city.

A great and pitiless slaughter ensued in Athens, the inhabitants, for want of nourishment, being too weak to escape. Sulla ordered an indiscriminate massacre, not sparing women or children. He was angry that they had so suddenly joined the barbarians without cause, and had displayed such violent animosity toward himself. Most of the Athenians, when they heard the order given, rushed upon the swords of the slayers voluntarily. Sulla forbade the burning of the city, but allowed the soldiers to plunder it. In many houses they found human flesh prepared for food. The next day Sulla sold the slaves at auction.[50]

Roman pride was, however, fully restored when Sulla moved into Boeotia and confronted Archelaus' Pontic army at Chaeronea in 86 BC and soundly defeated it, slaying 10,000 to their loss of an unbelievable twelve or thirteen. Sulla had closed the gap between the armies and rendered the scythe-wheeled chariots useless. Plutarch records a humorous scenario:

> [Sulla] robbed the scythe-bearing chariots of their efficiency. For these are of most avail after a long course, which gives them velocity and impetus for breaking through an opposing line but short starts are ineffectual and feeble, as in the case of missile which do not get full propulsion. And this proved to be true now in the case of Barbarians. The first of their chariots were driven along feebly and engaged sluggishly, so that the Romans, after repulsing them, clapped their hands and laughed and called for more, as they are wont to do at the races in the circus.[51]

Sulla then moved north into Thessaly and was met at Orchomenus by 80,000 crack Mithridatic troops who had arrived by sea at Chalcis in Euboea. In a bid to lessen the impact of Archelaus' cavalry by digging trenches down the sides of the plain, his engineers and their guards were cut down. Sulla rallied his army with a solo charge on foot into the ranks of the enemy and slew 15,000 of them.[52] Plutarch says that the slaughter was so great that the marshes were clogged with blood; weapons were still being found protruding out of the marshes 200 years later.[53] Archelaus defected to Rome. Mithridates' designs on Europe evaporated.

Mithridates had another opportunity to show his extreme cruelty. During the First Mithridatic War, there was a conspiracy to assassinate Mithridates by four of his so-called friends: Mynnio and Philotimus of Smyrna, and Cleisthenes and Asclepiodotus of Lesbos. Asclepiodotus had second thoughts and turned informant. When the time of the planned murder arrived, Mithridates hid under a couch to eavesdrop on the plot against him. The other three conspirators were tortured and executed. But Mithridates had not finished: he also killed all of the plotters' families and friends.

The Second Mithridatic War (83–81 BC) was largely between Mithridates and the Roman general Lucius Licinius Murena. As part of the settlement of the First Mithridatic War, Sulla was anxious to return to Rome to conduct his political business and agreed to allow Mithridates to retain control of Pontus, but to stay clear of Asia Minor. Independently, Murena invaded Pontus on the pretext that Mithridates was re-arming and posed a direct threat to Roman Asia Minor. Mithridates defeated Murena and expelled him from Pontus, after which Sulla ensured that peace was restored.

The Third Mithridatic War (73–63 BC) saw victory for the Romans, the demise of Pontus as a power, the death of Mithridates and Armenia absorbed as a client state into the Roman Empire. But not before the disaster at Zela, in which Mithridates defeated C. Valerius Triarius in 67 BC. The war was triggered when King Nicomedes IV of Bithynia bequeathed his kingdom to Rome on his death in 74 BC.

The Romans enjoyed victories at Cydonia in 69 BC over the Cretans and, more decisively, at Tigranocerta, where Tigranes raised an army of biblical proportions, numbering up to 250,000 infantry and 50,000 horse. Lucius Licinius Lucullus defeated Mithrobarnazes' small cavalry force at Tigranocerta, despite the fact that intelligence was in tatters because Tigranes executed anyone who brought him bad news about Lucullus' advance. Lucullus' army hurtled down from higher ground, sending Tigranes' baggage train into the ranks of his soldiers, causing utter mayhem. Lucullus' cavalry was able to massacre 100,000 enemy in the confusion, to the loss, incredibly, of five Romans, with 100 more wounded. Tigranocerta was taken by the Romans.[54]

When Lucullus heard of the success of his provision train and observed the enemy's flight, he sent out a large force of cavalry in pursuit of the fugitives. Those who were still collecting baggage in the camp he surrounded with his infantry, whom he ordered for the time to abstain from plunder, but to kill indiscriminately. But the soldiers, seeing vessels of gold and silver in abundance and much costly clothing, disregarded the order. Those who overtook Mithridates himself cut open the pack saddle of a mule that was loaded with gold, which fell out, and while they were busy with it they allowed him to escape to Comona.

From there, he fled to Tigranes with 2,000 horsemen. Tigranes did not admit him to his presence, but ordered that royal entertainment be provided for him on his estates. Mithridates, in utter despair of his kingdom, sent the eunuch Bacchus to his palace to put his sisters, wives, and concubines to death. These, with wonderful devotion, destroyed themselves with daggers, poison and ropes. When the garrison commanders of Mithridates saw these things, all but a few went over to Lucullus.

At Comana in 68 BC, the bridge there collapsed under the weight of Mithridates' army, thus robbing him of a fight with Valerius Triarius.[55]

By 67 BC, the Roman army had more or less pulled out of Pontus, leaving two Fimbrian legions amounting to 12,000 men. These were reinforced by Roman slaves, but to no avail. Mithridates attacked, slew 500 men and retreated. Mithridates took an arrow wound to the face but soon recovered.

The Romans tried to reassert their dominance at the Battle of Zela in 67 BC, which was characterised by meteorological and mystical intervention: it was preceded by a tornado which both sides interpreted as a definite call to battle, which the Romans initiated by a night attack on the camp of Mithridates. This was repulsed, the Romans being driven back into their trenches, which were soon 'clogged up with dead Romans.'[56] Mithridates was badly wounded again, but quickly restored to action by a shaman called Agari who applied snake venom to the wound. The Romans were forced to flee, leaving 7,000 dead, including twenty-four tribunes and 150 centurions. In 66 BC, after his successful campaign against the pirates, Cn. Pompeius Magnus – Pompey – was appointed sole commander to deal once and for all with Mithridates.

Defeats at Nicopolis, Cyris River and Abas River in 66 and 65 BC spelled the end for Mithridates. He was deserted and betrayed by his two sons. Machares, king of Cimmerian Bosporus, refused to help his father; Mithridates had him killed and took his land. Pharnaces II, under pressure from a war-weary population, rebelled against his father. Mithridates was wounded by all of this and attempted suicide by poison in Panticapaeum. However, his prudence earlier in life got the better of him. Mithridates was in the habit of taking sub-lethal doses of all known poisons to build up immunity against assassination. The poison he took now was ineffective.

Appian describes the scene:

Mithridates then took out some poison that he always carried next to his sword, and mixed it. There two of his daughters, who were still girls growing up together, named Roxana and Statira, who had been betrothed to the kings of Egypt and of Cyprus, asked him to let them have some of the poison first, and insisted strenuously and prevented him from drinking it until they had taken some and swallowed it. The drug took effect on them at once; but upon Mithridates, although he walked around rapidly to hasten its action, it had no effect, because he had accustomed himself to other drugs by continually trying them as a means of protection against poisoners. These are still called the Mithridatic drugs.[57]

Dio has a different version:

> Mithridates had tried to make away with himself, and after first removing
> his wives and remaining children by poison, he had swallowed all that was
> left; yet neither by that means nor by the sword was he able to perish by his
> own hands. For the poison, although deadly, did not prevail over him, since
> he had inured his constitution to it, taking precautionary antidotes in large
> doses every day; and the force of the sword blow was lessened on account of
> the weakness of his hand, caused by his age and present misfortunes, and as
> a result of taking the poison, whatever it was. When, therefore, he failed to
> take his life through his own efforts and seemed to linger beyond the proper
> time, those whom he had sent against his son fell upon him and hastened his
> end with their swords and spears. Thus Mithridates, who had experienced
> the most varied and remarkable fortune, had not even an ordinary end to
> his life. For he desired to die, albeit unwillingly, and though eager to kill
> himself was unable to do so; but partly by poison and partly by the sword
> he was at once self-slain and murdered by his foes.[58]

Mithridates concocted a complex 'universal antidote' against poisoning. Celsus
describes a version of it in his *De Medicina*, the *Antidotum Mithridaticum*.[59]
Our word 'mithridate' is derived from it.[60] Pliny the Elder's version described
fifty-four ingredients to be matured for at least two months. Mithridates' anti-
poison regimes were overseen by the *Agari*, the Scythian shamans who never
left his side. A horse, a bull and a stag, which would neigh and bellow whenever
anyone approached the royal bed, stood sentinel at his bedside when he was
asleep. Apparently, the recipe for the antidote was found written in his own
hand, and was taken to Rome by Pompey, who had it translated into Latin by
Pompey's freedman Lenaeus. Later, attempts to make it yet more efficacious
were made by Nero's physician Andromachus, and by Galen, physican to
Marcus Aurelius.

A.E. Housman describes Mithridates' antidote in the final stanza of his
poem 'Terence, This Is Stupid Stuff' in *A Shropshire Lad*:

> There was a king reigned in the East:
> There, when kings will sit to feast,
> They get their fill before they think
> With poisoned meat and poisoned drink.
> He gathered all that springs to birth
> From the many-venomed earth;
> First a little, thence to more,

He sampled all her killing store;
And easy, smiling, seasoned sound,
Sate the king when healths went round.
They put arsenic in his meat
And stared aghast to watch him eat;
They poured strychnine in his cup
And shook to see him drink it up:
They shook, they stared as white's their shirt:
Them it was their poison hurt.
– I tell the tale that I heard told.
Mithridates, he died old.[61]

Poison having failed, Appian tells us that Mithridates then ordered his Gallic bodyguard and friend, Bituitus, to stab him with his sword. Mithridates' body was buried in Sinope, his capital city, on the orders of Pompey. Pompey admired the king's achievements and paid for a royal funeral in the cave tombs of his ancestors in Amasya, the old capital of Pontus. Appian's epitaph, however, is uncompromising:

He was bloodthirsty and cruel to all – the slayer of his mother, his brother, three sons, and three daughters … When the Romans heard of his death they held a festival because they were delivered from a troublesome enemy.[62]

Carrhae 53 BC

Carrhae was the worst Roman disaster, and Rome's darkest day, since the catastrophic Battle of Cannae in 216 BC some 163 years earlier. The battle was fought against the Parthians, a monarchy founded about 250 BC when a band of migrants settled on the northern extremity of the Persian plateau. After the Battle of Magnesia in 190 BC, the Parthians took the whole of Persia from the dying Seleucid monarchy and extended their western border to the banks of the Euphrates. Negotiations with the expansive Chinese empire took place around 100 BC and a few years later Tigranes of Armenia took western Mesopotamia from them; thirty years after this, King Phraates III won the lost provinces back. Distrust of Mithridates and Tigranes united Rome and the Parthians to such an extent that an alliance was made with Sulla, then governor of Cilicia. An agreement with Pompey would have led to the recovery of all the lost territory in Mesopotamia, but the Roman reneged and partitioned the territory between Armenia and Parthia. This soured the relationship and marked the start of years of animosity and conflict between the two powers.

Pompey's second in command, Gabiius, made the situation worse when he, unsuccessfully, supported a usurper for the Parthian crown against King Orodes II in 56 BC.

The arrogance of Marcus Licinius Crassus was largely to blame for the calamity in which the precious standards were lost. Crassus had no mandate from the Roman senate for his invasion of Mesopotamia; moreover, he epitomized obscene wealth and ruthless materialism, the worst of all Roman vices at the time. Crassus started to amass his considerable fortune when he greedily bought up the houses of Sulla's proscription victims: these had been confiscated with their contents and sold at knock-down prices to Crassus who sold them on at eye-watering profits. He used his money to raise and keep a troop of 500 slaves, all skilled builders and other tradesmen, whom he would put to work rebuilding houses (and the damaged buildings next door) that had burnt down in Rome's frequent fires. Some believe that Crassus was also a serial arsonist. Again, these rebuilt houses would be sold at high profit or rented at extortionate rates. Add to this the lucrative silver mines in Spain, the cash cows that were the *latifundia* and the luxury, prestigious property in the city of Rome and we have a very rich man. He kept his own private army and used his money to magnetize political allies amongst obsequious senators and powerful men such as Julius Caesar and Pompey, his co-triumvirs. In the war against Spartacus, he had revived the much-feared punishment of decimation and made crucifixion popular again when he lined the road to Rome with 150 miles of prisoners rotting on their crosses.

But Crassus was not just an inordinately wealthy, odious monster of a man who bungled his way around Parthia, as often portrayed. Over the years, before Carrhae, which he fought when he was about 60 years old, he showed considerable political and military skill. He supported Sulla with a private army in the First Civil War, winning the decisive Battle of Colline Gate in 82 BC, and was ruthlessly effective in his terrible programme of proscriptions; he defeated Spartacus and brought an end to the slave rebellion, even though Pompey stole the glory and took the credit; he helped overthrow Sulla and was censor and consul twice. He was, of course, one third of the First Triumvirate.

Cicero was mistaken when he said there was 'no justification for the war' with the Parthians because the two nations were bound by treaty. Cicero's was not the only voice of discontent: the tribune Gaius Ateius Capito was so violently opposed that he conducted a public ritual of execration in November 55 BC as Crassus prepared to leave Rome. Crassus was on the Capitoline performing the required ritual vows before his army's departure; Capito claimed to have seen *dirae* – the most calamitous of portents. Crassus ignored him, so Capito tried to arrest him before he could set sail:

Ateius then ran on ahead to the city gate, where he set up a brazier with lighted fuel in it. When Crassus came to the gate, [Ateius] threw incense and libations on the brazier and called down on [Crassus] curses which were dreadful and frightening enough in themselves and made still more dreadful by the names of certain strange and terrible deities. ... The Romans believe that these mysterious and ancient curses are so powerful that no one who has had them laid upon him can escape from their effect. ... So on this occasion people blamed Ateius for what he had done; he had been angry with Crassus for the sake of Rome, yet he had involved Rome in these curses and in the terror which must be felt of supernatural intervention.[63]

Ateius Capito's execration became notorious as an instance of a successful curse with unintended consequences.

Actually, the prospect of confrontation between Rome and Parthia had been simmering away in the background for decades. Parthia had moved to restore the Persian Empire in a cavalier fashion, ignoring the interests of neighbouring nations as it annexed at will. Rome, on the other hand, was moving inexorably eastwards, absorbing Parthian lands through force and deception. Mithridates and Pontus, for example, saw Lucullus marching on the Armenian capital Tigranocerta (near Mardin); when he reached Parthia, he encouraged the Parthian king, whom Mithridates and Tigranes had asked for help, to stay neutral. The king suggested to Lucullus that the Euphrates should be recognized as the frontier between Parthia and Rome. Lucullus dissimulated and pretended to be taking note but instead planned an attack on Parthia which was only thwarted by the rebellion of his troops.[64] Pompey showed an interest in subjugating the East when he enquired about the distance to India, which was later invaded by the Parthian general Gorduene.[65] Gabinius, who commanded Syria, Arabia, Persia and Babylonia, aided Mithridates of Parthia in his rebellion against his newly-crowned brother, Orodes.[66] This interference led to clashes between the Romans and Parthians, who had hitherto remained their allies.

To the Romans, Parthia was nothing more than just another Asiatic state: this dismissive, arrogant judgement betrayed a serious lack of understanding or appreciation of Parthia's strong national identity, its prodigious natural resources and the determination of the Parthians to defend their independence. Indeed, Parthia and the Parthians were more like Rome and the Romans than the Romans could ever believe. The Romans assumed that the successful subjugation of the East was an inevitablility. This is the mindset that Crassus inherited. The Parthians, on the other hand, were militarily shrewd and had good intelligence of Roman expansionist strategies; they planned their defensive strategy accordingly.

Crucially, Crassus was desperate to match the military prowess of his co-triumvirs, Julius Caesar and Pompey. He insulted their military achievements when he pompously wrote them off as 'kid's stuff', declaring his ambition to conquer the East as far as Bactria and India.[67] Despite defeating Spartacus and a creditable victory at the Battle of the Colline Gate in 82 BC, Crassus had precious little to show on his military *curriculum vitae*.

The Battle of Carrhae was fought on an open, hot and dusty plain east of Harran in northern Mesopotamia. Here the Roman army was exposed and vulnerable – the last in a series of blunders which began when Crassus invaded and garrisoned the towns of western Mesopotamia with one-fifth of his army: all surrendered to the Romans, except for Zenodotia. Crassus reached Syria in late 55 BC, using his prodigious wealth to raise an army. He passed his first year fortifying towns and, no doubt, training his troops; he also cultivated local opposition and enmity when he rashly looted native sanctuaries. Crassus then returned to winter quarters in Syria instead of advancing on Seleucia or booty-rich Ctesiphon. He was joined in Syria by his son, Publius, a promising soldier who had served with distinction under Caesar in Gaul. He brought with him 1,000 Gallic cavalry. During the winter of 54–53 Crassus was rapacious in the extreme, weighing out the treasures from the local temples he had captured, accepting cash from the citizens, in lieu of military service in the forthcoming campaign. The temple at Jerusalem was just one of the sanctuaries remorselessly looted. Plutarch takes up the developments:

When he drew his army out of winter quarters, ambassadors came to him from Arsaces, with this short speech: If the army was sent by the people of Rome, he denounced mortal war, but if, as he understood was the case, against the consent of his country, Crassus for his own private profit had invaded his territory, then their king would be more merciful, and taking pity upon Crassus's dotage, would send those soldiers back who had been left not so truly to keep guard on him as to be his prisoners. Crassus boastfully told them he would return his answer at Seleucia, upon which Vagises, the eldest of them, laughed and showed the palm of his hand, saying, 'Hair will grow here before you will see Seleucia'; so they returned to their king, Hyrodes, telling him it was war [68].

Crassus was up against the Parthian general Surena, fighting for his king, Orodes II. Crassus knew that Surena was in the desert east of the Euphrates. He unwisely left the cover of the river, ignoring the advice of his Armenian allies under Artavasdes, king of Armenia. Artavasdes had the benefit of indisputable local knowledge; he recommended Crassus invade from the mountains to the north and so maximize the cover they would give against the Parthian cavalry. Instead, bull-headed Crassus, crossed the Euphrates at Zeugma to link up with his new garrisons. The objective was Seleucia, the commercial capital of Babylonia. His large force comprised 34,000 men in seven legions of heavy-armed infantry, 4,000 cavalry and some 4,000 lightly-armed foot soldiers. His quaestor Gaius Cassius Longinus saw the folly in this and warned that Crassus should advance along the river to Seleucia, where his flank would be protected and his water supply guaranteed by the river. The omens could not have been worse, according to Plutarch in Dryden's translation:

> He encountered preternaturally violent thunder, and the lightning flashed in the faces of the troops, and during the storm a hurricane broke upon the bridge, and carried part of it away; two thunderbolts fell upon the very place where the army was going to encamp; and one of the general's horses, magnificently caparisoned, dragged away the groom into the river and was drowned. It is said, too, that when they went to take up the first standard, the eagle of itself turned its head backward ... And when at the last general sacrifice the priest gave him the entrails, they slipped out of his hand.'[69]

Crassus blundered on and ingratiated himself with a local Arab chieftain named Ariamnes (or Abgar of Osrhoene), 'a cunning and wily fellow' who promised to escort the Romans across the Balicha (*Balīk*) river and Ḵabūr toward Ctesiphon and to provide him with cavalry.[70] Ariamnes duped Crassus into believing that he faced only a token force of Parthians, led not by King Orodes but by Surena. Crassus seriously underestimated the military skill of the precocious Surena. In fact, Surena was an adept cavalryman and cavalry was Parthia's strong suite; he clearly saw the advantages of deploying cavalry in the open plain. 'A brilliant idea,' according to Mommsen.[71] The Parthian nobility sponsored heavily armoured cuirassiers with horses specially bred to support their riders in terms of weight and strength. These were the forerunners of the heavily mailed mediaeval cavalries. Unfortunately, Crassus' army consisted mainly of infantry; apart from the cavalry brought from Gaul by Publius, Crassus was dependent on the horse promised by Artavasdes.

Futhermore, according to Tarn, Surena saw that 'archers were useless without arrows; this does not seem to have occurred to anyone before ... For the first time in history, so far as is known, there had appeared a trained professional force dependent solely on long-range weapons and with enough ammunition for a protracted fight.'[72]

Plutarch had the measure of Gaius Cassius Longinus: he has Caesar say of him, 'I am not much in fear of these fat, long-haired fellows, but rather of those pale, thin ones,' a statement famously paraphrased by Shakespeare in *Julius Caesar*, just before the assassination.[73]

Crassus blindly pursued the Parthian army into the desert under the dubious guidance of Ariamnes, who turned out to be a double agent, leading the Romans into the deep sand before he promptly melted away into the hot desert air. The promised Armenian support failed to materialize, as Artavasdes was himself under attack by Orodes and needed help himself from the Romans. Artavasdes advised a withdrawal into Armenia, from where the Romans could launch a new attack. Crassus was furious and threatened revenge on what he considered to be the perfidious Armenians. Crassus refused to allow his tired, hungry and increasingly nervous army to rest, opting instead to continue his pursuit of what he thought was the retreating Parthian army but was, in fact, just a squadron of scouts. Abgar and Alchaudonius deserted the Roman cause. Crassus' army, inexperienced in desert warfare and nothing like acclimatized to the searing heat, was routed at Carrhae. The standards were lost. Cassius, together with 500 cavalry, escaped that night and reached Syria. A destroyed and distraught Crassus ceded command to his legates, Vargunteius, Octavius and Cassius.

It took until 20 BC before Augustus negotiated the return of the precious and prestigious standards from the Parthians, a feat of diplomacy and a national triumph which was celebrated in 19 BC by the dedication of the Arch of Augustus.

Plutarch and Cassius Dio are our sources for the Battle of Carrhae, although there are snippets of information from Cicero, Caesar, Velleius Paterculus, Josephus and Appian. Tarn adds that the battle was witnessed at first hand by an unknown historian whose account is now lost but who provided the material for Plutarch's *Life of Crassus*.[74] According to Tarn, it 'gives us a better account of the battle of Carrhae and its preliminaries than we possess of most battles of antiquity; also we know what both sides were doing.'[75]

Plutarch tell us that Crassus marched into Parthia with seven legions, almost 4,000 cavalry and 4,000 light-armed troops; in total about 44,000 troops. He came out with 30,000 fewer men, 10,000 of whom were taken prisoner. The Romans had been confronted by the much smaller force of 10,000 Parthian cavalry – heavily armed and armoured cataphracts, and mounted archers, who were skilled in shooting even in retreat, hence the expression, 'Parthian shot'. Camels were crucial to the Parthian victory: Surenas had shrewdly brought along 1,000 Arabian camels, one for every ten men, laden with arrows, enabling the Parthians to replenish their quivers in a kind of relay. Crassus saw this, and, lacking provisions, tied to negotiate, but in vain. Dust too was important – raised in clouds by the Parthians to blind the Romans and exacerbate the intense June heat. Meanwhile, psychologically disturbing, relentless, rhythmic beating of drums was used to drive the Romans out of their minds. Here is Plutarch's terrifying account:

> all the field rung with a hideous noise and terrible clamour. For the Parthians do not encourage themselves to war with cornets and trumpets, but with a kind of kettle-drum, which they strike all at once in various quarters. With these they make a dead, hollow noise, like the bellowing of beasts, mixed with sounds resembling thunder, having, it would seem, very correctly observed that of all our senses hearing most confounds and disorders us, and that the feelings excited through it most quickly disturb and most entirely overpower the understanding. When they had sufficiently terrified the Romans with their noise, they threw off the covering of their armour, and shone like lightning in their breastplates and helmets of polished Margianian steel, and with their horses covered with brass and steel trappings ... Now as long as they had hopes that the enemy would exhaust their missiles and desist from battle or fight at close quarters, the Romans held out; but when they perceived that many camels laden with arrows were at hand, from which the Parthians who first encircled them took a fresh supply, then Crassus, seeing no end to this, began to lose heart. ... Then the Romans halted, supposing that the enemy would come to close quarters with them, since they were so few in number. But the Parthians stationed their mail-clad horsemen in front of the Romans, and then with the rest of their cavalry in loose array rode round them, tearing up the surface of the ground, and raising from the depths great heaps of sand which fell in limitless showers of dust, so that the Romans could neither see clearly nor speak plainly, but, being crowded into a narrow compass and feeling upon one another, were shot, and died no easy nor even speedy death. For, writhing in agonies of convulsive pain from the arrows, they would break them off in their wounds, and then in trying to pull out by force the barbed heads which had pierced their veins and sinews, they tore and disfigured themselves the more. Thus many died, and the survivors also were incapacitated for fighting. And when Publius urged them to charge the enemy's mail-clad horsemen, they showed him that their hands were riveted to their shields and their feet nailed through and through to the ground, so that they were helpless either for flight or for self-defence.[76]

Dio's account is no less horrific:

For if they decided to lock shields for the purpose of avoiding the arrows by the closeness of their array, the pikemen were upon them with a rush, striking down some, and at least scattering the others; and if they extended their ranks to avoid this, they would be struck with the arrows. Hereupon many died from fright at the very charge of the pikemen, and many perished hemmed in by the horsemen. Others were knocked over by the pikes or were carried off transfixed. The missiles falling thick upon them from all sides at once struck down many by a mortal blow, rendered many useless for battle, and caused distress to all. They flew into their eyes and pierced their hands and all the other parts of their body and, penetrating their armour, deprived them of their protection and compelled them to expose themselves to each new missile. Thus, while a man was guarding against arrows or pulling out one that had stuck fast he received more wounds, one after another. Consequently it was impracticable for them to move, and impracticable to remain at rest. Neither course afforded them safety but each was fraught with destruction, the one because it was out of their power, and the other because they were then more easily wounded. ... Finally, as the enemy continually assaulted them from all sides at once, and they were compelled to protect their exposed parts by the shields of those who stood beside them, they were shut up in so narrow a place that they could no longer move. Indeed, they could not even get a sure footing by reason of the number of corpses, but kept falling over them. The heat and thirst (it was midsummer and this action took place at noon) and the dust, of which the barbarians raised as much as possible by all riding around them, told fearfully up the survivors, and many succumbed from these causes, even though unwounded.[77]

Eran Spahbodh Rustaham Suren-Pahlav – Surena – was no ordinary general, or *spahbed*. His name means 'heroic one' and is still popular in Armenia and Iran today. Plutarch again:

Surena was an extremely distinguished man. In wealth, birth, and in the honour paid to him, he ranked next after the king; in courage and ability, he was the foremost Parthian of his time; and in stature and personal beauty, he had no equal. When he travelled about the country on his own affairs, he was always accompanied by a baggage train of 1,000 dromedaries; 200 wagons carried his harem; 1,000 armoured cavalry and still more light armed cavalry acted as his escort. The total number of his cavalry, his vassals, and his slaves came to at least 100,000 men. He had, as an ancient privilege of his family, the right to be the first to set the crown on the head of the king of Parthia at

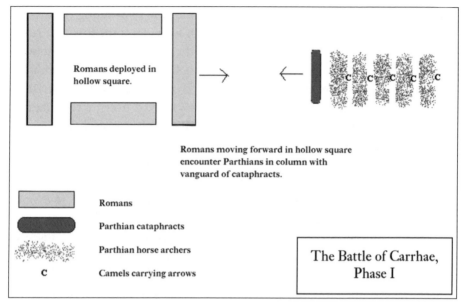

Diagram 2: The Battle of Carrhae, Phase I. (Courtesy of Pen & Sword; originally published in Gareth C. Sampson, *The Defeat of Rome*, 2008.)

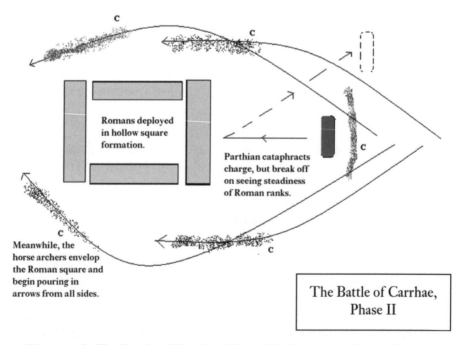

Diagram 3: The Battle of Carrhae, Phase II. (Courtesy of Pen & Sword; originally published in Gareth C. Sampson, *The Defeat of Rome*, 2008.)

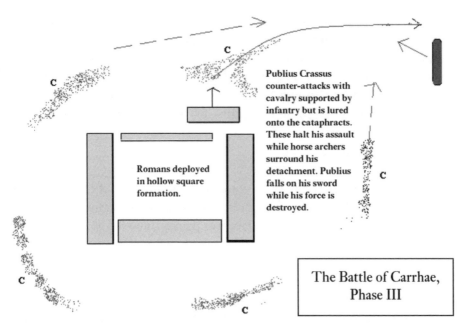

The horse archers once more encircle Crassus' main force and resume the barrage of arrows from all sides. Repeated charges by the cataphracts thwart any attempts to counterattack and force the Romans to remain huddled in close order, making an unmissable target for the Parthian arrows.

Publius Crassus counter-attacks with cavalry supported by infantry but is lured onto the cataphracts. These halt his assault while horse archers surround his detachment. Publius falls on his sword while his force is destroyed.

Romans deployed in hollow square formation.

The Battle of Carrhae, Phase III

Diagram 4: The Battle of Carrhae, Phase III. (Courtesy of Pen & Sword; originally published in Gareth C. Sampson, *The Defeat of Rome*, 2008.)

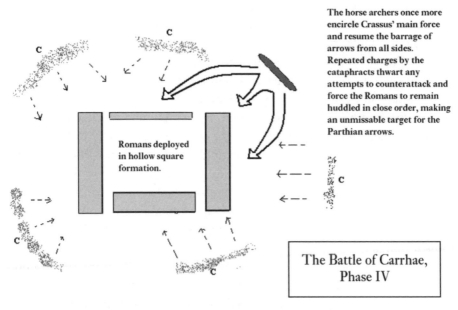

Romans deployed in hollow square formation.

The Battle of Carrhae, Phase IV

Diagram 5: The Battle of Carrhae, Phase IV. (Courtesy of Pen & Sword; originally published in Gareth C. Sampson, *The Defeat of Rome*, 2008.)

the coronation ... he, also, that took the great city of Seleucia, was the first man that scaled the walls, and with his own hand beat off the defenders. And though at this time he was not above thirty years old, he had a great name for wisdom and sagacity, and, indeed, by these qualities chiefly, he overthrew Crassus, who first through his overweening confidence, and afterwards because he was cowed by his calamities, fell a ready victim to his subtlety.[78]

Looks can be deceiving:

Surena was the tallest and finest looking man himself, but the delicacy of his looks and effeminacy of his dress did not promise so much manhood as he really was master of; or his face was painted, and his hair parted after the fashion of the Medes.

Publius Crassus fought valiantly on behalf of his father. He managed to rally his Gauls: some seized the Parthian cataphracts' lances and dragged them to the ground, where their heavy armour immobilized them. Some dismounted and crawled under the Parthian horses, which they promptly disembowelled. Publius, inevitably, was badly wounded and dragged off the field for a last stand. Two local Greeks, Hieronymus and Nicomachus urged him to flee to nearby Ichnae, a town friendly to the Romans but he refused, preferring to stay and die with his troops. Publius ordered his armour-bearer to run him through with his sword, his promising career tragically cut short.

The entrancing, persistent drum beating resumed as the Parthians rode towards Crassus with Publius' head on the end of a spear, asking where on earth could his parents be, as so brave and courageous a soldier could not possibly be the son of so wretched a coward as Crassus.

Octavius and his 5,000 men escaped, but sly Cassius and his 500 cavalry deserted, managing to escape that night and make their way to Syria. The Parthians let them go, but next morning they butchered 4,000 surviving wounded and stragglers lost on the night march to Carrhae. Refusing to negotiate with Surena while bound by the shackles that the Parthian demanded as a prerequisite, Crassus enlisted the help of another guide, Andromachus (who was later rewarded with the governorship of Carrhae for his duplicity), to help him and his 1,500 survivors through the tricky terrain complicating their escape. Andromachus too was a spy and misled the Romans straight into marshes. The Parthians attacked, but Crassus was saved when Octavius' unit, also lost, joined up with him and saved the day. Surena then offered Crassus a truce: peace and safe conduct and the restoration of relations with Rome. Urged on by his troops, Crassus accepted. He parleyed with Surena, who gave him a horse, as he could not negotiate with the enemy leader on foot, and asked for the treaty to be signed on the banks of the Euphrates, now the boundary between Rome and Parthia. Octavius, however, totally misread the situation, drew his sword, and killed the groom who was helping with Crassus' horse. The Romans died in the ensuing skirmish.

Crassus suffered the fate of all treaty breakers: his head and his hands were cut off by a Parthian, Pomaxathres, and sent to Orodes. According to Dio, the Parthians poured molten gold down his throat as a symbol of his avarice. Legend has it that his head arrived at an opportune moment, during the wedding of Artavasdes' sister to Orodes II's son and heir Pacorus, while they were enjoying a performance of Euripides' *The Bacchae*. A quick-witted actor, Jason of Tralles, took the head and quoted these appropriate lines from the play, bringing the performance to a happy conclusion:

> We bring from the mountain,
> A tendril fresh-cut to the palace,
> A wonderful prey.

Of the 42,000 Romans who entered the war with Crassus, 10,000 eventually reached Syria and were reorganized into a fighting force by Cassius, 10,000 were taken prisoners of war and held at Marv, and the rest died. So ended one of the worst disasters the Roman army ever suffered. Some others escaped with Cassius, who lived to conspire against Caesar and assassinate him in 44 BC.[79]

Crassus' death is described by Livy:

> [Crassus] was defeated in a battle in which his son also fell. With the remains of his army, he occupied a hill, and was summoned to a conference by the enemy leader, Surena, as if to speak about a truce. However, he was captured and killed to avoid suffering the indignity of remaining alive.[80]

Surena enjoyed his victory to the full and revelled in his success. He led his army back to Seleucia to celebrate a mock Roman triumph in which a Roman prisoner of war, Gaius Paccianus, bore a passing resemblance to Crassus and was placed at the head of the army, forced to wear women's clothes and to answer to the name of Crassus. Surena's soldiers marched behind, each carrying a decapitated Roman head, followed by Parthian women, singing abusive songs about the cowardice and effeminacy of Crassus. Surena got no thanks for this spectacle and was later executed by an increasingly jealous Orodes. Orodes suffered the same fate in 38 BC, literally, at the hands of his own son, Phraactes, who strangled him when the poison he administered failed.

The disaster of Carrhae has been called 'without doubt the most celebrated episode of Parthian history'.[81] On the other hand, it brought far-reaching and long-lasting humiliation and disgrace for Rome, and another serious loss of prestige. The only consolation for the Romans, who greeted the news with 'unwonted apathy', was that the disgrace was mitigated somewhat because Crassus' action was independent and unofficial. Nevertheless, the allies in the region and the tricky client kingdoms cannot have been impressed by Rome's performance. The evidence of Roman ignominy must have been there for all to see for a long time: visiting traders, officials and diplomats were probably only too aware of the bodies littering the battlefield and on the route of the disorderly retreat; the temples would have been filled with Roman booty and the captured standards would have taken pride of place in Parthia. The war between Parthia and Rome then slowly 'died of inanition'.[82] The campaign left the province of Syria undefended and leaderless: Crassus had deployed its legions in Parthia; all that remained now was 10,000 stunned survivors from Carrhae. In 52 BC, Orodes attacked Syria.

Most crucially, Carrhae was also responsible for destabilizing the delicate balance of power held by the First Triumvirate. Pompey had married Caesar's daughter, Julia, and when she died in childbirth in 54 BC, Caesar married the widow of Publius Crassus; a strong bond between the surviving triumvirs (now the duumvirs) had been irreparably broken. Where there were three, there were now two. A stand-off was inevitable.

Surena had put a decisive stop to Roman expansion in the east, restored Mesopotamia to the Parthians and established the Euphrates as the boundary between the two empires. Carrhae put Persia on an equal footing with Rome, making them political and military rivals for the next 700 years. The Romans did not go away completely empty-handed: they learnt the benefits and value of the fleet, mobile Parthian cavalry and adapted it to their own needs.

Whatever was thought of Crassus at the time, his reputation seems to have been restored quite soon after the disaster. Some Roman poets of the early Empire were unanimous in their praise. Ovid says, 'the pride of the nation had been fostered by the deaths of Crassus and his son,'[83] and, 'Parthia, thou shalt pay the penalty; rejoice you buried Crassi, and your standards that shamefully endured barbarian violence.'[84] Propertius chimes in with a reference to the cavalry skills of the Parthians: 'No longer does the Euphrates allow Parthian horsemen to glance behind their backs, and regrets keeping possession of the Crassi' and 'Rejoice Crassus, if any consciousness be yours amid the grave's black sands: now we may cross the Euphrates to your tomb.'[85]

Gergovia 52 BC

The following year, Julius Caesar was still immersed in his wars in Gaul (58–52 BC) and had concluded two speculative, propagandist invasions of Britannia in 55 and 54 BC. His co-triumvir, Pompey, was left to deal with a Rome that was engulfed in bribery scandals, gang warfare, cancelled elections and street fighting. As one of the two surviving members of the First Triumvirate, Caesar held the proconsulship of Cisalpine Gaul and Illyricum. Transalpine Gaul was added when the governor there, Metellus Celer, died suddenly. Caesar's governorships were, unusually, for five years.

Caesar, our source for the Gallic campaign, would have us believe that it was a pre-emptive, defensive war. In reality, it was used by Caesar as another stage on his *cursus honorum* and a means of paying off his substantial debts through booty. However, Gaul was of strategic importance to Rome, and Caesar was doing the state a favour if he quelled the troublesome natives and secured the Rhine as a natural frontier of the 'empire'.

Discontent had been brewing amongst the Gallic tribes for all the usual reasons: heavy-handed rule and depradation, oppressive taxation and unrealistic quotas for auxiliaries. In 53 BC, Ambiorix, leader of the Eburones in the Ardennes, ambushed and slew a legion and a half after he had enticed them out from their winter quarters in Liege. This had the effect of exciting other tribes to revolt. Another legion led by Quintus Tullius Cicero, the orator's brother, was holed up by the Nervii and only saved by a forced march by Caesar. Eventually, all the rebellious tribes were subdued, but not for long. The savagery with which Caesar conducted these reprisals served only to inflame the Gauls yet further.

Caesar's forces had won victories at Solonium at the start of the Gallic uprising in 61 BC, followed by success at Admagetobriga, the Arar River, Bibracte, Plain of Alsace in 58 BC, the Rivers Axona and Sabis and Octodurus in 57 BC, Morbihan Gulf and Sotium in 56 BC and at Noviodunum Biturigum in 52 BC, where Caesar encountered Vercingetorix for the first time.

Caesar describes his charismatic new opponent and his ruthless rise to the peak of Gallic military power:

Vercingetorix, son of Celtillus, an Arvernian youth of supreme influence ... summoned his own dependents and easily fired their spirit. Directly his design was known there was a general rush to arms. Gobannitio, his uncle, and the rest of the chiefs, who did not think this adventure should be hazarded, sought to prevent him. He was cast out of the town of Gergovia, but he did not give up for all that, and in the fields he held a levy of beggars and outcasts. Then, having got together a body of this sort, he brought over to his own way of thinking all the members of his state whom he approached, urging them to take up arms for the sake of general liberty ... by consent of all, the command was bestowed upon him ... he determined what amount of arms, and by what date, each state should manufacture at home, and he paid especial attention to the cavalry. To the utmost care he added the utmost strictness of command, compelling waverers by severity of punishment. Indeed, for the commission of a greater offence he put to death with fire and all manner of tortures; for a lesser case he sent a man home with his ears cut off or one eye gouged out, to point the moral to the rest and terrify others by the severity of the penalty.[86]

Caesar was to meet him again later that year at Gergovia, capital of the Averni tribe. The Gaul presented Caesar with a dilemma when, having been expelled from Gergovia the previous year, he attacked the *oppidum* (town) that winter.[87] Should Caesar wait until the spring and appear indecisive to his allies, the Aedui, or should he respond but risk running out of supplies? He chose the latter. After defeating Vercingetorix at Noviodunum, Caesar then took Avericum, where he resupplied and prepared to face his quarry at Gergovia, an easily defendable plateau 400m high with one way in and one way out.[88] It was crucial to get to Gergovia first and assume the advantage of such a strong fortress position. Veringetorix shadowed Caesar, destroying the bridges over the River Allier as he went. At Varennes, Caesar split his forces and ordered one third of his army to move north under Labienus to attack the Senones and Parisii, and himself took the remaining six legions south. Vercingetorix followed, believing that he was pursuing the whole force. Caesar then rebuilt the bridge at Varennes and recalled the larger contingent: the whole army was now able to cross the river and proceed to Gergovia. Caesar then laid siege and, in a night attack, took a small hill at the foot of the mountain which provided running water and corn. He then built a double trench, 12ft wide, between the newly-captured hill and his main camp. The plan was to encircle Gergovia and starve the Gauls inside. Vercingetorix, meanwhile, through a chief called Litavicus, had persuaded the Aedui, Rome's most loyal ally in the region, to desert Caesar and join him, lying that Caesar had butchered Aedui hostages surrendered in a peace treaty. Caesar reports the treachery:

All our horsemen, all our chivalry is perished; Eporedorix and Viridomarus, chief men of our state, have been accused of treachery by the Romans, and put to death with their cause unheard. This you shall learn from men who actually escaped from that same massacre; for all my own brethren and all my kindred have been put to death, and grief prevents me from declaring what was brought to pass ... let us avenge the death of those who have perished most shamefully, and let us slay these brigands. [Litavicus] pointed to Roman citizens, who were accompanying his force in reliance on his safeguard; he plundered a large quantity of corn and supplies, and put the Romans to death with cruel tortures.[89]

Caesar soon got the Aedui back on side in a meeting some 25 miles from Gergovia. Eporedorix, a high-ranking cavalry commander was one of the men Litavicus claimed had been killed; his presence disabused Caesar of this. Caesar led four of his six legions to confront the 10,000 Aeduan infantry. He sent Eporedorix into the Aeduan camp, at which point Litavicus's plan turned to dust. He fled to Vercingetorix, while the Aedui returned to Caesar. Meanwhile, Gaius Fabius, who was left in Gergovia, got word to Caesar that he was under attack. Caesar sped back to relieve his colleague. In the ensuing battle, Caesar was successful, but at a heavy price in terms of casualties.

Using one of his legions as a decoy, Caesar moved to remove the Gauls from the plateau by feigning a retreat. Unfortunately for Caesar, most of his men failed to hear the signal and continued their attempt to dislodge the Gauls from the mountain top. The resulting frontal assault was a disaster for the Romans: forty-six centurions and 700 legionaries died in the rout that followed, and over 6,000 were wounded, compared with a few hundred Gauls killed and wounded. Caesar was furious and harangued his surviving men for (apparently) disregarding his order to retreat, ordering them back into battle the next day.

Caesar describes the mayhem as the adrenalin rushed through the Roman soldiers:

Elated, however, and by the hope of a speedy victory, by the flight of the enemy, and their successful engagements on previous occasions, they thought that nothing was so difficult as to be unattainable by their valour, and they did not make an end of pursuing until they neared the wall and the gates of the town. Then, indeed, shouting arose from all parts of the city, and those who were farther away were terror-struck at the sudden uproar, and, believing that the enemy was within the gates, flung out of the town. Matrons cast clothing and silver from the wall, and with bare breasts and outstretched hands implored the Romans to spare them, and then not to do as they had done at Avaricum, where they slaughtered even women and children. Some of the women were lowered by hand from the wall, and gave themselves up to the troops. Lucius Fabius, a centurion of the VIIIth

Legion, who was known to have said that day among his company that he was spurred on by the rewards at Avaricum, and would allow no one to mount the wall before him, got three men of his company, was lifted up by them, and mounted the wall. Then he in turn took hold of them one by one and pulled them up on to the wall.

The Romans had little chance:

> When a great host of the [Gauls] had assembled, the matrons who a moment before were stretching out their hands to the Romans from the wall began to urge on their own men and, in Gallic fashion, to show dishevelled hair and to bring their children forward into view. The Romans had no fair contest in ground or numbers; they were tired out by the speedy march and the duration of the battle, and could not easily resist men that were fresh and unhurt.[90]

Caesar had to accept that, humiliating as it was, this was his first defeat in the campaign; he built a bridge across the Allier, and then, somewhat resignedly, advanced into Aedui territory:

> [Caesar] decided that enough had been done to reduce the bravado of the Gauls and to establish the spirit of the troops, and he moved camp accordingly into the territory of the Aedui. Even then the enemy did not pursue; and on the third day he reached the river Allier, rebuilt the bridge, and brought the army across to the other side.[91]

It was, nevertheless, to be Caesar's only reverse. He won back his pride and the army's reputation at Lutetia Parisiorum, at the decisive Battle of Alesia and finally at Uxellodunum.[92] Vercingetorix opted to occupy Alesia, at which point Caesar successfully besieged him, also fending off a huge Gallic relief force. This was effectively the end of the Gallic Wars. The last year of his procosulship was spent in reconciliation, winning back the trust and loyalty of the Gallic tribes – another lesson learnt. Additionally, Caesar imposed little more than a nominal tribute, which also helped to lower the temperature and bring the province to a state of peace and calm, allowing Caesar to withdraw most of his forces by 49 BC and later to enlist Gauls in the armies he needed to fight the civil wars.[93]

To put his achievement into perspective, the Transalpine Gaul he subdued and brought into Rome's orbit was double the size of the whole Italian peninsula and more populous than the whole of Spain. Caesar got the military glory he wanted in what was a critical juncture in his career, and the booty he acquired paid off his enormous debts and allowed him to buy political favours and alliances almost on a scale that would not have disppointed Crassus. On the other hand, Rome got stability in Gaul which lasted into the next century. Caesar returned to Italy, cast his die, crossed the Rubicon and died midst a salvo of stabbing daggers in the forum on the Ides of March, 44 BC.

Chapter 8

'Doom Monster' – Cleopatra VII

B y the end of the Republic, foreign women were a common sight in Roman towns and cities; they played an increasingly important part in the economy, society and arts. Many arrived on the tide of Hellenization which accompanied Rome's conquests and colonization of the Mediterranean and further afield, either as slaves or as skilled immigrant workers: doctors, midwives, shopkeepers, dancers, singers, prostitutes and the like.

In the early Empire, Martial tells of a Claudia Rufina, a lady from Britannia who embodied Latin chartacteristics, and could easily pass for a Roman or a Greek. Classic physical beauty apart, she was a perfect *matrona*: both *fecunda* (fertile) and *univira* (a one-man woman), and looking forward to sons and daughters-in-law to extend the family line yet further. If Martial's piece is typical and representative, foreign women were, by and large, welcomed by some Romans as they integrated into their increasingly cosmopolitan society.[1]

Tacitus acknowledges certain good points in German women: they considered birth control and infanticide to be evil – all very different to prevailing Roman practice and opinion.[2] He praised German women because they breastfed their own children, another implicit criticism of Roman women who, at least amongst the better off classes, tended to use wet nurses, and an appreciation of the nutritional and psychological benefits to both mother and child. Interestingly, in the same paragraph, he deprecates the Roman practice of marrying off daughters at an early age: Roman girls were married from the age of 12, something that no German would permit.

Some years earlier, though, a woman burst onto the scene who was to be somewhat less welcome. The Egyptian queen Cleopatra was a formidable foreign woman who had massive influence on Rome, both militarily and politically, and who changed the course of Roman history. For the Romans, Cleopatra was a disaster in more ways than one.

Up until the first century BC, relations between Rome and Egypt were mainly diplomatic and dependent on the payment of tribute, although, as Rome conquered more of the Hellenistic world, so her presence loomed larger in the background. Egypt remained the last tantalizing prize within Rome's orbit. She was a crucial source of supply for Rome, not least in grain. Macedonia,

Greece, Cyrene, Asia Minor, Syria and Cyprus – all former parts of Alexander the Great's Hellenistic empire – had fallen domino-like between 146 BC and 58 BC. Plans were laid to annex Egypt, but they came to nothing, and, in the first century BC, Rome continued to provide financial support to Ptolemy XII Auletes, Cleopatra's father, to keep him on side.

Greek as it was, the Ptolemaic dynasty was much more liberal and enlightened than Greece in its attitude to women and to women's role in society and in the monarchy. In law, Egyptian women were more or less equal to men. They could buy and sell property and make wills; they could adopt children, sign marriage contracts and make pre-nuptial agreements to avoid messy divorces and guarantee themselves and their children financial independence; they could sue for divorce, draw up commercial contracts, inherit and fight their own corner in a court of law. On marriage, a woman's property remained hers. Women could, and did, go right to the top, achieving pharaonic status. According to exhaustive work by Manetho, the third-century BC historian and Egyptologist, Sobekneferu (d. 1802 BC) was the first woman pharaoh; Hatshepsut (d. 1458 BC) ruled as pharaoh for twenty-two very successful years; Nefertiti (d. 1330 BC) was chief consort to Akhenaten and now has iconic status thanks to her bust in the Neues Museum in Berlin.[3] The high-ranking priestesses of the Amun Cult also wielded significant power and influence; they were referred to as 'God's Wife of Amun', prevalent from about 1550 BC.

The status and importance of the Egyptian woman inside and outside the house was very real. All property was inherited through the maternal line, perhaps reflecting that one always knew one's mother, while paternity was sometimes less exact. Egyptians always described themselves as sons or daughters of the mother, rather than of the father as is the case in many other societies. This all led to a reasonably liberal and liberated social life. There were no veils, guardians or chaperones; women were not confined to special quarters in the house, as in the Greek *gynaikon*. Herodotus is quite incredulous; to him the Egyptians have turned the world on its head:

> women go to market and do business; the men stay at home weaving ...
> Egyptian men carry loads on their heads, women on their shoulders; women
> stand up to urinate, men sit down ... they eat outside ... in other lands
> priests grow their hair long, in Egypt they shave their heads ... Egyptian
> men circumcise themselves for hygienic reasons, preferring cleanliness to
> comeliness.[4]

Their independence may be due to the fact that women, as noted above, aspired to important, inclusive roles in Egyptian society and government, particularly under the Ptolemys. Wall paintings show middle-class women working with their husbands and assisting in their businesses.

Cleopatra VII Philopator (69–30 BC) was born into the Ptolemaic dynasty, the Macedonian family that ruled Egypt after the death of Alexander in 323 BC. Cleopatra means 'famous for her forefathers'; Philopater means father or fatherland lover. As one of at least thirty-three Cleopatras we know about, this famous name resonates in mythology and Macedonian history. The first was the daughter of Boreas, the North Wind; another was the wife of the historical King Midas, king of Phrygia; another was the daughter of Philip II and Olympias and sister of Alexander the Great. Cleopatra VII, like all of her dynasty, had no Egyptian blood whatsoever: it is thought she was part Greek, part Macedonian and part Persian. Others believe that she was black African.

The identity of Cleopatra's mother remains a mystery: almost certainly, she was one of the many wives supported by Ptolemy, her father. Some have argued that she may have been Ptolemy's sister, Cleopatra V Tryphaena, Cleopatra's aunt. The fact that none of Cleopatra's fervent detractors in later years suggest that she was illegitimate would indicate that she was born within marriage.

Ptolemy XII Auletes set about funding a temple-building programme by re-establishing trade with India, the horn of Africa and re-exports to the rest of the Mediterranean world. This new wealth attracted the attention of the triumvirate – Pompey, Caesar and Crassus – and led to Auletes assisting Pompey in his highly lucrative victory over Mithridates VI. Other aspects of Auletes' reign were somewhat disastrous: the loss of Cyrene and Cyprus to the Romans and the ill-advised acceptance of the title 'friend and ally of the Roman people', which cost Ptolemy the best part of his country's wealth and forced him to lend huge amounts of money to Gaius Rabirius Postumus in order to render unto Caesar. A coup by Cleopatra V and a daughter, Berenike IV, in 58 BC, forced him and Cleopatra into exile in Rome via Rhodes and Athens. In 55 BC, after much bribery and intrigue between Auletes and the Romans, alternately playing and paying Berenike off, Alexandria was re-captured and Ptolemy XII was restored to the throne – but only at a price: it was with the support of the Roman general Aulus Gabinius and Mark Antony, sent to Egypt by Pompey. Auletes killed Berenike and her supporters, and Cleopatra, aged 14, was made joint ruler with her father.

Gabinius left some of his troops, the Gabiniani, in Egypt as a protection force for Ptolemy. This army of occupation was very unpopular with the Alexandrians, while the restoration of Ptolemy had drained the country's reserves and finances. Ptolemy died in March 51 BC during an ominous partial solar eclipse. He was still weighed down with debt, leaving Cleopatra and her brother, now Ptolemy XIII, joint monarchs. Economic problems, famine, low

ennus et sa part de but (Brennus and His Share
the Spoils) by Paul Jamin (1873).
is was one of Rome's first military disasters.
oulon Sculpture Workshop, Musée National de
Marine, Paris: 41OA74)

Brennus, sacker of Rome in 387 BC.
This is the figurehead of the French battleship,
Brennus. The ship was ultimately removed
from the naval register in 1919 and sold for
scrap in 1922.

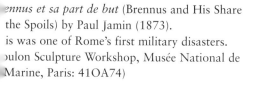

Hannibal looting slaughtered Romans after Cannae. (Time Life Pictures)

Miniature from a manuscript, *Speculum Humanae Salvationis*, depicting Eleazar killing an elephant with turret and then being crushed to death when it falls down dead on him. (Henri-Paul Motte, 1846–1922, originally published in *Das Wissen des 20. Jahrhunderts*, Bildungslexikon, Rheda, 1931)

Bronze statue of Surena, Parthian general and scourge of Crassus. (*National Museum of Iran*)

Persian scythe-wheeled chariots wreaking havoc amongst the Romans at the battle of Carrhae. (*Drawn by E. Castagne. Author's collection*)

...nus, the rebel slave who defeated the
...omans at the battle of Henna in 135 BC.
...e statue, titled *Cry for Freedom*, stands
...the town of Enna in Sicily.

Viriathus, the Lusitanian guerilla fighter
extraordinaire who defeated the Romans but was
never defeated by them, making him one of their most
successful foes. The statue is at Viseu in Portugal.

The road back to Rome with its rotting trail of crucified supporters of Spartacus after their defeat
by a vengeful Crassus. The painting, *The Crucified Slaves* (1878), is by Fyodor Andreyevich
Bronnikov (1827–1902) and hangs in the Tretyakov Gallery in Moscow.

A reconstruction of the Roman siege tower used at Masada. (Courtesy of Bibleplaces.com)

Spartacus' last stand. *The Death of Spartacus* (1882) by Hermann Vogel (1854–1921).

Tod des Spartacus. Zeichnung von Hermann Vogel.

man soldiers casting lots as to who should get
rist's robes at his crucifixion. Note the Victorian
ustaches sported by the soldiers. They are in St
phen's Chapel in York Minster. (Author's collection)

e rampart walk on the East Wall north of the Temple
unt with the Dome of the Rock in the background.
urtesy of Bibleplaces.com)

A statue of Boudica and her daughters.
She, a queen, was flogged, while the
daughters were raped by the Romans.
The statue was begun in 1910 and
created by James Havard Thomas
(1854–1921). Unusually for depictions
of Boudica, she is shown in a dignified
and maternal way. (Courtesy of Geoff
Cook at Cardiff City Hall)

Germanic Warriors Storm the Field in the Varusschlacht (or *Battle of Teutoburg Forest*) (1909) by Otto Albert Koch, now in the Lippisches Landsemuseum, Detmold, Germany.

First century AD marble frieze fragment showing Roman soldiers in their armour: tunic, armour plate, boots, shield and sword.

...ermannsdenkmal (1875), a huge copper monument to ...minius and his victory over the Romans at Teutoburger Wald. He is crowned with a winged helmet, brandishing his 203kg, 23ft sword ...nacingly in the direction of France. At 87ft high, and mounted on an 88ft stone ...se, it was the largest statue ...n the world until the *Statue of Liberty* rose up in 1886. ...Courtesy of Digital Park in Lage, Germany)

..s Siegreich Vordringende ...mann (The Victorious ...vancing Hermann) (1873) ...Peter Janssen (1844–1908). ..s now in the Kunstmuseen, ...efeld, Germany.

Alaric's river-bed burial after his reluctant sack of Rome. Drawing by H. Leutemann.

The end of the Roman Empire, as depicted in *The Course of Empire 4 – Destruction* by Thomas Cole (1836). (New York Historical Society)

Nile flood levels and political infighting continued to make life very difficult for Egypt and Cleopatra, who, despite being married to her brother, took steps to become sole ruler. Ptolemy's image was soon notably absent from Egyptian coinage.

Auletes' second term had seen something of a cultural renaissance in Alexandria. To complement the already world-famous library there, he financed the restoration of the equally renowned centre of excellence that was the Mouseion, an early university where more than 1,000 scholars lived and worked at any given time. Staff and scholars paid no taxes, received free meals and board, and free servants. All three of Auletes' surviving children – Ptolemy, Cleopatra and her half-sister Arsinoe – would have benefitted enormously from attendance at these institutions, and from their personal tutors; Cleopatra, we know, attended lectures in philosophy, delivered by Philostratus and others, eschatology, astronomy and astrology.

Perceptively, she set about winning back the support of her people. She astutely learned the local Egyptian language and spoke it, the first and only Ptolemy in 300 years to do so. She led the rites at Thebes celebrating the birth of Buchis, the earthly manifestation of the sun god as a bull, and was thereby seen to be taking an active and honest part in an important local tradition, the very foundation of Egyptian civilization. The Buchis celebration is indicative, too, of how important religion was to Cleopatra; throughout her life she associated herself very closely with Isis – she was in effect Isis on Earth – wife of Osiris. Her son, Caesarion, was, of course, their son, Horus. Coins were minted depicting her breast-feeding Caesarion-Horus; sculptures show mother and son as Isis and Horus. Later, Mark Antony was to link himself to Dionysus, the Roman equivalent of Osiris, thus forging a divine connection between himself and Aphrodite, the Roman Isis.

This, of course, was not Cleopatra being iconoclastic, arrogant, despotic or hubristic, although many Romans may have thought it so. Cleopatra was merely following in the Ptolemaic tradition whereby queens were routinely worshipped as goddesses and were honoured with temples and towns bearing their names and with coins depicting their image.

With prudent and skilful handling of the economy, combined with tax increases – tolerated by her subjects due to her growing popularity – Cleopatra began to turn around the ailing country she had inherited. Meanwhile, in Italy, Julius Caesar crossed the River Rubicon in 49 BC, while the armies of Pompey retreated south before requesting military support from Egypt. Cleopatra responded by sending a detachment of the Gabiniani and warships.

Later that year, relations between brother and sister broke down irreparably, with Ptolemy virtually ostracized and Cleopatra defying the Ptolemaic tradition that made female rulers subserviant to male. In 48 BC, Cleopatra incurred the wrath of the Gabiniani; when they killed the sons of the Roman governor of Syria, Marcus Calpurnius Bibulus, she handed the murderers over to Bibulus. This led to Cleopatra's fall from power: she fled Egypt with Arsinoe, while Ptolemy XIII assumed sole rule. Pompey ingratiated himself with Ptolemy.

The decisive Battle of Pharsalus saw Pompey defeated by Caesar in 48 BC. It was also the start of relations between Caesar and Cleopatra, who was making ready to win her country back from Ptolemy. Things started to go wrong between Pompey and Egypt when Pompey sought sanctuary in Alexandria with the remnants of his army in a bid to win support from his former ally. The 14-year-old Ptolemy XIII haughtily watched Pompey's arrival from a specially erected throne in the harbour. Pompey was stabbed in the back and beheaded in front of his wife and children; his body was burnt, his head embalmed. This half-baked attempt by Ptolemy to curry favour with Caesar backfired. Caesar sailed to Egypt to collect an outstanding debt owed to him by Auletes, only to be presented with Pompey's head. He was incensed and upset by the atrocity – Pompey, although an enemy, was still a Roman consul and the widower of Caesar's daughter, Julia, who had died in childbirth giving birth to Pompey's son, Caesar's grandson. Caesar's reaction was to take Alexandria and set himself up as mediator between Ptolemy and Cleopatra, an inevitable consequence of which was contact with Cleopatra.

Cleopatra was astute enough to interpret the animosity between Caesar and her brother as an opportunity; after her envoys had achieved little or nothing, she determined to meet Caesar face to face to plead her case. Cleopatra was only too aware of her sophistication and charm; Cassius Dio tells us that she 'reposed in her beauty all her claims to the throne.' Caesar agreed to a meeting, despite Ptolemy's attempts to thwart it.[5] Arriving regally at the palace in the royal boat (Ptolemy had blocked all the roads), Lucan says that she bribed the guards to unchain the harbour. Plutarch, improbably, insists that she, less than regally, inveigled her way in, rolled up in a carpet carried by Apollodorus the Sicilian, her faithful acolyte, to make the meeting with Caesar. According to Plutarch, it is Cleopatra's ingenuity here, her 'provocative impudence' that enthralled Caesar.[6] He cannot, though, have failed to be impressed by the appearance of Cleopatra. Lucan describes her as 'wearing the spoils of the Red Sea, treasures in her hair and around her neck, great pains taken on her refinement.'[7] Nine months later, Cleopatra gave birth to their son, Ptolemy Caesar, nicknamed Caesarion, 'little Caesar'. Caesar's paternity is doubted and was denied by him, possibly pending changes to the laws of marriage, which Caesar promised in order to have his 'marriage' to Cleopatra officially recognized. Instead, he opted to name Octavian, his grandnephew, as his heir and main beneficiary, despite Cleopatra's insistence on Caesarion.

Caesar now backed Cleopatra's claim to the throne but was besieged in Alexandria by the forces of Achillas and Pothinus, allies of Ptolemy. After Mithridates of Pergamum raised the siege, Caesar defeated Ptolemy's army at the Battle of the Nile; Ptolemy XIII drowned in the river. Caesar restored Cleopatra to her throne, with her younger brother Ptolemy XIV as co-ruler. Arsinoe, who had defected to Achillas, was taken prisoner, marched through Rome in disgrace, banished to the Temple of Artemis in Ephesus and later sacrilegiously executed by Cleopatra and Mark Antony on the temple steps. Caesar and Cleopatra married according to Egyptian rites – a polygamous union that initially went unrecognized in Rome as Caesar was still married to Calpurnia Pisonis, his third wife. Furthermore, it was illegal for a Roman citizen to marry a foreigner. When Caesar left Egypt some weeks later to prosecute the Civil War, he left behind him three legions (the XXVIIth, XXXVIIth and XXXIXth) under the command of Rufio, as much to keep Cleopatra under observation as to ensure the safety and security of Egypt, his new ally.[8]

A luxury cruise down the Nile gave Caesar an opportunity to display the naval might of Rome, and Cleopatra a chance to show Caesar the extent of her wealth and the treasures of Egypt. The queen further demonstrated her riches and her alliance with Caesar by building the monumental Caesareum in his honour, a huge, lofty building flanked by two ancient obelisks. One of these obelisks now stands on the Victoria embankment in London, while its pair is in Central Park, New York. They are popularly known as Cleopatra's Needles even though they were over 1,400 years old when Cleopatra had them re-sited at the Caesareum. The London obelisk was presented to Great Britain in 1819 by the then ruler of Egypt and Sudan, Muhammad Ali, to commemorate Nelson's victory at the Battle of the Nile and Abercromby's at the Battle of Alexandria in 1801. Their tour of Egypt ensued with an extensive building programme in the south of the country.

Already, at the age of twenty-one, Cleopatra was starting to exert influence on Rome, a world power. In 46 BC Cleopatra, Ptolemy XIV and Caesarion visited Rome, staying for two years in one of Caesar's houses on the fashionable Janiculum Hill.[9] It was an ill-judged move on Caesar's part, as sections of Roman society were beginning to wake up to the fact that Caesar was, scandalously, still married to Calpurnia. Caesar and Calpurnia had married in 59 BC; she was a sixteen-year-old virgin devoted to Caesar, and she typified the long-suffering, tolerant Roman *matrona* who clearly knew all about her husband's affair but kept quiet. She remained *univira* after he was assassinated.

Another famous example was Tertia Aemilia, wife of Scipio Africanus, who had full knowledge of her husband's affair with a slave girl but chose to turn a blind eye and, on Scipio's death, emancipated the girl and arranged her marriage to one of her freedmen.[10] Cleopatra left her most trusted advisors behind to govern the country in her absence.

Caesar could not have been more indiscreet and inappropriately honorific. He even went so far as to erect a golden statue of the queen in the guise of Isis in the temple of Venus Genetrix, the ancestor of his family, situated in the prestigious new Forum Julium he had promised to build after the Battle of Pharsalus.[11] The shock of a statue in honour of a living person, a woman at that, a foreigner and a queen and the religious association with Roman Venus, all in the middle of Rome, was incalculable.

It seems possible that Cleopatra would have met Mark Antony during her visit. At this time, Antony was married to the redoubtable Fulvia Flacca Bambula (c. 83 BC–40 BC). Ambitious and assertive, she is famous for gleefully pricking the decapitated Cicero's tongue with a hairpin. She had taken exception and exacted revenge after Cicero had insinuated that Antony, her third husband, only married her for her money. The great orator's tongue was the vehicle of his success; desecrating his tongue was the sweetest form of vengeance.

Cleopatra's party was still in Rome when Caesar was assassinated on 15 March 44 BC.[12] She and her retinue returned to Egypt, travelling via Cyprus to re-establish Egyptian control there. Cyprus had been restored to her by Caesar in 48 BC. Cicero, and many other Republicans besides, despised the foreign queen, Horace's *fatale monstrum* (doom monster), and was glad to see the back of her.

Young Ptolemy XIV died soon after – some allege that he was poisoned by Cleopatra. Whatever the case, she was anxious that her son, Caesarion, be a key player in her dealings with Rome. Accordingly, she made Caesarion her co-regent and successor, bestowing on him the titles Ptolemy XV Caesar Theos Philopator Philometor (Father-and-Mother-Loving God).[13] The Civil War raged on and Cleopatra sided with the Caesarian faction led by Mark Antony and Octavian, against the assassins of Caesar, under Marcus Junius Brutus and Gaius Cassius Longinus. In 43 BC, she allied with the leader of the Caesarian party in the east, the fickle Publius Cornelius Dolabella, who recognized Caesarion as her co-ruler. But soon after, Dolabella was defeated in Laodicea by Cassius and committed suicide by proxy by ordering one of his soldiers to kill him.[14]

In 41 BC, Cleopatra finally met with Mark Antony in Cilicia after a number of previous invitation requests had gone ignored. Ostensibly, Antony wanted to question the queen about the money she had allegedly paid to Cassius, and to win her support in his planned campaign against Parthia. Cleopatra arrived for the rendezvous in a blaze of astonishing extravagance and ceremony on the sumptuous royal barge, 'a get-up that beggared description,' Plutarch spluttered:

> she was going to visit Antony at the very time when women have the most brilliant beauty and are at the acme of intellectual power. Therefore she provided herself with many gifts, much money, and such ornaments as high position and prosperous kingdom made it natural for her to take; but she went putting her greatest confidence in herself, and in the charms and sorceries of her own person.[15]

Her magical boat he describes as having gold prows, purple sails, silver oars and a gold-studded canopy. Cleopatra's ostentatious display was so compelling that Antony, her second world leader, was so besotted that he spent the winter of 41–40 BC with her in Alexandria. Appian describes the overwhelming seduction of Mark Antony: he was astonished by her beauty; he was captivated by her as if he were a young man, even though he was forty.[16]

Antony attracted censure for dallying in Alexandria. Rumours of lavish entertaining percolated back to Rome and were exaggerated, excoriated and scandalized by a pious Cicero in his *Philippics*: Antony's house rang with the clamour of drunkards, the streets sloshed with wine; Antony was a booze-soaked, sex-sodden wreck of a man. Cleopatra's reputation suffered equally by association. The accusations of drunken debauchery persisted for years. According to Horace and Propertius, spokes-poets for the Augustan regime, Cleopatra was befuddled by Mareotic wine, her voice slurring with a wine-soaked tongue.

It was at this point that Cleopatra and Antony ordered the execution of her sister Arsinoe, carried out, as we have seen, sacrilegiously and scandalously on the steps of the Temple of Artemis. Apart from her fatal defection, she was, it seems, a pretender to the Egyptian throne. Cleopatra also had Sarapion, her top general in Cyprus, killed for his collusion with Cassius. Appian concludes that now Antony was putty in Cleopatra's hands: 'whatever Cleopatra wished it was done, regardless of the laws, human or divine.'[17] Cleopatra agreed the support Antony needed for his campaign against Parthia. The, possibly apocryphal, story where Antony tried to impress Cleopatra with his skills as a fisherman shows how easily she could humour and dupe him, ever urging him to focus his foreign policy to the benefit of Egypt. Antony surreptitiously had fish attached to his line by divers; she retaliated the next day by replicating the prank, thus exposing his unsuccessful efforts to impress her, much to the mirth of his audience.

Cleopatra gave birth to twins on December 25, 40 BC. The father was Mark Antony, and the children were named Alexander Helios and Cleopatra Selene II. There then followed a hiatus in the relationship. In 36 BC, Antony returned to Alexandria on his way to wage his war with the Parthians; the old acquaintance was renewed and Antony remained in the Egyptian capital, marrying Cleopatra even though he was at the time married to Octavia Minor, sister of Octavian. He and Cleopatra had another child, Ptolemy Philadelphus, during their stay in Antioch. Lucrative territories were signed over to Cleopatra to bolster the substantial natural resources and crops she already had access to. Crete, Cyrene, Cilicia, Phoenicia and part of Arabia corresponding to modern Jordan were all ceded to Egypt, as were parts of Syria and troublesome Judaea, ruled by Herod the Great (74–4 BC). Cedar from Lebanon for shipbuilding, the rare and priceless Balm of Gilead (*commiphora gileadensis* and *pistacia lentiscus*) from around Herod's Jericho, a key constituent in popular medicines and fine perfumes; Dead Sea bitumen, an essential ingredient in embalming fluid – all of this trade and produce came Cleopatra's way by the trireme load.

In 34 BC, another opulent and dazzling ceremony – again with Cleopatra symbolizing Isis – celebrated the carving up of the Egyptian empire, the so-called 'Donations of Alexandria'. Cleopatra was Queen of Kings over Egypt, while Caesarion took Cyprus as King of Kings; Alexander Helios and Philadelphus became kings east (Armenia, Media, and Parthia) and west (Phoenicia, Syria and Cilicia) of the Euphrates, while Cleopatra Selene II was made queen of Cyrene and Libya. Cleopatra added Philopatris, lover of her country, to her titles. Caesarion was depicted as the Egyptian god Horus, while Cleopatra called herself *Nea Isis*, meaning 'New Isis'.[18]

The increasingly fragile relationship between the triumvirates Octavian and Mark Antony finally shattered in 33 BC. Octavian succeeded in having the Senate vote a war against Egypt, culminating in 31 BC in the decisive naval action off Actium. Cleopatra took flight with her fleet, soon to be followed by Antony. Octavian then invaded Egypt; Antony's armies deserted to Octavian on August 1, 30 BC.

Antony had no choice but to take his own life. According to Plutarch, Cleopatra, fearing for her life from an Antony who believed that she had betrayed him, locked herself away in her mausoleum with her slave girls, sending messengers to Antony to misinform him that she was dead. Antony ordered a slave, Eros, to kill him but Eros selfishly elected to kill himself instead. Antony, following suite, stabbed himself in the stomach and lay down to die, but the wound proved not to be fatal. A further message arrived from Cleopatra with instructions to bring him to her; Antony agreed and was carried to the mausoleum. Inconveniently, Cleopatra had already closed the massive, cumbersome doors so he had to be secured to a stretcher and unceremoniously hauled up through a window by Cleopatra's slave-women, with some considerable difficulty. This, of course, only served to exacerbate his wound. Once inside, he was laid on a couch while a hysterical Cleopatra lamented at length. Antony calmed her down, drank a glass of wine and died.[19] Cleopatra committed suicide soon after.

Caesarion was proclaimed pharaoh by the Egyptians but soon after was captured and killed. One of Octavian's men neatly paraphrased Homer: 'It'not a good thing to have too many Caesars.'[20] There ended the Hellenistic, Ptolemaic line of Egyptian pharaohs, and with it all Egyptian pharaohs. The children of Cleopatra and Antony were taken back to Rome to live with Antony's widow, Octavia Minor. Cleopatra Selene was later married by Octavian to Juba II of Mauretania.[21]

Cleopatra was a powerful, successful, ruthless and influential woman who thrived at a time when Rome and the Mediterranean world were in turmoil, when political and military intrigue and activity were at their most intense. Cleopatra moved in the highest circles, forging alliances and pursuing affairs with the most powerful men of the day. Her fascinating life has been the subject of considerable interest, speculation and scrutiny for the last 2,000 or so years – by near contemporary historians and biographers, by classicists, historians, historical novelists and film-makers in the twentieth and twenty-first centuries. Only one thing matches this ongoing scrutiny of Cleopatra's life for intensity, and that is Cleopatra's death.

The consensus seems to be that Cleopatra killed herself by having a poisonous Egyptian cobra, an asp, bite her. The geographer Strabo, a contemporary, says that she either applied a poisonous ointment topically, or that she died from an asp bight on her breast.[22] Near contemporary Roman poets, Virgil, Horace and Propertius all mention asp bites; some sixty years later, Velleius Paterculus does too. Statius refers to Cleopatra's house as *anguifera* – serpent bearing – with Cleopatra slumped in seductive poison. Florus, the second century AD historian, also implicates an asp.[23] One scholar, at least, has argued that Octavian may have had her killed.[24] In 2012, the German historian Christoph Schaefer told *Discovery News* that Cleopatra died from drinking a cocktail of poisons. He argues that the asp could not have delivered the slow and painless death we so often hear about: asp venom induces paralysis in parts of the body, beginning with the eyes, before causing death. Schaefer and the toxicologist Dietrich Mebs, who worked with Schaefer, believe that Cleopatra took a mixture of hemlock, wolfsbane (*aconitum*) and opium. This would have induced the painless death sought by Cleopatra; asp venom, on the other hand, would have caused pain and unpleasant symptoms such as vomiting, diarrhoea and respiratory failure.[25] Plutarch records that a prescient Cleopatra carried out toxicological research to establish the least painful, efficacious and elegant way to commit suicide. This involved experimentation with various toxic herbs (*pharmaka*), which were cruelly tested on human guinea pigs: condemned prisoners of war. When this failed to produce a solution, she resorted to intensive animal experimentation, pitting venomous creatures against each other and observing the results:

> she found that the bite of the asp alone induced a sleepy torpor and sinking, where there was no spasm or groan, but a gentle perspiration on the face, while the perceptive faculties were easily relaxed and dimmed, and resisted all attempts to rouse and restore them, as is the case with those who are soundly asleep.[26]

Suicide had always been the likely cause of death. Cleopatra's first attempt was soon after Antony's death. Octavian wanted to take her alive, to parade her in Rome in his triumph, along with her many luxuries and treasures, which were now perilously poised on a funeral pyre awaiting ignition. In the event, he had to make do with an effigy of the queen. Proculeius was dispatched to the mausoleum to capture her and managed to stop her from stabbing herself with a hidden knife; he then took the precaution of searching her for concealed poisons. One of Octavian's freedmen, Epaphroditus, was left on close guard to prevent her suicide and keep her comfortable.[27] After Antony's funeral, Cleopatra contracted a fever and depression. The concomitant loss of appetite led her to hope for death through starvation, but this was dispelled when Octavian made cruel threats regarding the fate of her children. Plutarch adds that Cleopatra was known to carry poison in a hollow comb in her hair.[28]

In the end, Cleopatra managed to deceive not only Epaphroditus but also Octavian, who thought he had persuaded her to live on. Her guards, carelessly, allowed a meal of succulent figs to be delivered to her and two of her slave women. By the time the guards realized what was happening, Cleopatra was dead – 'upon a golden couch, arrayed in royal state' – and her maidservants, Iras and Charmian, were dying. Plutarch says that the snake was hidden in the fig leaves or that it had been concealed in a water jar, aggravated and released; Suetonius also says that an asp bite was responsible.[29] To Cleopatra, this would have been ideal: the bite of an asp was said to bestow divinity; elegantly dressed in all her finery as befitting a queen and destined for apotheosis, this, for Cleopatra, was the perfect final scene. A respectful Octavian had the 39-year-old buried alongside Mark Antony in a funeral fit for a queen. She thereby got what she wanted in death: the cults of Isis and Osiris bestowed immortality, an eternal life which she would be able to enjoy with Antony. Egypt, her beloved country, then became a Roman province.

Cleopatra was, of course, never popular in Rome. In her relationships with Julius Caesar and Mark Antony, she was viewed with considerable suspicion, a queen who evoked memories of the regal kings of early Rome and their tyranny. She was literally a living, inconvenient and embarassing disaster for Rome, militarily, socially and politically. Octavian, not surprisingly, made much of Cleopatra's reputation in a bid to slur and diminish her. He sacrilegiously took Antony's will from the safekeeping of the Vestal Virgins and read it out to the Senate, but not before he had carefully selected the extracts most likely to discredit Antony. He focused on Antony's state funeral preparations and the 'repatriation' of his body to Egypt; other damaging revelations included the news that he had left Cleopatra the 200,000 volumes deposited in the libraries at Pergamum. Furthermore, it was revealed that at a banquet he had stood up and annointed Cleopatra's feet as a bet, and he had allowed the Ephesians to salute Cleopatra as their queen; he would often receive love-letters from her on onyx or crystal, and read them while seated in tribunals when he was supposed to be dispensing justice. Once, when the famous orator Furnius was speaking, he saw Cleopatra outside being carried through the forum on a litter, abandoned the trial and escorted her on her way.[30]

Octavian ridiculed Antony and Cleopatra when he officially declared war on the queen and relieved Antony of the powers he had feebly ceded to a woman. He alleged that Antony's mind was befuddled by drugs, insinuating that Cleopatra was a witch. The war would be fought against a motley force comprising Mardian the eunuch, Potheinus, Iras, Cleopatra's hairdresser and Charmian, her lady-in-waiting, for they it was who were in charge in the Antony-and-Cleopatra camp.[31] Octavian's propaganda machine was highly effective, painting Cleopatra as the enemy of the state before and after Actium; the slurs were to achieve mythic proportions in the fiercely nationalist poems of Virgil, Horace and Propertius. The more Octavian exaggerated Cleopatra and the threat she posed to a paranoid Roman state, then the bigger his achievement when he eventually defeated her and extinguished that threat.

The poets at the end of the Republic and in the early Principate were unanimous in their contempt and derision. Virgil is perhaps the most restrained but, by the same token, the most eloquent. In Book 4 of the *Aeneid*, Dido is betrayed by Aeneas, sidelined by his dedication to the mission to found Rome. Dido is incandescent with rage and in a pit of misery and despair: 'she rages, out of her mind, and rushes through the city, mad as a Bacchant.'[32]

She confronts the treacherous Aeneas and promises to haunt him for ever:

When I'm gone I'll follow you into the black fire of Hell, when icy death draws out the spirit from my limbs; my ghost will be everywhere; you'll pay the price, you traitor, and I will hear about it – the news will reach me deep down among the deadmen.

Virgil's audience would have appreciated the poignancy of Dido's threats. Rome did indeed pay the price for Aeneas' duplicity; it paid with the devastating Punic Wars. Aeneas was indeed haunted by Dido, meeting again at arm's length in their frosty underworld encounter. The Dido episode resonates uncomfortably with the political upheaval caused so recently by Cleopatra, a foreign queen eerily reminiscent of Dido, whose facility for global power-play would be likened to the unnatural skills of Dido as sorceress.

More graphically, Cleopatra takes centre-stage on Aeneas' highly symbolic shield *ekphrasis*, which describes the armour given to him by Venus to fight for the establishment of Rome and the genesis of its proud history. She is called *regina* – 'the queen' – twice, still a dirty word so long after the fall of the monarchy; her gods are monsters, *monstra*, which assume the shape of all kinds of species and are ranged against the Roman pantheon; her defeat and her flight to Egypt are thrown into full relief.[33]

Horace excoriates the 'mad queen' – *regina demens* – in his famous poem celebrating her defeat at Actium: 'now the time has come to drink, get up and dance and feast!' Horace was sure that Cleopatra was plotting the death and destruction of Roman rule; her retinue is made up of eunuchs, squalid, diseased and drunk; she too is inebriated, she is a doom monster – *fatale monstrum*. Nevertherless, he concedes, patronisingly, that, in death, she does not act *muliebriter* (like a woman): she has no terror of the sword and bravely brings on the snakes, thus avoiding a humiliating appearance in a Roman triumph. The poem echoes sentiments first introduced in the *Epodes*, written soon after Actium, in which Horace sneers at the Roman soldiers under Antony and Cleopatra: they are enslaved by a woman and answer to eunuchs, and they have all gone soft with their un-Roman use of the *canopium*, the mosquito net.[34]

Propertius is no less hostile. Cleopatra features in a poem in which she is compared with Cynthia. Cynthia is the poet's *domina*; she dominated him just as Cleopatra dominated Antony; Propertius is enslaved by a woman, just as Antony was. Calling a mistress *domina*, and calling their love for that *domina* *servitium amoris* (slavery of love) were two of the outrageous ways in which the love poets controversially turned the usual man-woman relationship on its head. In the real world, the man was always the dominant partner; a real Roman would never be a slave to love. Insinuating Cleopatra into the poem embroils her in the decadent, un-Roman world of the love poets where women ruled, men were slaves, were love-sick or languished – '*exclusus*' – locked-out on the doorstep, were cuckolded as pathetic lovers whose only combat experience was in the war of love, '*militia amoris*'.[35] Propertius, of course, was one of the champions of this *roué* lifestyle; his portrait of Cleopatra here is probably one of the first instances of her as an embodiment of woman's domination of men, a symbol which has endured down the years.

Cleopatra comes at the end of a list of powerful women Propertius uses to justify Cynthia's domineering behaviour, but it is with Cleopatra that he piles on the invective when the poem turns into a celebration of Augustus. Chiming with Horace, we hear that she plotted to take over Rome, her marriage was sordid, Egypt a place of deceit and disaster; she is a whore of a queen – '*meretrix regina*' – she tried to supplant Roman gods with Egyptian, to influence the Tiber with the Nile before her death by asp. She has stained the reputation of the Macedonian house; she is 'shagged out' – '*trita*' – by sex with her own slaves, a cardinal sin and a crime which would have resonated with Propertius' audience. Centuries before, Lucretia lost her life at the mere prospect of such a heinous crime. This triumphalist tone is resumed by Propertius in his celebratory poem exulting at the victory of the Battle of Actium and the defeat of Cleopatra.[36]

Significantly, Virgil, Horace and Propertius all studiously avoid naming Cleopatra: she is *illa*, *Aegyptia coniunx* (the Egyptian wife), *regina* (queen), *femina* or *mulier* (woman); Cleopatra's identity has been half erased, she has become an opaque figure, *horrenda dictu* – too horrible to mention. Cicero too had exhibited the same depersonalizing, cringing horror at the thought of her.

Cleopatra is mentioned in Juvenal's list of effeminate pathics – grieving after Actium, *maesta* (dejected).[37] Martial, meanwhile, satirises her death.[38] In the epic *De Bello Civili*, Lucan's Cleopatra is evil: her beauty is sluttish (*incesta*) – a swipe at her marriage to her brother; her make-up is overdone and her jewels and clothing blingy; the banquet she lays on for Caesar is opulent beyond anything then known at Rome, and is described at length as the last word in *luxus*.[39] In the words of Pothinus, as he tries to foment war against Caesar, she is *inpia* – unholy, devoid of *pietas* – as she scuttles between husbands; she is selling off Rome and, witch-like seduces Caesar with potions; their affair is *incestus*, their love *obscaena* and impious. Unanimous as the poets are in their condemnation and vitriol, their opinions must, of course, be treated with caution. The exigencies of Augustan propaganda, patronage and nationalism, the universally held belief that women *per se* were inferior and should know their place, the exigencies of genre, particularly in satire, the subjectivity, fear and loathing – all this was never going to give an objective picture. Michael Grant called it all 'one of the most terrible outbursts of hatred in history'.[40]

As we know, the Romans were always unnerved by and uncomfortable with clever, educated, assertive women. Cornelia was acceptable, indeed pedastalized, because she was well-born, well-matched, clever and dignified, she was relatively unobtrusive and she was *univira*. Other women, though, were less compliant and clashed with the Romans' ideal perception of what a woman should be and how she ought to behave. For example, Sempronia, the Catiline conspirator, was as brave as any man; she too was well married with children; she was bilingual in Latin and Greek, an accomplished lyre player and a good dancer; she was a convivial conversationalist. For all that, Sallust sourly concludes that she was devoid of any of the qualities expected of the conventional *matrona*: she was impulsive, louche, truculent, passionate, a perjurer, an accessory to murder, a liar and a spendthrift. Sempronia to Sallust was a kind of anti-*matrona*: she broke the mould and stepped far beyond the traditional boundaries laid down for Roman women.[41] Cleopatra, too, came to embody everything the Roman man suspected, feared or despised about difficult and flamboyant women.

She was certainly gifted, highly intelligent, assertive, ambitious and conspicuous: after all, she was a (successful) head of state, a (respected) military commander and a (capable) strategist; she infatuated and manipulated two of Rome's leading generals and powerful politicians; she successfully assumed the guise of Isis, one of Egypt's most prominent deities. She restored the Egyptian Empire to its original boundaries, rebuilt the ailing economy and made it a force to be reckoned with again within the Mediterranean sphere. Quite simply, her actions helped form the shape of the Roman constitution and the establishment of the Roman Empire after the Battle of Actium. There was a stark and vivid contrast between her and the typically silent, publicly invisible and politically insignificant Roman woman. No wonder then that government propaganda and innate conservatism demanded that Cleopatra was commonly viewed as a *fatale monstrum*.

The Macedonian dynasty of Ptolemies was in some ways notoriously xenophobic throughout its 300-year reign in Egypt. Cleopatra bucked the trend: as noted, she was an adept linguist, the first and only Ptolemy to learn and speak Egyptian, her predecessors insisting on monolingual Greek alone. Her facility for language helps account for the fortunate appearance of Greek on the Rosetta Stone. She was well educated: Pliny the Elder reports that she introduced Caesar to her court astronomer, Sosigenes of Alexandria, who then helped with what became known as the Julian calendar comprising 365 days, leap days and leap years.[42]

Her beauty is legendary but it may be no more than that. We have seen how various poets describe her as beautiful, her beauty often intensifying the suspicion in which she was held. Plutarch, however, sees her differently. He believes that she was not the striking beauty she was reputed to be, but that it was her sophistication and manner that captivated men and accounted for her personal magnetism and attractiveness:

> conversation with her had an irresistible charm, and her presence, combined with the persuasiveness of her speech and the character which was somehow diffused about her behaviour towards others, had something stimulating about it. There was sweetness also in the tones of her voice; and her tongue, like an instrument of many strings, she could readily turn to whatever language she pleased.[43]

On the other hand, Dio Cassius, relying no doubt on earlier writers, had no doubts regarding her beauty. He says, with a swipe at Antony, that she was 'a woman of surpassing beauty ... she was most striking. Being brilliant to look upon and to listen to, with the power to subjugate everyone, even a love-sated man already past his prime.'[44] Her flattery knew no bounds and was particularly effective on the besotted Mark Antony: 'ever contributing some fresh delight and charm to Antony's hours of seriousness or mirth, kept him in constant tutelage, and released him neither night nor day.'[45] She shared in all of his pursuits – not for Cleopatra the traditional life of a stay-at-home wife. She played dice with him, drank with him, hunted with him and watched him in combat training. She even accompanied him when he anonymously visited the common people at night, he dressed as a servant, she as a slave girl.[46] Plutarch emphasizes her linguistic skills too, adding that she was rarely in need of an interpreter when talking with 'barbarians', be they Ethiopians, Troglodytes, Hebrews, Arabians, Syrians, Medes or Parthians. She was well-travelled; apart from the two years she spent in Rome, she also visited Athens, Ephesus, Tarsus and Antioch.

Alexandria was the centre of excellence in the Mediterranean world for medical science. Roman medicine was inhibited because human dissection was illegal there. No such restrictions prevailed in Egypt, and anyone who was anyone in the medical world studied in Alexandria. According to Galen, a lady called Cleopatra wrote the *On the Composition of Medicines by Place* (*Kosmetikon*), which included, amongst many other things, a remedy for male-pattern baldness involving the topical application of pulverised mouse skulls; an alternative therapy required the use of mouse droppings. She was also reputed in Jewish Talmudic texts to be an authority in foetal medicine and toxicology. The name Cleopatra here, though, is more likely to be coincidence or clever branding rather than to be of Ptolemaic provenance.

Cleopatra was born divine but her association with Isis was particularly unsettling to the Romans: Isis was linked with the Egyptian practice of honouring queens above kings. Most crucially for women, 'she made the power of women equal to that of men.'[47] Augustus saw in Isis a worrying reincarnation of Cleopatra and a threat to his license-curbing, moral legislation. In 28 BC, after Cleopatra's death, he banned the building of temples of Isis within the city of Rome, and in 21 BC he extended this to an exclusion zone outside Rome. Roman women would have sympathized with Isis' role as a mother, depicted as she often is with a baby in her arms, Horus, the offspring of her incestuous relationship with Osiris, her brother. Death and resurrection could be recognized in the rejuvenated, irrigated Egyptian lands and the death and rebirth of Osiris, also her husband. This flirtation with strange, oriental religions, intermarriage, incest, the elevation of women to something significant within society, the unpredictability and uncontrollability of the exotic rites, this Cleopatra, all of it was anathema to Octavian and to the Roman way of doing things.

Her behaviour in public would also have aroused concern. 'Silent' is a word that is sometimes used to describe Roman women, because of the paucity of first-hand, direct evidence for their lives. 'Silent' can also be used to describe how the typical Roman male liked his women: silent and unobtrusive.[48] Cleopatra was anything but: her skills as a glittering hostess of sumptuous banquets were beyond compare and her enjoyment at those extravagant feasts just as legendary. With Antony in Alexandria she founded the *Amimetobioi*, the 'Inimitable Livers', an exclusive dining club which convened every evening in unbelievable excess; defeat at Actium was met with impressive black humour when the 'Inimitable Livers' was disbanded and replaced with the 'Partners in Death', a club no less extravagant: 'for their friends enrolled themselves as those who would die together, and passed the time delightfully in a round of suppers.'[49]

Roman women of the elite classes, of course, would often attend dinners with their husbands, but their role there was usually discrete and dignified. Where a woman overstepped the mark, she was, if Juvenal is to be believed, the target of scorn and derision. In his excoriating sixth satire, he deplores the female pedant and the know-it-all; she should just go away and be a man.[50]

The extent to which Cleopatra made herself, and her opulence, the centre of attention is best illustrated by the story of the pearl, as narrated by Pliny the Elder some 100 years after the alleged event took place.[51] He starts by asserting that the world's two biggest pearls were both owned by Cleopatra, 'the royal whore'. During one of Antony's sumptuous dinners she bets him that she could outdo his efforts by spending ten million sesterces on a dinner. The next night, she serves up an unremarkable, relatively meagre meal, which Antony duly ridicules. The final course is the worst: a cup of vinegar, but she reassures him that she will still rack up the ten. At this point Cleopatra takes off one of her priceless pearl earrings and drops it into the vinegar; it dissolves, and she drinks the slushy mixture: ten million sesterces well spent.

Athenaeus, in the third century AD, quotes a description of a banquet attended by Antony and Cleopatra in his *Deipnosophistae – the Feast of the Philosophers*:

> The service was all made of gold and jewelled vessels of exquisite art; even the walls were draped with tapestries made of purple and gold threads ... [Antony] was taken aback by the opulence of the display: but she just quietly smiled saying that it was all a present for him. She invited him to come to dinner again the following night with his friends and his officers. This was an even more sumptuous dinner party; by comparison, the service on the previous evening seemed cheap; again, she presented him with these too. As for the officers, they were allowed to take away the couch they had reclined on ... she distributed fees, of one talent to buy roses, and the floors of the dining-rooms were strewn with them one cubit deep.[52]

Cleopatra represented everything the traditional Roman *matrona* was not, or could ever be: she was highly successful politically and militarily, she was a leader of men and she was head-of-state of a rich and bountiful country. She persisted in her single-minded determination to restore the Ptolemaic dynasty to its former glories and to win for Egypt a pivotal position in the Mediterranean world. She used her apparent beauty and social skills to allure and manipulate two of the world's most powerful men. Her education, refinement and sophistication, her ostentatious and extravagant behaviour, her obvious magnificent wealth, her exploitation of exotic religion all fanned the flames of the loathing and misogyny which she excited in Roman male contemporaries and in later writers.

Cleopatra was the anti-*matrona*, the anti-Roman. A few decades after her death, the emperors' women, of course, were able to assume a public prominence and political, dynastic profiles far and away above anything possible to women in the Republic. Only a foreign woman, Cleopatra, came close to the power wielded by the Julias, Livias, Agrippinas and the Mesallinas by virtue of their position at the heart of government and in the beds of the men running those governments.

Part Two: The Empire

Chapter 9

The Early Empire: *Clades Lolliana* 16 BC and the Teutoburg Forest AD 9

M ilitarily speaking, the 500 or so years of Empire made for a vastly quieter time for the Romans than the preceding 700 years or so of the Republic. The intractable doors of the Temple of Janus even remained closed for a while in the early years of Augustus' reign. Augustus wielded complete control over what had now become the Roman Empire; he also retained control of the Roman army – essentially to prevent a return to the bloody turmoil of the civil wars by covetous, power-hungry generals. He maintained a policy of limited expansion, largely keeping the new Empire within its existing boundaries. This was in the face of encouragement to invade Britannia and Parthia and a need to ensure that the legions were usefully employed to the benefit of the political establishment rather than to its detriment. As far as the Romans could see, there was little out there now which would earn a return on expensive military campaigns; lucrative booty and fertile lands not under Roman control were now in short supply. Why bother? Augustus had the financial resources to satisfy and resettle veterans out of his substantial windfalls from the Ptolemaic empire; he was naturally unwilling to allow ambitious commanders to launch insurrection on the back of victorious military campaigns. Fortuitously, it turns out that battle casualties and proscriptions from the civil wars had dramatically reduced the number of nobles agitating for a return to the Republic.

Policy in Asia Minor, Africa, Egypt, Spain and Gaul largely reflects this restraint, this military conservatism. Germany, however, was to prove an exception. In 17 BC, tribes led by the Sugambri, from near what is now the Dutch-German border on the right bank of the Rhine, defeated a Roman legion under the command of Marcus Lollius. This came to be known as the *Clades Lolliana* – the Lollius Massacre.[1]

Marcus Lollius is little known but he was probably a *homo novus* (new man), a friend of and indebted to Augustus who had saved him from proscription. Consul in 21 BC, he was the first governor of Galatia and enjoyed success over the Thracian Bersi tribe. In 17 BC, he was a governor on the Rhine leading the Vth (*Alaudae*) Legion, battle hardened from their campaigns against the Cantabri in Iberia. Soon after his arrival, a number of Romans were captured and crucified by the Tencteri, knowing quite well that this would not go unpunished. The Tencteri, noted for their skills as cavalrymen, joined with the Usipites and the Sugambri and launched attacks into Roman-occupied Gaul. For the Tencteri and Usipites, this was a long-awaited chance to avenge the slaughter visited on them some forty years earlier, in 55 BC, by Julius Caesar. According to Cato the Younger, Caesar murdered 400,000 of them and ought to be brought to book for the war crime. The Sugambri were led by Melo, brother of Baetorix; later the Sicambri under Deudorix, son of Baetorix, joined Arminius and were to help annihilate the three Roman legions under Publius Quinctilius Varus at the Teutoburg Forest.

Lollius was impatient and ill-prepared. He marched out with the Vth *Alaudae* and a small squadron of cavalry to confront the invaders; the cavalry were sent on ahead only to be massacred in a Tencteri ambush. The Germans pursued the survivors back to the ranks of the legion, which was taken by surprise and slaughtered. If the destruction of the Vth *Alaudae* was not bad enough, the Tencteri made things a lot worse when they triumphantly captured the coveted gold *aquila* standard – a most stigmatic, albeit rare, humiliation for the legion and its commander. There was further bad news when it transpired that Augustus was himself in that part of Gaul at the time. The emperor, no doubt furious at the loss of a standard and the best part of a legion, gathered an army to confront the Germans. Augustus took hostages and subsequently withdrew his army. Lollius, of course, was finished. Apart from this calamity, he had a torrid time as a guardian to Gaius Caesar, Augustus' nephew. Their strained relationship culminated in accusations of corruption and taking bribes from King Phraates of Parthia, after which he took his own life. He died a wealthy man, his considerable fortune being inherited by his granddaughter, Lollia Paulina. Predictably, history has not treated him well: Velleius Paterculus labelled him greedy and vicious – the inevitable epitaph for a commander who loses his eagle to the barbarians. His friend Horace, on the other hand, had praised him; to Pliny the Elder he was a hypocrite. With supreme understatement, Suetonius described the incident as 'disgraceful' rather than 'damaging'. Comparing it with the *Clades Varianas* (the Varus Massacre in the Teutoburg Forest), he says, 'But the Lollius debacle was more about dishonour than disaster.'

The Battle of Teutobug Forest, however, was to be a different matter altogether. The Romans should have taken *Clades Lolliana* as a stark and timely warning that, in this part of Gaul and in Germany, they were vulnerable, and, if they were to succeed, would have to demonstrate the utmost military skill and deploy the best strategies and the sharpest of tactics. If any good came out of Lollius's avoidable disaster it was that his *clades* eventually provided the Romans with a springboard for the invasion of western Germany in order to create a buffer against German attacks on Gaul. It allowed Augustus to extend the boundary of Empire to the Elbe and, incidentally, provided military opportunities for his stepsons, Tiberius and Drusus. Drusus was able to win a series of victories and reached the Elbe between 12 and 9 BC. From 11 BC, for seven years, German hostility between tribes deepened. Tacitus records that the Chatti defeated the Cherusci, but were themselves pacified from AD 4. Velleius Paterculus also notes unrest.[2] On the death of Drusus in 9 BC, Tiberius took over and consolidated these gains through ethnic cleansing, resettling the more refractory Germans in Gaul in 8 and 7 BC. Three years later L. Domitius Ahenobarbus was able to penetrate Germany by another route: the valley of the Saale in the upper Danube Valley.

Skillfully combining naval and land operations, in AD 6, Tiberius built on his successes, culminating in an attack against Maroboduus and his 75,000-strong Marcomanni army. Gaius Sentius Saturninus and Marcus Aemilius Lepidus led the 65,000 infantry and 10,000–20,000 cavalry and archers, along with 10,000–20,000 civilians, amounting to thirteen legions with entourage. In AD 4, Tiberius invaded Germania and subjugated the Cananefates, the Chatti near the upper Weser and the Bructeri, south of the Teutoburg Forest, before crossing the Weser. However, in that same year, a distracting and diverting rebellion erupted in Illyricum, led by the Daesitiate, the Breucians, the Pannonia and the Marcomanni; this *Bellum Batonianum* (War of the Batons) lasted for four years. Tiberius sent eight of his thirteen legions east to crush the revolt, which had been inflamed by neglect on the part of the Romans, food shortages and the heavy-handed exaction of oppressive taxes. Only three legions (the XVIIth, XVIIIth and XIXth), six independent cohorts and three squadrons of cavalry were left to Publius Quinctilius Varus, *legatus Augusti pro praetor* (envoy of the emperor, acting praetor), in Germany.

Varus, stepson and favourite of Augustus, was no diplomat. Indeed, he was vaguely reminiscent of some of Rome's worst and grasping governors from the Republican past, such as Galba and Lucullus in Lusitania.[3] He also had something of a reputation for crucifying inconvenient opponents: after occupying Jerusalem in 4 BC, he put some 2,000 Jewish rebels to the cross. Varus foolishly imposed burdensome taxation and restrictive Roman rule of law on the Germans, which, unsurprisingly, served only to ignite a rebellion. This was led by Arminius, a young member of the Cherusci who had been a Roman hostage and had actually been trained by the Romans and fought for them. He was a member of the *equester ordo* (equestrian order) and was now intent on putting his training to good use against the very army that had trained him. This disaster became known as the *Clades Variana* (Varus Massacre) which took place in the hilly Teutoburg Forest at Kalkriese, east of modern Osnabrück in the hills overlooking the modern road from Paderborn.[4]

Arminius returned from Rome to Germany, taking on the role of double agent: he became an advisor to Varus while at the same time duplicitously working with and for an alliance of Germanic tribes – former enemies of his – which included the Cherusci, the Marsi, Chatti, Bructeri, Chauci, Sicambri, and the Suebi. Taking advantage of the unrest fuelled by Varus' rapacious behaviour, Arminius united the tribes and channelled their animosity against the Romans. Arminius invented a fictional uprising to deceive Varus, who still believed the German to be loyal. The Roman decided on an immediate response and was accordingly led through unfamiliar Teutoburg land straight into an ambush by Arminius. Despite attempts by Segestes, the disaffected father-in-law of Arminius, to expose the treachery, Varus advanced while Arminius took his leave of the Romans, on the pretext of drumming up support from vacillating German tribes.[5] There was, of course, no support; instead, Arminius busied himself with a series of raids on Roman camps.

Many of Varus' troops lacked battle experience; the Germans, by contrast, were battle-hardened. Varus' columns were sloppy and disorganized. He entered the forest near modern-day Osnabrück, his troops mingling with camp followers extended dangerously over a vulnerable column of 20km and benefitting from little or no reconnaisance. Acording to Dio:

> The Romans were not proceeding in any regular order, but were mixed in helter-skelter with the waggons and the unarmed, and so, being unable to form readily anywhere in a body, and being fewer at every point than their assailants, they suffered greatly and could offer no resistance at all.[6]

The Romans marched blindfold into the waiting ambush, along a muddy, narrow forest trail the extent and direction of which they had no knowledge or intelligence. Rain poured constantly from the skies, producing a cloying mud bath.

The Germans struck, making good use of their close-combat weaponry: light swords and *fremae* – narrow-bladed short spears. Demonstrating his Roman military training, Arminius was able to anticipate Varus' tactics and surround his foe, wreaking havoc and dispensing carnage. After disastrous, heavy losses, the Romans camped for the night. The following day, some survivors were slaughtered in open country north of the Wiehen Hills, near modern Ostercappeln, yet more perished when the Romans resumed their rain-soaked march. The appalling weather favoured the Germans, as the Roman shields became waterlogged and their sinew bow strings went slack in the relentless rain.

An ill-advised night march led the Romans to Kalkriese Hill. A worse place for battle could not have been chosen, with little more than 100m between the hill and an extensive marsh. Add to that an intervening trench and earthwork which afforded the Germans cover from which to attack, and the Romans had walked into another calamity of their own making. Efforts to storm the wall failed; Varus' second-in-command, Numonius Vala, fled with his cavalry but was captured by the Germans and slain. The Germans pressed home their attack, annihilating the disintegrating Roman forces. Varus committed suicide. Another commander, Ceionius, surrendered, then took his own life, while his colleague Lucius Eggius salvaged some respect when he died a hero, leading his doomed soldiers. Here is the assessment of Velleius Paterculus:

> The details of this terrible calamity, the heaviest that had befallen the Romans on foreign soil since the disaster of Crassus in Parthia, I shall endeavour to set forth, as others have done, in my larger work. Here I can merely lament the disaster as a whole. An army unexcelled in bravery, the first of Roman armies in discipline, in energy, and in experience in the field, through the negligence of its general, the perfidy of the enemy, and the unkindness of fortune was surrounded, nor was as much opportunity as they had wished given to the soldiers either of fighting or of extricating themselves, except against heavy odds.[7]

The immediate aftermath was particularly unsavoury: there were up to 20,000 Roman dead, mass suicides by the officers and many instances of human sacrifice when survivors were cooked in pots, their bones preserved for magical rites. Others were ransomed or enslaved. Florus gives us some disturbing detail:

> Never was there slaughter more cruel than took place there in the marshes and woods, never were more intolerable insults inflicted by barbarians, especially those directed against the legal pleaders. They put out the eyes of some of them and cut off the hands of others; they sewed up the mouth of one of them after first cutting out his tongue, exclaiming, 'At last, you viper, you have ceased to hiss.' The body too of the consul himself, which

the dutiful affection of the soldiers had buried, was disinterred. As for the standards and eagles, the barbarians possess two to this day; the third eagle was wrenched from its pole, before it could fall into the hands of the enemy, by the standard-bearer, who, carrying it concealed in the folds round his belt, secreted himself in the blood-stained marsh. The result of this disaster was that the empire, which had not stopped on the shores of the Ocean, was checked on the banks of the Rhine.[8]

As might be expected, Romans shared Augustus' anger and sorrow at the disaster, although the main focus was unanimously on the duplicity of the Germans generally and the dissembling of Arminius in particular. Ovid speaks of a 'rebellious Germany' (*rebellatrix Germania*) in his *Tristia*, written in the spring of AD 10, just months after the defeat, from exile on the shores of the Black Sea. The following year he talks of 'this traitor who trapped our men in a treacherous place.'[9] Around the same time, Manilius describes in the *Astronomica*, where 'in foreign parts, when, its oaths forsworn, barbarous Germany made away with our commander Varus and stained the fields with three legions' blood.'[10]

Strabo in his *Geography*, from about AD 18, warns that:

In dealing with these peoples distrust has been a great advantage, whereas those who have been trusted have done the greatest harm, as, for instance, the Cherusci and their subjects, in whose country three Roman legions, with their general Quintilius Varus, were destroyed by ambush in violation of the treaty.[11]

The paucity of archaeological evidence (only part of one German spur has been uncovered) suggests very low German casualties. On the other hand, no less than 6,000 pieces of Roman equipment have been unearthed. That solitary spur, however, may be a red herring further confusing an already confused situation. The Germans possibly removed the bodies of their fallen from the battle sites. Or else, they may have buried their dead *in situ*, but they wore more perishable leathers than the Romans, who favoured more survivable metal. In addition, part of the German army had defected from the Roman force and wore Roman equipment and carried Roman kit.

The Germans then proceeded to erase any evidence of a Roman presence from the region, wiping out Roman forts, garrisons and the two cities east of the Rhine. Nevertheless, the two Roman legions left in Germania, commanded by Varus' nephew, Lucius Nonius Asprenas, tried to hold the river with the besieged garrison at Aliso under Lucius Caedicius. He held out against the

Germans for weeks, until, accompanied by survivors of the battle, he broke through the siege and reached the Rhine.

Back in a shocked and stunned Rome, the Battle of the Teutoburg Forest was seen as another *dies ater,* on a par with the sack of Rome in 390 BC, Lake Trasimene, Cannae and Carrhae. Augustus was beside himself: incandescent, distraught. According to Suetonius, he repeatedly bashed his head against a door, wailing '*Quintili Vare, legiones redde!*' – 'Quintilius Varus, give me back my legions!' He was so upset that for months he cut neither beard nor hair.[12] The anniversary of the disaster was met with mourning and gloom. Gauls and Germans living in Rome were expelled. As regards the three guilty legions, legion numbers XVII and XIX were expunged and never used again; XVIII was rebuilt under Nero, but disbanded under Vespasian. Teutoburger Wald marked the end of a period of Roman success in Germany extending over the previous forty years. Legions II (*Augusta*), XX (*Valeria Victrix*) and XIII (*Gemina*) were posted to the Rhine to replace the lost legions.

Varus, appropriately, fell on his sword, and his half-burned body was further mutilated by the Germans. Arminius sent Varus' severed head to Maroboduus, king of the Marcomanni, in a macabre attempt to forge an anti-Roman alliance. Maroboduus declined, sending the head to Rome for burial, and remaining neutral throughout the ensuing war. Augustus dignified the incident by burying the head in his own mausoleum.

As after the earlier 'black days' at the Allia River and Cannae, for example, the Romans were determined to lift themselves from this fathomless pit of military disaster and salvage some of their losses, dignity, prestige and military pride. How else to rebuild their shattered reputation and resume their position as leaders of the Mediterranean world and beyond? It is no consolation, nor mitigation, but the Battle of Teutoburg Forest was by no means Rome's greatest defeat.

As we have noted, this is what the ancient sources tell us: 'This terrible calamity, the heaviest that had befallen the Romans on foreign soil since the disaster of Crassus in Parthia'[13] was less costly in lives than the losses at Carrhae (53 BC), in which 20,000 soldiers were reputedly killed and 10,000 captured.[14] At Cannae (216 BC), 50,000 died;[15] Quintilian has 60,000; Polybius, 70,000.[16] Nearly a century before, Livy records 80,000 Roman casualties lost against Germanic tribes at Arausio in 105 BC.[17]

As we have seen, in AD 14 and 15, Tiberius mounted a number of campaigns commanded by his nephew, Germanicus. The first was a surprise attack on the Marsi, which drew in the Bructeri, Tubani and Usipeti, who ambushed Germanicus en route to his winter quarters. The Germans were soundly beaten.[18] More campaigns followed by land and sea, involving 70,000 men. Caecina Severus assaulted the Marsi again with about 25,000–30,000 men, wreaking havoc. Germanicus built a fort on Mount Taunus, whence he attacked and scattered the Chatti; he went on to attack Mattium, which he razed to the ground.[19] Among the captives were Arminius' wife, Thusnelda. Her father, an enemy of Arminius, handed her over to Germanicus. She was the daughter of the Cheruscan prince Segestes and had been intended for another but eloped with Arminius. In AD 17, while in captivity in Rome, she gave birth to Arminius' son, Thumelicus; mother and baby were paraded as trophies during Germanicus' triumph. While it is obvious that few Romans learnt anything from the *Clades Lolliana*, Tiberius, according to Suetonius, certainly took something away from the Teutoburg Forest:

> The next year he [Tiberius] returned to Germany, and realising that the disaster to Varus was due to that general's rashness and lack of care, he took no step without the approval of a council; while he had always before been a man of independent judgment and self-reliance, then contrary to his habit he consulted with many advisers about the conduct of the campaign. He also observed more scrupulous care than usual. When on the point of crossing the Rhine, he reduced all the baggage to a prescribed limit, and would not start without standing on the bank and inspecting the loads of the wagons, to make sure that nothing was taken except what was allowed or necessary. Once on the other side, he adopted the following manner of life: he took his meals sitting on the bare turf, often passed the night without a tent, and gave all his orders for the following day, as well as notice of any sudden emergency, in writing; adding the injunction that if anyone was in doubt about any matter, he was to consult him personally at any hour whatsoever, even of the night.[20]

During his campaign, Germanicus made a dignified but harrowing pilgrimage to the haunting site of the Battle of Teutoburg Forest. He and his soldiers came across piles of bleached bones, severed skulls nailed to trees and 'barbarous altars'. The traumatized Romans buried the remains; in the words of Tacitus, 'no soldier knowing whether he was burying the remains of a relative or a stranger, but looking on all as kinsfolk and of their own blood, while their anger rose higher than ever against the enemy.'[21]

In AD 16, Germanicus crossed the Weser near modern Minden, bringing Arminius to battle at Idistaviso in the Battle of the Weser River. Germanicus was victorious, routing the Germans; he was able to repeat the massacre at the Angivarian Wall to the west of modern Hanover with his eight legions. More success followed that year when Caius Silius engaged the Chatti with 33,000 men; meanwhile, Germanicus invaded the Marsi for a third time, laying waste their land.[22] Germanicus' successes were considerable: the Lippe Valley and the North Sea coast had been retaken and Arminius was defeated. Roman prestige was largely restored, but they took a cautious line. Tiberius withdrew from the Lippe Valley, leaving the Germans to themselves. They squabbled and Arminius was murdered.

Two of the three legions' eagles lost in AD 9 were recovered in subsequent raids. Germanicus was recalled to Rome to celebrate a triumph and receive a new command.[23] In a story reminiscent of Japanese soldiers finally surrendering decades after the end of the Second World War, Tacitus fascinatingly records that, in AD 50, when the Chatti invaded Roman territory in Germania Superior, the Roman commander, Publius Pomponius Secundus, repulsed them and found Roman prisoners, including a number from Varus' legions who had been held captive for forty years.

The most impressive piece of archaeological evidence for Teutoburg is the cenotaph of an officer called Marcus Caelius and two of his freedmen. It was found at Xanten in 1620, and is now in the Rheinisches Landesmuseum in Bonn. The relief and inscription are intact, and in the transcription below the extant wording is shown as capital letters:[24]

MarcoCAELIO Titi Filio LEMonia tribv BONonia
I Ordinis LEGionis XIIX ANNorvm LIII S
OCCIDIT BELLO VARIANO OSSA
INFERRE LICEBIT Pvblivs CAELIVS Titi Filivs
LEMonia tribv FRATER FECIT

To Marcus Caelius, son of Titus, of the Lemonian district, from
Bologna, first centurion of the eighteenth legion. Fifty-three years old.
He fell in the Varian War. His bones
may be interred here. Publius Caelius, son of Titus,
of the Lemonian district, his brother, erected (this monument).

As with Viriathus in Portugal and the rout of Lucius Cassius, who was 'sent under the yoke' by the Helvetii, Arminius and the Teutoburg Forest battle became symbols of national pride and unity. After the fifth century, the disaster was consigned to history and largely forgotten, until, that is, the fourteenth century, when Tacitus' *Germania* and *Annals* were rediscovered by German humanists who embraced the belief that Arminius was Germany's first national hero. Arminius is an object lesson in how history can be re-invented and turned into propaganda. He has been endlessly politicized by Germans of every peruasion. In 1530, even Martin Luther extolled him as a 'war leader'. In 1806, the Germans suffered another humiliation when Napoleon defeated the armies of the German states. Apparently, German eyes looked towards the Teutoburg Forest as their finest hour. Napoleon, of course, spoke a romance language and decked himself out as a Roman emperor, making it easy for the Germans to remember that they had already defeated the *welschen Erbfeind* – roughly meaning the Latin-speaking arch enemies of Germany. The Teutoburg Forest came to symbolize the dichotomy between the decadent Latin and the practical and dynamic Germanic people, between old France and new Germany.

Heinrich von Kleist's 1809 play *Die Hermannsschlacht* (*Hermann's Battle*) cast the hero as a national leader in the fight against Napoleon and the invading French hordes. Hermann, portrayed as a blond, muscular Teutonic warrior, was much in demand: he starred in more than fifty operas and plays during the eighteenth and nineteenth centuries. In 1875, four years after the unification of Germany, a huge copper monument, *Hermannsdenkmal*, was completed near Detmold – then the putative site of the battle – Hermann being a more suitably German name, derived as it is from Arminius and reminiscent of the German god of war, Herimannus. After many delays, Hermann was eventually crowned with a winged helmet, brandishing his 203kg, 23ft sword menacingly in the direction of France. At 87ft high, and mounted on an 88ft stone base, it was the largest statue in the world until the *Statue of Liberty* rose up in 1886. It was also a significant influence on the statue of *Justice* atop the Old Bailey in London. Hermann has one foot resting victoriously on a Roman eagle and a discarded *fasces*. The nationalist inscription reads '*Deutsche Einigkeit meine Starke, meine Starke Deutschlands Macht*' ('German unity my strength, my strength Germany's power'). Its completion marked an upsurge in German patriotism after German unification.

The monument became a popular Nazi pilgrimage site in the 1930s. Hitler described Arminius as 'the first architect of our liberty'. Unlike other nineteenth-century popular national war heroes (France's Vercingetorix, Belgium's Ambiorix, the Netherlands' Julius Civilis, Portugal's Viriathus and Britain's Boudica), Arminius was never beaten in battle by the Romans. Conscious of the sensitivity surrounding German nationalism, the 2,000th anniversary of the battle in 2009 was a decidedly low-key affair.

But is was not all Teutonic nationalism, solemnity and sobriety: Arminius did not escape the sharp tongue of satire, as Heinrich Heine in 1843 shows in his epic poem *Germany: A Winter's Tale*:

This is the Teutoburg Forest
as described by Tacitus,
and this is the classical swamp
where Varus got himself stuck.
It was here that the leader of the Cherusci
Hermann, the noble thane defeated him,
and German nationality
was victorious in all this mud.
If Hermann and his blonde hordes
had not won the battle,
there would be no more freedom
and we should all be Romans!
In our fatherland there would only be
Roman customs and language;
there would even be Vestal Virgins in Munich,
and the Swathians would be called Quirites.

Various suggestions (over 700) for the battle ground have been proposed over the years, with proposals ranging from the Netherlands to the outskirts of Paderborn, to Kalkriese Hill, the preferred option today.

The Teutoburg Forest was so catastrophic a disaster that it shook Rome to the core and brought the conquest of Germany to a grinding halt. As Peter S. Wells, author of *The Battle That Stopped Rome*, put it: 'This was a battle that changed the course of history.'[25]

It was one of the most devastating defeats ever suffered by the Roman Army, and its consequences were the most far-reaching. The battle led to the creation of a militarized frontier in the middle of Europe that endured for 400 years, and it created a boundary between Germanic and Latin cultures that lasted 2,000 years.

According to Herbert W. Benario, Emeritus Professor of classics at Emory University, a very different Europe would have emerged:

Almost all of modern Germany as well as much of the present-day Czech Republic would have come under Roman rule. All Europe west of the Elbe might well have remained Roman Catholic; Germans would be speaking a Romance language; the Thirty Years' War might never have occurred, and the long, bitter conflict between the French and the Germans might never have taken place.[26]

Tillmann Bendikowski provides a more considered analysis: 'It's typically German to say world history was shaped on German soil. ... We know that this was one battle among many and that there was a range of factors behind Rome's eventual retreat to the Rhine. Everyone who needed this myth regarded it as the turning point of history. For many it remains the turning point. But it wasn't.'[27]

Chapter 10

Boudica's Revolt AD 60

Britain first attracted serious attention when the Greeks, Phoenicians and Carthaginians began trading for Cornish tin. The Greeks called Britain the *Cassiterides*, or 'tin islands'. A rather sceptical Herodotus in the fifth century BC vaguely located them somewhere off the west coast of Europe. He declares no real evidence for this, though, but concedes that they must exist, as the Greeks get their tin from somewhere, probably from the ends of the earth. He prefers this explanation to the story that tin comes from the one-eyed Arimaspians who steal it from the griffins who guard it.[1]

The Carthaginian explorer Himilco probably visited in the fifth century BC and the Greek navigator Pytheas of Massalia around 325 BC. Strabo records that Pytheas circumnavigated the islands.[2] What he found here is recorded by Diodorus Siculus as a cold and frosty place where the people live in thatched cottages, store their grain underground and bake bread. They are a simple people and live plainly, ruled by many kings and princes who live in peace with each other. When they do fight, they do so from chariots, just like the Greeks in the Trojan War.[3] It was, however, a place shrouded in mystery, with some writers denying its existence completely, according to Plutarch.[4]

Despite the disinterest and mystery, an inquisitive Rome arrived in 55 BC with Julius Caesar. His purported aim was to put an end to the support the Britons had been giving to the Gauls, but in reality, it was another stage on his *cursus honorum*, as recorded in his *De Bello Gallico*, commentaries on the Gallic War. In what turned out to be more of a reconnaisance expedition than anything else, Caesar's stay was cut short by an equinoctial tide which destroyed part of his fleet, and by a shortage of cavalry. Nevertheless, the foray obviously won for Caesar the intended political kudos, as he was voted a twenty-day public holiday in Rome by the Senate for taking British hostages and defeating the Belgic tribes on his return to the continent.[5] The following year, Caesar came back to Britain.[6]

This time he was better prepared, with a more adventurous strategy; he brought with him a larger force. His strategy was to win over, or compel, native Celtic tribes to pay tribute and give hostages in return for non-aggression. The king of the Trinovantes, Mandubracius (also known as Imanuentius) was taken on side as an ally, while his rival, Cassivellaunus, king of the Catuvellauni, coordinated and led the British opposition to Caesar's forces. However, the Cenimagni, the Segontiaci, the Ancalites, the Bibroci and the Cassi all surrendered to Caesar and betrayed the location of Cassivellaunus's fortress at Wheathamstead. Cassivellaunus capitulated, was subjected to terms, and the hostages were taken.[7] There is no truth in the story told by Polyaenus that Caesar defeated Cassivellaunus's men while defending a river crossing, striking fear into their hearts when he deployed an armoured elephant with a turret, from which archers and slingers fired.[8]

Augustus toyed with the idea of invading in 34 (as Octavian), 27 and 25 BC, but with problems in Spain to deal with, the plans came to nothing and relations proceeded on the basis of diplomacy and trade.[9] Strabo reports lucrative tax revenues for Rome on British commercial activity; we have archaeological evidence for more and more imported luxury goods unearthed in southern Britain from that period. Sporadic references to Britannia include British kings who sent embassies to Augustus, and kings received by Augustus as refugees.[10] Tacitus adds to the mystique of Britannia in his reports that some of Tiberius' ships were blown off course to Britain during his German campaigns in AD 16; they were promptly sent back by local rulers, the startled Romans telling tales of hurricanes, strange birds, monsters and figures half man–half animal, imagined or otherwise.[11]

The diplomacy continued until AD 39, when an exile from the Catuvellauni, Adminius, son of Cymbeline, led Caligula to plan an invasion of Britain. Suetonius tells that it was a complete shambles and that the invaders never left Gaul. Caligula ranged his siege-engines on the Gallic coast facing Britannia, then, to everyone's astonishment, ordered his troops to gather sea shells from the beach – such was the booty due to Rome. This they did, a lighthouse was erected, a bounty of four gold pieces was announced and he bid the troops go rich and go happy![12]

Four years later, in AD 43, after a century of Roman indecision and hesitation, Claudius invaded, ostensibly to help the client king, Verica of the Atrebates, who had been exiled after a revolt by the Catuvellauni.[13]

Aulus Plautius was appointed commander-in-chief and governor of the province. The invasion force comprised four legions: the IXth (*Hispana*), the IInd (*Augusta*), the XIVth (*Gemina*), and the XXth (*Valeria Victrix*), supported by 20,000 auxiliary troops from Thrace and Batavia in Germany. The IInd was led by Vespasian, who was to become emperor in AD 69.[14] The invasion was not without its problems, however: the troops gathered on the coast of Gaul were apprehensive about sailing off the edge of the world and mutinied. Nevertheless, once reassured that the world did not end where they stood by Claudius's influential freedman and secretary Narcissus, and encouraged to see a former slave in place of their general, they shouted '*Io Saturnalia!*' (Saturnalia was the Roman festival in which social roles were reversed for the day). The mutiny ended and the force set sail, landing at Richborough and at Bosham harbour near Fishbourne, from where the Romans set about subduing the Catuvellauni, first on the Medway, and then on the Thames. The Medway battle was won by a flanking movement by the Batavians – special forces expert in swimming in full armour. Togodumnus, one of the Catuvellaunian leaders, was killed, but his brother Caratacus lived to fight another day. Claudius arrived with reinforcements, artillery and elephants for the attack on Camulodunum (Colchester) the Iron Age *oppidum* which was their key objective. After sixteen days, according to Dio, the stronghold fell, after which Cogidubnus was installed as a client king and Claudius returned to Rome, his victory celebrated with a triumphal arch.[15]

Aulus Plautius got on with the job of subduing Britannia, advancing inland. The IXth advanced through the north-eastern territories of the Catuvellauni into the Coritani lands in modern Leicestershire and Lincolnshire, establishing fortresses near the borders with the Iceni and the Brigantes, both client states. The XIVth marched north-west, quelling the remaining pockets of Catuvellaunian resistance before conquering the Dobunni in what is Gloucestershire today. The IInd went south-west, where they conquered first the Belgae of Wiltshire and Hampshire, then the Durotriges in Somerset and Dorset. It was assisted by the *Classis Britanniae* – 'the British Fleet' – whose role it was to build naval supply depots at Chichester, in the lands of the Regnenses, another client state. The XXth were kept in reserve at Colchester, the site of a future *colonia*.

Tacitus records that later, Plautius' wife, Pomponia Graecina, was tried before a family court for her alleged involvement in 'some foreign superstition' – probably dabbling in Christianity. As was standard procedure, Plautius presided over the court; she was aquitted. This was the theme of Sienkiewicz's novel *Quo Vadis?* and the subsequent film of the same name. Pomponia it was who remained in mourning for forty long years in stubborn defiance of the emperor after the execution of her relative Julia Drusi Caesaris by Claudius and Messalina on trumped up charges of incest and immorality. Suetonius gossips about the unfortunate fate of Plautius' son (also Aulus Plautius):

[Nero] put to death Antonia, daughter of Claudius [the emperor], for refusing to marry him after Poppaea's death, charging her with an attempt at revolution; and he treated in the same way all others who were in any way connected with him by blood or by marriage. Among these was the young Aulus Plautius, whom he forcibly defiled before his death saying 'Let my mother come now and kiss my successor,' openly charging that Agrippina had loved Plautius and that this had roused him to hopes of the throne.[16]

Tacitus describes the in-fighting and divisiveness that was characteristic of the British tribes and which was ultimately responsible for their conquest: 'and so they fight individually, and all are conquered.' Nevertheless, they are generally compliant and toe the line, so long as their trust is not abused (*iniuriae absint*).

Plautius was made governor of the new province, until AD 47, when he was replaced by Publius Ostorius Scapula. Dio records that, on his return to Rome in 46 AD, 'Plautius, for his skilfull and successful conduct of the war in Britain, not only was praised by Claudius but also obtained an ovation.'[17] The emperor walked with his friend to the Capitol.

Now that Augustus had reserved the triumph exclusively for members of the imperial family, Claudius honoured Plautius with the next best thing. In an *ovatio*, the conquering commander entered Rome on a caparisoned horse instead of the triumphal chariot; he did not redden his face with red lead in imitation of a terracotta image of triumphant Mars; but he did follow the same route through the city. Plautius' *ovatio* was to be the last time the distinction was granted to anyone outside of the imperial family. Claudius was related to Plautius through his first marriage to Plautia Urgulanilla.[18]

The area corresponding to modern-day Wales, however, proved particularly intractable, with fierce resistance coming from the Silures, Ordovices and Deceangli. Caratacus and his guerrilla attacks were a real problem; in northern England, the Brigantes and the Iceni were also troublesome. In AD 51, things came to a head when Publius Ostorius Scapula defeated the Silures under Caratacus. He fled to the Brigantes, but Queen Cartimandua treacherously handed him over to the Romans, whence he was sent to Rome, a reluctant star in Claudius' triumph. The Silures, however, would still not lie down, and Cartimandua's former husband, Venutius, a hater of the name of Rome – '*Romani nominis odium*' – took over the mantle of leader of British resistance against Rome.[19]

Cartimandua had probably been leader of the Brigantes well before Claudius invaded and may well be one of the eleven monarchs who surrendered to Rome without a fight, as described on Claudius' triumphal arch.[20] She was now considerably wealthy, due to her shrewd support of Rome and her betrayal of Caratacus. However, Venutius attacked the Brigantes, only failing to defeat them when the Romans sent Caesius Nasica and the IXth (*Hispana*) to help Cartimandua.[21]

She had married Vellocatus, former armour-bearer to Venutius, and made him her king. Although Tacitus records that Cartimandua was a good ally of Rome's and acknowledges her *nobilitas*, he savages her in much the same way as Propertius and Horace had destroyed Cleopatra.[22] He describes her treatment of Caratacus as *per dolum* – 'evilly-intended' – and highlights her wealth and luxurious lifestyle. Her liaison with Vellocatus is adulterous and driven by rage and lust; it is a disgraceful act – '*flagitium*' – which shook the very foundations of her dynasty. She is '*regina*' (a dirty word in Rome, thanks to Cleopatra) and is duplicitous in her behaviour towards Venutius and his family. Tacitus disparages the power that she wields as being ignominious to men. The next powerful woman, the next British queen the Romans encountered, was to prove even more belligerent and somewhat less compliant.

One of the ways in which local tribes could guarantee peaceful co-existence with Rome was to bequeath to the Romans their lands on the death of the king or queen. Prasutagus, prosperous king of the Iceni (inhabiting what is roughly today's East Anglia), did just that, citing Nero as heir but with a not unreasonable additional clause naming his daughters as co-heirs. The Iceni had been on friendly terms since the early days of the invasion. On the king's death in AD 60, however, the Romans chose to ignore the small print in the king's will and proceeded to take over the kingdom and plunder it. The Iceni's status as *civitas peregrine* – 'foreign state' – was annulled. Perhaps it was naive of the Iceni to expect an extension of the special relationship after Prasutagus' death, but the aftermath of the decision was shocking, brutal and highly provocative. Prasutagus' daughters were raped, Queen Boudica, his wife, was flogged, the family was treated like slaves and his Roman creditors called in their loans – loans which the Iceni had been led to believe were gifts.[23] According to Dio, Seneca the Younger was one such creditor, demanding payment of loans to the tune of 40 million sesterces. Boudica was humiliated and outraged.

Tacitus describes how trouble between the Britons and Rome had been brewing for some time.[24] A deplorable breach of trust, the high-handed treatment of Prasutagus' family and the growing burden of occupation provided the litmus paper that sparked revolution. We hear of *servitus*, *iniuriae*, *subiecti* and *contumelia*: slavery, injustice, subjugation and abuse. The Romans are greedy and rapacious cowards; they are driven by avarice and riotous living – *avaritia* and *luxuria*. The Iceni and other tribes had been disarmed by Ostorius Scapula, *legatus* from AD 57 to 62, a cause of great resentment to the Iceni, who believed they were a client kingdom and therefore immune from such treatment. The Roman veterans in Camulodunum behaved with contempt and arrogance towards the natives. The Britons had had enough: they had begun to plan a violent response.[25]

Tacitus describes Boudica as a woman of royal and noble birth, pointing out that it was, unlike in Rome, not unusual for a woman to lead a British army. The only other description we have of Boudica comes from Cassius Dio, writing at the end of the second century AD, who vividly describes her as follows:

> all this ruin was brought upon the Romans by a woman, a fact which in itself caused them the greatest shame. ... But the person who was chiefly instrumental in rousing the natives and persuading them to fight the Romans, the person who was thought worthy to be their leader and who directed the conduct of the entire war, was Buduica, a Briton woman of the royal family and possessed of greater intelligence than often belongs to women. ... In stature she was very tall, in appearance most terrifying, in the glance of her eye most fierce, and her voice was harsh; a great mass of the tawniest hair fell to her hips; around her neck was a large golden necklace; and she wore a tunic of divers colours over which a thick mantle was fastened with a brooch. This was her invariable attire. She now grasped a spear to aid her in terrifying all beholders.[26]

It is impossible to tell how true a representation of the woman this is. It probably depends as much on a Boudica legend that grew over the intervening 100 years as anything else. Dio would have been careful to build her up – the bigger the woman, the bigger Rome's success in defeating her. He echoes the typical Roman man's anxiety at being outclassed by a mere woman and grudgingly accepts that she was intelligent, unusual for a woman, and a capable strategist, something else to be feared. Physically she was big, frightening, a bit common and gaudily attired; like the elegant and classy Cleopatra, she was another unwelcome antithesis to the discrete, unobtrusive, compliant and modestly attired traditional Roman *matrona*.

At the time, Gaius Suetonius Paulinus, the Roman governor, was preoccupied with trying to take Mona, modern Anglesey. The objective was to eradicate the exiled druid community there and end the island's status as a haven for disaffected refugees. Druidism was feared by the Romans, not least because of its reputation for focusing opposition to Roman rule and the mystery surrounding the arcane rites; druids were also known for their veneration of the human head, which led to routine decapitation of corpses after battles. This head-hunting can be seen depicted on Trajan's Column. According to Tacitus, the druids had a reputation for 'soaking their altars in the blood of prisoners and using human entrails in their divination.'[27] Paulinus' soldiers lined up opposite an armed pack, among which were 'women dressed in black robes with dishevelled hair like Furies, brandishing torches. Next to them were the druids, their hands raised to the skies, screaming fearsome curses.' The Romans were at first paralyzed with fear but then attacked, slaughtered all before them and hacked down the sacred groves.[28]

The time was ripe for rebellion. The Iceni under Boudica marched on Camulodunum with its Temple of Claudius, a citadel symbolic of oppressive Roman rule and the seat of their servitude. The Iceni were joined by the disaffected Trinovantes, the tribe that had been displaced and enslaved to make way for the *colonia*. The omens were not good for the Romans: 'the statue of Victory in Camulodunum crashed to the ground, supine as if in flight; lamentations, though no mortal man had uttered the words or the groan,' hysterical women chanted impending doom, 'at night there was heard to issue from the senate-house foreign jargon mingled with laughter, and from the theatre outcries and a ghost town on the Thames was seen to be in ruins and the Channel turned blood red; shapes like bodies were washed up.'[29] More crucially, Camulodunum was not fortified and largely undefended – Suetonius Paulinus had fatefully posted the XXth legion to the Welsh borders. The procurator was found wanting: when the Roman inhabitants clamoured for reinforcements, Catus Decianus sent a mere 200 auxiliary troops.

The *colonia* was sacked and the temple fell after two days; the savagery of Boudica's forces was uncompromising. The IXth legion under Petillius Cerealis rushed to relieve the defenders but was annihilated. Catus Decianus fled to Gaul. Suetonius reached Londinium (London), an important but undefended trading port; he calculated that it was impossible to defend with the forces at his disposal. Londinium was abandoned and those left behind were slaughtered in the carnage that ensued. Tacitus paints a wretched picture of the doomed city, and of Suetonius' dilemma:

Alarmed by this disaster and by the fury of the province which he had goaded into war by his rapacity, the procurator Catus crossed over into Gaul.[30] Suetonius, however, with wonderful resolution, marched amidst a hostile population to Londinium, which, though undistinguished by the name of a colony, was much frequented by a number of merchants and trading vessels. Uncertain whether he should choose it as a seat of war, as he looked round on his scanty force of soldiers, and remembered with what a serious warning the rashness of Petilius had been punished, he resolved to save the province at the cost of a single town. Nor did the tears and weeping of the people, as they implored his aid, deter him from giving the signal of departure and receiving into his army all who would go with him. Those who were chained to the spot by the weakness of their sex, or the infirmity of age, or the attractions of the place, were cut off by the enemy.

Excavations have revealed a thick red layer of burnt detritus covering coins and pottery dating before AD 60.

Euphoric and drunk on their easy successes, the Britons then devastated Verulamium (St Albans), a stronghold of the pro-Roman Catuvellauni. According to (an exaggerating) Tacitus, up to 80,000 men, women and children were slain in the orgy of destruction visited on the three towns by Boudica's forces. The Britons were not in the habit of taking prisoners; they had no interest in selling slaves, and so they showed no quarter. The only options were slaughter, hanging, burning alive and crucifixion. Dio's account is even more graphic: he says that the noblest women were impaled on sharpened spikes the length of their bodies and that their breasts were hacked off and sewn onto their mouths, 'to the accompaniment of sacrifices, feasts, and lewd behaviour' sacrilegiously performed in sacred places, like the groves of Andraste, a British goddess of victory.[31]

Suetonius hurriedly assembled a force of around 10,000 men and prepared for battle, the Battle of Watling Street. His army included his own XIVth legion (*Gemina*) and units from the XXth (*Valeria Victrix*); the IInd legion under Poenius Postumus, near Exeter, did not respond. The 10,000 was massively outnumbered by Boudica's 230,000 – no doubt a huge exaggeration but Boudica had a substantial superiority. As Dio says, even if the Romans were lined up one-deep, they would not have reached the end of Boudica's line. So casual and confident was Boudica's army of victory that women were allowed to attend as spectators in wagons on the edge of the battlefield. Boudica herself rallied her troops from a chariot, her raped daughters before her: in a rousing speech recorded by Tacitus she declared that there was nothing unusual about a woman commander amongst the British and invoked her lineage from mighty men, 'and indeed it was usual for Britons to fight under the leadership of women.' She was fighting for her kingdom, her freedom and to avenge her battered body and her violated daughters, 'the chastity of the daughters violated.' She was intent in wiping out the *stuprum* (depravity) inflicted on her daughters and restoring their violated *pudicitia* (chastity). The Romans slay the elderly and rape virgins: 'They do not leave even the elderly or virgins undefiled.' The Romans are cowards, and the Iceni and she, a woman, will defeat them. She concludes by affirming her resolve, the resolve of a woman: men can live in servitude (if that is what they want), but she certainly will not.[32]

Paulinus' speech to his men takes up the gender theme when he disparagingly declares that there are more women in the ranks of the Britons than men. The speech is somewhat more sympathetic and respectful than Dio's description of the decidedly un-Roman queen. Tacitus, in what is no doubt a swipe at Roman imperialism, is, nevertheless, at pains to recognize Boudica's lineage and to emphasize her motives: she is driven by a will to extinguish the stain inflicted on her daughters' chastity, to avenge the humiliation of her flogging and to restore the liberty of her people. Such motives were very Roman: *pudicitia* (chastity), avoidance of *stuprum* (depravity) and *pietas* (duty) for the family were vital qualities in a Roman matron; freedom from tyranny and personal pride were good Roman aspirations and hallmarks of *Romanitas* (proper Roman conduct). Tacitus even plays down the enormity of the very thought of a woman with a successful military career, a woman with the temerity to do battle with men. Nothing could be more un-Roman, as exemplified only by two wives of the damned-from-memory and disgraced Mark Antony: Fulvia Furia Bibacula and that other exotic, foreign queen, Cleopatra VII.

Dio gives Boudica a less personal, more typically rhetorical battle speech: she appeals to the loss of freedom and relentless servitude imposed upon the Britons by the Romans and the grinding poverty they had caused. She outlines the strategic advantages held by the Britons: knowledge of the local area; versatility; no cumbersome, heavy armour; and sheer bravery. After divination to Adraste, in which Boudica let go a hare from the folds of her robe and interpreted the direction in which it ran, the battle commenced.[33]

Unfortunately, there was to be no victory; Boudica was soundly defeated. The Britons were hampered by their poor manoeuvrability and inexperience of disciplined open-field tactics. The narrowness of the battlefield restricted the numbers Boudica could deploy at any one time, thus reducing her numerical advantage. Moreover, the Britons were felled in their droves by the Roman *pilae*, which rained down on them.

Even women and animals were slain, and her retreating soldiers were hampered by the wagons nearby, full of spectators. According to Tacitus (exaggerating again), 80,000 Britons died that day, to the Romans' loss of 400. No doubt there was more rape; it is not known what happened to her daughters. Boudica committed suicide by poisoning. Dio disputes this, or at least paraphrases the detail out of the same story, and claims that Boudica fell ill and died, and was buried at great expense and with full honours.

Postumus fell on his sword. Catus Decianus was replaced by Gaius Julius Alpinus Classicianus. Suetonius instigated reprisals but was replaced by the more conciliatory Publius Petronius Turpilianus to avoid sparking another revolt. The pretext for his removal was that he had apparently lost some of the ships in the Roman fleet. If Suetonius, the historian, is to be believed, the crisis almost made Nero abandon Britannia.[34]

During his reprisals, Suetonius devastated Iceni territory, with many of the surviving rebels sold into slavery, and 'whatever tribes still wavered or were hostile were ravaged with fire and sword.'[35] The prospect, and reality, of famine was heightened because the Britons had apparently failed to sow the seeds for the year's harvest, over-optimistically assuming they could live off plundered Roman supplies. It is likely that Britannia went into recession, even depression: the agricultural workforce was severely depleted through casualties, disablement and enslavement. What little evidence we have of Romanization immediately after the revolt comes from the rebuilding of London, as a civil rather than a military community, as destroyed by Boudica. In the AD 70s there was reconstruction work at Verulamium and civic projects at Exeter and Cirencester. Nero sent over from Germany 2,000 legionaries, eight cohorts of auxiliaries, and 1,000 cavalry to make good the Roman losses. In the short term, the Romans had to win back the hearts and minds of the British aristocracy, something they had obviously lost during and after the revolt, particularly after Suetonius' savage reprisals. Tacitus hints that there was some success here when he says, not without a sneer, that the Britons were beginning to enjoy the fruits of peace and the allurements of civilization under Trebellius Maximus, governor from AD 63. The long-term effect of Boudica's revolt for the Romans was, quite simply, to increase their resolve to Romanize Britannia – a feat which was accomplished under the governorship of Agricola, Tacitus' father-in-law, some twenty years later after his victory at the decisive Battle of Mons Graupius in AD 83.

Tacitus' *Agricola 21* gives us something of a template for the process of Romanization, although it must be viewed in the light of the undeniable fact that Tacitus was keen to lionise his father-in-law, and that he cynically saw the process as just another form of servitude in which the locals turned soft:

The following winter passed without disturbance, and was employed in salutary measures. For, to accustom to rest and repose through the charms of luxury a population scattered and barbarous and therefore inclined to war, Agricola gave private encouragement and public aid to the building of temples, courts of justice and dwelling-houses, praising the energetic, and reproving the indolent. Thus an honourable rivalry took the place of compulsion. He likewise provided a liberal education for the sons of the chiefs, and showed such a preference for the natural powers of the Britons over the industry of the Gauls that they who lately disdained the tongue of Rome now coveted its eloquence. Hence, too, a liking sprang up for our style of dress, and the *toga* became fashionable. Step by step they were led to things which dispose to vice, the lounge, the bath, the elegant banquet. All this in their ignorance, they called civilization, when it was but a part of their servitude.[36]

If Boudica was loathed by some Romans in the years following her death, then the verdict of St Gildas (*c.* 500–570), or *Gildas Sapiens,* a British monk, probably outdoes them for vitriol. In his searing polemic *De Excidio et Conquestu Britanniae,* a history of the Britons before and during the the the Saxon period, he calls her 'a treacherous lioness' who 'butchered the governors' and had been left to give fuller voice and strength to the endeavours of Roman rule. The tract includes a description of the Roman occupation and the *Groans of the Britons,* in which the Britons request military assistance from the departed Roman army.[37]

The memory of Boudica faded and died until Victoria resurrected her as an icon of womanly bravery, patriotism and determination. Tennyson composed his *Boadicea* and Prince Albert commissioned Thomas Thornycroft to create a statue of Boudica and her daughters riding a war chariot, which now charges along the Embankment. The urban myth that she is buried beneath platforms nine and ten in King's Cross Station is just that, an urban myth. If anything, it probably stems from the fact that King's Cross was originally a village known as Battle Bridge, named after some battle or other – an ancient crossing of the River Fleet.

We have seen how war chariots had a part to play in reverses the Romans suffered at the hands of Mithridates, the Parthians and the Britons. In its early days, the war chariot was a highly mobile light vehicle, usually with two wheels, pulled by one or more horses or donkeys and driven by two standing combatants, a driver and a fighter using missiles such as bow-and-arrow or javelins.[38] It was the original artillery platform. A *biga* involved two horses, a *triga* three and a *quadriga* four horses. The spoked wheel, with its benefits of greater speed, helped in the deployment of the chariot. It seems likely that the chariot was developed to compensate for the fact that the considerably more manoeverable and fleeter horse was at the time not strong enough to support an armed and armoured soldier. Fighting from horseback came some 1,500 years after the invention of the chariot.

We hear first of war chariots from Syria around 1800 BC; the Hittites used chariots to establish their first kingdom about 1700 BC; Rameses II of Egypt sent 5,000 chariots to subdue the Hittites in 1286 BC. The Greeks used chariots to attack Troy, but by and large they never caught on as a weapon of war with the Greeks due to their mountainous terrain. In China, an aristocracy of charioteers was involved in setting up the first dynasty there, the Shang, from 1600 BC. Mycenaeans took on the chariot, which may have helped them in their fight against the Minoans in 1400 BC, as recorded in the arsenal inventories, and described in Linear B tablets from the fifteenth century BC. Herodotus tells us that chariots were used by the Sigynnae in the Pontic-Caspian steppe.

The chariot became a prestigious symbol of status, with kings commissioning images of themselves doing battle in a chariot; this soon filtered down into aristocracies where the chariot was a badge of wealth and power. Horse breeding was developed to obtain the right strength and horse power. At the famous Battle of Kadesh in 1294 BC, between Egypt and the Hittites, fifty chariots were deployed on each side. Decline in military use began about 500 BC due to the rise of the more versatile war horse pioneered by the Scythians. Iron weapons too were more effective aginst the chariot, while phalanx formations made it diffcult for charioteers to penetrate enemy infantry. We get our word 'car' from the Latin *carrum*, meaning 'wagon'.

Chariots were also used in hunting and in sporting contests, such as the Greek Olympic and Panathenaic Games and other public festivals, and in the 150,000-seat Circus Maximus in Rome. The first recorded Olympic chariot race was about 680 BC. The Olympia hippodrome could accommodate sixty chariot races, which could either be of the two- or four-horse variety. An intact Etruscan burial chariot dated to 530 BC was uncovered at Monteleone di Spoleto. Now in the Metropolitan Museum of Art, it is decorated with episodes from the life of Achilles.

In Greek mythology, the chariot was invented by Erichthonius of Athens to hide his feet, which took the form of a dragon. The most famous appearance is in the story of Phaëton, the son of Helios, who tried to drive the chariot of the sun, but only succeeded in setting the earth on fire. This gives us our word, *phaeton*, one who drives a chariot or coach at a dangerous speed. Plato has his *Chariot Allegory*, which shows a chariot pulled by two horses, one compliant, the other not, representing opposite aspects of human nature. The job of the charioteer, representing reason, was to keep the horses from going off in different directions and to guide them towards enlightenment.[39]

A particularly nasty development was the scythed chariot, introduced by the Persians, on which blades extend horizontally from the axle of the chariot. It was very effective against the tight phalanx formations of the Greeks between 467 BC and 458 BC, pulled by a team of four horses and manned by a crew of up to three men – a driver and two fighters. Xenophon (430–354 BC) saw them as an eyewitness at the Battle of Cunaxa, and describes them as 'thin scythes extending at an angle from the axles and also under the driver's seat, turned toward the ground.' The scythed chariot would literally scythe through infantry lines, cutting enemy soldiers in half, slicing off their legs and opening gaps in the line.

For the Romans, the chariot was, by and large, a weapon of war wielded by the enemy, for instance at the Battle of Zela in 47 BC, or else used ceremonially, such as in triumphal processions or in chariot racing. Pomponius Mela asserts they were used in Britain during Claudius' invasion: 'They make war not only on horseback but also from two-horse chariots and cars armed in the Gallic fashion – they call them *covinni* – on which they use axles equipped with scythes.'[40]

The Romans' answer to the scythed chariot was the caltrops; Frontinus tells us that the Romans fixed vertical posts in the ground behind which their infantry were safe. The *Scriptores Historiae Augustae* on Severus Alexander exaggerates that he captured 1,800 scythed chariots.[41]

In the late empire, *De Rebus Bellicis* may refer to cataphract-style fighters sitting on a chariot comprising just an axle with wheels, where the blades are lowered at the last moment in an attack.[42] The Celts were the undisputed champions of the chariot; they continued to use chariots until around the fourth century AD. Twenty or so iron-age chariot burials from between 500 BC and 100 BC have been excavated in Britain, mostly from East Yorkshire. Julius Caesar had first-hand battle experience of the British war chariot:

Their mode of fighting with their chariots is this: firstly, they drive about in all directions and throw their weapons and generally break the ranks of the enemy with the very dread of their horses and the noise of their wheels; and when they have worked themselves in between the troops of horse, leap from their chariots and engage on foot. The charioteers in the meantime withdraw some little distance from the battle, and so place themselves with the chariots that, if their masters are overpowered by the number of the enemy, they may have a ready retreat to their own troops. Thus they display in battle the speed of horse, [along with] the firmness of infantry; and by daily practice and exercise attain to such expertness that they are accustomed, even on a declining and steep place, to check their horses at full speed, and manage and turn them in an instant and run along the pole, and stand on the yoke, and thence betake themselves with the greatest celerity to their chariots again.[43]

In Britain, the chariot makes its last attested appearance soon after the destruction of Boudica's army, at the Battle of Mons Graupius where the Britons were defeated by Agricola:

The plain between resounded with the noise and with the rapid movements of chariots and cavalry. Meantime the enemy's cavalry had fled, and the charioteers had mingled in the engagement of the infantry.[44]

Chapter 11

Beth-Horon AD 66 and the Jewish War AD 68

S ome eight years after Boudica, the Romans had to deal with serious insurrection at the other extremity of their Empire. Judea first fell under Rome's gaze in 63 BC when, during the Third Mithridatic War, Pompey intervened in the civil war between Hyrcanus II, who supported the Pharisees, and Aristobulus II, who supported the Sadducees. Pompey and Hyrcanus II laid siege to Jerusalem, which fell after three months. Judea was secured for Rome.

Later, Herod the Great (r. 37–4 BC) was installed as client king of Judea by the Romans who, in 37 BC, helped him to oust the Parthian-backed leader Antigonus II Mattathias, the last Hasmonean king of Judea. Soon after Herod's death, Judea was partitioned among his sons to create a tetrarchy: Archelaus became ethnarch of Judea, Herod Antipas tetrarch of Galilee and Peraea, and Philip tetrarch of territories east of the River Jordan.

But, due to local difficulties, it all came under direct Roman control and in AD 6 became a Roman province, governed by Roman prefects. On one level there was stability – due in large part to the agreement fixed by Augustus whereby the Romans exercised religious tolerance with the Jews while the Jews, or rather the High Priest and the wealthy landowning Sanhedrin, tolerated Roman rule. On another level there was no such satisfaction; many Jews resented the occupation and looked forward to the day when the Messiah would return to deliver them from the Romans. They marked their anticipation with insurrection. From AD 6, bands of terrorists, *sicarii* – or knife-men – attacked Roman census officials, melting back into the desert after their assaults. These bandits were not only inimical to the Romans, they were the sworn enemies of the Zealots, the opposing faction of Jews who made up the majority of the rebels against Rome.

In AD 40, Caligula almost wrecked the fragile peace when he insisted the Jews raise a statue to him in the Temple of Jerusalem. It is difficult to imagine a more incendiary, iconoclastic and tactless act. Caligula vacillated, changing his mind twice, but avoided all-out rebellion by the Zealots. The general situation was, however, exacerbated by the appointment of a series of procurators notable for their corruption and reminiscent of the worst of the Republican perpetrators of provincial corruption. The main cause of the opposition, though, was the rapacity routinely deployed, often with impunity, by the Romans in suppressing the ongoing unrest. Notable was the case of Pontius Pilate (AD 26–36) who, through bungling incompetence, presided over an avoidable massacre of a number of Samaritans on Mount Gerizim.

Initially, the Romans had been mere spectators to the growing internecine ferment in Judea. Their client king Agrippa II tried to restore peace without success; some of those advocating peace, including the former High Priest Ananias, father of Eleazar ben Hanania, were murdered by the Zealots. The 600-strong Roman garrison tried to prevent further hostilities but were besieged in their Jerusalem headquarters for their troubles. Forced to surrender, they were allowed free passage on condition they gave up their weapons. The required oaths were taken and the commander Metilius marched out of the former palace of Herod the Great, believing he and his men were on the road to freedom. As soon as the Romans laid down their arms and armour they were brutally attacked by Eleazar and his fellow terrorists. Nonplussed, the Romans frantically appealed to the oaths and the agreement, but to no avail. They were butchered to a man – that is with the exception of Metilius, who promised to convert to Judaism (and circumcision – humiliating for a Roman). To the pacifist Jews, this atrocity was the end: war was now inevitable and an overwhelming cloak of gloom shrouded them in their guilt.[1]

In AD 66, simmering tensions between Greeks and Jews came to a head when Jewish worshippers suffered the indignity of witnessing Greeks blasphemously sacrificing birds in front of a synagogue in Caesarea and complained to the authorities.[2] The Roman procurator, the inept, venal and corrupt Gessius Florus, refused to intervene, which led to predictable protests against punitive Roman taxation. According to Josephus, swindling individuals was small fry to Florus; the extortion of whole towns was more his game. In one Jewish temple, Eleazar ben Hanania forbad the saying of prayers and the performance of sacrifices for the Romans. As we have seen, religious tolerance was a cornerstone of the political status quo and stability in Judea; prayers and sacrifices were the visible demonstration of this. To Josephus, this was the ultimate slap in the face for the Roman administration and laid 'the foundation of the war with the Romans'.[3]

It seems, though, that the incident was of much greater moment to the Jews than to the Romans. Accordingly, the Romans ignored these protests as well, and it was only when Jews in Jerusalem started attacking Roman citizens that the garrison reacted. The soldiers sent in defence were also assaulted: 6,000 Jews were whipped and crucified in reprisal, while the Temple was looted in an act of iconoclasm. The Jews humiliated and mocked Florus after his raid (he had stolen an insignificant amount of money, purportedly for Caesar's coffers). Florus' response was as swift as it was brutal: he released his troops to wreak rapine and death in the upper market in Jerusalem. The result was wholesale slaughter, in which Jewish homes were looted and 3,600 men, women and children were slain, the women raped, no doubt, beforehand. Others were crushed to death in the narrow alleyways. This marked the beginning of four years of serial atrocity, culminating in the sack of Jerusalem.[4]

But Florus had not quite finished; his savagery continued unabated when he insisted on a humiliating demonstration of Jewish subjugation. A group of Jews were detailed to meet and greet two cohorts of Roman soldiers as they approached Jerusalem. Predictably, the Romans were met with some abuse – the signal for them to lay into the reception committee; the Jews were summarily clubbed to death or suffocated in the crush, or mangled under the horses' hooves. The carnage was such that many of the corpses were unrecognisable.[5]

The news of the riots spread, fanning insurrection in other towns and cities: the pro-Roman king Agrippa II (Herod Agrippa) and his sister Berenice fled Jerusalem to Galilee. After the destruction of the Temple in AD 70, members of the Sicarii fled Jerusalem and settled on Masada. Josephus reports that the Sicarii raided nearby Jewish villages, including Ein Gedi, where they massacred 700 women and children.[6]

Further Roman reaction eventually came in the form of the Nero-sponsored, inexperienced Cestius Gallus, the legate of Syria. He marched on Jerusalem with the XIIth (*Fulminata*) legion, units from the three other legions based in Syria – IIIrd (*Gallica*), IVth (*Scythica*) and VIth (*Ferrata*) – six cohorts of auxiliary infantry and four *alae* of cavalry. These regulars were reinforced by 14,000 allies provided by Agrippa II, Antiochus II and other client rulers. Gallus had first tried diplomacy when he visited the year before, during Passover. He agreed to curb the excesses of Florus and took time gathering intelligence with which to form a rational strategy, even sending an envoy, Neapolitanus, to explore the situation.[7] But the Jews were impetuous: Gallus approached Jerusalem with something of a reputation for massacring civilians and razing villages, notably Lydda during the feast of Tabernacles. To the rebels, this was a red rag to a bull, and they attacked the Romans, killing 550 to their twenty-two casualties.

Agrippa persisted in his rather clumsy attempts to broker a peace. Rome, however, was a willing party, offering an amnesty on condition that the Jews reverted to the original political arrangement. But the rebels were dismissive to the extent that they murdered one of the envoys and injured the other. Gallus took Acre and then Caesarea and Jaffa, where he massacred some

8,400 citizens. Gallus then razed Bezetha and advanced as far as Mount Scopus on the outskirts of Jerusalem. Failing to take the Temple Mount, he halted his advance and prepared to besiege the inner city, deploying a *testudo* to good effect, undermining the wall and burning down the gate. Inside, panic set in, with some inhabitants clamouring to surrender the city to the enemy.

Astonishingly, the Romans suddenly withdrew from Jerusalem and headed towards the coast, always under surveillance by Jewish scouts, through difficult and dangerous territory. Why the seemingly inexplicable change of plan? Josephus alleges that Gallus was bribed by Florus to conceal the latter's corruption and indiscretions. Gallus had apparently lost his siege equipment in an ambush, so he was quite unable to prosecute a siege of Jerusalem; moreover, he was reluctant to be cut off from escape during the coming winter. Whatever, Gallus had been within an ace of bringing the war to a comparatively bloodless end; this extension was certainly going to make it much worse for the Jews, as they were to discover to their bloody cost in AD 70.

The ignominious retreat from Jerusalem was always going to be fraught with peril. It was a terrible strategic decision. When the Romans reached the Beth-Horon pass, 12 miles from Jerusalem, the rebels, under Simon Bar-Giora, predicatably sprang an ambush: missiles and arrows rained down on the Romans before a mass infantry attack by the Judaean infantry. The narrow confines of the pass prevented the Romans from forming any credible defensive formation: 6,000 men and the legion's *aquila* were lost, with the remainder wounded or fleeing in confusion. Gallus escaped with a small contingent back to Antioch, but not before he had sacrificed most of his army and lost tons of *matériel*. The Jewish rebels systematically plundered the Roman dead. This disaster served as a very effective recruitment campaign for the Jews, as more and more towns joined the rebel cause.

For a time, Jerusalem became a hotbed of industry, with the rebels frantically training, churning out arms and building defences to defend against and oppose the inevitable attack.[8] Bad omens were defiantly 'interpreted' as good. The capable Simon, son of Gorias, was given sole command of the defence of the city.

Josephus was in no doubt regarding the false hopes the victory gave to his more pugnacious, deluded countrymen:

Fear we had in no small measure, when we saw the populace in arms, and we were at an impasse as to what to do, having no power to stop the revolutionaries. Being in clear and present danger, we claimed to share their convictions. We did so hoping it would not be long before Cestius would come up with a great force to stop the revolution. But, coming and engaging in battle, he was defeated, and a great many of those that were with him fell. This failure of Cestius was a calamity for our whole nation; for those who loved war were so excited by it that they had hopes in the end of conquering the Romans.[9]

Retribution would be terrible; reprisals would be without mercy. The Romans would make the Jewish people pay dearly for this humiliation – and so it transpired, in AD 70.

Gallus had started his campaign the classic Roman way: terrorizing the locals, scorching crops and torching buildings to undermine the enemy's ability to do battle. His inexperience, however, was clearly evident and critical: he dallied in camp indecisively rather than acting, thus giving the enemy time to rally and plan. Amazingly, he failed to position his baggage train in the middle of his column, thus exposing it to attack and capture. The loss of siege equipment in particular compromised his ability to besiege Jerusalem. He also failed to secure the high ground through which he had to pass.

Gallus died in AD 67. Josephus says he died of shame, having taken full responsibility for the disaster.[10] Tacitus says he died of natural causes or from anxiety.[11] He was succeeded as governor of Syria by Licinius Mucianus. Nero appointed the future emperor Vespasian to the command of the Roman forces in Judaea, with a brief to crush the rebellion. Titus Flavius Vespasian, a veteran of Claudius' invasion of Britain, represented a safe pair of hands. Meanwhile, Menahem ben Yehuda, leader of the Sicarii, attempted to take control of Jerusalem but failed. He was executed, and the remaining Sicarii were expelled from the city.

All Judaea was now caught up in the rebellion, as were Galilee and parts of Transjordania, with wholescale massacres regular events. The appointment of the competent Vespasian was inspired; he was able to suppress Galilee in AD 67 and Transjordania the following year, with an army exceeding 50,000 men. Judaea was now surrounded. However, when Nero committed suicide back in Rome, Vespasian, distracted by the resulting political turmoil, paused, allowing the Jews the opportunity to rally. Internal division and fighting, however, amongst the rebels meant that they squandered the reprieve and their insurrection slowly evaporated.

The predicted revenge exacted by the Romans in Jerusalem soon came. The siege was led by the future emperor Titus and Tiberius Julius Alexander. Simon ben Gioras, Jacob ben Sosias, Eleazar ben Simon and Simon ben Cathlas led the doomed Jews and a combined force of about 25,000 Zealots and Idumeans. The siege ended with the sacking of the city and the destruction of its Second Temple. The sack of Jerusalem and the Temple by Titus can still be seen today on his arch in the forum in Rome.

The city was surrounded with three legions: the Vth (*Macedonica*), XIIth (*Fulminata*) and the XVth (*Apollinaris*). The Xth (*Fretensis*) stood on the Mount of Olives. Titus cleverly turned up the pressure on the food and water supplies when he permitted pilgrims to enter the city for Passover, and then refused to allow them to go back out. Titus sent Josephus to negotiate with the defenders but he came away with nothing more than an arrow wound in the arm. In the fighting, Titus was nearly captured but escaped. Titus then battered to destruction both the newly-built Third Wall and the Second Wall, moving on to the Fortress of Antonia north of the Temple Mount; street fighting with the Zealots followed. Food and water were getting perilously low, but this was offset in a small way by foraging parties bringing supplies into the city. To stop this, the Romans built a new wall and a new siege tower.

Josephus' description of the most harrowing aspects of the predicted famine is truly Lucanesque in its horror. These are the lengths to which the Romans were prepared to go to avenge Beth-Horon:

Children pulled the morsels that their fathers were eating out of their very mouths, and what was still more to be pitied, so did the mothers to their infants; and when those that were most dear were perishing under their hands, they were not ashamed to take from them the very last drops that might preserve their lives: and while they ate after this manner, yet were they not concealed in so doing; but the seditious everywhere came upon them immediately, and snatched away from them what they had got from others; for when they saw any house shut up, this was to them a signal that the people within had got some food; whereupon they broke open the doors, and ran in, and took pieces of what they were eating almost up out of their very throats, and this by force: the old men, who held their food fast, were beaten; and if the women hid what they had within their hands, their hair was torn for so doing; nor was there any commiseration shown either to the aged or to the infants, but they lifted up children from the ground as they hung upon the morsels they had got, and shook them down upon the floor. But still they were more barbarously cruel to those that had prevented their coming in, and had actually swallowed down what they were going to seize upon, as if they had been unjustly defrauded of their right. They also invented terrible methods of torments to discover where any food was, and they were these: to stop up the passages of the privy parts of the miserable wretches, and to drive sharp stakes up their fundaments; and a man was forced to bear what it is terrible even to hear, in order to make him confess that he had but one loaf of bread, or that he might discover a handful of barley-meal that was concealed; and this was done when these tormentors were not themselves hungry; for the thing had been less barbarous had necessity forced them to it; but this was done to keep their madness in exercise, and as making preparation of provisions for themselves for the following days.[12]

Incredible as it may be, the description is eclipsed by Josephus when he gives an illustration of a woman called Mary who is forced by starvation into cannibalism. She roasts her breastfeeding baby and devours half the body:

As soon as she had said this, she slew her son, and then roasted him, and ate the one half of him, and kept the other half by her concealed. Upon this the seditious came in presently, and smelling the horrid scent of this food, they threatened her that they would cut her throat immediately if she did not show them what food she had gotten ready. She replied that she had saved a very fine portion of it for them, and withal uncovered what was left of her son. Hereupon they were seized with a horror and amazement of mind, and stood astonished at the sight ... those men went out trembling, being never so much affrighted at any thing as they were at this, and with some difficulty they left the rest of that meat to the mother.[13]

The city eventually fell to the Romans on September 7 and was systematically destroyed. Josephus records that 1.1 million people were butchered after the siege, most of whom were Jewish; 97,000 were captured and sold into slavery.[14] He sums up the carnage as follows:

The slaughter inside was even more awful than the spectacle seen from outside. Men and women, old and young, insurgents and priests, combatants and those who wanted mercy, were mowed down in indiscriminate carnage. There was more slain than slayers. The legionaries had to clamber over heaps of dead to proceed with their extermination.

Josephus – a priest from Jerusalem (*c.* AD 37–AD 100) – is our principal source for Beth-Horon and for the Jewish Wars generally. He was born Joseph ben Mattathias. Josephus was well placed to write his seven-book *Jewish War* since he had the dubious privilege of seeing the conflict from both the Jewish and the Roman side. Initially something of a guerilla, he fought as a (somewhat indifferent) rebel general for the Jews until his capture in AD 67 at Yodfat, the besieged Jewish garrison. After this, he was able to observe the progress of the uprising from inside Roman headquarters, later as a Roman citizen blessed with a pension. Yodfat fell after forty-seven days through treachery, the Romans butchering 40,000 Jews and enslaving 1,200 women and children. Yodfat was razed and the survivors committed suicide.

According to Josephus, he was trapped in a cave there with forty of his companions. The Romans led by Vespasian and his son Titus offered the group surrender, only to be refused. Josephus' cunning plan was to try collective suicide: the group would draw lots and kill each other, one by one, counting to every third person. The only survivor was Josephus, who surrendered to the Romans and was taken prisoner, then released in AD 69. Josephus explained away his dissimulation in the cave and apparent treachery in deserting to the Romans through visions of God telling him to accept the inevitability of Roman rule and to join the winning side.

His influence in Rome was such that he had found himself negotiating with the influential Poppaea, Nero's wife at the time, on the release of Jewish priests, and then ingratiating himself with Vespasian in AD 69, and Titus.[15] Josephus had prophesied through Jewish Messianic prophecies the elevation of Vespasian to the purple – a shrewd prediction which did his later career no harm. A flattered Vespasian assumed that Josephus had divine qualites and made him a slave and interpreter. On becoming emperor in AD 69, Vespasian gave Josephus his freedom; Josephus assumed the emperor's family name of Flavius. Josephus quickly latched on to his own good fortune: he believed that his revelation had taught him three things: that God, the creator of the Jewish people, had decided to 'punish' them; that 'fortune' had been given to the Romans; and that God had chosen him 'to announce the things that are to come.' He was obviously in good favour, installed in Vespasian's former residence with plenty of time to write his *Jewish War*, *Jewish Antiquities* and other works.

Given Josephus' hinterland, we can hardly expect him always to be objective. Indeed, he himself admits that his work is inevitably infused with and freighted by emotion and sentiment for the country of his birth. Josephus does indeed look boths ways, and it is this dichotomy which must be kept in mind as we read through his *War* and the sometimes contradictory *Antiquities*. Mary Smallwood assesses the man well:

[Josephus] was conceited, not only about his own learning but also about the opinions held of him as commander both by the Galileans and by the Romans; he was guilty of shocking duplicity at Jotapata [Yodfat], saving himself by sacrifice of his companions; he was too naive to see how he stood condemned out of his own mouth for his conduct, and yet no words were too harsh when he was blackening his opponents; and after landing, however involuntarily, in the Roman camp, he turned his captivity to his own advantage, and benefited for the rest of his days from his change of side.[16]

The Romans were determined to wipe out Jewish resistance once and for all. What little opposition remained after Jerusalem emanated from Herodium, to the south of Jerusalem, Machaerus on the east bank of the Dead Sea and Masada on the west bank. Vespasian deputed Lucilius Bassus to exterminate the resistance. Herodium and Machaerus quickly surrendered. Refugees from Jerusalem who had escaped through the city's sewers were annihilated at the Forest of Jardes. This left Masada as the sole pocket of Jewish opposition, to be dealt with by Flavius Silva. As we have seen, Masada was occupied by the Sicarii; these rebels had estranged themselves from the Jewish cause, content to devastate and plunder and kill their compatriots in the surrounding region, which they reduced to a desert. As noted, the massacre at Ein Gedi was the pinnacle of their five-year-long atrocity.

Lucius Flavius Silva arrived with the Xth legion at fortress Masada in 73 AD, faced with about 1,000 Sicarii and various refugees from Jerusalem and Qumran, including women and children. The citadel was well provisioned with water, weapons and ammunition, but the seemingly impregnable Masada was effectively a dead end: the rebels had no means of escape – defeat was only a matter of time. The Romans raised their 114m ramp on the western face to the level of the plateau and destroyed the two defensive walls with a battering ram in a day. During its construction, the Jews threw down rocks and boulders onto the Roman builders, who quickly replaced them with Jewish prisoners. Masada fell to Silva: Josephus reports that when the Romans troops entered the fortress, they found that all the buildings except the food stores had been torched; the 960 defenders had committed mass suicide or killed each other. The few Sicarii who survived fled to rebellious communities in Alexandria and Cyrenaica, but they were soon exposed and murdered.

The Romans never let the Jews forget the Jewish Revolt; their reprisals were severe, designed to emasculate the Jewish nation and deny the Jews their nationhood. The temple would not be rebuilt and the Sanhedrin and the High Priesthood were abolished. Jews were still paying the Jewish tax, *Fiscus Judaicus*, in the third century AD, imposed as punishment for the events of AD 66–70, after which it was extended to all Jewish women and children and the elderly, irrespective of where they lived in the empire. Originally, it was levied only on Jewish males between the ages of 20 and 50 living in Judaea. All Jews in Judaea were dispossessed, refugees in their own country. The massacre of the Jews and the sacking of Jerusalem, despite Titus' unsuccessful attempts at restraint, would serve as a poignant and vivid reminder to all those peoples living within the borders of the Roman Empire. This is what can happen if and when Roman rule is rejected; indeed, what can happen, as recently did in Britain, when anyone has the temerity to defeat a Roman legion and inflict a disaster on Rome.[17]

The fall of Jerusalem, of course, was not just a Roman triumph taken as revenge for a Roman disaster. It had far-reaching, inestimable repercussions and ramifications on the western world and it galvanized the spread of Christianity through a hostile and punitive world. Many Jews fled to other parts of the empire, thus marking the start of the diaspora; Judaea was effectively erased from the map in a kind of national *damnatio memoriae*; Hadrian changed the name of Judaea to Syria Palaestina. The teachings of the *Torah*, the Sabbath, circumcision, the Gezeirah and the Age of the Decree were all outlawed. Jews were only allowed to enter Jerusalem once a year, in order to mourn their calamity; the Romans built a temple to Jupiter on the site of Herod's temple. The pagan city of Aelia Capitolina was built on the ashes of Jerusalem.

Jewish and Christan scholars alike see the Jewish revolt and its consequences as the point at which the schism opened up between the followers of Jesus (no more than a sect of Judaism until then) and mainstream Judaism. The savage reprisals imposed on the Jews led to a second revolt under Simon Bar Kokhba, Son of the Star, and seen as the Messiah. Over time, weapons had been stockpiled and a honeycomb of tunnels was built. The Jews rose up in AD 132 and established an independent sovereign state, minting their own coinage, restoring the Sanhedrin and the High Priesthood, annexing Roman estates and sub-letting them to Jewish peasants. This final Jewish revolt was effectively suppressed by Hadrian at the siege of Bethar – a strategic town near to Jerusalem – in AD 135, but not without serious Roman losses earlier in the campaign, according to Dio, and the deployment of no fewer than twelve legions. Every Jew was slain: the *Talmud* tells us that the Romans persisted with their slaughter 'until their horses were submerged in blood up to their nostrils.' Fifty Jewish strongholds and nearly 1,000 villages were wiped off the map. The death toll amongst the Jews was 580,000 according to Dio; we do not know for certain if that huge number included the many children who were wrapped in *Torah* scrolls and burnt alive by the Romans:

> There were four hundred synagogues in the city of Bethar, and in every one were four hundred teachers of children, and each one had under him four hundred pupils [400 × 400 × 400 = 64 million Jewish children], and when the enemy entered there they pierced them with their staves, and when the enemy prevailed and captured them, they wrapped them in their scrolls and burnt them with fire.[18]

Jerusalem and Masada are two of history's most atrocious sieges. Siege warfare started when communities such as the Assyrians from around 3500 BC started building city walls and other such fortifications. Famous examples include the Sumerian city of Uruk, whose walls were 9.5km in length and up to 12m (39ft) high. Later, the walls of Babylon were reinforced by towers, moats and ditches; the Hittites erected huge stone walls around their hilltop cities. The earliest images of siege warfare originate from Egypt in around 3000 BC. The first known siege equipment is shown on Egyptian tomb reliefs of the twenty-fourth century BC, depicting Egyptian troops storming Canaanite town walls on wheeled siege ladders. Temple reliefs of the thirteenth century BC illustrate the siege of Dapur in Syria, with Egyptian soldiers climbing scaling ladders with back-up from archers. The simple but effective battering ram was introduced in the ninth century by the Assyrians, who developed siege warfare and used, among other things, enormous wooden tower-shaped battering rams with archers on top. The best-known piece of siege machinery is the Trojan Horse, as described in the *Iliad* of Homer and the *Aeneid* of Virgil. This owes something to the description of the fifteenth century BC Canaanite city of Joppa, which was taken by the Egyptians. The *Book of Joshua* features the famous story of the Battle of Jericho:

> Now Jericho was straitly shut up because of the children of Israel: none went out, and none came in ... And the Lord said unto Joshua: And seven priests shall bear seven rams' horns before the ark; and the seventh day ye shall compass the city seven times, and the priests shall blow with the horns. And it shall be, that when they make a long blast with the ram's horn, and when ye hear the sound of the horn, all the people shall shout with a great shout; and the wall of the city shall fall down flat ... So the people shouted, and [the priests] blew with the horns ... and the wall fell down flat, so that the people went up into the city, every man straight before him, and they took the city. And they utterly destroyed all that was in the city, both man and woman, both young and old, and ox, and sheep, and ass, with the edge of the sword.[19]

This miraculous Biblical story is, in its aftermath, something of a template for many a subsequent siege in antiquity and right through history: total destruction of the besieged city, murder of the male inhabitants regardless of age, rape of their women, infanticide and the butchery of all domestic animals. King Priam had no doubts about the atrocious fate that awaited him (eaten by his own dogs) and his family (murdered and raped) if and when Troy fell to the Greeks:

Moreover, pity me, wretched, yet still preserving my senses, unhappy, whom the Saturnian sire will destroy by grievous fate, upon the threshold of old age, having seen many evils, my sons slain, my daughters dragged captives, their chambers plundered, and my infant children dashed upon the earth in dire hostility, and my daughters-in-law torn away by the pernicious hands of the Greeks. And myself perhaps the last – the raw-devouring dogs, whom I have nourished in my palaces, the attendants of my table, the guards of my portals, will tear at the entrance of the gates, after some one, having stricken or wounded me with the sharp brass, shall take away my soul from my limbs; and who, drinking my blood, will lie in the porch, infuriated in mind.[20]

Thucydides' anguish is palapable when he describes a similar scenario of wholesale rapine and slaughter that had become all too familiar – the fate of Mycalessus after it fell to the Thracians in 413 BC: 'so now there was ... death in every shape and form ... a disaster more complete than any, more sudden and more horrible.'[21] Most shocking is how the Thracian soldiers, 'like all the most bloodthirsty barabarians, are always particularly bloothirsty,' burst into a large boys' school as it opened for the day and butchered everyone inside.

Alexander the Great and his armies were serial besiegers. Two of the most notorious blockades were the Siege of Tyre and the Siege of the Sogdian Rock. Tyre was virtually impregnable: it saw his engineers build a causeway that was originally 60m (200ft) wide backed up with siege towers housing stone-throwers and catapults with which to bombard the city walls. He constructed a mole, which the Tyrians attacked with a fire-ship. Nevertheless, seven months later, Tyre fell. Sogdian Rock was captured by a commando-style assault up the cliffs.

Alba was one of Rome's first sieges, in 672 BC, and it provided the template for much of what was to follow. The Romans pulled all the houses down and expelled the inhabitants – erasing everything the Alabans ever had and totally destabilizing their community and culture. Even their temples and gods had been appropriated. Sometimes the Romans made what was often a difficult and draining operation look easy. In their early battles with the Aequi, they stormed thirty-one hill forts in fifty days, according to Livy, or forty fortifications according to Diodorus Siculus.[22] Julius Caesar pulled off a masterful siege at the Battle of Alesia when he built two immense fortified walls around the city and a system of booby traps to deter the besieged from attacking him and his walls. The inner circumvallation, 16km long, penned in Vercingetorix's forces, while the outer contravallation prevented external relief from reaching them. The Romans occupied the ground in between the two. The besieged Gauls were on the brink of starvation and surrendered when their relief force was destroyed by Caesar's cavalry.

Starvation was a powerful and deadly weapon in the Roman armoury. Stopping food getting into a besieged city, imposing demands on the food supply by herding people in and then locking them in, slaying foraging parties and adopting scorched-earth tactics in the vicinity to destroy anything and everything that the enemy might eat, even if it was growing on Roman land – all of these were adopted on a routine basis to the extreme detriment of the besieged, for whom the sack of their city was the ultimate disaster. The retribution handed out to the survivors of a fallen city had become such a routine event that by the first century AD it was a popular topos in the manuals of rhetorical training, with source material going all the way back to Troy. Quintilian explains how to embroider a sacking with melodramatic language and images:

> So, too, we may move our hearers to tears by the picture of a captured town. For the mere statement that the town was stormed, while no doubt it embraces all that such a calamity involves, has all the curtness of a dispatch, and fails to penetrate to the emotions of the hearer. But if we expand all that the one word 'stormed' includes, we shall see the flames pouring from house and temple, and hear the crash of falling roofs and one confused clamour blent of many cries: we shall behold some in doubt whither to fly, others clinging to their nearest and dearest in one last embrace, while the wailing of women and children and the laments of old men that the cruelty of fate should have spared them to see that day will strike upon our ears. Then will come the pillage of treasure sacred and profane, the hurrying to and fro of the plunderers as they carry off their booty or return to seek for more, the prisoners driven each before his own inhuman captor, the mother struggling to keep her child, and the victors fighting over the richest of the spoil. For though, as I have already said, the sack of a city includes all these things, it is less effective to tell the whole news at once than to recount it detail by detail.[23]

To the Romans, the atrocities they routinely perpetrated after a successful siege had become so normalized that they felt comfortable including them as case studies in a text book for students of declamation. The Christians were not much better, as we shall see, using the horrific aftermath of a siege to illustrate and explain their beliefs about the Judgement Day.

The siege of Amida (in modern south-east Turkey) in AD 505 and its consequences were particularly repellent. The siege lasted three months and

80,000 inhabitants died in the ensuing reprisals. The Persians tied up all the men and incarcerated them in the local amphitheatre; many died of starvation or of its effects. The women, meanwhile, were famished as well and took to eating stones, the soles of old boots 'and other horrible things from the streets and squares'. Prostitution was a way out for many who exchanged sex for food, but when the food began to run out the Persians deserted the women and left them to starve. According to our reporter, Pseudo-Joshua, what happened next was quite unbeliebable: the women got together and planned acts of cannibalism where they would go out and overpower the vulnerable: other women, children and the old and infirm. Once boiled or roasted, these victims would be eaten. The 'odour of the roasting' told the Persians what was going on; they tried to stop it through torture or execution.

The aftermath was no less horrific. The wildlife there got so used to feeding off the numerous corpses scattered around that, at the end of the war, when the corpses had rotted away, they began attacking the inhabitants in order to satisfy their taste for human flesh. They would run off with children and devour them; farmers and solitary travellers were also attacked and eaten to death.[24]

All of this may well have happened, and it illustrates well the depths to which besiegers and the besieged will sink to win or to survive. At the same time, though, it may be an example of a Christian writer using fictitious stories of such depravity to illustrate the dystopian world we all apparently live in and the repugnant things that go on which typify what may await us after Judgement Day.

True or not, we learn that the very threat of siege had terrible consequences. In AD 560, rumours were put about in Amida that the Persians were on their way back. John of Ephesus calls the reaction this caused 'rage, madness and frenzy'. It was the last straw for a town that in the last fifty years had endured the depradations of one siege, and the loss of 30,000 more inhabitants during a three-month plague and the collapse of its economy. Women and children were the main sufferers of the madness and frenzy: 'barking like dogs, bleating like goats, meowing like cats, cock-a-doodle-dooing like cocks and imitating the sounds of all dumb animals.' More social anxiety set in with huddled groups 'confused, troubled, disturbed,' staggering about at night, visiting the cemetery. They 'sang and raged and bit each other,' their voices sounded like horns and trumpets; they swore 'as if from devils in person'. Involuntary gales of laughter, 'immodest talk and evil blasphemy' rang out. They leapt about and jumped on walls 'hanging themselves upside down, falling and rolling around in the nude.' None of them knew where he or she lived.[25]

Chapter 12

Carnuntum AD 170; the Crisis of the Third Century – Abritus AD 251, Edessa AD 260

One hundred years after the sack of Jerusalem, the Romans had to face rampaging Germans overrunnng their defences along the Danube. Carnuntum (Ptolemy calls it Καρνους; today it is Petronell) was one such Roman garrison camp in the province of Noricum. We first hear of it during the reign of Augustus, when Tiberius made it his headquarters in the campaigns against Maroboduus. The town became the garrison of the XVth legion (*Apollinaris*) and the centre of the Roman fortifications along the Danube from Vindobona (Vienna) to Brigetio (Ó-Szőny). Under either Trajan or Hadrian it became the HQ of XIVth legion (*Gemina*) and the capital of Pannonia Superior. Today, its ruins are located halfway between Vienna and Bratislava.

The Battle of Carnuntum took place in AD 170 during the Marcomannic Wars – *bellum Germanicum et Sarmaticum* – which lasted from AD 166 to AD 180. In the spring of AD 170, when the German hordes raided Roman provinces along the Danube, the king of the Marcomanni, Ballomar (AD 140–AD 170-180), a long-standing client of Rome's since AD 19, allied with the Quadi, Vandals, and Sarmatian Iazyges tribes. The Germans came in search of new lands in which to settle. For three years they overwhelmed the defences between Vindobona and Carnuntum, penetrated the border between Pannonia and Noricum, devastated Flavia Solva and were only halted in Italy just outside Aquileia on the Adriatic. Marcus Aurelius' response to the incursions was to raise a war chest and an army comprising citizens from all classes, slaves and gladiators; fortifications were thrown up at vulnerable points. The emperor was an ever-present figure on the Danube front line from AD 167. The war saw the death of two Praetorian Guard commanders and lasted until Marcus Aurelius' death in AD 180.

Eutropius tells us that Marcus Aurelius crossed the Danube with his son-in-law and chief military adviser Tiberius Claudius Pompeianus in a bid to repel the raiders. The Romans and Germans clashed outside Carnuntum. The Roman army was inexperienced and hopelessly outmatched by the Germans: the ensuing battle was a disaster for the Romans, with 20,000 Romans killed.

The victorious German war machine rolled on to besiege Aquileia and sack Opitergium. Carnuntum was the worst Roman defeat in a century.

However, Rome bounced back, with victories over the Marcomanni in AD 17. The Quadi were finally subdued in AD 174 in what has survived in Christian legend as the Thundering Legion when thirsty Christian soldiers in the (*Fulminata*) Legion prayed for rain. God obliged and the resulting storm allowed them to defeat the Quadi. Roman territory was cleared of German insurgents by AD 178.

Our source for Carnuntum is Lucian, in his *Alexander.*[1] After the battle, Marcus Aurelius began work on his *Meditations* at Carnuntum; Book 1 carries the note, 'Among the Quadi at the Granua.' From AD 171 to 173, Marcus Aurelius lived in Carnuntum. The governor Septimius Severus was proclaimed emperor by his troops in Carnuntum in AD 193. The city was awarded the status of *colonia*. Other evidence regarding the wars is decidely scarce. There is little else besides a possible episode depicted on the column of Marcus Aurelius in Rome.

Abritus AD 251

The Battle of Abritus (otherwise known as the Battle of Forum Terebronii) marked the beginning of a period of increased military activity for the Romans. Abritus was located in Moesia Inferior (modern Razgrad in Bulgaria), and the battle took place in July AD 251, between the Romans and a coalition of Scythian tribesmen led by the Goth king Cniva. The Romans were convincingly defeated, and the joint Roman emperors Decius and his son Herennius Etruscus (*c.* AD 227–251) both fell during battle.[2]

They have gone down in history footnoted with the dubious privilege of being the first Roman emperors to die in battle against a foreign enemy. Jordanes and Aurelius Victor assert that Herennius Etruscus was killed by an arrow before the battle and that his father showed little filial devotion when he addressed his men: 'Let no one mourn. The death of one soldier is not a great loss to the Republic.' However, others believe that Herennius died with his father.[3]

Cniva began his invasion of the Roman Empire when he crossed the Danube with contingents of Goths, Germans and Sarmatians. Cnivus was no doubt aggrieved when Decius' predecessor, Philip the Arab, discontinued the payments of annual subsidies to the tribes of the region instigated by Emperor Maximinus Thrax in AD 238. Decius may also have taken troops from the Danube frontier, for deployment in his campaign to depose Philip in AD 249, leaving the region vulnerable to invaders.

Cniva demanded an audience with Decius and was laying siege to Nicopolis when Decius arrived, while the Goths departed for Philippopolis (Plovdiv). Decius pursued Cniva through the difficult terrain; Cniva soon turned on Decius. The Romans were surprised and Decius fled while his army suffered heavy casualties. Cniva then laid siege to Philippopolis and finally conquered the city, (apparently) slaying 100,000 citizens, and taking a subtantial number of prisoners.

Decius retaliated by battling with several bands of Germans and strengthening his fortifications along the Danube, with a view to fighting Cniva. The Romans surrounded the Goths, who were now making moves to retreat from Roman territory. Decius, however, wanted revenge and so attacked the Goths at Forum Terebronii. At this devastating battle, the Battle of Abritus, Cniva cleverly divided his army into three smaller, more versatile units with one posted out of sight behind a swamp. He pushed the Roman army back into the swamp, whence they were attacked by the Gothic army.[4] The substantial casualties included the two emperors. Decius won the earlier part of the battle when he attacked from the front, but made a tactical error of some magnitude when he was led by the fleeing enemy into the swamp. Decius was routed. The disastrous carnage marked one of the most catastrophic defeats in the history of the Roman Empire. It has attracted much attention from the historians, all more or less in agreement. First Zonaras:

> He and his son and a large number of Romans fell into the marshland; all of them perished there, none of their bodies to be found, as they were covered by the mud.[5]

Zosimus, in his *Historia Nova* says:

> Proceeding therefore incautiously in an unknown place, he and his army became entangled in the mire, and under that disadvantage were so assailed by the missiles of the Barbarians, that not one of them escaped with life. Thus ended the life of the excellent emperor Decius.[6]

Lactantius, the fourth-century AD early Christian and advisor to Constantine the Great, describes it thus:

> He was suddenly surrounded by the barbarians, and slain, together with great part of his army; nor could he be honoured with the rites of sepulture, but, stripped and naked, he lay to be devoured by wild beasts and birds, a fit end for the enemy of God.[7]

The new emperor, Trebonianus Gallus (r. AD 251–253), amidst allegations of treachery against Decius, made a feeble peace agreement with the Goths: he allowed Cniva to leave laden with his booty, even assisting the Goths' departure. He paid tribute to Cniva, so long as he desisted from invading the empire again.

For Ammianus Marcellinus, the soldier and historian (AD 330 to after 391), this defeat ranked on the same level as Varus' defeat at the Battle of the Teutoburg Forest, the invasions of the Marcomanni during the reign of Marcus Aurelius and the Battle of Adrianople.[8] The Romans won in the end, though: in AD 271, the Emperor Aurelian soundly vanquished the Goths and slew their king, Cannobaudes, in battle.

The Third Century Crisis: Barbalissos AD 253 and Edessa AD 260

The Third Century Crisis also goes by the names Military Anarchy or the Imperial Crisis. It was a disaster of the first magnitude, lasting from AD 235 to 284 and involving military and economic catastrophe, as well as plague. Indeed, this toxic combination and unhappy coincidence almost brought the empire to its knees. Alexander Severus was assassinated by his own army in AD 235 after a period of civil war and an invasion by barbarians. This triggered a fifty-year period of imperial anarchy in which there were twenty-six or so claimants to the throne, led by Roman military commanders, the so-called 'barrack' commanders. None of them lasted very long, their reigns averaging less than two years each. Severus paid the price of trying to negotiate with barbarian invaders while his armies thought he should be punishing them. According to Herodian, 'In their opinion Alexander showed no honourable intention to pursue the war and preferred a life of ease, when he should have marched out to punish the Germans for their previous insolence.'[9]

Politically, by AD 260, the empire was split into three hostile states: the Gallic Empire (Gaul, Britannia and, for a short while, Hispania); the Palmyrene Empire (Syria, Palaestina and Aegyptus); and the Italian Roman Empire. Aurelian (AD 270–75) eventually reunited the empire, and the reforms of Diocletian brought the Crisis to an end in AD 284. These brought such extreme and significant change to all espects of the Roman Empire, its society, economics and religion that historians regard it as the end of the classical period and the dawn of late antiquity.

The Severan emperors had raised new legions and increased the salaries of the soldiers by something like 200 per cent, devaluing the currency and raising taxes to pay for it all. The Third Century Crisis emperors continued with these policies, bribing armies to ensure their support in the civil wars. They debased the coinage, igniting rampant inflation and wrecking the economy. The people resorted to bartering, thus depriving the treasury of essential taxes; taxes were paid in kind in food or goods.

The schisms within the empire meant that the armies of Rome were so distracted by their own internecine differences and battles that they neglected the incursions on their borders by the Carpians, Goths, Vandals and Alamanni on the Rhine and Danube, with raids by the Sassanids in the east. Climate changes in what are now the Low Countries caused sea levels to rise, forcing the displacement of inhabitants there in search of new land. In AD 251, the Plague of Cyprian (probably smallpox) laid low with a vengeance the populations in the empire, causing further problems for unified defence.

At the height of the pandemic, from AD 250 to 266, 5,000 people a day were said to be dying in Rome. St Cyprian's biographer, Pontius of Carthage, described its terrible effect in Carthage:

Afterwards there broke out a dreadful plague, and excessive destruction of a hateful disease invaded every house in succession of the trembling populace, carrying off day by day with abrupt attack numberless people, every one from his own house. All were shuddering, fleeing, shunning the contagion, impiously exposing their own friends, as if with the exclusion of the person who was sure to die of the plague, one could exclude death itself also. There lay about the meanwhile, over the whole city, no longer bodies, but the carcasses of many, and, by the contemplation of a lot which in their turn would be theirs, demanded the pity of the passers-by for themselves. No one regarded anything besides his cruel gains. No one trembled at the remembrance of a similar event. No one did to another what he himself wished to experience.[10]

The usual scapegoating ran riot and the 'Decian persecution' was blamed on the Christians. Cyprian, in his attempts to moralize, gives graphic descriptions of the horrible physical symptoms in his *De Mortalitate*:

This trial, that now the bowels, relaxed into a constant flux, discharge the bodily strength; that a fire originated in the marrow ferments into wounds of the fauces; that the intestines are shaken with a continual vomiting; that the eyes are on fire with the injected blood; that in some cases the feet or some parts of the limbs are taken off by the contagion of diseased putrefaction; that from the weakness arising by the maiming and loss of the body, either the gait is enfeebled, or the hearing is obstructed, or the sight darkened; – is profitable as a proof of faith. What a grandeur of spirit it is to struggle with all the powers of an unshaken mind against so many onsets of devastation and death! ... but rather to rejoice, and to embrace the benefit of the occasion.[11]

The plague was still raging in AD 270.

The crisis led to wholesale changes in the military – if anything, the Romans were going to learn from this chaos and mayhem and try to prevent it from recurring. The army had failed singularly to deal with the many external threats and it had been misused for personal gain and benefit. Under Gallienus (r. AD 253–268), senators were stopped from serving in the army: this had the dual benefit of reducing the likelihood of senatorial insurrection against Gallienus and eliminating the old hoary aristocratic hierarchy in the military. Officers would now have to work their way up through the ranks, no longer depending on their privileged status. The benefit was a much more experienced officer corps. To win his victories over the Gallic and Palmyrene secessionists, Aurelian deployed fleet, cavalry-based soldiers rather than the usual infantry. Diocletian increased even further the cavalry element to ensure speedy and flexible deployment wherever armies were required. Diocletian also reigned from the regions as well as Rome so that his fast reaction forces were nearer to potential trouble spots. He ruled from cities in the East, forming the Tetrarchy, a system of four reigning emperors, who each ruled from a region close to the borders.

The disaster at Edessa in AD 260 is notable and unique in military history for two reasons: first, a Roman army was lost in its entirety; second, a Roman emporer, Valerian (r. AD 253–259), was taken prisoner by a foreign enemy – the first time that this had happened. The Battle of Edessa took place between Valerian and Sassanid forces under Shahanshah (King of Kings) Shapur I (r. AD 240–270).[12]

Using Roman incursions into Armenia as a pretext, the Sassanids had attacked the Romans in AD 253; Shapur had Chosroes, the Armenian king, assassinated and replaced with one of his own. The Sassanids assaulted a Roman force at Barbalissos in the province of Mesopotamia and soundly defeated the Roman army. Allegedly 70,000 Romans died that day but no Roman sources record the fact. Perhaps the bad news blackout was in response to Roman shame at the magnitude of the disaster. The number butchered was a significant part of the Roman infantry forces of 350,000 at the time. We can only speculate, but perhaps the Romans were caught up in attacks by the notorious rapid Persian heavy cavalry, the *clibinarii*, or *savaran* in Farsi. As we have seen, the Persian success here and at Edessa led the Romans to bring the shock troops, the *cataphractarii*, into the Roman war machine.[13]

Barbalissos left the Roman east open to attack and led to the sacking of Antioch, Tarsus and Dura Europos (known as the Pompeii of the East) in AD 256. By AD 257, Valerian had retaken Antioch and restored Syria to Roman control. The emperor, his army decimated by plague, pursued the Persians to Edessa where he was routed; Valerian, along with the remnants of the Roman army, was captured by Shapur and sent to Pars. Edessa is only known to us through Shapur's mural inscription at Naqš-e Rostam.[14] Here Shapur is mounted on horseback, resplendent in royal armour and a crown. Valerian kneels in shaming supplication before him. The scene is repeated in other rock-face inscriptions. According to Lactantius, Shapur allegedly publicly humiliated Valerian by using him as a footstool when mounting his horse. Valerian's body was later skinned and stuffed with manure – a bizarre trophy of Roman submission which was preserved in a Persian temple. Sources contradict this: in other stone carvings Valerian is shown with respect and is never on his knees; Valerian and elements of his army lived in relatively good conditions in Bishapur, and Shapur made use of Roman engineers. Band-e Kaisar (Caesar's Dam) near Susa is living evidence of this.[15]

Shapur then advanced into Asia Minor and took Caesarea, removing 400,000 of its citizens to the southern Sassanian provinces. He then invaded Cilicia but the Romans rallied, and he was repulsed by Macrianus, Callistus and Odenathus of Palmyra. Macrianus proclaimed his sons, Macrianus and Quietus, joint emperors, while in the Balkans Ingenuus and Regalianus rose up too, but were defeated by an army sent by Gallienus, the son of Valerian. The Persians were now pushed to withdraw from Roman territory, surrendering Armenia and Antioch.[16]

Chapter 13

The Theban Legion Massacre AD 286

According to Eucherius of Lyon (*c*. AD 380 – *c*. 499), in AD 286, a legion of soldiers made up of 6,666 men was massacred in its entirety.[1] Two significant factors set this legion apart from other Roman legions of the time: first, the high number of legionnaires and the special number of soldiers; second, it was made up exclusively of Christians.[2] It was called the Theban Legion (*Alkateeba al Teebia*) because the men were Egyptian Christian Copts recruited from and stationed in Thebes in Upper Egypt. There they stayed until the emperor Maximian posted them to Gaul, to fight against a rebellious Gallic tribe, the Bagaude, which is around modern Burgundy. This was in line with standard Roman policy of not having Roman armies fight in their own recruiting grounds for fear of uprisings to liberate their homelands.

The Theban legion served at a time when Christianity was very popular amongst Copts, and just as unpopular amongst the Roman authorities; so much so that there were a number of persecutory measures to suppress Christianity around this time. An edict of AD 202 decreed that an end should be put to all conversions, while the edict of AD 250 decreed that all citizens were required, by means of an official certificate, to show evidence that he or she had offered sacrifice to the pagan gods. *Thebaei* is the name of Legio I (*Maximiana*), or the *Maximiana Thebaeorum*, as recorded in the *Notitia Dignitatum* (Register of Dignities).

There were two legions with the name 'Theban', both formed by Diocletian (co-ruler with Maximian) and stationed at Alexandria.[3] A papyrus found at Panopolis, on the Nile just north of Thebes, contained a delivery note and invoice dated 'In the Sixth year of our Lord the Emperor Caesar Marcus Aurelius Probus Pius Augustus, Tubi sixteenth' (13 January 282 CE). The delivery was for 38,496 *modii* (measure) of bread (about 577,440lb, or 384,490 daily rations), which would feed a legion for about three months; it was to be delivered to Panopolis to the 'mobilized soldiers and sailors'.

Dissenters against official Roman religion, regardless of age or sex, were cruelly tortured: some were decapitated, while others were thrown to the lions or else burnt alive. The Catechetical School of Alexandria was shut down, although this only led to clandestine meetings taking place elsewhere; the number of bishops was restricted to three. Persecutions reached their high point during the reign of Diocletian (AD 284–305). Such was the ferocity of his programme of mass executions and torture that the Copts adopted the day of Diocletian's election as emperor to mark the beginning of the era of the Coptic martyrs. This became the start of the Coptic Calendar known as *Anno Martyrum* (AM), the year of the Martyrs. Eusebius describes some of the torture in a campaign of eye-watering atrocity which, it is estimated, claimed 20,000 lives:

> They were torn to bits from head to foot with broken pottery like claws till death released them. Women were tied by one foot and hoisted in the air, head downwards, their bodies completely nude ... the most shameful, brutal and inhuman of all spectacles to anyone watching. Others again were tied to trees and stumps and died horribly; for with the aid of machines they drew together the very stoutest of boughs, fastened one of the martyr's legs to each and let the boughs fly back to their normal position ... in this they continued not for a few days or weeks but year after year.[4]

Thebes was a hotbed of Christianity. Some of the first Christian 'monks', The Desert Fathers, were largely made up of Thebans. Historically, Theban Christians honour a number of martyrs who defied the authorities during these persecutions. The purge of Christians from the military between AD 284 and 299 under Diocletian suggests that non-compliance to emperor worship was a common way of revealing Christian soldiers and bringing them to eventual execution.

The Theban Legion reached Maximian's army in Gaul to engage the Bagaude by way of the St Bernard's Pass in the Alps. The leaders of the Theban Legion were Mauritius (St Maurice or St Moritz), Candidus and Exupernis (Exuperantius). The Gallic revolt was quashed, the legion camping at Agaunum (what is now St Maurice). Here Maximian, smelling religious dissent, organized a universal sacrifice, in which the whole army was required to participate and swear an oath of allegiance, as well as promise to assist in the extermination of Christianity from Gaul. Maximian was uncompromising: he organized the un-Roman rite of *adoratio* (*proskynesis* in Greek), which was the Persian rite of worship to the Shah-I-Shah as a living god, translated over to the Roman emperor.[5] Worshippers were obliged to prostrate themselves before the emperor three times, ironically and poignantly for the Christians, as it was just as Satan had asked of Jesus.[6]

This, of course, presented insoluble problems for the all-Christian Theban legion. They all refused point-blank to sacrifice or take the oaths, incensing

Maximian, who immediately ordered the decimation of the legion at Martigny. But it was not to be any ordinary decimation. When every tenth man had been butchered, the survivors bucked the trend and enthusiastically reasserted their Christian faith, further enraging Maximian; 666 more soldiers then met their deaths, their blood turning the Rhone and its flood plain crimson. This was repeated until all the soldiers were dead.

Mauritius spoke to the survivors of the first round of decimation, firing their enthusiasm for martyrdom, urging them to join their newly-murdered comrades in death and reminding them of their baptismal vow: to renounce Satan, to worship only God. Before the decimation had started, the Christians had compromised when they agreed to swear loyalty to Maximian:

> Emperor, we are your soldiers but also the soldiers of the true God. We owe you military service and obedience, but we cannot renounce Him who is our Creator and Master, and also yours even though you reject Him. In all things which are not against His law, we most willingly obey you, as we have done hitherto. We readily oppose your enemies whoever they are, but we cannot stain our hands with the blood of innocent people (Christians). We have taken an oath to God before we took one to you, you cannot place any confidence in our second oath if we violate the other (the first). You commanded us to execute Christians, behold we are such. We confess God the Father the creator of all things and His Son Jesus Christ, God. We have seen our comrades slain with the sword, we do not weep for them but rather rejoice at their honour. Neither this, nor any other provocation have tempted us to revolt. Behold, we have arms in our hands, but we do not resist, because we would rather die innocent than live by any sin.[7]

But Maximian remained implacable and slew them all. The Maximian atrocity is what is known as the Sixth Primitive Persecution in *Foxe's Book of Martyrs*.[8] Thousands of Christians were slaughtered without trial and buried unceremoniously in unmarked mass graves; there was no resistance: they simply put down their weapons and offered their necks to their executioners.

> The principal persons who perished under this reign were: Pontianus, bishop of Rome; Anteros, a Grecian, his successor, who gave offence to the government by collecting the acts of the martyrs Pammachius and Quiritus, Roman senators, with all their families, and many other Christians; Simplicius, a senator; Calepodius, a Christian minister, thrown into the Tyber; Martina, a noble and beautiful virgin; and Hippolitus, a Christian prelate, tied to a wild horse, and dragged until he expired. During

this persecution, raised by Maximinus, numberless Christians were slain without trial and buried indiscriminately in heaps, sometimes fifty or sixty being cast into a pit together, without the least decency.[9]

Not all the members of the legion were at Aguanum at the time of the massacre. Some were posted at various points along the military road linking Switzerland with Germany and Italy. These were systematically martyred wherever they were found. Eucherius records that during the massacre and martyrdom, there were a series of miracles: in Zurich, the three decapitated saints Felix, Regula and Exuperantius rose from the dead and carried their heads to the top of a hill, where they knelt, prayed and lay down.[10] A cathedral was later built here. The three saints, their heads in their hands, feature on the coat of arms and seal of Zurich today. When saints Victor, Orsus and their comrades were tortured by Hirtacus, the Roman governor of Solothurn, their shackles snapped and a fire was extinguished. The bodies of the saints which were thrown in the river Aar stepped out of the waters, and knelt and prayed at the spot where the Basilica of St Peter was later built. The bodies of the martyrs of Aguanum were discovered and identified by Saint Theodore, the Bishop of Octudurm, around AD 350. He built a basilica in their honour at Aguanum, the remains of which still can be seen. This later became the focal point of a monastery, built about the year AD 515 on land donated by King Sigismund of Burgundy.

There is much controversy surrounding the historicity of the Theban Legion and the disaster which befell it. Some scholars believe it to be a fiction, as seems likely, born out of Christian hagiography, notably that of Saint Maurice, the chief among the Legion's saints. Others argue that it was an actual event.[11] Either way, it was a catastrophe of the first order, although it seems that many of the soldiers would not have seen it that way, delighting as they did in their martyrdom. Their feast day is on 22 September. Sigebert of Gembloux (d. AD 1112) wrote a poem on the martyrdom of the Theban Legion.

One of the strongest arguments against the story is that, at this time, the Romans did not execute complete legions for insubordination. Decimation had not been used to discipline a Roman legion for centuries, since the reign of Galba, who ordered this done to a formation of marines that Nero had formed into a legion, and who demanded an eagle and standards. It was less than successful in terms of morale and discipline. An eleventh-century monk called Otto of Freising wrote that most of the legionaries escaped, and only some were executed. It may be that the legion was simply re-organized during Diocletian's reforming of units (breaking up legions of 6,000 men to create smaller units of 1,000), and that some of the soldiers had been executed. Some argue that it was only a *vexillatio* that was decimated.[12] Furthermore, the soldiers' god was typically Isis or Mithras (Sol Invictus), until the reign of Constantine at least (AD 306–337), making it unlikely that Christians filled an entire legion.

Gregory of Tours (AD 538–594) gloried in the miraculous powers of the Theban Legion, though he transplanted the event to Cologne where there was an earlier cult devoted to Maurice and the Theban Legion:

> At Cologne there is a church in which the fifty men from the holy Theban Legion are said to have consummated their martyrdom for the name of Christ. And because the church, with its wonderful construction and mosaics, shines as if somehow gilded, the inhabitants prefer to call it the 'Church of the Golden Saints'. Once Eberigisilus, who was at the time bishop of Cologne, was racked with severe pains in half his head. He was then in a villa near a village. Eberigisilus sent his deacon to the church of the saints. Since there was said to be in the middle of the church a pit into which the saints were thrown together after their martyrdom, the deacon collected some dust there and brought it to the bishop. As soon as the dust touched Eberigisilus' head, immediately all pain was gone.

Alexander of Bergamo is a good example of how the Romans relentlessly pursued the Theban legionaries. He is said to have been a survivor of the decimation and escaped to Milan, where he was recognized and imprisoned until he renounced his Christian faith. Nevertheless, Alexander escaped and fled to Como, only to be captured again and brought back to Milan; he was condemned to death by decapitation, but during the execution the executioner's arms went stiff. He was imprisoned again and once again managed to escape, ending up in Bergamo. Alexander was once again captured and was finally decapitated on 26 August AD 303, where the church of San Alessandro in Colonna now stands.

Saint Maurice is one of the most popular saints in Western Europe, with over 650 foundations in his name in France alone. Five cathedrals, countless churches, chapels and altars are consecrated in his name all over Europe. Aguanum (Saint Maurice en Valais) has always remained the capital city of veneration of the Thebans and a major pilgrimage resort. An all-night vigil on the night before the feast is regularly attended by up to 1,000 people. On the actual feast day, they carry the relics of the martyrs in the ancient silver caskets. Over seventy towns bear the name of Saint Maurice. In the monastery carrying his name in Switzerland, the vigil 'Tasbeha' has been chanted continuously twenty-four hours a day without stopping for more than 500 years now. On 19 July 1941, Pope Pius XII declared Saint Maurice patron Saint of the Italian Army's Alpini Mountain Infantry Corps.

Chapter 14

Adrianople AD 378

The disaster which befell the Romans at the Battle of Adrianople, fought on 9 August AD 378, is often considered by some to be the beginning of the end for the Roman Empire. Eunapius and Ammianus would have it thus. At this time, the Western Empire was ruled by the precocious and gifted Flavius Gratianus (Gratian), while the Eastern Empire was governed by his uncle, Flavius Valens, somewhat less talented in the arts of war and peace, fair but firm and sometimes cruel. Adrianople was a key moment in the Gothic War (AD 376–382); the battle took place about 13km north of Adrianople (modern Edirne in Turkey, near the Graeco-Bulgarian border) in the Roman province of Thracia. It was fought between Valens and Gothic rebels, largely Thervings, Greutungs, non-Gothic Alans and various local rebels led by Fritigern (d. *c.* AD 380) a Thervingian Gothic chieftain, and Alavivus.

Who were these Goths? They were Germanic, originating in the lands of modern Scandinavia, or Scandza as Jordanes calls it, migrating south through Poland and Ukraine in the second century AD before settling on the shores of the Black Sea. They subdued the Vandals – an eastern German tribe – and moved west, where they inevitably came up against the Romans in the third century. Their opening conflict against Rome occurred when they sacked Histria, a Greek *polis* on the Danube delta in AD 238; Cniva, as we have seen, annihilated a Roman army in AD 251, an action in which the emperor Decius was killed; raids followed on coastal districts of Asia Minor, Greece, Macedonia and Cyprus, but they were soundly repulsed by Claudius at Naissus in AD 269. Alliances, truces, the payment of tribute and the supply of troops followed between the two adversaries. Contrary to popular belief, the Goths, like other barbarians, were relatively civilized, most of them Arian Christians. The Huns arrived from the east to find an already complicated and fragile political scene in the 370s when they subdued the Alans, nomads from the Central Asian steppes. This forced the Alans to attack the Greuthungi, Goths from the northern shores of the Black Sea, led by Alatheus and Saphrax, who in turn retreated into Tervingi territory between the Dniester and the Dnieper in the north-east corner of the Roman Empire. The Huns returned and attacked the Tervingi and the Greuthingi, who retreated into the Carpathians to defend against the Huns. Ammianus, no doubt in common with many Romans, had no time for the Huns, calling them 'abnormally savage', 'a wild race ... consumed by a wild passion to pillage ... uprooting and destroying everything ... like a whirlwind.'[1]

By this time, the Goths – ever a disparate bunch of tribes – were led by the charismatic Fritigern, a cautious leader with something of the Fabius Cunctator about his military style. Ammianus describes him as 'skillful at divining the future and [wary of] a doubtful struggle,' meaning that he only did battle when certain of victory. It was at this pivotal point in their history that the Goths, tired of eking out their sparse existence, came down from the mountains in search of more fertile lands and security, asking the Romans for permission to settle within the empire as asylum seekers.

Valens' predecessor, Julian, had lost lands to the Persians in a dispute over Armenia, including five provinces to the east of the Tigris, various forts and the cities of Nisibis, Singara and Castra Maurorum. Valens' mission was to reclaim it all back, but he was distracted by revolts within the Eastern Empire. One of the revolts was caused by the the usurper Procopius; he was a relative of Julian, the last of the line of Constantine. Procopius persuaded many of Valens' troops to defect, but in AD 366, Valens defeated Procopius, killed him and sent his head to Valentinian, his brother.

In AD 376, tens of thousands of Fritigern's displaced Goths turned up on the banks of the Danube River, the eastern frontier of the Roman Empire, requesting asylum from the Huns and seeking to settle on the south bank of the Danube as refugees. Ominously, but not surprisingly, Valens agreed, even facilitating the crossing of the river by the Goths at the fortress of Durostorum (modern Silistra in Bulgaria). The Goths promised to coexist peacefully and provide auxiliaries. The Tervingi probably made up most of the Goths; their leaders were Fritigern and Alavivus. When later the Greuthungi turned up requesting permission to cross over under Alatheus and Sphrax, they were refused entry: perhaps Valens thought that there were enough Goths within his borders already. The disappointed and affronted Greuthungi moved on to the Transylvanian Alps to consider their options and bide their time.

The emperor promised the first wave of immigrant Goths farming land, grain, and protection as *foederati*.[2] Valens, however, was no altruist. His true aim in this apparent show of generosity was to boost his army and to levy new taxes. The Goths would be very useful as recruits to the army he was building for his impending war with Persia. To that end, the Romans were cruelly selective with regard to who was allowed to cross the Danube and who was not: the old and infirm were left deserted on the far bank, defenceless against the Huns. Eunapius exaggerates that 200,000 Goths made the crossing. Apart from being an instantly successful army recruitment campaign, the new immigrants would be useful workers on the land where population decline and labour shortage had left Valens' agricultural output in a parlous state. The intention was that those allowed across were to surrender their weapons, as was the normal practice with potentially belligerent immigrants, but this went by the wayside when the Romans took bribes to allow the Goths to remain in arms. To Ammianus, the Roman officials in charge of the arms surrender – Lupicinus the *comes rei militaris* and Maximus, *dux* of Moesia or Scythia – were *homines maculosi*, tainted men.[3]

With so many people confined in such a small area, it was not long before the Goths were struck by famine. The Romans diverted the provisions intended for the asylum-seekers for personal gain and sold instead poor quality food at vastly inflated prices. The Goths were herded into a small holding compound, guarded by armed Roman soldiers – and slowly starved. In response, the Romans offered two hideous options: the exchange of dog meat for enslavement, mainly of young women and children including the children of Goth nobles: one dog for one child sold as a slave; or else endure a death march to distant Marcianople, where food and the chance to barter were said to be freely available. Those who survived the march found the gates of Marcianople slammed in their faces.[4]

To make matters even worse, during a working banquet, the unscrupulous Lupicinus tried clumsily to divide and rule the Goths with a bungled assassination attempt on Alavivus and Fritigern who were blithely unaware of any possible treachery. Roman troops were posted between the main Gothic force and the city walls. Scuffles and riots broke out when the Goths tried to enter the city to purchase supplies and the Goths' bodyguard was murdered: the Goths laid siege to the city. Fritigern survived but Alavivus was never heard of again. The outraged Goths began systematically to plunder the Roman territories in Scythia over the next two years, in AD 376 and 377. All negotiations were off. Ammianus now talks of *Gothi*, rather than of individual Gothic tribes. Goths allied to the Romans in the Thracian army under Sueridus and Colias quartered at Adrianople then defected in another bungle: the chief magistrate of the city, the *curia*, wanted to move them – 'the dregs of the populace' – east to prevent them from joining the advancing Fritigern and to support Valens in his forthcoming war against the Persians. He recklessly refused them supplies for the journey, instead arming and inciting armaments workers in the city, *fabricenses*, to attack them. Pelted by stones, the army of Sueridus and Cokias stood firm and then massacred the workers, at the same time helping themselves to supplies for the journey to join Fritigern.

Rashly, Lupicinus went in pursuit of Fritigern but suffered a disastrous loss 14km south of Marcianopole, in which the Goths eliminated the entire Roman junior officer complement and seized the standard. All of the Goths who had crossed the Danube now joined Fritigern in revolt, killing many Roman citizens and helping themselves to Roman weapons and armour from the bodies. What had originally been a little local difficulty with independent Gothic tribes had quickly escalated into a serious threat to Roman rule in the region from a combined force of hitherto disparate Gothic armies that was now a unified, well-provisioned, highly mobile and very antagonized force, determined to win revenge. Valens, meanwhile, remained obsessed with his designs on Persia, leaving his commanders floundering. Jordanes describes the dire scenario:

> Soon famine and want came upon them, as often happens to a people not yet well settled in a country. Their princes and the leaders who ruled them in place of kings, that is Fritigern, Alatheus and Safrac, began to lament the plight of their army and begged Lupicinus and Maximus, the Roman commanders, to open a market. But to what will not the 'cursed lust for gold' compel men to assent? The generals, swayed by avarice, sold them at a high price not only the flesh of sheep and oxen, but even the carcasses of dogs and unclean animals, so that a slave would be bartered for a loaf of bread or ten pounds of meat.[5]

After a chaotic, unsuccessful siege attempt on Adrianopole, Fritigern split his armies for the forthcoming winter. All the while, his forces were being supplemented by Gothic defection on a large scale: prisoners escaped, slaves ran away, gold miners from Thrace and Macedonia went over and all provided an invaluable source of local intelligence.

By the close of AD 377, it began to dawn on the Romans that their duplicitous hospitality on the banks of the Danube had serious ramifications: rather than just accommodating a mob of fugitive semi-barbarian asylum seekers, they now had a well-organized, albeit starving, army camped in their back yard. Lupicinus did his best to assemble an army, but the main Roman force was still away, busy fighting the Persians in Armenia. His aim was to destroy the Goths, but his army was routed, leaving Thrace in Fritigern's control and the borders gaping open to hoards of yet more Goths pouring in across the Danube. Fritigern, however, was seriously impeded by the parlous state of his army as it approached starvation; it was virtually impossible to open viable lines of supply, and foraging parties were easily picked off by the Romans. More defections to his cause meant that more food was needed; a growing baggage train had to be fed. Peace, it seems, was the only option – in return for farm land on which to settle. Nothing had changed since the massing of the Goths on the banks of the Danube.

Initially, Valens completely misread the situation, delegating subordinates and auxiliaries to deal with the negotiation. His *magister equitum*, Victor, was despatched to Persia to negotiate a settlement there; Profuturus and Trajan led squads of guerrillas against the Goths, taken from Armenia. Valens asked Gratian to send reinforcements: Gratian sent the general Frigeridus with auxiliaries and the leader of his guards, his *comes domesticorum*, Richomeres, to contain the trouble.[6] Such complicity and co-operation between east and west, between emperor and junior co-emperor, was rare, and served to underline the seriousness of the situation which the Romans found staring them in the face. Richomeres, Frigeridus, Profuturus and Trajan all joined forces near Ad Salices, to find themselves confronted by a massive horde of Goths drawn up inside a circle of wagons. Frigeridus withdrew through illness. The Romans were content to wait until the Goths were forced to break out of the *laager* – whether from hunger or disease. The Goths, however, were attracting more and more reinforcements; this encouraged them to burst from the *laager* and attack. The battle was inconclusive; it lasted all day, until the armies, heavily depleted and exhausted, withdrew at nightfall. Rome, nevertheless, had clearly compromised its only viable fighting force in the region. Profuturus was killed in action.

The Romans returned to Marcianople and Frigeridus returned east, fortified Beroe and heavily defeated the Gothic leader Farnobius. The remnants of the Gothic army wintered in the Haemus Mountains, while Richomeres went back to Gaul to raise an army for the following year.

Meanwhile, Valens left Antioch for Constantinople, arriving on 30 May. He appointed the *magister equitum*, Saturninus, who had just arrived from Italy, to lead the Roman armies already in Thrace. He and Traianus blockaded the Goths in the Haemus Mountains, hoping to starve them to death and draw them out into a pitched battle (not the Goth's strongest point). However, the plan failed when Frigeridus marched south and devastated the provinces of Moesia and Scythia. Saturninus marched towards Adrianople with 2,000 legionaries. Fritigern mustered the Gothic forces at Nicopolis and Beroe (Stara Zagora) to face the Romans.[7] Despite early successes, which contained Fritigern in Dobrudja with his largely infantry-based army, things soon started to go wrong for the Romans.

In the summer of AD 377, Fritigern persuaded the cavalry armies of Altheus and Saphrax to join him; the Goths burst out into Thrace, again causing the Roman army to retreat westwards. Other bands of Goths moved south from the Danube to confront the Romans at Marcianople and Adrianople. At last, Valens realized the enormity of the situation; he sued for peace with the Persians and hurried back to Adrianople, arriving there in mid-July AD 378. Things then seemed to be improving for the Romans: Gratian sent auxiliaries under Richomeres. He himself was held up by a revolt by the Letienses when they crossed the frozen Rhine in February AD 378, so invading the Roman Empire. They were defeated by Gratian in the Battle of Argentovaria (modern Colmar in Alsace), where their king, Priarius, was killed. This battle was the last campaign by any Roman Emperor behind the Limes area. By now, Gratian was on his way from the west with a large army of regular troops; his subordinates dealt a hefty defeat on a Gothic force engaged on a looting expedition in southern Thrace. Gratian arrived at Sirmium in Pannonia and at the Camp of Mars, 400km from Adrianople, where they were attacked by a squadron of Alans. Gratian withdrew.[8]

Valens, meanwhile, was encouraged by what he saw as signs of progress; moreover, he was eager for his own victory. Leaving his base in Antioch, he arrived in Constantinople in spring AD 378, where he crushed a revolt by inhabitants anxious about the ominous presence of the Goths on their doorstep. Valens reorganized his officers, replacing Traianus (whom he blamed for not winning at Ad Silices) with Sebstianus. He joined up with Sebastianus' force; reconnaissance alerted Valens that about 10,000 Goths were marching towards Adrianople from the north, about 25km away. Despite the unforgiving terrain, Valens reached the battle site north of Adrianople after a gruelling seven-hour march, where he fortified his camp with ditch and rampart.[9]

Astonishingly – and stupidly – Valens decided on an immediate attack, arrogantly dispensing with the invaluable help Gratian could bring to the battlefield.[10] This flew in the face of the advice from all around him. Richomeres delivered a letter asking Valens to wait for the arrival of reinforcements from Gratian before engaging in battle. Valens' officers, led by Victor, the *magister equitum*, also recommended that he wait for Gratian. However, Valens saw it all very differently: *carpe diem*, and why share the glory and spoils when he could have it all to himself? And there was a vocal faction led by Sebastianus, which urged immediate action. Ammianus describes the vanity shown by Valens:

> The fatal obstinacy of the emperor and the flattery of some of his courtiers prevailed. They urged immediate action to prevent Gratian sharing in a victory which in their opinion was already as good as won.

Valens broke two cardinal military rules: astonishingly over-confident and seriously underestimating his enemy, he led his army out from behind

Adrianople's walls to engage a small faction of the Goth army encamped there, numbering around 10,000 men.

Everyone anticipated a Roman victory. Open battle, as we have noted, was not the Goth's strong suite. Even Fritigern was pessimistic. On 8 August, Fritigern, waiting for the much-needed Greuthung to arrive, sent a Christian priest to Valens offering peace and an alliance in exchange for Roman territory to settle on. Wary of a possible trap, and confident of success because of his misguided assumption that he had numerical superiority in the shape of more than 40,000 troops, Valens rejected the proposals. He wanted to look strong and was somewhat insulted by the humility of the diplomacy. Regrettably, however, his estimates did not take into account that significant elements of the Gothic cavalry were still absent on a scouting and foraging expedition. Ammianus records the fateful miscalculation:

> When the barbarians ... arrived within fifteen miles from the station of Nike, ... the emperor, with wanton impetuosity, resolved on attacking them instantly, because those who had been sent forward to reconnoiter – what led to such a mistake is unknown – affirmed that their entire body did not exceed ten thousand men.[11]

It was not long before things started to go badly wrong for the Romans. The Romans were exhausted after their march; the Gauls, rested, had pitched camp on top of a hill. The Goths set up a smoke screen, then delayed proceedings with an exchange of hostages, in the hope of seeing the Greuthungi arrive: Fritigern himself would come and negotiate in exchange for a senior Roman officer as hostage. The Romans, meanwhile, were suffering in the full glare of the midday sun, their ordeal much worsened by the smoky fires Fritigern had lit to punish and irritate them further. Richimer was sent as hostage, but during the exchange, an unauthorized, treacherous pre-emptive strike was made by auxiliary archers, the Sagitarii, under the Iberian prince Bacurius. They were joined by crack units of the *scholae palatinae*, and the Scutarii led by Casio. The damage was done: the Romans were rapidly surrounded when the foraging cavalry returned. Ammianus again:

> Our left wing had advanced actually up to the wagons, with the intent to push on still further if they were properly supported; but they were deserted by the rest of the cavalry, and so pressed upon by the superior numbers of the enemy, that they were overwhelmed and beaten down ... And by this time such clouds of dust arose that it was scarcely possible to see the sky, which resounded with horrible cries; and in consequence, the darts, which were

bearing death on every side, reached their mark, and fell with deadly effect, because no one could see them beforehand so as to guard against them.[12]

To make matters yet worse for the Romans, Alatheus and Saphax had finally arrived with the Greuthungi, themselves augmented by detachments of Alans. The substantial Gothic reinforcements hurtled down from the mountains in a *blitzkrieg*; this effectively sealed the fate of the Romans who were squeezed in on themselves and at the mercy of friendly fire in which Roman slaughtered Roman. The Roman left wing over-extended itself, was cut off and wiped out, as were the *scholae*. Victor, Richomeres and Saturninus fled; the massacre continued until nightfall. A somewhat deluded Ammianus is at pains to show both sides of the battle:

> Then you might see the barbarian towering in his fierceness, hissing or shouting, fall with his legs pierced through, his right hand cut off, sword and all, or his side transfixed, and still, in the last gasp of life, casting round him defiant glances. The plain was covered with carcasses, strewing the mutual ruin of the combatants; while the groans of the dying, or of men fearfully wounded, were intense.[13]

Sebastianus and Traianus both fell, along with thirty-five tribunes. Themistius added a bleak and gloomy footnote: 'Thrace was overrun, Illiricum was overrun, armies vanished altogether, like shadows.'[14]

According to Ammianus, Valens died, deserted by the remnants of his bodyguard along with two-thirds of the Eastern army; sixteen divisions were slaughtered. He was killed by an arrow when seeking refuge with the remnants of two legions, the Lanccarii and the Mattiarii. A more embellished version has it that Valens was removed injured from the battlefield with bodyguards and some eunuchs, and hid in a peasant's cottage. The enemy attacked the cottage while the Roman archers fired on them. Unaware that Valens was inside, the Goths torched the cottage in reply. Valens died in the blaze; only one Goth escaped, and lived to tell the tale.[15]

Ammianus Marcellinus called the battle 'the beginning of evils for the Roman empire then and thereafter.' He graphically describes the immediate aftermath:

> After this disastrous battle, when night had veiled the earth in darkness, those who survived fled, some to the right, some to the left, or wherever fear guided them, each man seeking refuge among his relations, as no one could think of anything but himself, while all fancied the lances of the

enemy sticking in their backs. And far off were heard the miserable wailing of those who were left behind – the sobs of the dying, and the agonizing groans of the wounded. But when daylight returned, the conquerors, like wild beasts rendered still more savage by the blood they had tasted, and allured by the temptations of groundless hope, marched in a dense column upon Hadrianopolis, resolved to run any risk in order to take it, having been informed by traitors and deserters that the principal officers of state, the insignia of the imperial authority, and the treasures of Valens had all been placed there for safety, as in an impregnable fortress.

And to prevent the ardour of the soldiers from being cooled by delay, the whole city was blockaded by the fourth hour; and the siege from that time was carried on with great vigour, the besiegers, from their innate ferocity, pressing in to complete its destruction, while, on the other hand, the garrison was stimulated to great exertions by their natural courage.[16]

The whole of the Balkan region was now vulnerable to Gothic attack; the response from what was left of the remaining Roman garrisons was negligible. They were 'more easily slaughtered than sheep.'[17] Roman cities survived intact only because the Goths had no expertise in siege warfare and carried no siege equipment.

Ammianus Marcellinus is more or less our solitary source for the battle and its preamble. His account forms the climax of his history and is complemented by material from Eunapius' fragments and later by Zosimus, but Eunapius relies heavily on Ammianus, and Zosimus relies on Eunapius. To Ammianus, Adrianople was as dark a day as Cannae had been back in 216 BC. Generally speaking, though, caution is required, because Ammianus, no doubt aggrieved to be on the losing side, is naturally biased towards the Roman view of events, and because there is little or no corroboration of Ammianus from other sources. This has led to exaggeration amongst some historians, leaving others to unravel the hyperbole from the facts. This colourful description of battle-scene carnage gives some idea of the epic Lucanesque melodrama, stereotyping and hyperbole of which Ammianus was capable:

The plain was covered with carcasses, strewing the mutual ruin of the combatants; while the groans of the dying, or of men fearfully wounded, were intense, and caused great dismay all around ... The ground, covered with streams of blood, made their feet slip, so that all they endeavoured to do was to sell their lives as dearly as possible; and with such vehemence did they resist their enemies who pressed on them, that some were even killed by their own weapons. At last one black pool of blood disfigured everything, and wherever the eye turned, it could see nothing but piled up heaps of dead, and lifeless corpses trampled on without mercy.[18]

Ammianus' description of the Huns, Goths and Alans – the peoples queuing up to enter the empire in AD 376 – is clearly suspect, riddled as it is with clichés and very much in the anecdotal style of ethnography typical of Herodotus writing some 800 years earlier. The Huns were little more than 'two-legged beasts' – *bipedes bestias* – and walked oddly because they literally lived on horseback; they scarred the faces of their children and drank only the milk of mares; their food was never cooked but meat was warmed up by placing it between their thighs and the backs of their horses.[19] Zosimus adds that the Huns were incapable of fighting on foot because of their preference for life on the backs of horses, on which they even slept. It is unlikely that Ammianus had ever seen a Hun.

On the morning after their victory, the Goths woke up to learn that Adrianopole was theirs for the taking. The resulting siege was, however, unsuccessful, despite many Roman defections, including members of Valens' bodyguard, the *candidati*. The Goths, along with Roman deserters, Alans and Huns, proceded to devastate the fertile Thracian plain around Perinthus (modern Marmora Ereglisi in Turkey). Next, they ambitiously turned their attentions to Constantinople, contemplating a siege there. The voluminous city walls, the formidable straits of Bosphorus and a surprise attack by Arab mercenaries defending the city all conspired to disabuse them of the strategic sense of such an action. Ammianus describes a bizarre episode during the attack, barbaric even by Gothic standards:

> One of the [warriors from the East] a man with long hair wearing nothing but a loin cloth, drew his dagger and hurled himself with blood–curdling yells into the midst of the Gothic host. He cut a man's throat then put his lips to the ground and sucked the streaming blood. This appalling sight terrified the barbarians [the Goths].

The Goths now retreated back into Thrace, Illyricum and Dacia. In AD 379, Gratian appointed Theodosius I Emperor in the East (r. AD 379–395), and with it responsibility for the prosecution of the war. All Gothic soldiers serving in the Roman army were butchered. Four years of virtual deadlock followed.

The disaster that was Adrianopole had incalcuble consequences for the Romans. Not only had they lost a significant part of their army in the east, and their emperor, but many of their officers , including thirty-five tribunes and the generals Trajan and Sebastian, were slain in one of Rome's worst defeats and one of the darker of her *ateres dies*. Many experienced officials were also lost, as were many of the Roman arsenals along the Danube. There was now also a shortage of troops and a recruitment crisis. The Roman war machine in the east had been crippled for the time being. The Goths were now significant adversaries and a credible threat to Roman hegemony. Theodosius kept them in check to some degree with a series of alliances, the final one being in AD 382 which gave the Goths what they first demanded in 376. As *foederati*, the Goths in the future routinely provided military support, most notably in Theodosius' suppression of the upstart Maximus, as described in Pacatus' famous panegyric to Theodosius.[20]

This was the first time a whole ethnic group had been settled in Roman territory, armed and operating under their own laws and fielding their own army led by their own commanders. But the harmony did not last long: the Goths rose up again once they had helped extinguish the threats posed by Maximus and Eugenius. Alaric took over the command and invaded Greece and Illyricum; his ambition was to win a degree of military control within the empire. He was awarded the position of *magister militum* of Illyricum by Theodosius' successor, Arcadius. He then attacked Stilicho's Roman army in the West and attempted an invasion of Italy, then changed sides and held Illyricum for the West. In AD 409, he invaded Italy for a second time, leading ultimately to the sack of Rome.

The disaster at Adrianople did not mark the end of the Roman Empire, but it may just have signified the beginning of the end. Ammianus' graphic description of the battle highlights the physical constriction and immobility endured by the Roman infantry, the choking dust, the wailing of the injured and the overwhelming superiority of the enemy. As Toner argues, this becomes an eloquent metaphor for the dysfunction of the wider Roman Empire.[21] It should be remembered, though, that Adrianople was an Eastern disaster and the Eastern Empire survived for another 1,000 years, while it was the West which quickly declined and fell. In the longer term, Adrianople was important because it demonstrated that a fairly *ad hoc* army composed of deserters and disparate tribes could beat the Roman army and remain undefeated by the Roman army. This did not go unnoticed by Franks, Alamanni, Burgundians, Vandals, Sarmatians, Alans and Suebi, who followed the Goths over the increasingly porous Roman frontiers. After Adrianople, Goths, along with other barbarians in other parts of the empire, would have to be accommodated, organized, managed and controlled in a different, perhaps more tolerant and understanding way.

From a military history viewpoint, some argue that Adrianople marked the end of the dependence of armies on infantry, heralding the advent of the mediaeval knight and helping to elevate the cavalry to something like the position it was to enjoy for the next 1,500 years or so. Standing armies declined in importance as the vital role of auxiliary units of German allies increased. Citizens, commanders and emperors turned to militias (often German) to defend against usurpers or else to mount challenges to ruling emperors. Allegiance shifted from the state to the warlord, a situation more akin to feudal rather than classical warfare.

It is important to note, however, the causes for the disaster at Adrianople. It was not brought about by a seething horde of war-crazed Goths overrunning the Romans. Nor was it the vengeance of the pagan gods, angry and sulking at being supplanted by Christianity, as some, like Eunapius, would contend. The Romans lost so catastrophically at Adrianople due to serial incompetence. The victorious Goths were the same Goths, to a large extent, who had been received into the empire as immigrants from the wrong bank of the Danube in AD 376. There was nothing particularly unusual about allowing them entry, but it was a mistake to allow them to keep their weapons instead of disarming and re-arming them as and when required from Roman arsenals. The war crime perpetrated when food and other necessities were requisitioned by the Romans and replaced with dog meat in exchange for a child slave would obviously rankle for years to come; the bungled assassination attempt and the forced removal of Goths from Adrianople without provisions were all avoidable Roman errors and misinterpretations of the facts before them. Valens' obsession with a potentially booty-rich Persian campaign and his subsequent underestimation of the seriousness of the Gothic threat to Rome was similarly diverting. Impatience, selfishness and venality defined his decision to do battle before the essential support from Gratian arrived.[22]

Chapter 15

Alaric's Sack of Rome AD 410

Alaric I was the Christian King of the Visigoths from AD 395 until his death in 410.[1] He emerged on the scene as leader of a motley band of Goths who invaded Thrace in AD 391, but was halted by the half-Vandal Roman general Stilicho. Alaric then joined the Roman army, serving under the Gothic general Gainas. In AD 394, he led a 20,000-strong Gothic army which helped Theodosius subdue the usurper Flavius Eugenius at the Battle of Frigidus. Alaric's was something of a Pyrrhic victory; he lost a quarter of his troops. To add insult to injury, Theodosius was distinctly unimpressed with Alaric's contribution to his war effort, so Alaric left the army and was elected *reiks* (tribal leader or king) of the Visigoths in AD 395. That same year, Theodosius died of heart failure; the empire was divided between his two sons: Flavius Arcadius in the east and Flavius Honorius in the west. Arcadius showed no interest in empire building, while Honorius was still a minor – Theodosius had appointed Flavius Stilicho *magister equitum* and guardian of Honorius. Honorius cemented the bond by marrying Stilicho's daughter, Maria. A disappointed and angry Alaric was passed over in his hoped-for permanent command of a Roman army. Alaric was one of those educated and clever Goths who became career Romans, excelling in the Roman military hierarchy, taking sides when necessary, winning all or losing all. Alaric was different, though, because his aspirations to get close to Rome were that much higher than was typical for a barbarian.

Hoping to win his permanent Roman command, Alaric marched on Constantinople with an army which snowballed in size as he progressed, in much the same way as Fritigern's had before him. But Constantinople was too daunting a challenge and the Romans blocked him anyway. He then moved on Greece, where he sacked the more vulnerable Piraeus and devastated Corinth, Megara, Argos and Sparta. Athens capitulated and was spared devastation. To prevent further death and destruction, Arcadius appointed Alaric *magister militum* in Illyricum. Alaric had finally got the command he craved.

In AD 401, Alaric invaded Italy[2] and laid siege to Milan, but he was later defeated by Stilicho, first at Pollentia (modern Pollenza) and then, accused of violating the treaty signed after Pollentia, at the Battle of Verona the following year. Amongst Stilicho's prisoners were Alaric's wife and children, and ten year's worth of pillaged booty. Honorius moved the western capital from Rome to Ravenna, believing it to be more secure against attacks from the Goths.

Alaric, as it happened, was something of a Romanophile and, as we have seen, entertained hopes of getting closer to the city – militarily and politically. His military command helped him to achieve this. Invasion would assist him further. He even encouraged use of the Latinized name Alaricus. It was because of Alaric's subsequent invasion that the capital city was transferred from Mediolanum (Milan) to Ravenna (it had been moved from Rome to Mediolanum in AD 286); Legio XX (*Valeria Victrix*) was recalled from Britannia. Alaric and Stilicho became allies of sorts.

Tensions between Roman west and east had risen sharply: Stilicho proposed using Alaric's army to realize Honorius' claim to the prefecture of Illyricum. Alaric, now in Noricum, threatened that he would only refrain from war with Rome if he was paid the extortionate sum of 4,000lb of gold in compensation. The Roman Senate consented to pay, under pressure from Stilicho, who did not want to add to his list of belligerent enemies. There was trouble in Gaul with Constantine, who had crossed the Channel from Britannia, and with the Vandals, Sueves and Alans who had crossed the Rhine and invaded.

In AD 408, Arcadius died after a short illness. Stilicho and Honorius squabbled over who should travel east to settle the succession of the Eastern Empire. There were rumours abroad that Stilicho wanted to place his son, Eucherius, on the eastern throne. When his first wife Maria died, Stilicho insisted that the emperor marry his younger daughter, Thermantia.[3] But Honorius had had enough. Soon after, Olympius, his stooge, provoked a mutiny of the army during which most of Stilicho's people were killed; Olympius persuaded Honorius that Stilicho was an enemy of the state and was appointed *magister officium*. Stilicho took refuge in a church in Ravenna but, faithful to Honorius to the end, was arrested and executed; his son was also slain. Honorius inflamed the Roman people to massacre tens of thousands of wives and children of Goths serving in the Roman army. Unsurprisingly, this atrocity led to around 30,000 Gothic soldiers defecting to Alaric, joining him on his march on Rome over the Julian Alps to avenge their murdered families.[4] Honorius had rejected Alaric's demand for a sum of gold and an exchange of prisoners. *En route*, Alaric sacked Aquileia and Cremona and laid waste to the lands along the Adriatic. In September AD 408, Alaric was menacingly encamped ouside the walls of Rome whence he began his siege of the city and blockaded the Tiber.[5] The hunt was on for scapegoats and one of the victims was Stilicho's widow, Serena, strangled in an act of post-mortem justice.[6]

Alaric's greatest ally was starvation. It was not long before the Senate capitulated, agreeing in exchange for food to send an envoy to Honorius in Ravenna to urge peace. Alaric agreed, but not before the Senate's failed attempt to unsettle Alaric; their flaccid threats were met with derision and a loud guffaw when the Goth retorted: 'The thicker the hay, the easier it's cut down!' The Romans eventually agreed a huge ransom of 5,000lb of gold, 30,000lb of silver, 4,000 silken tunics, 3,000 hides dyed scarlet, 3,000 pounds of pepper and 40,000 Gothic slaves. According to Gibbon, 'the Senate presumed to ask, in modest and suppliant tone, "If such, O king! are your demands, what do you intend to leave us?" "Your lives," replied the haughty conqueror.'[7] Prodigious as it may seem, the ransom was probably not beyond the deep pockets of some of Rome's more affluent senators. They made little contribution – the bill was paid by the official ransacking of pagan temples.

As we have seen, Alaric had hopes of insinuating himself into the Roman political machine and winning land within the Roman borders. The Senate sent envoys, including Pope Innocent I, to Ravenna to encourage the emperor to make a deal with the Goths. Alaric was much more conciliatory this time and went to Ariminum, where he discussed terms with Honorius' diplomats. He demanded, quite reasonably, the provinces of Rhaetia and Noricum as a homeland for the Visigoths – a strip of territory 200 miles long and 150 miles wide between the Danube and the Gulf of Venice. He also demanded grain and – prize of them all – the rank of *magisterium utriusque militae*, commander-in-chief of the Imperial Army, just as Stilicho had been. Jovius, leader of the imperial delegation, agreed, but predictably, Honorius refused to see the long-term picture and declined. He did not want another barbarian in the imperial hierarchy, and he subsequently tried to infiltrate a unit of Illyrian soldiers into Rome.[8] The army was intercepted by Alaric and, infuriated by these insults, he just as predictably reacted by besieging Rome a second time, this time destroying the Roman granaries at Portus for good measure. Starvation loomed again: the high price of relief this time was permission from the Senate for Alaric to install a rival emperor to Honorius – the Greek Priscus Attalus, prefect of the city (*praefectus urbi*), something of a star in Rome. Alaric took Galla Placidia, Honorius' sister, prisoner. Usurpers were always a sure way to concentrate the mind of an emperor.

Alaric had Attalus make him *magister utriusque militium*, and his brother-in-law Ataulf, who had arrived with reinforcements, was given the rank of *comes domesticorum equitum*. They then marched on Ravenna to overthrow Honorius and place Attalus on the imperial throne.

Victory was in Alaric's grasp: Honorius was on the point of surrender when an army from the Eastern Empire arrived to defend Ravenna. Heraclian, who was governor of Africa, turned off Rome's grain supply, threatening the city with more famine. Jerome rumoured cannibalism within the walls. Alaric wanted to send a modest Gothic force of 500 men to invade Africa and secure food for Rome, but perversely Attalus vetoed this, fearing that the Goths would seize Africa for themselves. Attalus marched on Ravenna with Alaric and succeeded in getting Honorius to propose some form of power-sharing arrangement – a clear indication of the legitimate emperor's feebleness. Attalus stubbornly insisted that Honorius be deposed and go into exile on an island. This was not in Alaric's script, so he had the reactionary and ineffective Attalus deposed and reopened negotiations with Honorius.[9]

This time he was confounded by the inconvenient emergence on the scene of the malevolent Gothic general Sarus. He was of the Amalis, a clan which harboured eternal hostility against Alaric's people. His intervention at this critical juncture may be explained by the possibility that he now felt threatened by Alaric.[10] Sensing duplicity on the part of Honorius, an outraged Alaric thundered south with his army and stormed through the Porta Salaria to threaten the very existence of the city. Some say that Alaric bribed elderly senators inside with the promise of Goth slave boys if they opened the gates to him. In any event, Rome was taken. Jerome lamented: 'My voice sticks in my throat, and, as I dictate, sobs choke me. The City which had taken the whole world has itself been taken.'[11] Alaric, a Christian, was busy desecrating a Christian city with his Christian Goths.

It seems that the storming of Rome in AD 410 was not nearly as catastrophic and horrendous as it might have been. Indeed, it goes down as one of the most benign and least destructive of pivotal sackings in history. There are stories of clemency, churches (for example, the basilicas of St Peter and St Paul) being saved; the sparing of those seeking sanctuary therein, even to the extent of escorting holy women there to safety, for example one Marcella, before systematically looting their homes; pots of gold and silver and other liturgical vessels remaining untouched because they 'belonged to St Peter'; and a *matrona* appealing successfully to the better nature of a Goth who was on the point of raping her. One nun was given help returning gold and silver, God's gold and silver, to her church; she had concealed it from the looters.[12] Nevertheless, it was still a disaster of the first order, with three days of unrelenting looting and rapine. Casualties included the mausoleums of Augustus and Hadrian, where the ashes of many Roman emperors and their families and friends were scattered to the four winds. The Goths also removed a huge silver *ciborium* weighing 2,025lb, a gift from the Emperor Constantine, from the Lateran Palace. Most of the vandalism occurred around the Salarian Gate, where the old senate house and Gardens of Sallust were wrecked along with the Basilicas Aemilia and Julia.[13]

The taking of movables apart, most of Rome's magnificent buildings escaped unscathed, in direct contrast to the Gaulish sack of Rome in 390 BC, where only the Capitol survived. So why is it that Alaric's assault was seemingly so half-hearted and fails to live up to the stereotype we have of Goths running rampage in an orgy of unremitting rape and pillage? We have already noted that Alaric was anxious to ingratiate himself with Rome and win some sort of military and political standing there. Alaric was a civilized man; he acted with restraint and patience time and time again when confounded by events over which he had little control, by a stubborn Honorius and implacable Stilicho. He was astute enough to opt for short-term compromise in his long-term mission to settle the Goths. Alaric sacked Rome reluctantly because he had to satisfy, to some extent at least, the appetite and expectation of his army for booty, but more as a signal to Honorius, hoping that the emperor would install and accommodate him in some capacity or other. He used his assault on the city as a gambling counter, in the belief that Honorius would be persuaded to bring him into his circle by the threat that was posed to his city. Alaric, however, misread the situation completely: Rome was no longer Honorius' city – Ravenna was. To a pragmatic Honorius, Rome was political history, no longer the powerful hub it had been for centuries. So Alaric got nowhere and Rome was more or less saved from destruction. Alaric had failed: he might possess Rome but he was no nearer winning for himself the inside position within the Roman establishment. He had no permanent imperial command and now he would be excluded from the imperial court forever. Just as importantly, the Goths were still a displaced people with nowhere to go and nowhere to call home. It was not until AD 417 that the Visigoths were able to found an autonomous kingdom of their own within the boundaries of the Western Empire. Alaric's fervid ambition to find for the Goths a permanent, sustainable homeland was finally realized.

After Rome, Alaric headed into Calabria with designs on invading Africa, the bread-basket of Rome, and of Italy. His plans were thrown into confusion by a storm which smashed his fleet; many of his troops drowned. Alaric himself died soon after in Cosenza. According to Jordanes, his body and some precious spoils were buried under the river bed of the Busento in accordance with the funerary practices of the Visigoths. The stream was temporarily dammed while his grave was dug; the river was then restored to its natural course. The prisoners who did the work were put to death so that the location of the king's final resting place remained as much a secret as possible.[14] Alaric's brother-in-law Ataulf succeeded him; he married Honorius' sister Galla Placidia three years later.

Rome soon responded; there was the same old grain shortages within two years of the sacking and the returning Gallic nobleman Rutilius Namatianus seeing what he described as an *ordo renascendi* – a brave new world.[15] Two years after the death of Alaric, Ataulf led the Visigoths into south-western Gaul, where, in AD 418, Honorius was forced to recognize their kingdom at Toulouse. In AD 423, Honorius died and was succeeded by Valentinian III, though still a child at the time. The Vandals invaded North Africa, defeated the Romans and, in AD 439, took Carthage, which Genseric, their leader, made his capital. In AD 451, Attila and the Huns, already so powerful that they were paid an annual tribute by Rome, invaded Gaul with the Vandals. They were defeated at the Battle of Châlons by the Visigoths under Flavius Aetius, military commander of the West. In AD 455, on the death of Valentinian III, the Vandals walked into an undefended Rome, which they plundered at liberty for two weeks. If Alaric's sack was restrained, this was even more so, despite the length of time spent plundering. The Vandals did, though, make off with treasures from the Temple of Peace and lifted the gilded bronze tiles from the Temple of Jupiter Optimus Maximus. This outrage gives us the word 'vandalism'. They took Licinia Eudoxia (AD 422–462) and her daughters hostage; she was the Roman empress daughter of Eastern Emperor Theodosius II. Her husbands included the Western Emperors Valentinian III and Petronius Maximus.

Rome had held sway in the Mediterranean region for 600 years or so. The city had remained unmolested for 800 years. Alaric's sacking exposed the Western Roman Empire's increasing vulnerability and military fragility. The political and cultural shock waves must have been overwhelming to all those who viewed Rome as the Eternal City.[16] Rome was home to the richest senatorial noble families and the centre of their civilized, cultured world; to pagans it was the sacred origin of the empire, and to Christians the seat of the heir of Saint Peter, Pope Innocent I, the leading bishop of the West. Jerome summed it up for many when he asked, 'If Rome can perish, what can be safe?' To many Romans, the destruction of their city was seen as divine retribution for rejecting the traditional pagan gods for Christianity. This provided the impetus for Saint Augustine to write *The City of God*, questioning the role of the pagan gods as history-makers. Non-Christians clung to the belief that Rome had succumbed because the old gods had withdrawn their protection. But Augustine was far from convinced. Where were the gods when the Romans could not break the siege of Veii? Where were the gods when the Gauls sacked Rome under Brennus? These were just two of the leading questions he asked.

Orosius too, in his *History Against the Pagans*, proved that Rome suffered many disasters before the coming of Christ. On a more mundane level, Stilicho's military failings were also blamed.[17] Perhaps Alaric's greatest legacy was that he, through the disaster he visited on the city of Rome and on the Romans, was the man who made it possible for the Goths to make history, whereas before they were mere participants in other people's histories.

Epilogue

It took Rome some 1,200 years to finally fail and fall but, as we have seen, there were many decisive Roman military disasters along the way. The reasons for, and causes of, disaster are many and various, and the Romans had their share: incompetence, myopia, surprise, poor intelligence, unsuitable terrain, arrogance, impetuousness, glory-seeking, bad luck – all of these played their part in the disasters described here. However, Roman military disasters allowed the Romans to learn lessons. Where they scored time and time again was in their ability to learn from military mistakes and to take and adapt the good things from their victorious enemies, to swallow their collective, national pride and react with vision and versatility; to ensure, through political and miltary sagacity, an endless supply of new recruits to revivify and replenish armies which had been depleted by disaster on a scale that would have destroyed most other nations; to rise with steely determination from the depths of disaster and put their dark days behind them – to forget their Cannaes, their Carrhaes and their Teutoburg Forests and respond with a vengeance. Rome's military disasters were just as critical and crucial to them over the centuries as their numerous victories. Without their disasters there would have been no enduring Roman success.

Typical *cursus honorum* in the second century BC

Position Attained	Typical Age
Ten years of military service in the cavalry or on the political staff of a relative or friend.	—
quaestor, eight–twelve in number. Financial administration in Rome or in a province as second-in-command to the Governor.	30 (minimum age)
tribune of the plebs, ten in number. Presided over the concilium plebis.	—
aedile, four in number, two curule and two plebeian. Administrative role in Rome, with responsibility for the corn supply, festivals etc. (Optional role.)	36
praetor, six in number. Judicial role in Rome, in charge of provinces not allocated to consuls. Commanded one legion and allies.	39
consul, two in number. Governed larger provinces and held major commands in all wars: led two legions and two allied *alae*. Other role was to preside over the Senate and assemblies.	40
censor, two in office for five years. Magistracy held by most distinguished ex-consuls. Their fuction was to carry out the census.	—

Appendix 2

Roman Assemblies

Senate – Consisted of 300 members regulated by the censors. Members were from the eighteen senior centuries, i.e. they had property worth more than 400,000 HS. Its role was to advise magistrates, especially the consuls.

Concilium Plebis – Made up of plebeians and divided into thirty-five tribes, with membership based on ancestry. Its role was to elect the tribune and the aedile, as well as passing laws.

Comitia Tributa – Made up of citizens, including patricians. Its role was the same as above, but it elected curule aediles and quaestors.

Comitia Centuriata – Comprised citizens divided into 193 voting centuries. It was originally formed from citizen militia with membership based on possession of military equipment. It was presided over by a consul or praetor. Its functions included: the election of consuls, praetors and censors; declarations of war; and ratification of peace treaties.

Appendix 3

The Seven Kings of Rome

Romulus (753–715 BC) – The fabled founder of Rome.

Numa Pompilius (715–673 BC) – The unusually peaceful Roman king.

Tullius Hostilius (673–642 BC) – Responsible for the destruction of Alba Longa and the migration of its inhabitants to Rome.

Ancus Marcius (642–617 BC) – Extended the city, built the first bridge across the Tiber and founded Ostia to give Rome a seaport.

Tarquinius Priscus (617–579 BC) – An Etruscan who built Rome's first sewer, the Cloaca Maxima, laid out the Circus Maximus and started work on a temple to Jupiter on the Capitoline Hill.

Servius Tullius (579–535 BC) – Divided the Romans into tribes and classes, and so established a constitution in which wealth was the main factor. Built the city walls, five miles in circumference with nineteen gates, and embracing all seven hills of Rome. He transferred the regional festival of Diana from Aricia to the Aventine Hill.

Tarquinius Superbus (534–510 BC) Rome's last king. His son, Sextus, raped Lucretia, a virtuous *matrona*, with the consequence that Tarquinius was exiled and the monarchy gave way to the Roman Republic.

Appendix 4

Some Carthaginian Generals

Hamilcar Barca (*c.* 275–228 BC) – Leader of the Barcid family and father of Hannibal, Hasdrubal and Mago. He was father-in-law to Hasdrubal the Fair. Barca means 'thunderbolt'.

Hannibal (died 238 BC) – Took part in the Mercenary War between Carthage and rebel mercenaries. Not be confused with the more famous Hannibal Barca, son of Hamilcar Barca. During the Mercenary War, he took over from Hanno II the Great as a commander of the Carthaginian army. During the siege of Tunis, he was captured in a night raid and crucified, along with other high-ranking Carthaginians.

Hasdrubal the Fair (*c.* 270 BC–221 BC) – Governor in Iberia after Hamilcar Barca's death and founder of Cartagena. He was the brother-in-law of Hannibal and son-in-law of Hamilcar Barca.

Adherbal (died 230 BC) – The admiral of the Carthaginian fleet during the First Punic War. He defeated Publius Claudius Pulcher in the Battle of Drepana in 249 BC.

Hanno II the Great (*fl.* third century BC) – Leader of the faction in Carthage opposed to continuing the war against Rome and opposed by Hamilcar Barca. He is blamed for preventing reinforcements reaching Hamilcar's son Hannibal after his victory at the Battle of Cannae. Hanno stood down the Carthaginian navy in 244 BC, crucially allowing Rome time to rebuild its navy and finally defeat Carthage. After the Second Punic War, Hanno withheld payment to his Berber mercenaries, who revolted; Hanno took control of the Carthaginian army in order to defeat them, but he failed and returned the army to the control of Hamilcar. The two joined together to crush the rebels in 238 BC. After the defeat of Carthage at the Battle of Zama in 202 BC, he was among the ambassadors at the peace talks with the Romans.

Hannibal Barca (247 – *c.* 181 BC) – Son of Hamilcar Barca and generally considered one of the greatest military commanders in history. After the defeat of Carthage, Hannibal took refuge with Prusias I of Bithynia, who was at war with Rome's ally, King Eumenes II of Pergamon. Hannibal served Prusias and on one occasion had large pots filled with poisonous snakes thrown into Eumenes' ships. Under pressure from the Romans, Prusias gave him up, but Hannibal took poison at Libyssa on the Sea of Marmara; Hannibal had long carried the poison about with him in a ring. He left behind a letter that read, 'Let us relieve the Romans from the anxiety they have so long experienced, since they think it tries their patience too much to wait for an old man's death.'

Hasdrubal II (245–207 BC) – Hamilcar Barca's second son and the brother of the famous general Hannibal, and of Mago. When Hannibal crossed the Alps to Italy in 218 BC, Hasdrubal was left in command of Hispania. For the next six years, he would be embroiled in fighting against the brothers Gnaeus and Publius Cornelius Scipio. In 207 BC, he was trounced at the Battle of the Metaurus, where he was killed. His corpse was beheaded, the head put in a sack and thrown into Hannibal's camp.

Mago (243–203 BC) – Third son of Hamilcar Barca, he was influential in the Second Punic War, with commands in Hispania, Gallia Cisalpina and Italy. He excelled himself at Lake Trasimene and Cannae. Mago lives on with us to this day: on Menorca he founded the city today called Port Mahon, which has given its name to the sauce known as mayonnaise.

Hasdrubal Gisco (died 202 BC) – Fought against Rome in Hispania and North Africa during the Second Punic War. Livy describes him as 'the best and most distinguished general this war produced after the three sons of Hamilcar.'[1] Elsewhere, Livy quotes Fabius Maximus, who described Hasdrubal as 'a general who showed his speed chiefly in retreat.'[2] He was an able diplomat and raised three large armies, in Iberia and in Africa, after heavy defeats.

Hasdrubal Beotarch – A general during the Third Punic War. Hasdrubal was in command at the Siege of Carthage in 146 BC, where he was defeated by Scipio Aemilianus and lost the war to the Romans. According to Polybius, Hasdrubal's wife and two sons hurled themselves into a burning temple on news of the defeat and Hasdrubal's surrender to the Romans. He was taken to Rome and paraded at Scipio's triumph, but was later allowed to live in Italy.

Hanno – Son of Hannibal, and a general during the First Punic War (264 to 241 BC). Hanno was sent to relieve Hannibal Gisco who was holed up under siege at Agrigentum. Hanno concentrated his troops at Heraclea Minoa and captured the Roman supply base at Herbesos. He duped the Romans when he ordered his Numidian cavalry to attack the Roman cavalry and then feign retreat. The Romans pursued the Numidians as they retreated, only to find themselves face-to-face with the main Carthaginian column, which inflicted heavy casualties. The siege lasted several months before the Romans won the day and forced Hanno to retreat.

Appendix 5

Greek and Roman Authors

Aelian (Claudius Aelianus, *c*. AD 175 – *c*. 235) – Roman author of *De Natura Animalium* and *Varia Historia*.

Aeneas Tacticus (fourth century BC) – Greek writer on the art of war who wrote a number of treatises (*hypomnemata*) on the subject. The only extant one, *How to Survive under Siege*, describes the best ways of defending a fortified city.

Aeschylus (525 – *c*. 456 BC) – Greek tragedian.

Ammianus Marcellinus (AD 325/330 – after 391) – Late-Empire historian. Author of *Res Gestae*.

Appian (Appianus of Alexandria, *c*. AD 95–165) – Politician and historian whose *Bellum Civili*, a history of the late Republic, arranged geographically, survives in fragmentary form. Written in Greek, it covers the Spanish and Mithridatic Wars.

Aristophanes (*c*. 446 BCE – *c*. 386 BCE) – Athenian comic playwright.

Aristotle (384–322 BC) – Prolific Greek philosopher and tutor of Alexander the Great.

Arrian (Lucius Flavius Arrianus, *c*. AD 86–160) – Roman general and historian from Bithynia, noted for his account of the campaigns of Alexander the Great, the *Anabasis* and *Contra Alanos* (*Order of March Against the Alans*). Also wrote *Ars Tactica*.

Athenaeus (late second century AD) – Greek grammarian and author of the fifteen-book *Deipnosophistai* (*Dinner-table Philosophers*).

Augustine of Hippo (AD 354–430) – Also known as Saint Augustine, author of *De Civitate Dei*, amongst many other works.

Aulus Gellius (*c*. AD 125 – after 180) – Latin author of *Noctes Atticae*, a miscellany of notes on grammar, philosophy, history and antiquarianism.

Aurelius Victor (Sextus Aurelius Victor, *c.* AD 320 – *c.* 390) – Author of *De Caesaribus*, covering the period from Augustus to Constantius II, and *De Viris Illustribus Romae.*

Ausonius (Decimius Magnus Ausonius, *c.* AD 310 – *c.* 395) – A Latin poet and teacher of rhetoric. He also wrote on the workings of a marble-cutting water mill.

Caesar (Gaius Julius Caesar, 100–44 BC) – General, politician and writer, famous for his commentaries on the Gallic and Civil Wars: *De Bello Gallico* and *Bellum Civile.*

Cassius Dio – *See* Dio Cassius.

Cato the Elder (234–149 BC) – Author of what was probably Rome's first military treatise, the *De Re Militari*, as well as other works, including the *Origines*, the first history of Rome in Latin. The *De Re Militari* only survives in fifteen fragments covering battle formations and discipline.

Catullus (*c.* 84–54 BC) – Poet who espoused the life of *otium* and was one of the first writers of Roman personal love poetry in his *Carmina.*

Celsus (*c.* 25 BC – *c.* AD 50) – Medical writer and author of *De Medicina*, the sole surviving section of a much larger encyclopedia. The *De Medicina* is a primary source on diet, pharmacy, surgery and other specialties, and it is one of the prime sources for medical knowledge in the Roman world. The lost portions of his encyclopedia probably included agriculture, law, rhetoric and military arts. He made contributions to the classification of human skin disorders in dermatology.

Chrysostom (John, *c.* AD 347–407) – Monk pupil of Libanius, author of *The Type of Women Who Ought to be Taken as Wives*, written in Greek.

Cicero (Marcus Tullius Cicero, 106–43 BC) – Roman politician and orator, author of numerous works on politics and philosophy. A large part of his copious correspondence survives.

Clement of Alexandria (Titus Flavius Clemens, *c.* AD 150 – *c.* 215) – Christian theologian who taught at the Catechetical School of Alexandria.

Ctesias of Cnidus (fifth century BC) – Greek physician and historian from Cnidus in Caria. Author of the *Persica* and *Indica.*

De Viris Illustribus or ***De Hominibus Illustribus*** – Various works go by this name, including those by Aurelius Victor, Jerome and an anonymous version. There is also *Liber De Excellentibus Ducibus Gentium* by Cornelius Nepos.

Dio Cassius Cocceianus (*c.* AD 155–230) – Roman senator and author of an eighty-book history of Rome, written in Greek. *Historia Romanae* is our principle source for the wars of the second century BC. It took twenty-two years of research.

Diodorus Siculus (*fl.* 30s BC) – Sicilian Greek who wrote the forty-book *Bibliotheca Historica* (*The Library of History*) down to the mid-first century BC.

Diogenes Laertius (after AD 200) – Author of *Lives and Opinions of Eminent Philosophers*.

Dionysius of Halicarnassus (*fl.* 30s BC) – Wrote the *Roman Antiquities*, a history of Rome down to 264 BC, in Greek.

Ennius (*c.* 239 – *c.* 169 BC) – Rome's first epic poet; composed the *Annales*.

Epictetus (AD 55–135) – Greek Stoic philosopher.

Eunapius of Sardis (b. AD 346) – Wrote a contemporary history soon after the Battle of Adrianople in AD 378, used by Zosimus as a key source. Also wrote Lives of the Sophists, which adumbrates Alaric's invasion of Greece.

Euripides (*c.* 480 – 406 BC) – Greek tragedian.

Eutropius (*fl.* second half of the fourth century AD) – Wrote his summary of Roman history around AD 380.

Fabius (Q. Fabius Pictor, *fl.* 225–200 BC) – Rome's first historian and the source for many who came after him.

Fasti Triumphales published around 12 BC. They are a list of triumphs from the foundation of Rome down to the reign of Augustus; now part of the larger *Fasti Capitolini*.

Festus (*fl.* AD 370) – Wrote a summary of Roman history, *Breviarum Rerum Gestarum Populi Romani*.

Florus (Lucius Annaeus, *c.* AD 74 – *c.* 130) – Author of *Epitome de T. Livio Bellorum omnium annorum DCC Libri duo* (*Epitome of Roman History*).

Frontinus (Sextus Julius Frontinus, *c.* AD 40–103) – Governor of Britannia AD 74–78; author of a military treatise, the *Strategemata*, and a seminal work on the water supply of Rome, *De Aquis*. The *Strategemata* comprises four books with over 400 strategems described, including preparations for battle, ambushes, retreats, sieges, discipline, sayings and justice. His other military work, non extant, is *De Scientia Militari*.

Herodotus (*c*. 484-420 BC) – A Greek from Halicarnassus, he is known as the father of history. He wrote his *Histories* covering the Persian Wars.

Homer (seventh or eighth century BC) – Greek epic poet and author of the *Iliad* and the *Odyssey*.

Horace (Quintus Horatius Flaccus, 65–8 BC) – Poet who wrote the *Odes, Epodes, Satires, Carmen Saeculare*, etc.

Jerome (Saint Jerome or Eusebius Sophronius Hieronymus, *c*. AD 347–420) – Priest, theologian and historian whose many works include the *De Viris Illustribus*.

Jordanes (sixth century AD) – Roman bureaucrat who turned to history. He wrote *Romana* on the history of Rome. His best-known work, however, is the *De origine actibusque Getarum*, written in Constantinople about AD 551. It is the only extant ancient work dealing with the early history of the Goths.

Josephus (Flavius Josephus, *c*. AD 37–100) – Jewish general who fought against Rome, and historian; wrote an account, in Greek, of the Jewish War of AD 66–73 (*Bellum Judaicum*) in which he fought. Also wrote *Antiquitates Judaicum (Jewish Antiquities)*.

Juvenal (Decimus Iunius Iuvenalis, late first century/early second century AD) – Satirist who demolished many aspects of Roman life.

Livy (Titus Livius, 59 BC – AD 17) – Born in Padova, his *Ab Urbe Condita* in Latin takes us down to 9 BC and is our main source for the early history of Rome and the Carthaginian Wars. Of the 142 books, only thirty-five survive (1-10, 21-45); all but two of the *Epitomes and Periochae* do survive, however.

Lucan (Marcus Annaeus Lucanus, AD 39–65) – Latin epic poet who composed the *Bellum Civile*, on the wars between Julius Caesar and Pompey.

Lucian (*c*. AD 125 – after 180) – There are seventy extant surviving works attributed to Lucian. He wrote comic dialogues, rhetorical essays and prose fiction and is one of the earliest novelists in Western culture. In *A True Story* he parodies some of the tales told by Homer in the *Odyssey* and also stories from Thucydides. He anticipated fictional themes like voyages to the moon and Venus, extra-terrestrial life and wars between planets, nearly two millennia before Jules Verne and H.G. Wells. His novel is widely regarded as the earliest work of science fiction.

Manetho (third century BC) – Egyptian historian, author of *Aegyptiaca*.

Manilius (*fl*. first century AD) – Author of five-volume poem, the *Astronomica*.

Martial (Marcus Valerius Martialis, *c.* AD 40–100) – Writer of epigrams and the *Spectacula.*

Nepos (Cornelius Nepos, *c.* 110–24 BC) – Cisalpine Gaul who wrote biographies, including those of foreign generals: *De Viris Illustribus* and *Prologue to the Lives of Foreign Generals.*

Olympiodorus of Thebes (*fl.* before AD 380 – after 425) – Greek historian who wrote a detailed history of AD 407–425, sourced by Sozomen, Philostorgius and Zosimus, to give an important understanding of Alaric before the sack of Rome.

Onasander (first century AD) – A Greek philosopher and the author of *Strategikos*, a comprehensive work on the duties of a general.

Orosius (Paulus Orosius, fifth century AD) – Portuguese author of *Historiarum Adversum Paganos* (*Histories Against the Pagans*).

Ovid (P. Ovidius Naso, 43 BC – AD 18) – Poet whose works include the *Fasti,* an invaluable poetic description of the Roman religious calendar.

Pacatus Drepanius (fourth century AD) – Panegyricist.

Palatine Anthology or **Anthologia Palatina** – A collection of Greek poems and epigrams which comprises material from the seventh century BC to 600 AD, later forming the basis of the *Greek Anthology.*

Pausanias (*fl.* AD 150–180) – Greek author of the *Description of Greece.*

Petronius (*c.* AD 27–66 AD) Roman author of the novel *Satyricon.*

Philostorgius (*c.* AD 368 – *c.* 440) – Author of a homoean Greek church history leaning heavily on Olympiodorus.

Pindar (*c.* 522–443 BC) – Greek lyric poet.

Plato (*c.* 428 – *c.* 348 BC) – Athenian philosopher.

Pliny the Elder (C. Plinius Secundus Maior, AD 23–79) – Roman author of the *Historia Naturalis*, thirty-seven books of which survive. His *De Iaculatione Equestri* (*On Throwing A Javelin from a Horse*) is lost. He wrote it while a prefect of a cavalry unit in Germany, and it is quoted in his *Historia Naturalis* at 8, 159, 162.

Pliny the Younger (Gaius Plinius Caecilius Secundus, AD 61 – *c.* 112) – Lawyer, author, magistrate and nephew of the elder Pliny. His letters are a major historical source for the period. Pliny served as an imperial magistrate under Trajan and his letters to the emperor provide a rare record of the relationship between the imperial office and provincial governors.

Plutarch (Lucius Mestrius Plutarchus, *c.* AD 50–120) – His *Parallel Lives* is a fund of information in Greek on politicians and military commanders (e.g. Romulus, Coriolanus, Camillus) amongst other famous Greeks and Romans.

Polyaenus (second century AD) – Macedonian author, best known for his *Stratagems in War.*

Polybius (*c.* 200–118 BC) – Greek politician from Arcadia and historian of the Republic. Fought against the Romans in the Third Macedonian War and was then sent to Rome as a hostage.

Procopius of Caesarea (*c.* AD 500 – *c.* 560) – Accompanying the Roman general Belisarius in the wars of the Emperor Justinian, he became the principal historian of the sixth century AD, writing the *Wars of Justinian*, the *Buildings of Justinian* and the *Secret History*. He is the last major historian of the ancient world.

Propertius (Sextus Propertius, *c.* 50– 15 BC) – Roman elegist and love poet who wrote about his love for Cynthia – and poems about Tarpeia and Cleopatra.

Quintilian (Marcus Fabius Quintilianus, *c.* AD 35 – *c.* 100) – Author of the twelve-volume *Institutio Oratoria*, a study of rhetoric.

Quintus Curtius Rufus (*fl.* AD 41–54 or AD 69–79) – Roman historian whose only surviving work, *Historiae Alexandri Magni*, is an incomplete biography of Alexander the Great in ten books, written in Latin.

Sallust (Gaius Sallustius Crispus, 86–35 BC) – Author of works in Latin on the Jugurthine War (*Bellum Jugurthinum*) and the conspiracy led by Catiline (*Bellum Catalinae*) as well as the *Histories* covering 78– 67 BC, which survives in fragments. Served under Caesar in Gaul.

Seneca the Elder (Marcus Annaeus Seneca, 54 BC – *c.* AD 39) – Rhetorician and writer, father of Seneca the Younger.

Seneca the Younger (Lucius Annaeus Seneca, *c.* 4 BC – AD 65) – Stoic philosopher, politician and dramatist; tutor and advisor to Emperor Nero.

Servius (Maurus Servius Honoratus, late fourth century and early fifth century AD) – Grammarian and the author of commentaries on the works of Virgil, the *In tria Virgilii Opera Expositio.*

Silius Italicus (*c.* AD 28 – *c.* 103) – Author of the epic *Punica.*

Socrates Scholasticus or **Socrates of Constantinople** (born *c.* AD 380; d. after 439) – A fifth-century Christian church historian. He is the author of a

Historia Ecclesiastica (*Church History*), which covers the history of late ancient Christianity during the years AD 305–439.

Sophocles (*c.* 497 BC – 406 BC) – Greek tragedian.

Sozomen (fifth century AD) – Lawyer and church historian whose work is parallel to that of Socrates Scholasticus (above) but very different. Relies heavily on Olympiodorus.

Statius (Publius Papinius Statius, *c.* AD 45 – *c.* 96) – His surviving works are the epic poems the *Thebaid* and the unfinished *Achilleid*, and a collection of occasional poetry, the *Silvae*.

Strabo (Aelius Strabo, *c.* 64 BC – AD 25) – Greek author of the seventeen-book *Geography*. His *History* is not extant.

Suetonius (b. *c.* AD 69) – Biographer of Roman rulers and emperors, from Caesar to Domitian.

Tacitus (Publius Cornelius Tacitus, *c.* AD 55–120) – Important source in Latin for the wars of the first century AD in his *Annals* (AD 14–68, most of which survives) and *Histories* (only AD 68–70 survives) and the biography of his father-in-law, the *Agricola*. His ethnographic *Germania* informs us a great deal about the German tribes.

Tertullian (Quintus Septimius Florens Tertullianus, *c.* AD 160 – *c.* 225) – A prolific early Christian author from Carthage.

Themistius (*c.* AD 317 – 388) – Greek philosopher; thirty-four surviving speeches shed light on Roman policy towards the Goths.

Thucydides (*c.* 460–400 BC) – Athenian author of the monumental *History of the Peloponnesian War*.

Tibullus (*c.* 55 – 19 BC) – Roman writer of love *Elegies*.

Gnaeus Pompeius Trogus (first-century BC) – Roman historian of the Celtic tribe, the Vocontii in Gallia Narbonensis, and a near contemporary to Livy. Justin wrote an epitome of Trogus' lost work, and in the manuscripts of Justin's work an anonymous series of *prologi* or summaries of the books is extant. The last event recorded by Justin is the recovery of the Roman standards captured by the Parthians in 20 BC.

Valerius Antias (first century BC) – Roman historian and one of Livy's sources.

Valerius Flaccus (died *c.* AD 90) – Author of the epic poem *Argonautica*.

Valerius Maximus (first century AD) – Author of a collection of memorable deeds and quotations: *Factorum et Dictorum Memorabilium.*

Varro (Marcus Terentius Varro, 116–27 BC) – Author of *De Lingua Latina* and *Rerum Rusticarum.*

Vegetius (Flavius Vegetius Renatus, late fourth century AD) – Latin author of a seminal work on Roman military matters, *Epitoma Rei Militaris*, and a book on veterinary medicine.

Velleius Paterculus (b. *c.* 20 BC) – Wrote a summary of Roman history to AD 29 in Latin: *Historiae Romanae.*

Virgil (P. Vergilius Maro, 70–19 BC) – Rome's most celebrated poet, author of the *Aeneid.*

Vitruvius (first century BC) – Author of *De Architectura* – on architecture and engineering.

Xenophon (*c.* 430–355 BC) – Athenian author of the *Hellenica, Cyripaedia* and the *Anabasis* (*The Persian Expedition*).

Zonaras (Johannes Zonaras, twelfth century AD) – Byzantine historian whose eighteen-book *Historical Epitome* is based on Dio and extends from the Creation to AD 1118.

Zosimus (*fl.* AD 490s–510s) – A Byzantine historian who lived in Constantinople. His *Historia Nova* (*New History*) is written in Greek in six books. For the period from AD 238 to 270, he apparently uses Dexippus; for the period from AD 270 to 404, Eunapius; and after AD 407, Olympiodorus.

Appendix 6

Glossary of Greek and Latin Terms

aedile – public officer responsible for public works, entertainments and the distribution of grain, markets etc.

aerarium – the public treasury.

ager publicus – Roman land in Italy, public land belonging to the Roman people.

ager Romanus – Roman territory comprising *ager publicus* and *ager privatus*.

ala (pl. *alae*) – wing of an army; usually a contingent of allies about the size of a legion.

amicitia – friendship without any further obligations; it could be concluded by a treaty but also without.

aristeia – (ἀριστεία) epic poetry convention in which a hero in battle has his or her finest hour. An *aristeia* can conclude with the death of the hero.

auctoritas – influence or prestige, especially in the early Empire.

auxilia – troops provided by Rome's allies (*socii*).

candidati – imperial body guards.

capite censi – the head count or *proletarii* of Roman citizens who did not have sufficient property to qualify for military service and featured as numbers in the census. Marius changed all that and included the *proletarii* in his armies.

Capitol – one of the seven hills of Rome, the religious and symbolic centre of Rome.

castra – military camp.

centuria – a unit of the Roman legion; of varying size, around 80–100 men. A voting unit in the *comitia centuriata*. See Appendix 2 above.

centurio – commander of a century.

civitas sine suffragio – citizenship without suffrage, a form of citizenship granted to towns (e.g. Capua in 338 BC) who were subject to Roman taxation and military service but were denied the right to vote or hold political office.

classis – fleet; also the Roman soldiers who made up the bulk of the armies. The *infra classem* were less wealthy, lightly armed skirmishers.

cognomen – a man's third name; a woman's second. The name of a legion.

cohors – one of ten sub-units of a legion.

colonia – a town founded at a strategic place (e.g. a river crossing) populated with Romans and/or Latins.

comes domesticorum – imperial household troops.

comes rei militaris – military companion.

Comitia Centuriata – the assembly of citizens which legislated, elected magistrates, declared war, ratified treaties and judged capital offences.

consul – the highest political office on the *cursus honorum*; two elected annually (usually). Consuls held *imperium*.

corvus – bridge-shaped grappling/boarding device on warships.

cursus honorum – the sequence of public offices held by men of senatorial class.

damnatio memoriae – the erasing of records, statuary and the memory of unpopular individuals after their death.

decimatio – the execution of every tenth man, chosen by lot from the ranks.

deditio – surrender, with the assumption that the victor would extend *fides* and spare the lives of the defeated.

delator – informer, particularly prevalent and successful in the early Empire.

devotio – an extreme act of bravery in which a Roman gave himself up in battle in what was a suicidal attack on the enemy.

dictator – temporary absolute leader appointed for a limited period to resolve a crisis; also known as *magister populi*.

dies nefasti – inauspicious days.

dignitas – political dignity related to tenure of offices in the *cursus honorum*.

dilectus – the annual military levy.

dominae – the domineering mistresses of Catullus and the love poets.

dona militaria – military decorations.

dux – leader.

ecphrasis – description of a work of art, often a conventional device in epic.

equester ordo – the same as *equites*.

equites – the equestrian order ranked below senators; the equites were middle-class businessmen and farmers; also means cavalry.

exclusus amator (or *paraklausithyron*) – the love poet locked out by his mistress.

exercitus – army.

fetialis – war priest responsible for ensuring that Rome's wars were just in the eyes of the gods. Responsible for the rites performed for declaring war and concluding peace.

fides – trustworthiness, good faith, loyalty, a quality the Romans were anxious to be seen to uphold, including respect for the law and *fides* in foreign relations.

foederati – nations to which Rome provided benefits in exchange for military assistance.

foedus – originally a sacred oath made by a fetial priest on behalf of the Roman people; a treaty.

gens – family, clan, e.g. Claudii.

gladius – short sword.

glans – slingshot.

haruspex – soothsayer.

hasta – spear.

hastati – soldiers of the second class who stood in the front line; green, raw recruits.

Hellenism – the culture of classical Greece which percolated into Rome in the second century BC.

hoplite – heavily-armed infantryman.

imagines – portraits of ancestors.

imperium – power, command, empire; particularly power that bestowed on consuls, generals and praetors.

incestum – unchastity, particularly in Vestal Virgins; incest.

indutia – cease-fire.

latifundia – large estates in Italy and Sicily.

Latin League – an association of communities in Latium who were allied militarily.

latrones – bandits, pirates.

laudatio – eulogy.

legio – legion; a levy of troops.

lex – law.

magister equitum – second-in-command to the dictator; the master of the horse usually commanded the cavalry, as the dictator was forbidden to ride a horse.

maiestas – power, authority, treason.

manipulus – maniple; sub-unit of the legion comprising two centuries.

manubiae – the general's share of the booty.

miles – soldier.

miles amoris – a soldier in the war of love, as described by the Roman elegists of the first century BC.

mimula – a little female mime artist.

modii – measure.

momento mori – remember that you too have to die.

municipium – a town in which the duties, or *munera*, were a communal obligation assumed by the *municipes* in exchange for the privileges and protections of citizenship.

naumachia – naval warfare.

novus homo – a 'new man', a man not of the aristocracy, a self-made man.

onager – stone-lobbing torsion catapult.

oppidum – town.

otium – a lifestyle of ease and commercial, political or military inactivity.

patricius – patrician: the dominant political class; aristocratic families.

pax – peace.

phalanx – close-knit body of heavily-armed infantry.

pietas – dutifulness in all aspects of life.

pilum – javelin.

Plebeian – non-patricians.

polis – Greek city state.

pontifex maximus – chief priest.

praefectus – prefect, commander of an auxiliary force.

preafectus urbi – prefect of the city.

praetexta – the white robe with a purple border worn by a Roman boy before he was entitled to wear the *toga virilis*, around his fourteenth year, and by girls until their marriage. Also worn by magistrates and priests.

praetor – public office, responsible for justice. Second highest political and military office.

Principate – the period of the Emperors, from 27 BC.

principes – troops in their twenties and thirties.

proconsul – acting consul.

proletarii – volunteer soldiers of the poorer orders, recruited first by Marius.

psiloi – light infantry skirmishers.

raptus – seized, abducted, raped.

Republic – the period of Republican government, 509–43 BC.

res gestae – political and military achievements.

rex – king.

Salii – the 'leaping priests' of Mars supposed to have been introduced by King Numa Pompilius.

scutum – shield.

secessio plebis – a general strike in which the plebeians downed tools, shut up shop and deserted Rome, leaving the patricians to get on with running the city on their own. All business and services ground to a halt; there were five between 494 BC and 287 BC.

Sibylline Books – three sacred scrolls kept under guard and only consulted when decreed by the senate to give oracular advice in times of crisis, or to interpret portents and omens.

signifer – standard bearer.

societas – synonymous with amicitia: peace and neutrality with an obligation to military support.

socius – ally.

spolia opima – the highest award for gallantry, won when a commander defeated an enemy leader in unarmed combat.

sub iugum missi – sent under the yoke, the ultimate humiliation for an army in defeat.

synoikism – the amalgamation of villages, usually in Ancient Greece into *poleis*, or city-states.

testudo – tortoise-shaped formation in which shields are interlocked above the head.

toga virilis – the plain white toga worn on formal occasions by Roman men from between fourteen and eighteen years of age; also worn by senators. The first wearing of the *toga virilis* was one of the rites of passage of reaching maturity. See *praetexta*.

triarii – veteran troops.

tribuni plebei – officials responsible for protecting their fellow plebeians against injustices from the patricians; had a veto and sacrosanctity.

tribunus militum – military tribune.

trireme – standard warship with three banks of oars.

triumphator – a general who had been awarded a triumph.

triumphus – triumph: the military procession along the Via Sacra in Rome for victorious generals in which spoils of war, prisoners and captured chieftains were paraded. The enemy chieftains were sometimes executed; the triumphator rode in a chariot and was dressed as Jupiter.

tumultus – crisis.

vates – soothsayer, prophetess, priestess.

velites – lightly armed skirmishing troops; 1,200 or so in a legion.

via – road, as in Via Appia.

virtus – manliness, courage, virtue.

vis – force, rape; military strength.

Notes

Introduction

1. Arrian, *Tactica* 33, 2–3.

Chapter 1: Rome's Peninsular Wars

1. Livy 1, 19, 2–3. For a description of the gates, the *geminae Belli portae*, and the procedure, see Virgil, *Aeneid* 7, 601–15. See Fordyce, *Virgil Aeneid VII-VIII ad loc.*
2. G. Williamson (tr.), Josephus, *The Jewish War*, 1959, p. 378. Adcock, *The Roman Art of War*, pp. 4–5. The Romans were not the only serial warmongers. As Finley, *Ancient History*, p. 67, points out: 'Athens ... was at war on average more than two years out of every three between the Persian wars and the defeat... at Chaeronea in 338 BC, and ... it never enjoyed ten consecutive years of peace in all that period.'
3. Livy 10, 1, 4.
4. See Ogilvie, *The Etruscans*; Cornell, *The Beginnings of Rome* for details of these early days.
5. Livy 2, 6–7; *Fasti Triumphales*; Plutarch, *Life of Poplicola*.
6. Livy 1, 9.
7. Livy 1, 13.
8. Polybius 3, 22.
9. Livy 1, 32ff.
10. Livy 1, 37.
11. Livy 2, 18. See Lintott, *The Constitution of the Roman Republic*, p. 110. Livy 22, 8, 5–6.
12. Livy 2, 16.
13. Livy 2, 19–22; Dionysius of Halicarnassus, *Roman Antiquities* 6, 4–12; Florus 1, 5, 1–4.
14. Cicero, *Pro Balbo* 53. Dionysius summarizes its contents at 6, 95. Around this time it seems likely that the eleven towns in the League were: Arretium, Caere, Clusium, Cortona, Perusia, Rusellae, Tarquinii, Veii, Vetulonia, Volsinii and Vulci.
15. Livy 2, 33, 9; Dionysius 5, 75; 6, 20.
16. Livy 2, 26; Dionysius 6, 32–33.
17. Dionysius 8, 83–85.
18. Dionysius 9, 57–8; Livy 2, 64–5.
19. Dionysius 9, 5–13.
20. Livy 3, 26–9. See Ward Fowler, *Passing Under the Yoke*.
21. Livy 4, 28–30. Plutarch, *Life of Metellus* 8, 1–3.
22. Livy 4, 30–34; 51. See Ogilvie, *Commentary ad. Loc.*
23. Livy 4, 21–2; 4, 31–33.

24. Livy 5, 10; 6, 4; 5, 15. Plutarch, *Life of Camillus*.
25. Cary, *A History of Rome*, p. 72.
26. For the Fasti Triumphales see Attilio Degrassi, *Inscriptiones Italiae, vol.XIII, fasc.1* (Rome, 1947).
27. See Toner, *Roman Disasters*, p. 143ff.
28. Scene 43. See Ferris, *Hate and War*, p. 118.
29. See, for example, Jesus Christ at Matthew 24, 7–8: 'For nation will rise against nation, and kingdom against kingdom. And there will be famines, pestilences, and earthquakes in various places ... All these are the beginning of sorrows.' Jesus would not have been the first to predict the inevitability of military and man-made disaster.
30. Dio Chrysostom, *Orationes* 38, 20.

Chapter 2: The Roman War Machine

1. Festus 100; Livy 4, 34, 6.
2. For the association of the land with the army and Roman agronomy, see the detailed treatment by Nathan Rosenstein in his *Rome at War*.
3. Oakley, *The Roman Conquest of Italy*, p. 25.
4. Livy 2, 22–33.
5. See Cornell, *The Beginnings of Rome*, pp. 179–197; Ogilvie, *Early Rome and the Etruscans*, p. 45ff. Livy 1, 43; Dionysius of Halicarnassus 4, 16; Cicero, *De Re Publica* 1, 39.
6. See Vegetius 3, 6; Caesar, *De Bello Gallico* 6, 40; Frontinus, *Strategemata*, 2, 4, 8; Livy 7, 14; Frontinus, *op. cit.* 2, 4, 1; 2, 4, 6. Spain: Livy 27, 18; Nervi: Caesar, *op. cit.* 2, 27. Q. Cicero: Caesar, *op. cit.* 6, 37.
7. Brunt, *Italian Manpower*, pp. 44–60. Livy 10, 27, 10–11. Hopkins, *Conquerors and Slaves*, pp. 31–5.
8. Lewis and Short, *ad loc.* See Chrystal, *Women in Ancient Rome*, pp. 20, 22: 'Women also exhibit *virtus*, with its connotations of manliness (*vir*) and traditional male attributes of strength and bravery, as well as of virtue. Seneca describes the conspicuous valour of Cornelia and Rutilia as *conspecta virtus*. In the *Ad Marciam* he spells out his belief that women are just as capable of displaying *virtutes* as men. The elderly Ummidia Quadratilla shows vitality (*viridis*) and a physique unusual in an octogenarian woman.' See also Cicero, *Fam.* 14, 11 and *Att.* 10, 8; *Fam.* 14, 1. Also McDonnell, *Roman Manliness* (Cambridge, 2006).
9. For a litany of anti-Carthaginian and anti-Greek vitriol, see Sidebottom, *Ancient Warfare*, pp. 8–14.
10. Tacitus, *Histories* 3, 47; Lucan, *De Bello Civili* 7, 400–10.
11. Polybius 6, 39, 1–11; Aulus Gellius 5, 6–5, 26; Caesar, *op.cit.* 3, 56.
12. Dio *fr.* 36, 28; Zonaras 8, 1; Livy 10, 29, 14; 10, 33, 9.
13. Brunt *op.cit.* pp. 44–60.
14. See G. Colin, *Rome et la Grece*; J. Griffin, *Augustan Poetry*, p. 88ff. and the Appendix, *Some Imperial Servants*. Various suggestions for the start and or cause of the decline have been made: Polybius, 31, 25 ascribes it to the victory over Macedonia; L. Calpurnius Piso (Pliny *NH* 17, 38, 244) goes with 154 BC; Appian, *Bellum Civile* 1, 7 for the end of the war in Italy; Livy 39, 6, 7 prefers 186 BC; Velleius Paterculus, *Historiae Romanae*, and Sallust, *Catilina* 10, 1 and *Jugurtha* 41, 1 opt for the end of the Third Punic War. See also Catullus 51.

15. Suetonius, *Augustus* 38, 2.
16. See Phang, *Marriage*.
17. *Bowman and Thomas* No. 5, 1987.
18. Tacitus, *Agricola* 30, 4–5.
19. Livy 21, 57, 13–14.
20. Livy 26, 13, 15
21. Livy 29, 17, 15–16.
22. Livy 26, 13, 15; 26, 50, 7–14.
23. Cicero, *In Verrem* 2, 1.
24. *In Verrem*, 2, 1, 65.
25. Cicero, *In Verrem* 2, 1, 62; 2, 1, 64; 4, 116.
26. Unruly soldiers: Juvenal, 16; Petronius, *Satyricon* 82; 62; *cf.*: in the *New Testament*: *Matthew* 27, 26–35; *Mark* 15, 15–19; *John* 19, 23–4; *Luke* 3–14; Epictetus, *Discourses* 4, 1, 79. Vitellius: Tacitus, *Histories* 2, 56.
27. Tacitus, *op. cit.* 2, 73; 4, 14; 3, 34. See Ziolkowski, Urbs Direpta, for an analysis of rape and plunder and 'how the Romans sacked cities.'
28. Frontinus, *op. cit.* 2, 9, 3. Appian, *Bellum Civile* 1, 93–4.
29. Frontinus, *op. cit.* 2, 9, 5.
30. Frontinus, *op. cit.* 2, 9, 4.
31. Livy 2, 17, 2; 37, 2.
32. Polybius 10, 15.
33. Livy 23, 7.
34. Caesar, *op.cit.* 8, 44.
35. Tacitus, *op. cit.* 18.
36. Livy 4, 59; 11, 60, 6; Polybius 6, 39, 12–15; Varro, *De Lingua Latina* 5, 86; Dionysius 4, 19, 1–4.

Chapter 3: The Sources

1. See Cicero, *de Imperio* 28 and 36, and Onasander on the qualities of generals. Polybius tells us where he got his military knowledge from at 11, 18, 1; Cicero on military manuals at *Pro Fonteio* 42, *Pro Balbo* 47, and Plutarch, *Lucullus* 1.
2. Polybius 6, 19–42.
3. Onasander 38.
4. Zosimus 1, 69.
5. Frontinus, *Strategemata* 2, 9, 2–5; Tacitus, *Agricola* 20.
6. For examples of Livy's faults see Yardley, *Livy: Hannibal's War*.
7. Livy 28, 46.

Chapter 4: The Fourth Century: the Gallic Invasion and the Samnite Wars

1. Strabo 4, 4, 2–5.
2. Strabo 5, 30, 2–4.
3. Livy 5, 37.

4. Livy 5, 36, 1.
5. Livy 5, 38.
6. Livy 5, 37, 1.
7. Plutarch, *op cit.* 22; Livy 5, 39. Livy 5, 40. Translation by Rev. Canon Roberts, J.M. Dent & Sons, Ltd., London, 1905.
8. Livy 5, 40. See Gardiner, *The Blitz*, pp. 126–7; 184–5.
9. Livy 5, 41. Plutarch, *op cit.* 22.
10. Plutarch, *Camillus* 22, 6.
11. Livy 5, 42. Plutarch, *op cit.* Trans. Bernadotte Perrin, *Plutarch, Parallel Lives, Vol. 2* (Loeb, 1916).
12. Livy 5, 43.
13. Livy 5, 43–45. Plutarch, *op cit.* 23, 9.
14. Livy 5, 10; 6, 4; 5, 15. Plutarch, *op cit.*
15. Livy 5, 47. Plutarch, *op cit.* 25–26. Diodorus Siculus 116.
16. Livy 5, 48.
17. Livy 5, 49. Plutarch, *op cit.* 29.
18. Cornell, *The Beginnings of Rome*, p. 317.
19. Livy 5, 55; 5, 51.
20. Plutarch, *op cit.* 31.
21. Livy 5, 50. Diodorus *op. cit.* says that the women donors were given the privilege of riding through Rome in a chariot.
22. Livy 5, 55. Plutarch, *op cit.* 32. Diodorus, *op cit.* blames the urban mess on the fact that all Romans were given permission to build a house wherever they liked.
23. See Cary, *A History of Rome*, pp. 84–5.
24. Livy 9, 2ff.
25. Livy 9, 6.
26. Appian's *History of Rome: The Samnite Wars*, 1.
27. Caesar, *De Bello Gallico* 1, 12.
28. Sallust, *Bellum Jugurthinum.*
29. Livy 9, 23, 15; Diodorus Siculus 19, 72, 6–7.

Chapter 5: The Third Century: the Wars with Pyrrhus, the Punic Wars and the Gallic Invasion

1. Livy, 10, 26; Polybius, 2, 19, 5.
2. Polybius 2, 20.
3. Pliny, *NH* 6, 22, 4.
4. 1 *Maccabees*, 6:43–46.
5. Caesar, *De Bello Africo* 30, 2, 41; 2, 86, 1.
6. J. Mazard, *Corpus Nummorum Numidiae Mauretaniaeque* (Paris, 1955) 103, n°. 276, pl. 247.
7. Polybius 84, 2–7.
8. See Kistler, *War Elephants*, p.100. Horace, *Odes* 3, 5; Aulus Gellius, *Noctes Atticae* 7 4; Augustine, *De Civitate Dei* 1, 5; see also Aurelius Victor, *De Viris Illustribus Romae*, 40, Tertullian, *To the Martyrs* Chapter 4. Later depictions in art include *Regulus in the Spiked Cask* by Salvatore Rosa, *c.* 1651.

9. Pliny NH 8, 127.

10. Aelian, *de Natura Animalium* 16, 36

11. Plutarch, *Pyrrhus*.

12. Plutarch, *op. cit.* 16–17; 21, 5–10; Zonaras 8, 3; 5; Orosius 4, 1, 8–15; 19–23; Livy, *Epitome* 13.

13. Thucydides 22.

14. Polyaenus 8, 23, 5.

15. Quintus Curtius Rufus, *Historiae Alexandri Magni* 7, 19.

16. Polybius 1, 21; Zonaras 8, 10; Livy, *Epitome* 17.

17. Polybius 1, 25–34; Florus 2, 2; Cicero, *De Officiis* 3, 26; Livy, *Epitome* 18; Valerius Maximus 9, 2; Silius Italicus, *Punica* 6, 299–550; Appian, *Punica* 4; Zonaras 8, 15; see also O. Jager, *M. Atilius Regulus* (1878).

18. Polybius 1, 32–4; Zonaras 8, 13; Appian, *op.cit.* 3; Livy, *op.cit.*

19. Polybius 2, 25–6.

20. Polybius 3, 65; Livy 21, 45–6.

21. Livy 21, 54–6; Polybius 3, 71–4.

22. Sir Walter Raleigh, *The Works of Sir Walter Ralegh, Kt; Now First Collected: to which are Prefixed The Lives of the Author. VI. The History of the World*, Book V, Chapters 1–3, (Oxford, 1829) p. 242.

23. Livy 3, 83-84; Livy 22, 4–7.

24. See Elliott, *Ennius' Fabius Maximus Cunctator and the History of an Ablative Gerund in the Roman Historiographical Tradition.*

25. Virgil, *Aeneid* 6, 846.

26. Ennius *Annales* 363. See Elliott, *op.cit.* See its use in Cicero, *De Officiis* 1, 84; *De Senectute* 10; *Ad Atticum* 2, 19, 2; Virgil, *Aeneid* 6, 846; Ovid, *Fasti* 2, 240; Suetonius, *Tiberius* 21; Livy 22, 14, 14; 22, 24, 10; 22, 53, 7; 25, 23, 15; Sallust, *Histories fr.* 1, 55, 7; 1, 77, 17; 2, 98, 2; 4, 69, 20–21. The name of Fabius also lives on in the Fabian Society, the British socialist organization which promotes socialism through reform.

27. Polybius 3, 92; Livy 22, 15.

28. Polybius 3, 104–5; Livy 22, 28–29; Plutarch, *Fabius Maximus* 11–12.

29. Polybius 3, 110–117; Livy 22, 43–9; Plutarch, *op. cit.* 15–16; 16, 8; Appian, *Punic Wars* 19–26; Zonaras 9, 1; Appian, *op. cit.* 4, 25; Quintilian, *Institutio Oratoria*, 8, 6, 26; Eutropius, *Abridgement of Roman History*, 3, 10.

30. Polybius 27, 8, 8.

31. Livy 22, 51; Translation adapted from Rev Canon Roberts, *Livy History of Rome*, Vol. 3.

32. Livy 22, 51, 5.

33. Paret, *Makers of Modern Strategy*, p. 337.

34. Livy 25, 20-21.

35. Livy 25, 34.

36. Livy 26, 39.

37. Livy 27, 1; Appian, *op.cit.* 48.

38. Livy 27, 12; Plutarch, *Marcellus* 25.

39. Livy 27, 26; Plutarch, *op.cit.* 29.

40. Livy 27, 28.

Chapter 6: The Second Century: the Spanish Wars, Viriathus and the Invasion of the Northmen

1. Appian 46.
2. Appian 61–3; Livy, *Epitome* 52; Orosius 5, 5.
3. Appian 69.
4. Mommsen, *History of Rome*, p. 214.
5. Livy, *Epitome* 33.
6. Florus 2, 7, 1–8
7. Diodorus 36, 7–8.
8. Livy, *Epitome* 54.
9. Cary, *A History of Rome*, pp. 217–218.
10. Strabo 4, 1, 11; Livy, *Epitome* 61; Orosius 5, 14; Florus 1, 37.

Chapter 7: The First Century: the Social War, Spartacus, Mithridates, assus, the Parthians and the Gauls

1. Plutarch, *Tiberius Gracchus* 8.
2. Velleius Paterculus 2, 15.
3. Appian, *Civil Wars* 1, 41; Livy, *Epitomes* 72 and 73; Orosius 5, 18, 14.
4. Appian 1, 42.
5. Appian 1, 43; Orosius 5, 18, 11–12; Livy, *Epitome* 73. Ovid, *Fasti* 6, 555.
6. Appian 1, 45; Orosius 5, 18, 11.
7. Appian 1, 50; Velleius Paterculus 2, 15; Orosius 5, 18, 24.
8. Appian 1, 47.
9. Appian 1, 47–48; Orosius 5, 18, 18; Livy, *Epitome* 76; Florus 3, 18.
10. Orosius 5, 18, 24
11. Appian 1, 50; 1, 52; Orosius 5, 18, 23.
12. Matyszak, *Cataclysm 90 BC*, p. vii.
13. Appian 1, 7. Trans. Horace White (Loeb, 1913).
14. Plutarch, *Life of Crassus* 8. Trans. Rex Warner (Penguin, 1958).
15. Florus, *History of Rome*; Livy, *Epitome* 2, 8. Trans. Edward Forster (Loeb).
16. Sallust, *Historiae* 3, 96; Frontinus, *Strategemata* 1, 5, 22.
17. Appian estimates, or exaggerates, an army 70,000 strong.
18. *Cf.* Plutarch, *op.cit.* 9, 6; Livy, *Periochae* 96. Sallust, *ibid.;* 3, 106.
19. Appian 1, 116–117.
20. Florus *ibid.* Orosius, *Histories* 5, 24, 1–8.
21. Plutarch, *op. cit.* 9.
22. Frontinus 2, 4, 7. Plutarch *op.cit.* 10, 1–3.
23. Pirates: Plutarch, *ibid.* Barrels: Florus, Epitome, 2, 8; Cicero, *Oratio Pro Sextio Roscio* 5, 2. Trench: *cf.* Sallust, *op.cit.* 4, 25.
24. Appian 1, 119.
25. Plutarch, *Crassus* 8–11.
26. Frontinus 2, 5, 34; Orosius 5, 24, 6; Plutarch, *op. cit.* 11, 2–3; Livy, *Epitome* 97.
27. Crassus: Appian, 1, 120. Plutarch, *op.cit.* 11, 4–5.
28. Orosius 5, 24, 5–8; Livy, *ibid.*; Appian, 1, 120; Plutarch, *op.cit.* 11, 6–7. Florus *ibid.*

29. Plutarch, *Pompey* 21, 5. See Cicero, *In Pisonem* 58; Pliny, *NH* 15, 125; Plutarch, *Crassus* 11, 8; *Pompey* 22.
30. Cicero, *Philippics* 3, 21; 4, 15; 13, 22. Horace, *Epodes* 16, 5; *Odes* 3, 14, 18–20.
31. Cicero, *Ad Atticum* 7, 14, 2.
32. Seneca, *Ad Marciam* 6, 20, 3.
33. Tacitus, *Annals* 2, 32, 2.
34. Josephus, *Jewish War* 5, 2.
35. Cicero, *Pro Rabirio Perduellionis Reo* 5, 16.
36. In John Granger Cook, *Crucifixion in the Mediterranean World*, p. 430, n. 72.
37. Josephus, *The Life of Flavus Josephus* 75.
38. F.P. Retief and L. Cilliers, 'The History and Pathology of Crucifixion', in *South African Medical Journal*, 93:12 (December 2002), pp. 938–41.
39. Plautus, *Miles Gloriousus* 359.
40. Bernard Joseph Saurin, *Spartacus, tragédie. En cinq actes, et en vers. Représentée, pour le première fois, par les Comédiens ordinaires du Roi, 1760.* The text of the play is in the standard collections, e.g., *Répertoire Générale du Théâtre français*, vol. 32, (Paris, 1818), 71–134.
41. Voltaire, *Correspondance General* 461–463, letter 283, 5, 4.1769.
42. After Patrick Leigh Fermor in *The Traveller's Tree*: 'the foremost of the Negro chain-breakers'.
43. K. Marx and F. Engels, *Collected Works*, Vol. 41, p. 265.
44. K. Marx and F. Engels, *Collected Works*, Vol. 41, p. 265.
45. Runciman, *Sicilian Vespers*, p. 212.
46. Appian, *Mithridatic Wars* 18; 21. Trans. Horace White (Loeb, 1989).
47. Appian, *op.cit.* 19.
48. Appian, *op.cit.* 22.
49. Appian, *op.cit.* 23.
50. Plutarch, *Sulla* 14, 7. Appian, *op.cit.* 38.
51. Plutarch, *Sulla* 18, 2.
52. Plutarch, *op.cit.* 15–19; 20–21; Appian, *op. cit.* 41–45; 49. Frontinus, *op.cit.* 2, 3, 17.
53. Plutarch, *op.cit.* 21.
54. Appian, *Sicily fr.* 6; Appian, *op.cit.* 84–85; Plutarch, *Lucullus* 25–28, 6.
55. Appian, *op.cit.* 82.
56. A. Mayor, *The Poison King: The Life and Legend of Mithradates, Rome's Deadliest Enemy*, p. 310.
57. Appian, *op.cit.* 111.
58. Dio 37, 13.
59. Celsus, *De Medicina* 5, 23, 3.
60. A remedy with as many as sixty-five or so constituents, used as an antidote for poisoning. It was much in demand in the Middle Ages (against plague) and the Renaissance, in Italy and France for centuries. A revised recipe, theriac (*Theriacum Andromachi*), was prevalent in the nineteenth century.
61. A.E. Housman, 'Terence, This is Stupid Stuff', *A Shropshire Lad* (1896).
62. Appian, *op.cit.* 112–113.
63. Plutarch, *Crassus* 16, 5–6. Translation in Sarah Iles Johnston, *Religions of the Ancient World*, (Harvard, 2004), p. 510. See Cicero, *De Divinatione* 1, 29–30; Velleius Paterculus

2, 46, 3, the commentary by A.J. Woodman (Cambridge, 2004); Appian, *op.cit.* 2, 18; Florus 1, 46, 3. For the departure, see Cicero, *Ad Atticum* 4, 13, 2 and *Ad Familiares* 1, 9, 20, and Lucan, *Bellum Civile* 3,43ff. and 3, 126–127.

64. Cicero, *De Finibus Bonorum et Malorum* 3, 22; 3, 75. Plutarch, *Lucullus*, 25ff.; Appian, *Mithridates* 87; Dio, 36, 1ff.; Sallust, *Histories* 4, *fr.* 69; Plutarch, *op.cit.* 30; Dio 36; Cicero, *Oratio Pro Lege Manila* 23–24.

65. Plutarch, *Pompey* 36; Pliny, *NH* 6, 52; Dio, 37, 5, 2.

66. Cicero, *De Domo Sua* 60, 124; Dio, 39–56; Justin, 42, 4, 1; Appian, *Syriaca* 51, *cf.* Plutarch, *Crassus* 21.

67. Plutarch, *op.cit.* 16.

68. Plutarch, *Crassus* 18

69. Translation by John Dryden. Dio 32, 2; 40, 20; *cf.* Plutarch, *op.cit.* 22.

70. Plutarch, *op.cit.* 19.

71. T. Mommsen, *Romische Geschichte, Vol. 3*, (1817–1903) p. 328.

72. Mommsen, p. 328. Tarn (1932) p. 607.

73. Plutarch, *op.cit.* 42, 10. Shakespeare, *Julius Caesar* 1, 2, 193.

74. Gnaeus Pompeius Trogus, a first-century BC Roman historian of the Celtic tribe, the Vocontii in Gallia Narbonensis; a near contemporary to Livy. His *magnum opus* was the forty-four book *Historiae Philippicae*, so called because the Macedonian empire founded by Philip II forms the central theme of the narrative. This was a general history of lands ruled by Alexander and his successors. Justin wrote an *epitome* of Trogus' lost work, and in the manuscript a series of anonymous *prologi* of the books by an unknown hand is extant. The last event recorded by Justin is the recovery of the Roman standards captured by the Parthians in 20 BC.

75. Caesar, *Bellum Civile* 3, 31, 3; Velleius Paterculus, *History of Rome* 2, 46, 4; Appian, *Syrian Wars* 3, 9, 1. Tarn, *Greeks*, p. 51.

76. Plutarch, *op. cit.* 25. From *Plutarch: Parallel Lives* (1916). Trans. Bernadotte Perrin (Loeb).

77. Dio, 40, 22–23. Trans. Earnest Cary and Herbert B. Foster, *Dio Cassius: Roman History* (Loeb, 1914).

78. Plutarch, *op.cit.* 21, 6–21, 7.

79. Tarn (1932), p. 611. Dio 40, 26, 3.

80. Livy, *Periochae* 106.

81. H Bivar, *The Political History of Iran under the Arsacids*, 21–99.

82. Cary, *A History of Rome*, p. 256–257.

83. Ovid, *Fasti* 5, 581ff.

84. Ovid, *Ars Amatoria* 1, 177–184.

85. Ovid, *Fasti* 5, 583–585; *Ars Amatoria* 1, 179–180; Propertius 2, 10, 13–14; 4, 7, 83–85.

86. Caesar, *De Bello Gallica* 7, 4. Trans. H.J. Edwards (Loeb, 1917).

87. *Idem* 7, 4; 7, 9; 7, 10.

88. *Idem* 7, 12.

89. *Idem* 7, 38.

90. *Idem* 7, 47.

91. *Idem* 7, 48.

92. *Idem* 7, 41–51.

93. *Idem* 7, 57–62; 79–80; 8, 32–36.

Chapter 8: 'Doom Monster' – Cleopatra VII

1. Martial 11, 53.
2. Tacitus, *Germania* 19–20. For infant burials in Roman Britain, see Allason-Jones, *Women in Roman Britain* (1989), 42ff.
3. Manetho, *Aegyptiaca*.
4. Herodotus, *Histories* 2, 35ff.
5. Cassius Dio, *Historia Romanae* 42, 34, 3–6. Trans. E. Cary. Caesar, *Bellum Civile* 3, 109.
6. Plutarch, *Caesar* 49.1–3; Lucan, *De Bello Civili* 10, 56–58. *Cf.* Dio, *op. cit.* 42.34.6–35.1. Trans. Rex Warner, *Plutarch, the Fall of the Roman Republic*, p. 290.
7. Lucan, *op. cit.* 10, 139–140.
8. Suetonius, *Caesar* 76.3.
9. Dio, *op. cit.* 43, 27, 3; Cicero, *Ad Atticum* 15, 15, 2.
10. Valerius Maximus, *Facta et Dicta Memorabilia*, 6.7. 1–3.
11. Appian, *Bellum Civile* 2, 102, 424; Dio, *op. cit.* 51.22.3.
12. Cicero, *op. cit.* 15, 15, 2; 14, 8, 1.
13. Josephus, *Antiquities of the Jews* 15, 89.
14. Appian, *op. cit.* 4, 61, 262–263; Dio, *op. cit.* 47, 30, 4 and 47, 31, 5.
15. Plutarch, *Antony* 25.
16. Plutarch, *Life of Antony* 25–29; Trans. Bernadotte Perrin, Vol. IX (Loeb, 1920); Appian, *op. cit.* 5, 8–11; Dio, *op. cit.* 48, 24.
17. Appian, *op. cit.* 5, 9, 35.
18. For the importance of balsam see Pliny *NH* 12, 111 and Josephus, *op. cit.* 15, 4, 2; bitumen, Diodorus Siculus 19, 98–99. Plutarch, *op. cit.* 54, 9.
19. Plutarch, *op. cit.*, 86, 3.
20. Plutarch, *op. cit.* 81, 4–82, 1; Dio, *op. cit.* 51, 15, 5; Suetonius, *Augustus* 17, 5.
21. Plutarch, *op. cit.* 87, 1–2; Dio, *op. cit.* 51, 15, 6; Suetonius, *op. cit.* and *Caligula* 26, 1.
22. Strabo, *Geography*, 17, 10.
23. Virgil, *Aeneid*, 8, 696–697; Horace, *Odes*, 1, 37; Propertius, 3, 11; Florus, *Epitome of Roman History*, 2, 21; Velleius Paterculus, *Compendium of Roman History* 2,87. Statius, *Silvae* 3, 2, 119–120.
24. Everitt, *Augustus: The Life of Rome's First Emperor*, pp. 194–195.
25. CNN News, *Cleopatra Killed by Drug cocktail?* 27 November, 2012.
26. Plutarch, *op. cit.* 71. Trans. Bernadotte Perrin, *op. cit.*
27. Plutarch, *op. cit.* 78–79.
28. *ibid.*, 82; 86.
29. *ibid.*, 85–86. Trans. Perrin, *op. cit.* Suetonius, *Augustus* 17, 4.
30. Plutarch, *op.cit.* 58.
31. *ibid.*, 60.
32. Virgil *Aeneid* 4, 300–301; 384–387; 450–473; 483ff.
33. For Dido's curse see O'Gorman, *Does Dido's Curse Work?; Virgil.* 8, 696ff.
34. Horace, *op. cit. Epodes* 9, 11–16.
35. For themes used by the love poets and their significance see Chrystal, *Differences.*
36. Propertius, *op. cit.*; 4, 6, 57–66.
37. Juvenal 2, 109.
38. Martial 4, 59.

39. Lucan, *op. cit.* 10, 104–106; 107ff.
40. *ibid.* 353ff. Grant, *Cleopatra* p. xvii.
41. Sallust, *Catilina* 25. See Chrystal, *Women in Ancient Rome,* p. 68
42. Pliny, *Historia Naturalis* 18, 210–212.
43. Plutarch, *Antony* 27.
44. Dio, *Roman History,* (42, 34, 4).
45. Plutarch, *Antony,* 29, 1.
46. Plutarch, *op. cit.* 27; 29. Trans. Perrin, *op. cit.* with adaptations. Dio, *op.cit.* Trans. Cary.
47. The Oxyrhynchus Papyri Collection, 11, 1380, 214–216.
48. Notably, by Finley, *The Silent Women of Rome*; Fraschetti, *Roman Women,* Introduction.
49. Plutarch, *op.cit.* 28 and 71.
50. Juvenal 6, 434ff.
51. Pliny, *op. cit.* 9, 59, 119–121. See Ullman, *Cleopatra's Pearls.*
52. Athenaeus, *The Deipnosophists,* 4.147–148

Chapter 9: The Early Empire: *Clades Lolliana* 16 BC, the Teutoburg Forest AD 9

1. For the Sugambri in the time of Caesar see Caesar, *Commentarii de Bello Gallico* 6, 35. *Clades Lolliana* is coined by Tacitus, *Annals* 1, 10, 4.
2. Horace, *Odes* 4, 9; Velleius Paterculus 2, 97, 102; Pliny, *Nat. Hist.* 9, 35 (58); Tacitus, *Annals* 1, 10, 3, 48; Suetonius, *Augustus* 23; *Tiberius* 12; Velleius Paterculus 2, 104, 2.
3. Tacitus, *Annals* 4, 66.
4. The Germans call it variously *Schlacht im Teutoburger Wald, Hermannsschlacht* or *Varusschlacht.*
5. Tacitus, *op. cit.* 1, 71.
6. Dio, 56.
7. Dio, 61, 5; Velleius Paterculus 2, 119. From *Dio's Roman History.* Trans. Earnest Cary (Loeb, 1924); *Velleius Paterculus: Compendium of Roman History.* Trans. F.W. Shipley (Loeb, 1924).
8. Florus, *Epitome* 2, 30, 39.
9. Ovid, *Tristia* 4, 31–32.
10. Manilius, *Astronomica* 898–900.
11. Tacitus, *op. cit.* 1, 61. Florus, *Epitome of Roman History* 30, 36. Trans. Edward Forster (Loeb). Ovid *Tristia* 3, 12, 45ff; 4, 2, 31ff. Manilius, *Astronomica,* 1, 898ff. Strabo, *Geography* 7, 1, 4. See also Seneca The Younger, *Epistulae* 47, 10.
12. Suetonius, *Augustus* 23. This is one of the most memorable scenes in the BBC adaptation of Robert Graves' *I Claudius.*
13. Velleius Paterculus, 2, 119.
14. Plutarch, *Crassus* 25; Dio, 40, 14ff.
15. Livy, 32, 49; 25, 6; also Appian, *Roman History* 7, 25 and Plutarch, *Fabius Maximus* 16, 8.
16. Quintilian, *Institutio Oratoria* 8, 6, 26; Polybius, *The Histories* 3, 117.
17. Livy, *Periochae,* 67.
18. Tacitus, *op. cit.* 1, 50.
19. *Idem.* 1, 56.

20. *Idem.* 1, 57. Suetonius, *Tiberius* from *The Lives of the Twelve Caesars.* Trans. J.C. Rolfe (Loeb, 1913).
21. Tacitus, *Annals* 1.60–62. Trans. Alfred John Church and William Jackson Brodribb.
22. Tacitus, *op. cit.* 2, 25.
23. One eagle was recovered from the Marsi in AD 14; the XIX's Eagle was recovered from the Bructeri in AD 15 by troops led by Lucius Stertinius. A coin showing Germanicus with a recovered standard can be seen at http://www.livius.org/le-lh/legio/xvii.html.
24. *CIL* 13, 8648.
25. Peter S. Wells, *The Battle That Stopped Rome.*
26. www.smithsonianmag.com/.../the-ambush-that-changed-history-726367. Accessed 15 June 2015.
27. 'Battle of the Teutoburg Forest: Germany Recalls Myth That Created the Nation', David Crossland, *Spiegel Online International*, 28 August, 2009.

Chapter 10: Boudica's Revolt AD 60

1. Herodotus, *Histories* 3, 115. See Alonso-Nunez, *Herodotus on the Far West.*
2. Strabo, *Geography* 2, 4, 1.
3. Diodorus Siculus, 5, 21–22.
4. Plutarch, *Caesar* 23, 2.
5. Caesar, *De Bello Gallico* 4, 20–36.
6. *idem.* 5, 8–23.
7. *idem.* 5, 20. Dio Cassius, *Roman History* 40, 1–3; Orosius, *Histories Against the Pagans* 6, 9.
8. Polyaenus, *Strategemata* 8, 23, 5.
9. Dio, *op. cit.* 49, 38, 53, 22, 53, 25.
10. Augustus, *Res Gestae Divi Augusti* 32. On trade, see Webster, *Boudica* p. 38ff.
11. Tacitus, *Annals* 2, 24.
12. Suetonius, *Caligula* 44–46; Dio *op. cit.* 59, 25.
13. Dio, *op. cit.* 60, 19–22.
14. Tacitus, *Histories* 3, 45; *Annals* 14, 32; 14, 34.
15. Suetonius, *Vespasian* 4; Tacitus, *Agricola* 14.
16. Suetonius, *Nero* 35, 4.
17. Dio, 61, 30.
18. Tacitus, *op. cit.* 12, 13; 13, 22. Suetonius, *Nero* 35, 4. Dio, *op.cit.* 61, 30. Suetonius, *Claudius* 24, 2.
19. Tacitus, *Annals* 12, 36; *Agricola* 14–17; *Annals* 14, 29–39; Dio, *op. cit.* 62, 1–12. Venutius: Tacitus, *Histories* 4, 25.
20. *The Roman Senate and People to Tiberius Claudius Caesar Augustus Germanicus, son of Drusus, Pontifex Maximus, Tribunician power eleven times, Consul five times, Imperator twenty-two times, Censor, Father of the Fatherland, for taking the surrender of eleven kings of the Britons defeated without any loss, and first brought barbarian peoples across the Ocean under the sway of the Roman people.* ILS 216–7; *cf.* Suetonius, *Claudius* 25.
21. Tacitus, *Annals* 12, 40.
22. Tacitus, *Histories* 3, 45; *Annals* 12, 40.
23. *Op.cit.* 12, 31; 14, 31; Dio, *op. cit.* 62, 2.

24. Tacitus, *Annals* 14.
25. Tacitus, *Agricola* 15.
26. Tacitus, *op. cit.* 16. Dio, *op. cit.* Trans. E. Cary.
27. Tacitus, *Annals* 14, 30.
28. Tacitus, *Annals* 14, 29–30.
29. Dio, *op. cit.* 62, 1.
30. Tacitus, *Annals* 14, 33.
31. Tacitus, *op. cit.* 14, 33.
32. Tacitus, *op. cit.* 14, 35.
33. Dio, *op. cit.* 62, 3–5.
34. *Op. cit.* 62, 12, 6; Tacitus, *op. cit.* 14, 39; Suetonius, *Nero* 18, 39–40.
35. Tacitus, *Annals* 14, 38.
36. Tacitus, *Agricola* 21. Trans. Sara Bryant, *Complete Works of Tacitus* (New York, 1876, reprinted 1942).
37. See R. Hingley, *Boudica: Iron Age Warrior Queen*, (2006), pp. 41, 61.
38. Plutarch describes a lion pulling a chariot in his *Antony*.
39. Plato, *Phaedrus*, 246a–254e.
40. Pomponius Mela *De Chorographia* 3, 6, 52.
41. Pomponius Mela 3, 52; Frontinus, *Stratagems* 2, 3, 17–18.
42. *De Rebus Bellicis*, 12–14.
43. Caesar, *op. cit.* 4, 31.
44. Tacitus, *op. cit.* 1, 35–36.

Chapter 11: Beth-Horon and the Jewish War AD 68

1. Josephus, *Bellum Judaicum* 2, 41, 5.
2. *Ibid.* 2, 14, 5.
3. *Ibid.* 2, 409.
4. *Ibid.* 2, 305–7.
5. *Ibid.* 3, 326–7.
6. *Ibid.* 2, 408; 4, 7, 2.
7. *Ibid.* 2, 14, 3; 2, 16, 1.
8. *Ibid.* 2, 648–9.
9. Josephus, *Life* 5–6, 22–24.
10. See Gichon, 'Cestius Gallus' Campaign in Judaea', *Palestine Exploration Quarterly*, p. 56. Goodman, *The Ruling Class of Judaea*, 'Chapter 7: The Outbreak of Revolt'.
11. Tacitus, *Histories* 5, 10.
12. Josephus, *Bellum Judaicum* 5, 10, 3. Trans. William Whiston, *Wars of the Jews*. Such horrors, of course, are not confined to the ancient world.
13. Josephus, *op.cit.* 6, 201–13.
14. *Idem.* 6, 9, 3.
15. For Josephus, see Rajak, *Josephus: The Historian and His Society*. Josephus, *Life* 3.
16. Flavius Josephus, *The Jewish War*. Trans. G.A. Williamson, introduction by E. Mary Smallwood, p. 24.
17. Cassius Dio 66, 7, 2. Josephus *op.cit.* 7, 218.
18. *Tractate Gittin* 58a. Four hundred was long hand for 'a great number'.

19. *Book of Joshua* 6, 1–27.
20. Homer, *Iliad* 22, 58–71.
21. Thucydides 7, 29. Translation by Rex Warner (London, 1954).
22. Livy 9, 45, 17; Diodorus Siculus 20, 101, 5. Alba: Livy 1, 29.
23. Quintilian, *Institutio Oratoria* 8, 3, 67–70. Vol. III of the Loeb Classical Library edition (1920).
24. *The Chronicle of Pseudo-Joshua the Stylite*, 85.
25. For John of Ephesus, see Harvey, *Ascetism and Society in Crisis,* pp. 55–75.

Chapter 12: Carnuntum AD 170; the Crisis of the Third Century – Abritus AD 251, Edessa AD 260

1. See Steger, *Die Chronologie der Markomannenkriege.*
2. Full Latin name is Quintus Herennius Etruscus Messius Decius Augustus. In 251, Decius elevated Herennius to the title of *Augustus,* making him his co-emperor, and one of the year's consuls.
3. Jordanes, *Getica* 103; Aurelius Victor, *De Caesaribus* 29; Potter, *The Roman Empire at Bay,* p. 247.
4. See Potter, *op. cit.* p. 246.
5. Zonaras, *Epitome Historiarum* 12, 20.
6. Zosimus 1.
7. Lactantius, *De Mortibus Persecutorum* 4.
8. Ammianus Marcellinus, *Res Gestae* 31, 12, 13.
9. Herodian 6, 7, 10.
10. Pontius of Carthage, *Life of Cyprian.* Trans. Ernest Wallis (1885). Available online at Christian Classics Ethereal Library.
11. Cyprian, *De Mortalitate.* Trans. Ernest Wallis (1885). Available online at Christian Classics Ethereal Library.
12. The Sasanian Empire was the last Iranian empire before the rise of Islam, ruled by the Sasanian dynasty from AD 224 to 651. The Sasanian Empire, which succeeded the Parthian Empire, was one of the main powers in Western and Central Asia, along with the Roman–Byzantine Empire, for more than 400 years.
13. Vegetius, *Epitoma Rei Militaris* 26.
14. Naqŝe Rostamſ is an ancient necropolis about 12km northwest of Persepolis, in Fars Province, Iran.
15. See R. Grishman, *Iran From the Beginning Until Islam* (1995).
16. Lactantius, *De Mortibus Persecutorum,* 5; *Sibylline Oracles,* XIII, 155–171; Frye, *The Sassanians,* p. 126; Southern, *Beyond the Eastern Empire,* p. 238.

Chapter 13: The Theban Legion Massacre AD 286

1. 'Codex Parisiensis', Bibliothèque National, 9550, reproduced in Louis Dupraz, *Les passions de st Maurice d'Agaune: Essai sur l'historicité de la tradition et contribution à l'étude de l'armée pré-Dioclétienne (260–286) et des canonisations tardives de la fin du IVe siècle* (Fribourg, 1961), Appendix I. Dupraz writes to confirm the historicity of the Theban Legion.

2. Note the similarity with 666 – a number with a very different significance when it appears as the Number of the Beast in the *Book of Revelations*.
3. S.F. Girgis, 'Theban Legion', *The Coptic Encyclopedia*, Vol. 7, (Macmillan, 1991).
4. Eusebius, *Historia Ecclesia* 8, 19.
5. Livy 5, 11; 9, 8; 30, 16; Suetonius, *Vitellius* 2.
6. *Luke* 7, 20.
7. R. Van Dam, *Gregory of Tours: Glory of the Martyrs* (Liverpool, 1988), p. 85.
8. J. Foxe, *Fox's Book of Martyrs*, 'The Sixth Persecution, Under Maximus, AD 235', (1563).
9. *Ibid.*
10. 'Codex Parisiensis', Bibliothèque National, 9550, reproduced in Louis Dupraz, *Les passions de st Maurice d'Agaune: Essai sur l'historicité de la tradition et contribution à l'étude de l'armée pré-Dioclétienne (260–286) et des canonisations tardives de la fin du IVe siècle* (Fribourg, 1961).
11. See Van Berchem, *The Martyrdom of the Theban Legion* (1956); Woods, *The Origin of the Legend of Maurice and the Theban Legion* (1994); O'Reilly, *Lost Legion Rediscovered* (2011).
12. A *vexillatio* was a detachment of a Roman legion formed as a temporary task force for a particular emergency. It was named from the standard carried by legionary detachments, the *vexillum*, which bore the emblem and name of the parent legion. They varied in size and composition, but usually consisted of about 1,000 infantry and/or 500 cavalry. As soon as the crisis was taken care of, these *vexillationes* were disbanded and the troops returned to their parent legions.

Chapter 14: Adrianople AD 378

1. Ammianus, *Res Gestae* 14.
2. *Foederati*: nations to which Rome provided benefits in exchange for military assistance. Ammianus, *Historiae* 31, 4, 12–13.
3. Ammianus, *op. cit.* 31, 4.
4. Modern Devnya in Bulgaria. Trajan had renamed Parthenopolis after the Second Dacian War in AD 106. The city was named after Trajan's sister, Ulpia Marciana. See Ammianus Marcellinus, *op. cit.* 27, 4, 12; 31, 4, 11. Zosimus, *Historia* 4, 20, 6.
5. Jordanes, 134.
6. Ammianus, 31, 3–9.
7. Ammianus, 31, 11. Zosimus, 4; Socrates Scholasticus, *Church History* 1, 38.
8. Zosimus, *op. cit.*; Ammianus Marcellinus 31, 10–11.
9. Ammianus, 31, 12.
10. Ammianus, 31, 7–11.
11. Trans. C.D. Yonge, *The Roman History of Ammianus Marcellinus During the Reigns of The Emperors Constantius, Julian, Jovianus, Valentinian, and Valens* (London, 1911), pp. 609–618.
12. Trans. C.D. Yonge, *op. cit.*
13. Ammianus, *op. cit.* 31, 13.
14. Themistius, *Orations* 16, 206d.
15. Ammianus, 31, 13.
16. Ammianus, 31, 12–14.

17. Ammianus, *op. cit.* 16.
18. Trans. C.D. Yonge, *op. cit.*
19. Ammianus 31, 2. Zosimus, *op.cit.* 4, 20, 4.
20. Ed. R.A.B. Mynors, *XII Panegyrici Latini* (Oxford, 1964), No. 2; Trans. C.E.V. Nixon, *In Praise of Later Roman Emperors* (Berkeley, 1994).
21. Toner, *Roman Disasters*, p. 134.
22. Zosimus, *op.cit.* 4, 20, 6; Eunapius *fr.* 42.

Chapter 15: Alaric's Sack of Rome AD 410

1. Alaric means 'King of All'.
2. *Fasti Vindobonenses Priores*, 532 (Chron. Min. 1, 299).
3. Olympiodorus *fr.* 3 (Blockley) = 2 (Muller).
4. Olympiodorus *fr.* 5, 1 (Blockley) = 2 (Muller); Sozomen, *HE* 9, 4; Philostorgius, *Historia Ecclesiastica* 12, 3. Zosimus, *Nova Historia* 5, 35, 5–6.
5. Zosimus, *op. cit.* 5, 36, 1–3. Sozomen *HE* 9, 6–7.
6. Olympiodorus *fr.* 7, 3 (Blockley) = 6 Muller; Zosimus, *op. cit.* 5, 38.
7. Gibbon, *Decline and Fall of the Roman Empire*, Chapter 31. Zosimus, *op. cit.* 5, 40.
8. Sozomen, *HE* 9, 7.
9. Sozomen, *HE* 9, 8; Zosimus, *op. cit.* 6, 12, 2.
10. Sozomen, *HE* 9, 9; Philostrogius, *HE* 12, 3.
11. *Nicene and Post-Nicene Fathers: Series II, Volume VI, The Letters of St. Jerome*, Letter 127, paragraph 12.
12. Orosius, *Historiarum adversum Paganos* 7, 39, 4–14.
13. See Courcelle, *Histoire Litteraire* for details.
14. Jordanes, *Getica* 158.
15. Olympiodorus *fr.* 25 (Blockley) = 25 (Muller) ; *fr.* 16 (Blockley) = 15 (Muller).
16. As described by Tibullus, *Elegies*, 2, 5 300 years previously.
17. Zosimus, *op. cit.* Augustine, *City of God* 3, 17.

Appendix 4: Some Carthaginian Generals

1. Livy, 28, 12.
2. Livy, 30, 28.

Bibliography

Abbreviations:

ABSA = *Annual of the British School at Athens.*
AC = *L'Antiquite Classique.*
Ad Att. = *Cicero Ad Atticum.*
Ad Fam. = *Cicero Ad Familiares.*
AJAH = *Americal Journal of Ancient History.*
AJPh = *American Journal of Philology.*
Annales ESC = *Annales: Histoire, Sciences Sociales.*
Anc Soc = *Ancient Society* (Louvain).
AncW = *The Ancient World.*
BICS = *Bulletin of the Institute of Classical Studies.*
BStudLat = *Bollettino di Studi Latini.*
CAH = *Cambridge Ancient History.*
CB = *Classical Bulletin.*
CIL = *Corpus Inscriptionum Latinarum*, Berlin 1863.
CJ = *Classical Journal.*
Cl. Ant = *Classical Antiquity.*
CPh = *Classical Philology.*
CQ = *Classical Quarterly.*
CW = *Classical World.*
G&R = *Greece and Rome.*
GRBS = *Greek, Roman and Byzantine Studies.*
HSCPh = *Harvard Studies in Classical Philology.*
ILS = *Inscriptiones Latinae Selectae*, ed. H. Dessau.
JHS = *Journal of Hellenic Studies.*
JRS = *Journal of Roman Studies.*
L&S = *Lewis & Short, A Latin Dictionary.*
MAAR = *Memoirs of the American Academy in Rome.*
NH = *Naturalis Historia*, Pliny the Elder.
Olympiodorus = RC Blockley, *The Fragmentary Classicising Historians of the Later Roman Empire*, vol. 2 (Liverpool, 1983).
PBSR = *Papers of the British School at Rome.*

Philostorgius HE = Philostorgius Kirchengeschichte, ed. J.D. Bidez, rev. 1972, Berlin.
PNAS = Proceedings of the National Academy of Science of the USA.
RE = Real Encyclopedia der Classischen Altertumswissenschaft, Pauly-Wissowa.
RhM = Rheinisches Museum fur Philologie.
SO = Symbolae Osloensis.
Sozomen HE = Sozomenus Kirchengeschichte, ed. J.D. Bidez, rev. 1960, Berlin.
TAPhA = Transactions of the Proceedings of the American Philological Association.
WS = Wiener Studien.
ZPE = Zeitschrift fur Papyrologie und Epigraphik.

Primary Sources

Greek = [Gk]
Latin = [L]

Aelian – [L] (*c.* AD 175 – *c.* 235) *De Natura Animalium.*
Ammianus Marcellinus – [L] (AD 325/330 – after 391) *Res Gestae.*
Anonymous – [L] *De Bello Africo* (40 BC).
Appian – [Gk] (late first century AD – 160+ AD) *Bellum Civile*; *Syriaca*; *Mithridatic Wars.*
Asclepias of Mendes – [Gk] (*fl.* AD 10?) *Theologoumena.*
Asconius, Quintus Asconius Pedianus – [L] (*c.* 9 BC – *c.* AD 76) *Pro Milone.*
Athenaeus of Naucratis – [Gk] (*fl.* end second century AD) *Deipnosophistae.*
Augustine of Hippo – [L] (354 BC – 30 AD) *De Civitate Dei.*
Augustus – [L] (63 BC – AD 14) *Res Gestae Divi Augusti.*
Aulus Gellius – [L] (*c.* AD 125 – after 180) *Noctes Atticae.*
Aurelius Victor – [L] (*c.* AD 320 – *c.* 390) *De Viris Illustribus Romae*; *De Caesaribus.*
The Bible – *Matthew; Mark; Luke; Joshua; Revelation; 1 Maccabees.*
Caesar – [L] (100 – 44 BC) *De Bello Gallico; De Bello Civili.*
Catullus – [L] (*c.* 84–54 BC) *Carmina.*
Celsus – [L] (*c.* 25 BC – *c.* AD 50) *De Medicina.*
Chrysostom, John – [Gk] (*c.* AD 347–407), *The Type of Women Who Ought to be Taken as Wives.*
Cicero – [L] (106 – 43 BC), *Ad Atticum; Ad Familiares; De Divitatione; De Domo Sua; De Officiis; De Oratore; De Re Publica; In Catilinam; Oratio de Doma Sua; Oratio Pro Sexto Roscio; Philippics; Pro Fonteio; In Verrem; Pro Milone; Pro Balbo; Pro Lege Manila; De Senectute; Pro Rabirio Perduellionis Reo; In Pisonem.*
Cornelia Africana – [L] the alleged author of *The Cornelia Fragments* (*c.* 122 BC).

Dio Cassius – [Gk] (*c.* AD 155–235) *Historia Romanae.*

Dio Chrysostom – [Gk] (AD 40–120) *Orationes.*

Diodorus Siculus – [Gk] (*fl.* between 60 and 30 BC) *Bibliotheca Historica.*

Diogenes Laertius – [Gk] (after AD 200) *Lives and Opinions of Eminent Philosophers.*

Dionysius of Halicarnassus – [Gk] (*c.* 60 BC – after 7 BC) *Roman Antiquities; On Composition.*

Donatus – [L] (*fl.* AD 350) *Life of Virgil.*

Ennius – [L] (*c.* 239 BC – *c.* 169 BC) *Annales.*

Epictetus – [G] (*c.* AD 55–135) *Discourses.*

Euripides – [Gk] (*c.* 480–406 BC) *Bacchae.*

Eusebius – [Gk] (AD 260/265–339) *Historia Ecclesiastica.*

Eutropius – [L] (*fl.* AD 360) *Abridgement of Roman History.*

Fasti Triumphales – [L] (12 BC) *The Fasti Triumphales* were published in about 12 BC. They contain a list of triumphs from the foundation of Rome down to the reign of Augustus. They are preserved as part of a larger inscription, the *Fasti Capitolini,* which is now displayed in the Capitoline Museums in Rome.

Fasti Vindobonenses Priores – [L] The *Fasti Vindobonenses* are two sets of late antique consular annals (*fasti*) found in the *Vindobonensis* manuscript MS. 3416, together with the Chronography of 354. The first collection is entitled *Fasti Vindobonenses Priores* and covers the periods 44 BC – AD 403 and 455–493. The second is called *Fasti Vindobonenses Posteriores* and covers the periods 44 BC – AD 397, 439–455 and 495–539. Later additions were included for years 390–473 in a copy conserved in the *Sangallensis* MS. 878.

Festus – [L] (*fl.* late second century AD) *Epitome.*

Florus – [L] (*c.* AD 74 – *c.* 130), *Epitome of Roman History.*

Frontinus – [L] (*c.* AD 40 – 103) *Strategemata.*

Herodian – [Gk] (*c.* 170–240), *History of the Empire from the Death of Marcus Aurelius.*

Herodotus – [Gk] (*c.* 484–425 BC) *Histories.*

Homer – [Gk] (*c.* 850 BC) *The Iliad.*

Horace – [L] (65 – 8 BC) *Epodes; Odes.*

Jerome – [L] (fourth century AD) *De Viris Illustribus.*

John of Ephesus – [Syriac] (*c.* AD 507 – *c.* 588) *Ecclesiastical History.*

Jordanes – [L] (*fl.* AD 551) *Getica.*

Josephus – [Gk] (AD 37 – *c.* 100) *Jewish Antiquities; Bellum Judaicum; The Life of Flavius Josephus.*

Juvenal – [L] (*fl.* early second century AD) *Satires.*

Lactantius – [L] (*c.* AD 240 – *c.* 320) *Institutiones Divinae; Oracula Sybillina; De Mortibus Persecutorum.*

Livy – [L] (59 BC – AD 17), *Ab Urbe Condita.*

Lucan – [L] (AD 39 – 65), *Bellum Civile.*

Lucian – [Gk] (*c.* AD 125 – after AD 180) *Alexander.*

Macrobius – [L] (*fl.* fifth century AD) *Saturnalia.*

Manetho – [Gk] (third century BC) *Aegyptiaca.*

Manilius – [L] (*fl.* first century AD) *Astronomica.*

Martial – [L] (*c.* AD 40–100) *Epigrams.*

Minucius Felix – [L] (*fl.* AD 200?) *Octavius.*

Nepos – [L] (*c.* 110 – *c.* 25 BC) *Atticus; De Viris Illustribus; Prologue to the Lives of Foreign Generals.*

Nicene and Post-Nicene Fathers – A set of books containing translations of early Christian writings into English published between 1886 and 1900.

Olympiodorus of Thebes – [Gk] (born AD 380, *fl. c.* 412–425) *History of the Western Empire.*

Onasander – [Gk] (*fl.* first century AD) *Strategikos.*

Orosius – [L] (born *c.* AD 375) *Histories Against the Pagans.*

Ovid – [L] (43 BC – AD 17) *Fasti; Ars Amatoria.*

Pacatus Drepanius – [L] (*fl.* end of fourth century AD) *In Praise of Later Roman Emperors.*

Petronius – [L] (*c.* AD 27 – 66) *Satyricon.*

Philostorgius – [Gk] (AD 368–439) *Historia Ecclesiastica.*

Plato – [Gk] (424–348 BC) *Phaedrus.*

Plautus – [L] (*c.* 254–184 BC) *Bacchae; Miles Gloriosus.*

Pliny the Elder – [L] (AD 23–79) *Historia Naturalis.*

Plutarch – [Gk] (*c.* AD 45–125), *Antony; Caesar; Camillus; Lucullus; Poplicola; Metellus; Pyrrhus; Fabius Maximus; Marcellus; Crassus; Pompey.*

Polyaenus – [Gk] (*fl.* second century AD) *Strategemata.*

Polybius – [Gk] (*c.* 204–122 BC) *Histories.*

Pomponius Mela – (*fl.* 43 BC) *De Situ Orbis libri III.*

Propertius – [L] (b. 50–45 BC – d. 15 BC) *Elegies.*

Pseudo-Hyginus – [L] (*fl.* third century AD) *De Munitionibus Castrorum.*

Pseudo-Joshua the Stylite – [Syriac] (*fl.* AD 500) *Chronicle.*

Quintilian – [L] (*c.* AD 35–90) *Institutiones Oratoriae.*

Quintus Curtius Rufus – (*fl.* first century AD) *Historiae Alexandri Magni.*

Sallust – [L] (*c.* 86–35 BC) *Bellum Catilinae; Jugurtha; Historia.*

Senatus Consultum de Cn. Pisone Patre – [L] (AD 20). Text of a decision of the Senate dated 10 December AD 20, recording the trial of Cn. Calpurnius Piso and the verdict of the Senate against him. Piso had been accused of poisoning Germanicus and of *maiestas* (treason) and had taken his own life on 8 December.

Seneca, L – [L] (*c.* 4 BC–65 AD) *Ad Marciam.*

Silius Italicus – [L] (*c.* AD 28 – *c.* 103) *Punica.*

Socrates Scholasticus – [L] (b. *c.* AD 380- d. after 439) *Historia Ecclesiastica.*

Statius – [L] (*c.* AD 45 – *c.* 96) *Silvae.*

Strabo – [Gk] (64 BC – *c*. AD 24) *Geography*.
Suetonius – [L] (*c*. AD 69–140) *Augustus; Caligula; Claudius; Julius Caesar; Nero; Tiberius; Vitellius; Vespasian*.
Tacitus – [L] (AD 56–118) *Agricola; Annals; Germania; Histories*.
Tertullian – (*c*. AD 160 – *c*. 225) *Ad Martyras*.
Themistius – [Gk] (AD 317 – *c*. 390) *Orations*.
Thucydides – [Gk] (*c*. 460 – *c*. 395 BC) *History of the Peloponnesian War*.
Tibullus – [L] (*c*. 55 – 19 BC) *Elegies*.
Trajan's Column – (AD 113) 24, 57, 72, 147.
Valerius Maximus – [L] (14–27 AD) *Memorable Deeds and Sayings*.
Varro – [L] (116 – 27 BC) *De Lingua Latina*.
Vegetius – [L] (*fl.* late fourth century) *De Re Militari*.
Velleius Paterculus – [L] (*c*. 19 BC – *c*. AD 31) *Historiae Romanae*.
Virgil – [L] (70 – 19 BC) *Aeneid*.
Zonaras – [Gk] (*fl.* twelfth century AD) *Epitome Historiarum*.
Zosimus – [Gk] (*fl.* AD 490) *Historia Nova*.

Secondary Sources

Aberbach, D, *The Roman-Jewish Wars and Hebrew Cultural Nationalism* (Basingstoke, 2000).
Abramson, E, *Roman Legionaries at the Time of Julius Caesar* (London, 1979).
Achaud, G, 'Bellum iustum, bellum sceleratum Sous les Rois et Sous la Republique', *BStudLat* 24 (1994), pp. 474–86.
Adams, C, 'War and Society' in Sabin, *The Cambridge History of Greek and Roman Warfare, Vol. 2* (Cambridge, 2007), pp. 198–234.
Adams, JP, *Logistics of the Roman Army* (London, 1976).
Adcock, FE, *The Greek and Macedonian Art of War* (Berkeley, 1957).
———, 'Delenda est Carthago', *Cambridge Historical Jnl* 8 (1946), p. 117f.
———, *The Roman Art of War Under the Republic* (Cambridge, MA, 1940).
Adie, K, *Corsets to Camouflage: Women and War* (London, 2003).
Adler, E, *Valorizing the Barbarians: Enemy Speeches in Roman Historiography* (Austin, 2011).
———, 'Boudica's Speeches in Tacitus and Dio', *CW* 101 (2008), pp. 173–195.
Afflerbach, H (ed), *How Fighting Ends: A History Of Surrender* (Oxford, 2012).
Alfoldi, A, *Early Rome and the Latins* (Ann Arbor, 1965).
Allason-Jones, L, 'Women in Roman Britain', in James, *Companion to Women in the Ancient World* (Chichester, 2012), pp. 467–477.
———, *Women in Roman Britain* (London, 1989).
Allison, PM, *People and Spaces in Roman Military Bases* (Cambridge, 2013).
Alonso-Nunez, J, 'Herodotus on the Far West', *Ant. Class.* 56 (1987), pp. 243–249.

Aly, AA, 'Cleopatra and Caesar at Alexandria and Rome', in Caratelli (1989), pp. 47–61.

Anglim, S, *Fighting Techniques of the Ancient World, 3000 BC – AD 500* (London, 2002).

Alston R, 'Warfare and the State B: The Military and Politics', in Sabin, *The Cambridge History of Greek and Roman Warfare, Vol. 2* (Cambridge, 2007), pp. 176–197.

———, *Soldier and Society in Roman Egypt: A Social History* (London, 1995).

———, 'Roman Military Pay from Caesar to Diocletian', *JRS* 84 (1994), pp. 113–123.

Anderson, A, *Roman Military Tombstones* (Oxford, 1983).

Annas, J, 'Plato's *Republic* and Feminism', *Philosophy* 51 (1976), pp. 307–321.

Appels, A, *Roman Buckles and Military Fittings* (Witham, 2007).

Archimedes, 'Archimedes Death Ray: Testing with Myth Busters', *The Discovery Channel*, January 25, 2006. *http://web.mit.edu/2.009/www//experiments/deathray/10_Mythbusters.html*

Arieti, JA, 'Rape and Livy's View of Roman History', in Deacy, *Rape in Antiquity*, (London, 1997) pp. 209–229.

Arthur, MB, 'Early Greece: The Origins of the Western Attitude Toward Women', *Arethusa* 6 (1973), p. 7–58.

Ash, R, 'Epic Encounters? Ancient Historical Battle Narratives and the Epic Tradition', in Levine, *Clio and the Poets: Augustan Poetry and the Traditions of Ancient Historiography* (Leiden, 2002), pp. 253–73.

Ashley, JR, *The Macedonian Empire: The Era of Warfare Under Philip II and Alexander the Great* (Jefferson, NC, 2004).

Askin, KD, *War Crimes Against Women: Prosecution in International War Crimes Tribunal* (Amsterdam, 1997).

Astin, AE (ed.) *CAH Volume 8, Rome and the Mediterranean to 133 BC* (Cambridge, 1989).

———, *Cato the Censor* (Oxford, 1978).

———, *Scipio Aemilianus* (Oxford, 1967).

———, 'Saguntum and the Origins of the Second Punic War', *Latomus* 26 (1967), pp. 577–96.

Austin, NJE, 'Ammianus on Warfare', *Latomus* 165 (1979).

———, 'Ammianus' Account of the Adrianople Campaign: Some Strategic Observations', *Ant. Class* 15 (1972), pp. 77–83.

Babcock, C, 'The Early Career of Fulvia', *AJPh* 86 (1965), pp. 1–32.

Badian, E, 'Rome, Athens and Mithridates', *AJAH* 1 (1976), pp. 105–128.

———, *Roman Imperialism in the Late Republic* (Oxford, 1968).

———, 'The Early Historians', in Dorey, *Latin Historians* (London, 1966), pp. 1–38.

———, *Foreign Clientelae* (London, 1958).

Bagnall, N, *The Peloponnesian War: Athens, Sparta, And The Struggle For Greece* (New York, 2006).

———, *The Punic Wars: Rome, Carthage and the Struggle for the Mediterranean*, (London, 1999).

Bahmanyar, M, *Vanquished: Crushing Defeats from Ancient Rome to the 21st Century* (Oxford, 2009).

Bahrani, Z, *Women of Babylon: Gender and Representation in Mesopotamia*, (London, 2001).

Baldwin, B, 'Women in Tacitus', *Prudentia* 4 (1972), pp. 83–101.

———, 'Two Aspects of the Spartacus Slave Revolt', *CJ* 62 (1966), p. 289ff.

Ball, W, *Rome in the East: The Transformation of an Empire* (London, 2001).

Balsdon, JPVD, *Romans and Aliens* (London, 1979).

Barber, EW, *Women's Work: The First 20,000 Years – Women, Cloth and Society in Early Times* (New York, 1994).

Barbero, A, *The Day of the Barbarians: The Battle That Led to the Fall of the Roman Empire* (London, 2007).

Barker, P, *The Armies and Enemies of Imperial Rome* (Worthing, 1981).

Bar-Kochva, B, *The Seleucid Army* (Cambridge, 1976).

Barnes, J, 'Ciceron et la Guerre Juste', *Bulletin de la Societe Française de Philosophie* 80 (1986), pp. 41–81.

Barnes, TD, *Ammianus and the Representation of Historical Reality* (Ithaca, 1998).

Baronowski, DW, *Polybius and Roman Imperialism* (London, 2013).

———, 'Roman Military Forces in 225 BC (Polybius 2, 23–4)', *Historia* 42 (1993), pp. 81–201.

Barrow, R, 'Faithful Unto Death: Picturing a Roman Soldier in Victorian Britain', *Omnibus* 66 (2013), pp. 1–3.

Barton, CA, 'The Price of Peace in Ancient Rome', in Raaflaub, *War and Peace in the Ancient World* (Chichester, 2007), pp. 245–255.

Basch, L, 'Another Punic Wreck in Sicily: Its Ram', *International Jnl of Nautical Archaeology* 4 (1976), pp. 201–208.

Bauman, RA *Crime and Punishment in Ancient Rome* (London, 1996).

———, *Women and Politics in Ancient Rome* (London, 1992).

Bayless, WN, 'The Visigothic Invasion of Italy in 401', *CJ* 72 (1976), pp. 65–67.

Beaver, J, *The Roman Military Punishments* (Cambridge, MA, 2011 reprint).

Beard, M, *The Roman Triumph* (Harvard, MA, 2009).

Beard, MR, *Women as a Force in History: A Study in Tradition and Realities* (New York, 1946).

Beck, H (ed.), *Consuls and* Res Publica: *Holding High Office in the Roman Republic* (Cambridge, 2011).

Becker, TH, 'Ambiguity and the Female Warrior: Virgil's Camilla', *Electronic Antiquity*, 4 (1997). http://www.scholar.lib.vt.edu/ejournals/ElAnt/V4N1/becker.html

Beevor, A, *Stalingrad* (London, 2007).

———, *Berlin: The Downfall 1945* (London, 2002).

Belhassen, I, 'Revision and Reconstruction in the Punic Wars: Cannae Revisited', *International Jnl of the Humanities*, 4, 2 (2006), pp. 103–110.

Bell, MJV, 'Tactical Reform in the Roman Republican Army', *Historia* 14 (1965), pp. 404–22.

Beloch, KJ, *Romische Geschichte bis zum Beginn der Punische Kriege* (Berlin, 1926).

Benario, HW, 'Boudica Warrior Queen', *Classical Outlook* 82 (2007), pp. 70–73.

Berlin, A (ed.) *The First Jewish Revolt: Archaeology, History and Ideology* (London, 2002).

Berry, J, *The Complete Roman Legions* (London, 2012).

Bertrand, AC, 'Stumbling Through Gaul: Intelligence and Caesar's *Bellum Gallicum*', *Ancient History Bulletin* 2, 4 (1997), pp. 107–22.

Best, EE, 'Cicero, Livy and Educated Roman Women', *CJ* 65 (1970), pp. 199–204.

Billows, R. 'International Relations', in Sabin, *The Cambridge History of Greek and Roman Warfare, Vol. 1* (Cambridge, 2007), pp. 303–324.

Bishop, M, *Roman Military Equipment*, 2nd edition (Oxford, 2005).

Bishop, P, *Fighter Boys: Saving Britain 1940* (London, 2003).

Bivar, H, 'The Political History of Iran under the Arsacids', in *CAH*, Iran III/1 (1983), pp. 21–99.

Blanshard, AJL, *Classics on Screen: Ancient Greece and Rome on Film* (London, 2011).

Bloch, R, *Combats Singuliers Entre Gaulois et Romans* (Paris, 1968).

Blok, J, *The Early Amazons* (Leiden, 1994).

Bloom, JJ, *The Jewish Revolts Against Rome AD 66–115: A Military Analysis* (Jefferson, 2010).

Bluestone, NH, *Women and the Ideal Society: Plato's Republic and Modern Myths of Gender* (Oxford, 1997).

Boardman, J, *The Greeks Overseas* (Harmondsworth, 1964).

Bonfante, WL, 'Roman Triumphs and Etruscan Kings', *JRS* 60 (1980), pp. 49–66.

———, 'The Women of Etruria', *Arethusa* 6 (1973), pp. 91–102.

———, 'Etruscan Couples and Their Aristocratic Society', in Foley, *Reflections* (London, 1981), pp. 323–342.

———, 'Etruscan Women', in Fantham, *Women in the Classical World* (Oxford, 1994), pp. 243–259.

Boot, M, *Invisible Armies: An Epic History of Guerilla Warfare from Ancient Times to the Present* (London, 2014).

Bordewich, FM, 'The Ambush That Changed History', *Smithsonian Magazine*, (September 2006).

Bosworth, AB, *The Legacy of Alexander: Politics, Warfare, and Propaganda Under the Successors* (Oxford, 2005).

Boudet, J, *The Ancient Art of Warfare* (London, 1966).

Bourriau, J (ed.), *Understanding Catastrophe* (Cambridge, 1992).

Bowman, AK, *The Roman Agricultural Economy* (Oxford, 2013).

———, *The Vindolanda Writing Tablets* (London, 2003).

Bradley, G (ed.), *Greek and Roman Colonization: Origins, Ideologies and Interactions* (Swansea, 2005).

Bradley, H, *The Goths: from the Earliest Times to the End of the Gothic Dominion in Spain*, 2nd edition, (New York, 1883).

Bradley, KR, *Slavery and Rebellion in the Roman World (140 BC – 40 BC)* (London, 1989).

Bragg, E, 'Beyond the Battlefield: Caesar on Massacres, Executions and Mutilations', *Omnibus* 54 (2007), pp. 15–18.

Bragg, M, (presenter) 'Spartacus', *In Our Time*, BBC Radio 4, 6 March, 2014.

Brand, CE, *Roman Military Law* (Austin, 1968).

Branigan, K, *The Catuvellauni* (Stroud, 1985).

Brauer, GC, *Judea Weeping: The Jewish Struggle Against Rome from Pompey to Masada, 63 BC to AD 73* (New York, 1970).

Braund, DC, *Ruling Roman Britain: Kings, Queens, Governors, and Emperors from Julius Caesar to Agricola* (New York, 1996).

———, *Rome and the Friendly King: The Character of the Client Kingship* (London, 1984).

Braund, S (ed.), *Ancient Anger: Perspectives from Homer to Galen* (Cambridge, 2003).

Breeze, D, 'The Organization of the Legion: The First Cohort and the Equites Legionis', *JRS* 59 (1980), pp. 50–55.

Brennan, TC, 'Perception of Women's Power in the Late Republic: Terentia, Fulvia and the Generation of 63 BC', in James, *Companion* (2012), pp. 354–366.

Brewer, R, *Roman Legions and Their Fortresses* (London, 2000).

Brier, R, *Daily Life of the Ancient Egyptians* (New York, 1999).

Brighton, MA, 'The Sicarii in Josephus' Judean War: Rhetorical Analysis and Historical Observations', *Society of Biblical Literature* (Atlanta, 2009).

Brion, M, *Alaric the Goth* (RM McBride & Co., 1930).

Briscoe, J, 'The First Decade', in Dorey, *Livy* (London, 1971).

Broadhead, W, 'Colonisation, Land Distribution and Veteran Settlement', in Erdkamp, *A Companion to the Roman Army* (Oxford, 2007).

Brosius, M, *Women in Ancient Persia: 559–331 BC* (Oxford, 1998).

Broughton, TRS, *The Magistrates of the Roman Republic Vol 1: 509 BC – 100 BC* (Cleveland, 1951).

Brown, C, 'The Search for Cleopatra', *National Geographic* (July 2011), pp. 40–63.

Brown, JET, 'Hannibal's Route Across the Alps', *G&R* 10 (1963), pp. 38–46.

Brown, RD, 'Livy's Sabine Women and the Ideal of *Concordia*', *TAPhA* 125 (1995), pp. 291–319.

Brownmiller, S, *Against Our Will: Men, Women and Rape* (Harmondsworth, 1975).

Brule, P, *Women of Ancient Greece* (Edinburgh, 2003).

Brunt, PA, *The Fall of the Roman Republic and Related Essays* (Oxford, 1988).

——, 'Conscription and Volunteering in the Roman Army', *Scripta Classica Israelica* 1 (1974), pp. 90–115.

——, *Italian Manpower* (Oxford, 1971).

——, 'The Army and the Land in the Roman Revolution', *JRS* 52 (1962), pp. 69–86.

Bruun, P, *Studies in the Romanization of Etruria* (Rome, 1975).

Bryant, S, (trans.) *Complete Works of Tacitus* (New York, 1876, reprinted 1942).

Buitelaar, M, 'Widow's Worlds', in Bremmer J, *Between Poverty and the Pyre* (London, 1995) pp. 1–18.

Bulst, C, 'The Revolt of Queen Boudicca in AD 60: Roman Politics and the Iceni', *Historia* 10 (1961), pp. 496–509.

Burns, TS, *Rome and the Barbarians, 100 B.C. – A.D. 400* (Baltimore, MD, 2009).

——, *Barbarians Within the Gates of Rome* (Bloomington, IN, 1995).

——, *A History of the Ostrogoths* (Bloomington, IN, 1984).

——, 'The Battle of Adrianople: A Reconsideration', *Historia* 22 (1973), pp, 336–45.

Bury, JB, *Later Roman Empire* (London, 1923).

Buruma, I, *Year Zero: the History of 1945* (London, 2014).

Cadoux, CJ, *The Early Christian Attitude towards War* (New York, 1912).

Cadoux, TJ, 'Marcus Crassus: A Reevaluation', *G&R* 3 (1956), pp. 153–161.

Cairns, F, 'Propertius and the Battle of Actium (4, 6)', in Woodman, *Poetry and Politics in the Age of Augustus* (Cambridge, 1984), pp. 129–68.

Campbell, B (ed.) *Oxford Handbook of Warfare in the Classical World* (Oxford, 2013).

——, *Greek & Roman Military Writers* (London, 2004).

——, 'Teach Yourself How to be a General', *JRS* 77 (1987), pp. 13–29.

——, *The Roman Army, 31 BC – AD 337: A Sourcebook* (London, 1984).

——, 'The Marriage of Roman Soldiers Under the Empire', *JRS* 68 (1978), pp. 153–66.

Campbell, DB, *Besieged: Siege Warfare Ancient World* (Oxford, 2006).

——, *Ancient Siege Warfare: Persians, Greeks, Carthaginians* (Oxford, 2005).

——, *Greek and Roman Siege Machinery 399 BC – AD 363* (Oxford, 2003).

Capponi, L, 'Signed Cleopatra – Fact or Factoid?', *Ad Familiares* 32 (2007), pp. 15–16.

Carey, BT, *Warfare in the Ancient World* (London, 2005).

Carney, E, *Olympias: Mother of Alexander the Great* (London, 2006).

——, 'Women and Dunasteia in Caria', *AJPh* 126 (2005), pp. 65–91.

————, 'Women and Military Leadership in Macedonia', *AncW* 35 (2004), pp. 184–95.

————, 'The Career of Adea Eurydice', *Historia* 36 (1987), pp. 496–502.

Carney, TF, *A Biography of C. Marius* (Chicago, 1970).

Carroll, M, *Celts and Germans: The German Provinces of Rome* (Stroud, 2001).

Carson, A, 'Putting Her in Her Place: Women, Dirt and Desire', in Halperin, *Before Sexuality* (Princeton, NJ, 1990) pp. 35–69.

Carter, J, *The Battle of Actium: The Rise and Triumph of Augustus Caesar* (London, 1970).

Cartledge, P, 'Surrender in Ancient Greece', in Afflerbach, *How Fighting Ends* (Oxford, 2012) pp. 15–28.

————, 'Spartan Wives: Liberation or Licence?', *CQ* 31 (1981), pp. 84–105.

Cary, M, *A History of Rome, 3rd edition* (London, 1975).

Casson, L, *Ships and Seamanship in the Ancient World* (Princeton, 1971).

Caven, BM, *The Punic Wars* (London, 1980).

Cerchiai, L, *The Greek Cities of Magna Graecia and Sicily* (New York, 2004).

Chadwick, N, *The Celts* (London, 1970).

Chakravarti, P, *The Art of War in Ancient India* (2003, reprint).

Champion CB, *Roman Imperialism: Readings and Sources* (Chichester, 2003).

Chapman, A, *The Female Principle in Plutarch's Moralia* (Dublin, 2007).

Chaniotis, A (ed.), *Army and Power in the Ancient World* (Stuttgart, 2002).

Chaplin, D (ed.), *Livy: Oxford Readings in Classical Studies* (Oxford, 2009).

————, *Livy's Exemplary History* (Oxford, 2000).

Charles, MB, '*Magister Elephantorum*: A Reappraisal of Hannibal's Use of Elephants', *CW* 100 (2007), pp. 363–89.

Chavalas, MV, *Women in the Ancient Near East* (London, 2013).

Cheeseman, GL, *Auxilia of the Roman Army* (Oxford, 1914).

Chrystal, P, 'A Powerful Body of Women', *Minerva*, January–February (2014), pp. 10–13.

————, 'Roman Women Go to War, I-IV', *Omnibus*, October (2014).

————, *Women at War in the Classical World* (Barnsley, in press 2016).

————, *Roman Women: The Women Who Influenced the History of Rome* (Stroud, 2015).

————, *Wars and Battles of the Roman Republic* (Stroud, 2015).

————, *In Bed with the Romans* (Stroud, in press 2015).

————, *Women in Ancient Rome* (Stroud, 2014).

————, *Differences in Attitude to Women as Reflected in the Work of Catullus, Propertius, the Corpus Tibullianum, Horace and Ovid*, diss., University of Southampton (Southampton, 1982).

Church, AJ, *Stories from Livy* (London, 1902).

Churchill, B, '*Ex Qua Quod Vellent Facerent*: Roman Magistrates' Authority over *Praeda* and *Manubiae*', *TAPhA* 129 (1999), pp. 85–116.

Clarke, K, 'History and Histrionics: Staging Nero's Reign', *Omnibus* 67 (2014), pp. 12–14.

Clayton, EC, *Female Warrior* (London, 1879).

Cloud, D, 'Roman Poetry and Anti-Militarism', in Rich, *War and Society in the Ancient World*, pp. 113–138.

Cloutier, G, 'Andromache: Denial and Despair', *The First-Year Papers (2013)*, Trinity College Digital Repository (Hartford, CT). http://www.digitalrepository.trincoll.edu/fypapers/37

Clunn, JAS, *In Quest of the Lost Legions, The Varussschlacht*, (London, 1999).

Clutton-Brock, J, *Horse Power: A History of the Horse and the Donkey in Human Societies* (Harvard, 1992).

Cohen, EA, *Military Misfortunes: The Anatomy of Failure in War* (New York, 1990).

Colin, G, *Rome et la Gréce de 200 a 146 BC avant JC* (Paris, 1905).

———, 'Luxe Oriental et Parfums Masculins dans la Rome Alexandrine', *RBPH* 33 (1935), pp. 5–19.

Collins, JH, *Propaganda, Ethics and Psychological Assumptions in Caesar's Writings* (Frankfurt, 1952).

Connolly, P, *Greece and Rome at War* (London, 2006).

———, *Hannibal and the Enemies of Rome* (London, 1978).

Cook, BA (ed.), *Women and War: A Historical Encyclopedia from Antiquity to the Present, 2 Vols.* (Oxford, 2006).

Cook, SA (ed.), *Hellenistic Monarchies and the Rise of Rome* (Cambridge, 1928).

Cooke, D, *Battlefield Yorkshire: From the Romans to the English Civil Wars* (Barnsley, 2006).

Cooper, HM (ed.), *Arms and the Woman: War, Gender, and Literary Representation* (Chapel Hill, NC, 1989).

Copper, JS, *The Curse of Agade* (Baltimore, MD, 1983).

Corbett, JH, 'Rome and the Gauls 285–280 BC', *Historia* 20 (1971), pp. 656–64.

Cornell, TJ, *Gender and Ethnicity in Ancient Italy* (London, 1997).

———, (ed.) *The Second Punic War: A Reappraisal* (London, 1996).

———, *The Beginnings of Rome* (London, 1995).

Cotterell, A, *The Chariot: The Astounding Rise and Fall of the World's First War Machine* (London, 2004). This should be a new entry on a new line Cottrell, L, 'The Battle of Trebbia' in *Hannibal: Enemy of Rome* (London, 1992).

———, *Hannibal: Enemy of Rome* (London, 1992).

Coulston, JC, *Roman Military Equipment from the Punic Wars to the Fall of Rome* (Oxford, 2005).

Courcelle, P, *Histoire Litteraire des Grandes Invasions Germaniques* (Paris, 1964).

Courtney, E, 'Virgil's Military Catalogues and their Antecedents', *Vergilius* 34 (1988), pp. 3–8.

Cowan, R, *The Roman Conquests: Italy* (Barnsley, 2009).

————, *Roman Battle Tactics 109 BC – AD 313* (Oxford, 2007).

————, 'Wounds to the Front', *Ad Familiares* 33 (2007), pp. 7–9.

————, *For the Glory of Rome: A History of Warriors and Warfare* (London, 2007).

Crawford, H, *Sumer and Sumerians* (Cambridge, 2004).

Crawford, MH, 'War and Finance', *JRS* 54 (1964), pp. 29–32.

Crowley, J, *The Psychology of the Athenian Hoplite: The Culture of Combat in Classical Athens* (Cambridge, 2012).

Crump, G, *Ammianus Marcellinus as Military Historian* (Wiesbaden, 1975).

Cuff, PJ, 'Caesar the Soldier', *G&R* 4 (1957), pp. 29–35.

Curchin, LA, *The Romanization of Central Spain: Complexity, Diversity and Change in a Provincial Hinterland* (London, 2004).

————, *Roman Spain: Conquest and Assimilation* (New York, 1995).

Curran, JR, 'The Jewish War: Some Neglected Regional Factors', *CW* 101 (2007), pp. 75–91.

Curto, S, *The Military Art of the Ancient Egyptians* (Milan, 1971).

D'Agostino, B, 'Military Organization and Social Structure in Archaic Etruria', in Murray, *The Greek City*, (Oxford, 1990) pp. 59–82.

Daly, G, *Cannae: The Experience of Battle in the Second Punic War* (London, 2002).

Dando-Collins, S, *Legions of Rome: The Definitive History of Every Roman Legion* (London, 2010).

David, JM, *The Roman Conquest of Italy* (Oxford, 1997).

Davies, G, *Roman Siege Works* (Stroud, 2006).

Davies, RW, *Service in the Roman Army* (Edinburgh, 1989).

————, 'The Roman Military Medical Service', *Sonderdruck aus dem Saalburg Jahrbuch* 27 (1970), pp. 84–104.

Davis, PK, *Besieged: 100 Great Sieges from Jericho to Sarajevo* (Oxford, (2001).

————, *100 Decisive Battles from Ancient Times to the Present: The World's Major Battles and How They Shaped History* (Oxford, 1999).

Dawson, D, *The Origins Of Western Warfare: Militarism And Morality In The Ancient World* (Boulder, CO, 1997).

Deacy, S (ed.) *Rape in Antiquity* (London, 1997).

de Beer, G, *Hannibal Challenging Rome's Supremacy* (New York, 1969).

————, *Hannibal's March* (London, 1967).

de Blois, L, 'Army and General in the Late Roman Republic', in Erdkamp, *A Companion to the Roman Army* (Chichester, 2007).

de Brohun, 'The Gates of War (and Peace)', in Raaflaub, *War and Peace in the Ancient World* (2007), pp. 256–278.

DeGroot, G, 'Punic Enemy Number One', *The Times* 14 February 2015, review of Macdonald, *Hannibal: A Hellenistic Life*.

de la Bedoyere, G, *Defying Rome: The Rebels of Roman Britain* (Stroud, 2003).

Delbrück, H, *The Barbarian Invasions* (Lincoln, NE, 1990).

———, H, *Warfare in Antiquity: History of the Art of War, Volume 1* (Lincoln, NE, 1920).

Delia, D, 'Fulvia Reconsidered', in Pomeroy, *Women's History and Ancient History* (Chapel Hill, NC, 1991) pp. 197–217.

de Libero, L, 'Surrender in Ancient Rome', in Afflerbach, *How Fighting Ends,* (Oxford, 2012), pp. 29–40.

de Ligt, L, *Peasants, Citizens and Soldiers: Studies in the Demographic History of Roman Italy* (Cambridge, 2012).

———, 'Roman Manpower and Recruitment During the Middle Republic', in Erdkamp, P, *A Companion to the Roman Army* (Chichester, 2007).

de Neeve, PW, *Peasants in Peril: Location and Economy in 2nd Century BC Italy* (Amsterdam, 1984).

den Hengst, D, *Emperors and Historiography: Collected Essays on the Literature of the Roman Empire* (Leiden, 2009).

Desmond, AC, *Cleopatra's Children* (New York, 1971).

de Souza, P (ed.) *War and Peace in Ancient and Medieval History* (Cambridge, 2011).

———, 'Military Forces, B: Naval Forces', in Sabin, *The Cambridge History of Greek and Roman Warfare Vol. 1* (Cambridge, 2007) pp. 357–367.

———, 'Battle, B: Naval Battles and Sieges', in Sabin, *The Cambridge History of Greek and Roman Warfare Vol. 1* (Cambridge, 2007) pp. 434–460.

———, *Piracy in the Greco-Roman World* (Cambridge, 1999).

———, 'Romans and Pirates in a Late Hellenistic Oracle from Pamphylia', *CQ* 47 (1997), pp. 477–481.

Dillon, S (ed.) *Representations of War in Ancient Rome* (Cambridge, 2006).

Dixon K, *The Roman Cavalry* (London, 1992).

Dodge, TA, *Warfare in the Age of Gaius Julius Caesar – Volume 1: Arar & Bibracte to Uxellodunum, 110 BC to 50 BC* (New York, 2013).

———, *Warfare in the Age of Gaius Julius Caesar – Volume 2: Brundisium & Massilia to Munda, 49 BC to 45 BC* (New York, 2013).

———, *Hannibal: A History of the Art of War Among the Carthaginians and Romans Down to the Battle of Pydna, 168 BC, with a Detailed Account of the Second Punic War* (London, 1994 reprint).

———, *The Battle of the Trebia. December, 218 B.C.* (Boston, 1891).

Donaldson, I, *The Rapes of Lucretia: A Myth and Its Transformations* (Oxford, 1982).

Donato, G, *The Fragrant Past: Perfumes of Cleopatra and Julius Caesar* (Rome, 1989).

Dorey, T.A. (1971) *Rome Against Carthage* (London).

———, (ed.), *Livy* (London, 1971).

———, (ed.), *Tacitus* (London, 1969).

———, (ed.), *The Latin Historians* (London, 1966).

———, 'Hannibal's Route Across the Alps', *Romanitas* 3 (1961), pp. 325–30.

———, 'The Treaty with Saguntum', *Humanitas* (1959), pp. 1–10.

———, 'Macedonian Troops at the Battle of Zama', *AJPh* 78 (1957), pp. 185–7.

Dougherty, C, 'Sowing the Seeds of Violence: Rape, Women and the Land', in Wyke, *Parchments of Gender* (Oxford, 1998), pp. 267–84.

Dowden, K, 'The Amazons: Development and Function', *RhM* 140 (1997), pp. 97–128.

Drinkwater, JF, *The Gallic Empire: Separation and Continuity in the North-west Provinces of the Roman Empire AD 260-274* (Stuttgart, 1987).

Du Bois, P, *Centaurs and Amazons: Women and the Pre-History of the Great Chain of Being* (Ann Arbor, 1982).

Duggan, A, *He Died Old: Mithridates Eupator, King of Pontus* (London, 1958).

Dunbabin, TJ, *The Western Greeks* (Oxford, 1948).

Druett, J, *She Captains: Heroines and Hellions of the Sea* (New York, 2005).

Dudley, DR, *The Rebellion of Boudicca* (London, 1962).

Dyck, A, *A Commentary on Cicero, de Officiis* (Ann Arbor, 1996).

Eck, W, 'The Bar Kokhba Revolt: The Roman Point of View', *JRS* 89 (1999), pp. 76–89.

Eckstein, AM, *Mediterranean Anarchy, Interstate War, and the Rise of Rome* (Berkeley, 2009).

———, 'Polybius, Demetrius of Pharus and the Origins of the Second Illyria War', *CPh* 89 (1994), pp. 46–59.

———, 'Human Sacrifice and the Fear of Military Disaster in Republican Rome', *AJAH* 7 (1982), pp. 69–95.

Eder, W (ed.) *Staat und Staatlichkeit in der Fruhen Romische Republik* (Stuttgart, 1979).

Eggenberger, D, *Encyclopaedia of Battles: Accounts of Over 1560 Battles from 1479 B.C. to the Present* (New York, 1986).

Elliott, J, 'Ennius' Fabius Maximus Cunctator and the History of an Ablative Gerund in the Roman Historiographical Tradition', *CQ* 59 (2009), pp. 532–542.

Ellis, PB, *A Brief History of the Celts* (London, 2003).

———, *Celt and Roman: The Celts in Italy* (London, 1998).

Elton, H, *Warfare in Roman Europe AD 350-425* (Oxford, 1996).

Erdkamp, P (ed.) *A Companion to the Roman Army* (Chichester, 2007).

———, 'War and State Formation in the Late Republic', in Erdkamp, *A Companion to the Roman Army* (Chichester, 2007).

———, *Hunger and the Sword: Warfare and Food Supply in Roman Republican Warfare (264–30 BC)* (Amsterdam, 1998).

Errington, RM, *The Dawn of Empire* (Ithaca, 1972).

Erskine, A, *Roman Imperialism* (Edinburgh, 2008).

Freepost Plus RTKE-RGRJ-KTTX
Pen & Sword Books Ltd
47 Church Street
BARNSLEY
S70 2AS

DISCOVER MORE ABOUT MILITARY HISTORY

Pen & Sword Books have over 4000 books currently available, our imprints include; Aviation, Naval, Military, Archaeology, Transport, Frontline, Seaforth and the Battleground series, and we cover all periods of history on land, sea and air.

Keep up to date with our new releases by completing and returning the form below (no stamp required if posting in the UK).

Alternatively, if you have access to the internet, please complete your details online via our website at **www.pen-and-sword.co.uk.**

All those subscribing to our mailing list will receive a free e-book, *Mosquito Missions* by Martin W Bowman. Please enter code number ACC1 when subscribing to receive your free e-book.

Mr/Mrs/Ms ....

Address...

....

Postcode... Email address..

Website: www.pen-and-sword.co.uk Email: enquiries@pen-and-sword.co.uk
Telephone: 01226 734555 Fax: 01226 734438
Stay in touch: facebook.com/penandswordbooks or follow us on Twitter @penswordbooks

Evans, JA, *The Power Game in Byzantium: Antonina and the Empress Theodor* (London, 2011).

Evans, JK, *War, Women and Children in Ancient Rome* (London, 1991).

Evans, RF, *Soldiers of Rome: Praetorians & Legionnaires* (Washington, DC, 1986).

Evans, RJ, *Roman Conquests: Asia Minor, Syria and Armenia* (Barnsley, 2011).

―――, *Gaius Marius: A Political Biography* (Pretoria, 1994).

Everson, T, *Warfare in Ancient Greece* (Stroud, 2007).

Fabia, P, *Titii Livii loci qui sunt de praeda belli Romana* (Lyons, 1903), pp. 305–68.

Fagan, GG (ed.), *New Perspectives on Ancient Warfare* (Leiden, 2010).

Fantham, E, *Women in the Classical World: Image and Text* (New York, 1994).

Fast, H, *Spartacus* (London, 1996 reprint).

Faulkner, N, *Apocalypse: The Great Jewish Revolt against Rome* (Stroud, 2004).

Feeney, D *Caesar's Calendar: Ancient Time and the Beginnings of History* (Berkeley, 2007).

Fielding, S (ed.), *The Lives of Cleopatra and Octavia* (Lewisburg, 1757).

Feldherr, A (ed.), *Cambridge Companion to the Roman Historians* (Cambridge, 2009).

―――, *Spectacle and Society in Livy's History* (Berkeley, 1998).

Ferrill, A, *The Origins of War: From the Stone Age to Alexander the Great* (Boulder, CO, 1997).

Ferris, I, *Hate and War: The Column of Marcus Aurelius* (Stroud, 2009).

Feugere, M, *Weapons of the Romans* (Stroud, 2002).

Fields, N, *Roman Conquests: North Africa* (Barnsley, 2010).

―――, *Spartacus and the Slave War 73–71 BC* (Oxford, 2009).

―――, *The Roman Army of the Punic Wars 264–146 BC* (Oxford, 2007).

Finley, M, *Ancient History: Evidence and Models* (London, 1985).

Fischer, NRE, *Social Values in Classical Athens* (London, 1976).

Fitton-Brown, AD, 'After Cannae', *Historia* 4 1955, p. 365ff.

Fletcher, J, *Cleopatra The Great: The Woman Behind the Legend* (London, 2008).

Foley, H (ed.), *Reflections of Women in Antiquity* (London, 1992).

―――, 'Women in Ancient Epic', in Foley, *A Companion to Ancient Epic* (Oxford, 2008), pp. 105–118.

Flory, MB, 'The Integration of Women into the Roman Triumph', *Historia* 47 (1998), pp. 489–94.

Flower, HI (ed.), *The Cambridge Companion to the Roman Republic* (Cambridge, 2004).

―――, 'The Tradition of the *Spolia Opima*: M. Claudius Marcellus and Augustus', *Cl Ant* 37 (2000).

Ford, MC, *The Last King: Rome's Greatest Enemy* (New York, 2004).

Fordyce, CJ (ed.) *P Vergili Maronis Aeneidos Libri VII–VIII* (Glasgow, 1977).

Forsythe, G, 'The Army and Centurate Organisation in Early Rome', in Erdkamp, *A Companion to the Roman Army* (Oxford, 2007).

————, *A Critical History of Early Rome: From Prehistory to the First Punic War* (Berkeley, 2005).

————, *Livy and Early Rome* (Stuttgart, 1999).

Fowler, R, 'How the *Lysistrata* Works', *EMC* 15 (1996), pp. 245–259.

Fox, M, *Roman Historical Myths: The Regal Period in Augustan Literature* (Oxford, 1996).

Foxe, J, *Foxe's Book of Martyrs* (1563).

Frank, E, 'Marius and the Roman Nobility', *CJ* 50 (1955), pp. 149–152.

Frank, T, 'Roman Historiography Before Caesar', *American Historical Review* 32 (1927), pp. 232–240.

Fraschetti, A (ed.), *Roman Women* (Chicago, 2001).

Fraser, A, *The Warrior Queens: Boadicea's Chariot* (London, 2002).

Frederiksen, MW, *Campania* (London, 1984).

Freeman, P, *War, Women, and Druids* (Austin, TX, 2002).

Fronda, MP, *Between Rome and Carthage: Southern Italy During the Second Punic War* (Cambridge, 2010).

Fry, PS, *Rebellion Against Rome* (Lavenham, 1982).

Frye, RN, 'The Sassanians', in Iorwerth Eiddon, *CAH – XII – The Crisis of Empire* (Cambridge, 2005).

Fuller, JFC, *Decisive Battles of the Western World and Their Influence upon History: Vol. 1* (London, 1970).

————, *Julius Caesar: Man, Soldier and Tyrant* (London, 1965).

Furneaux, R, *The Roman Siege of Jerusalem* (London, 2004).

Gabba, E, 'True History and False History in Classical Antiquity', *JRS* 61 (1981), pp. 50–62.

————, *Republican Rome, the Army and the Allies* (Oxford, 1976).

————, 'The Origins of the Professional Army at Rome: The Proletarii and Marius' Reforms', in Gabba, *Republican Rome* (1976), pp. 1–19.

————, 'The Perusine War and Triumviral Italy', *HSCP* 75 (1971), pp. 139–60.

Gabriel, RA, *Scipio Africanus: Rome's Greatest General* (Washington, 2008).

————, *The Great Battles of Antiquity: A Strategic and Tactical Guide to Great Battles That Shaped the Development of War* (London, 1994).

————, *The Great Armies of Antiquity* (London, 1992).

————, *A History of Military Medicine Vol. 1: From Ancient Times to the Middle Ages* (New York, 1992).

Gale, M, 'Propertius 2, 7: *Militia Amoris* and the Ironies of Elegy', *JRS* 87 (1997), pp. 77–91.

Gardiner, J, *The Blitz: The British Under Attack* (London, 2010).

Garlan, Y, *War in the Ancient World* (London, 1975).

Garlick, B (ed.) *Stereotypes of Women in Power* (New York, 1992).

Garouphalias, P, *Pyrrhus: King of Epirus* (London, 1979).

Gelzer, M, *Caesar: Politician and Statesman* (Oxford, 1968).

Gentili, A, *The Wars of the Romans: A Critical Edition and Translation of* De Armis Romanis, B. Kingsbury (ed.) (Oxford, 2011).

Gera, DL, *Warrior Women: The Anonymous* Tractatus De Mulieribus (Leiden, 1997).

Gibbon, E, *Decline and Fall of the Roman Empire* (1776–1781).

Gichon, M, 'Aspects of a Roman Army in War According to the *Bellum Iudaicum* of Josephus', in Freeman, P, *The Defence of the Roman and Byzantine East*, British ArchaeologicalReports Int. Series 279 (i) (1986), pp. 287–310.

———, 'Cestius Gallus' Campaign in Judaea', *Palestine Exploration Quarterly* 113 (1981), p. 56.

Gilbert, CD, 'Marius and Fortuna', *CQ* 23 (1973), pp. 104–107.

Gill, C (ed.), *Lies and Fiction in the Ancient World* (Liverpool, 1993).

Gilliver, CM, 'Combat in the Late Republic and Empire', in Sabin, *The Cambridge History of Greek and Roman Warfare Vol. 2* (Cambridge, 2007), pp. 122–157.

———, 'Display in Roman Warfare: The Appearance of Armies and Individuals on the Battlefield', *War in History* 14, 1 (2007), pp. 1–21.

———, *Caesar's Gallic Wars 58–50 BC* (Oxford, 2002).

———, *The Roman Art of War* (Stroud, 1999).

———, 'The Roman Army and Morality in War', in Lloyd (ed.), *Battle in Antiquity* (Swansea, 1996).

Glew, DG, 'Mithridates Eupator and Rome: A Study of the Background of the First Mithridatic War,' *Athenaeum* (1977), pp. 380–405.

Goldsworthy, A, *War* in Sabin, *The Cambridge History of Greek and Roman Warfare, Vol. 2* (2007), pp. 76–121.

———, *Cannae: Hannibal's Greatest Victory* (London, 2007).

———, *Caesar: The Life of a Colossus* (New Haven, CT, 2006).

———, *The Complete Roman Army* (London, 2003).

———, *In the Name of Rome* (London, 2003).

———, *The Punic Wars* (London, 2000).

———, *Roman Warfare* (London, 2000).

———, (ed.) 'The Roman Army as Community', *Jnl of Roman Archaeology* 34 (1999).

———, '"Instinctive Genius" – The Depiction of Caesar the General', in Welch, *Julius Caesar as Artful Reporter* (Swansea, 1998), pp. 193–219.

———, *The Roman Army at War*, 3rd edition (Oxford, 1996).

———, *The Roman Imperial Army of the First and Second Centuries A.D.* (London, 1985).

Goodman, MD, *Rome and Jerusalem: The Clash of Ancient Civilizations* (London, 2007).

———, (ed.), *Jews in a Graeco-Roman World* (Oxford, 2004).

———, 'Religious Scruples in Ancient Warfare', *CQ* 36 (1986), pp. 151–1.

————, *The Ruling Class of Judaea: The Origins of the Jewish War Against Rome* (Cambridge, 1987).

Goudchaux, GW, 'Cleopatra's Subtle Religious Strategy', in Walker (ed.), *Cleopatra of Egypt* (London, 2001).

————, 'Was Cleopatra Beautiful?', in Walker (ed.), *Cleopatra of Egypt* (London, 2001).

Gould, J, 'Women in Classical Athens', *JHS* 100 (1980), pp. 38–59.

Gowers, W, 'The African Elephant in Warfare', *African Affairs*, 46 (1947), pp. 42–49.

Graf, F, 'Women, War and Warlike Divinities', *ZPE* 55 (1984), pp, 245–54.

Graham, F, *Dictionary of Roman Military Terms* (Morpeth, 1989).

Grainger, JD, *Rome, Parthia and India: The Violent Emergence of a New World Order 150–140 BC* (Barnsley, 2013).

————, *Roman Conquests: Egypt and Judaea* (Barnsley, 2013).

————, *Hellenistic and Roman Naval Wars 336-31 BC* (Barnsley, 2011).

————, *The Syrian Wars* (Leiden, 2010).

————, *The Roman War of Antiochus the Great*, Mnemosyne 239 (Leiden, 2002).

Gransden, K (ed.) *Virgil*, Aeneid Book XI (Cambridge, 1991).

Grant, M, *Greek and Roman Historians: Information and Misinformation* (Abingdon, 1995).

————, *Cleopatra* (New York, 1992).

————, *The Jews in the Roman World* (London, 1973).

Grant de Pauw, L, *Battle Cries and Lullabies: Women in War from Prehistory to the Present* (Oklahoma, 2000).

Greatrex, G, *The Roman Eastern Frontier and the Persian Wars: Part 2: AD 363–630, A Narrative Sourcebook* (London, 2007).

Green, M, *Celtic Goddesses: Warriors, Virgins and Mothers* (London, 1995).

Greene, E, *The Erotics of Domination: Male Desire and the Mistress in Latin Love Poetry* (Baltimore, 1998).

Greenhalgh, P, *Pompey: The Republican Prince* (London, 1981).

————, *Pompey: The Roman Alexander* (London, 1980).

Griffin J, 'Augustan Poetry and the Life of Luxury', *JRS* 66 (1976), pp. 87–105.

Groenman-van-Waateringe, W (ed.), *Roman Frontier Studies 1995* (Oxford, 1997).

Gruen, ES, *Culture and National Identity in Republican Rome* (Ithaca, 1992).

————, *The Hellenistic War and the Coming of Rome* (Berkeley, 1984).

————, 'M. Licinius Crassus: A Review Article', *AH* 2 (1977), p. 125.

Grundy, GB, 'The Trebbia and Lake Trasimene', *Journal of Philology* 24 (1896), pp. 83–118.

Grunewald, T, *Bandits in the Roman Empire: Myth and Reality* (London, 2008).

Gurval, RA, 'Dying Like a Queen: the Story of Cleopatra and the Asp(s)', in Miles, *Cleopatra: A Spinx Revisited* (Berkeley, CA, 2011), p. 54ff.

Haberling, W, 'Army Prostitution and Its Control', in Robinson, *Morals* (1943), pp. 3–90.

Hackett, J, *Warfare in the Ancient World* (London, 1989).

Haggard, HR, *Cleopatra* (London, 1889).

Haley, SP, 'The Five Wives of Pompey the Great', *G&R* 32 (1985), pp. 49–59.

Hallet, J, '*Perusinae Glandes* and the Changing Image of Augustus', *AJAH* 2 (1977), pp. 151–171.

Halliday, WR, '*Passing under* the Yoke', *Folklore*, 35 (1924), pp. 93–95.

Halperin, D, *Before Sexuality: The Construction of Erotic Experience in the Ancient Greek World* (Princeton, 1990).

Halsall, G, *Barbarian Migrations and the Roman West* (Cambridge, 2007), pp. 376–568.

Hamblin, JW, *Warfare in the Ancient Near East to 1600 BC* (New York, 2006).

Hamer, M, *Signs of Cleopatra: Reading an Icon Historically, 2nd edition* (Liverpool, 2008).

Hammerton, JA (ed.), *Universal History of the World Vol. 3* (London, 1930).

Hammond, NGL, 'The Campaign and Battle of Cynoscephalae in 197 BC', *JHS* 108 (1988), pp. 60–82.

———, *History of Macedonia* (Oxford, 1988).

———, 'The Battle of Pydna', *JHS* 104 (1984), pp. 31–47.

———, 'The Two Battles of Chaeronea (338 B.C. and 86 B.C.)', *Klio* 31 (1938), pp. 186–218.

Hansen, EV, *The Attalids of Pergamon*, (New York, 1971).

Hansen, MH, 'The Battle Exhortation in Ancient Historiography: Fact or Fiction?' *Historia* 42 (1993), pp. 161–180.

Hanson, A, '*The Medical Writers' Woman*', in Halperin, *Before Sexuality*, pp. 309–338.

Hanson, VD, *Why the West Has Won: Carnage and Culture from Salamis to Vietnam* (Oxford, 2001).

———, *The Western Way of War: Infantry Battle in Ancient Greece, 2nd edition* (Oxford, 2000).

———, *The Wars of the Ancient Greeks* (London, 1999).

———, 'The Status of Ancient Military History', *Journal of Military History* 63 (1999), pp. 399–414.

——— (ed.), *Hoplites: The Classical Greek Battle Experience* (London, 1991).

Hanson, WS (ed.), *Roman Frontier Studies* (Oxford, 1979).

———, *Agricola & the Conquest of North Britain* (London, 1987).

Harbottle, T, *Harbottle's Dictionary of Battles from 743 BC to the Present* (London, 1980).

Hardwick, L, 'Ancient-Amazon Heroes: Outsiders or Women?', *G&R* 37 (1990), pp. 14–36.

Harkness, A, *The Military System of the Romans* (Miami, 2004).

Harl, K, 'The Roman Experience in Iraq', *Journal of the Historical Society* 7 (2007), pp. 213–227.

Harris, R, '*Independent Women in Ancient Mesopotamia*', in BS Lesko, *Women's Earliest Records* (Atlanta, 1989), pp. 145–56.

Harris, WV, 'The Rage of Women', in Braund, *Ancient Anger: Perspectives from Homer to Galen* (New Haven, CT, 2003), pp. 121–43.

———, 'Roman Warfare in the Economic and Social Context of the 4th Century BC' (1979), in Eder, W (ed.), *Staat und Staatlichkeit in der Fruhen Romische Republik* (Stuttgart, 1990).

——— (ed.), *The Italians and the Empire* (Rome, 1984).

———, 'Current Directions in the Study of Roman Imperialism', in Harris, *The Italians and the Empire* (1984), pp. 89–113.

———, *War and Imperialism in Republican Rome 327–70 BC* (Oxford, 1979).

———, *Rome in Etruria and Umbria* (Oxford, 1971).

Harrison, T, 'Herodotus and the Ancient Greek Idea of Rape', in Deacy, *Rape in Antiquity* (1997), pp. 185–208.

Harvey, D, 'Women in Thucydides', *Arethusa* 18 (1985), pp. 67–90.

Harvey, SA, *Ascetism and Society in Crisis: John of Ephesus and the Lives of the Eastern Saints* (Berkeley, CA, 1990).

Hassall, M, 'Rome and the Eastern Provinces at the End of the 2nd Century BC', *JRS* 64, pp. 195–220.

Hatke, G, *Aksum and Nubia: Warfare, Commerce, and Political Fictions in Ancient Northeast Africa* (New York, 2013).

Havell, HL, *Republican Rome: Her Conquests Manners and Institutions from the Earliest Times to the Death of Caesar* (London, 1914).

Hawkes, C (ed.), *Greeks, Celts and Romans, Studies in Venture and Resistance* (London, 1973).

Haynes, DEL, *Ancient Tripolitania* (London, 1923).

Haynes, I, *Blood of the Provinces: The Roman Auxilia and the Making of Provincial Society from Augustus to the Severans* (Oxford, 2013).

Hayward, R, *Cleopatra's Needles* (London, 1978).

Haywood, J, 'Alaric I', in Roberts (ed.) *Great Commanders of the Ancient World* (2008).

Healy, M, *Cannae 216 BC* (Oxford, 1994).

Heath, EG, *Archery: A Military History* (London, 1980).

Heather, P, *The Fall of the Roman Empire: A New History of Rome and the Barbarians* (London, 2006).

———, *Goths and Romans 332–489* (Oxford, 1991).

———, *The Goths in the Fourth Century*, Translated Texts for Historians 11 (Liverpool, 1991).

Helgeland, J, *Christians and the Roman Army* (Chicago, 1974).

Henderson, B, 'The Campaign of the Metaurus', *The English Historical Review* (1898).

Henderson, J, *Fighting for Rome: Poets and Caesars, History and Civil War* (Cambridge, 1998).

Hendry, M, 'Three Problems in the Cleopatra Ode', *CJ* 82 (1930), pp. 137–146.

Hengel, M, *Crucifixion in the Ancient World* (Minneapolis, MN, 1977).

Hermann, P, *Historicorum Romanorum Reliquae* (Leipzig, 1870).

Herwig, H (ed.), *Cassell's World History of Warfare* (London, 2002).

Herzog, C, *Battles of the Bible* (London, 1978).

Heurgon, J, *The Rise of Rome to 264 BC* (London, 1973).

Higgins, C, 'Roman Britain under Attack', *BBC History*, August 2013, pp. 20–26.

Hildinger, E, *Swords Against the Senate: The Rise of the Roman Army and the Fall of the Republic* (Cambridge, MA, 2002 reprint).

Hindley, C, 'Eros and Military Command in Xenophon', *CQ* 44 (1994), pp. 347–66.

Hinds, K, *Ancient Celts* (London, 2009).

Hingley, R, *Boudica: Iron Age Warrior Queen* (London, 2005).

Hodkinson, S (ed.), *Sparta and War* (Swansea, 2006).

Hogg, OF, *Clubs to Cannon: Warfare and Weapons Before the Introduction of Gunpowder* (London, 1968).

Holder, PA, *Studies in the* Auxilia *of the Roman Army* (Oxford, 1980).

Holland, T, 'Hannibal', in Roberts (ed.) *Great Commanders of the Ancient World* (2008).

Holmes, R, *Acts of War: The Behaviour of Men in Battle* (London, 2004).

Holscher, T, 'Images of War in Greece and Rome', *JRS* 93 (2003), pp. 1–17.

Holum, KG, *Theodosian Empresses* (Berkeley, 1982).

Hooper, F, *Roman Realities* (Detroit, 1979).

Hopkins, M, *Conquerors and Slaves* (Cambridge, 1978).

Hopwood, K, *Organised Crime in the Ancient World* (Swansea, 1999).

———, *Death and Renewal: Sociological Studies in Roman History v. 2* (Cambridge, 1985).

Hornblower, S, 'War and the Development of Ancient Historiography', in Sabin, *The Cambridge History of Greek and Roman Warfare* (2005).

——— (ed.), *The Oxford Classical Dictionary* 3rd edition (Oxford, 2003).

———, *The Greek World 479–323 BC* (London, 1983).

Horsley, RA, 'Josephus and the Bandits', *Journal for the Study of Judaism* 10 (1979), pp. 37–63.

Howarth, N, *Cartimandua, Queen of the Brigantes* (Stroud, 2008).

Hoyos, BD, *Roman Imperialism* (London, 2013).

———, *A Companion to the Punic Wars* (Chichester, 2011).

———, 'The Age of Overseas Expansion (264–146 BC)', in Erdkamp, *A Companion to the Roman Army* (Oxford, 2007).

————, *Truceless War: Carthage's Fight for Survival, 241 to 237 BC* (Leiden, 2007).

————, *Hannibal: Rome's Greatest Enemy* (Bristol, 2005).

————, *Hannibal's Dynasty: Power and Politics in the Western Mediterranean, 247–183 BC* (London, 2005).

————, *Unplanned Wars: The Origins of the First and Second Punic Wars* (Berlin, 1998).

Hubbard, TK (ed.), *A Companion to Greek and Roman Sexualities* (Chichester, 2014).

Hunt, P, *Slaves, Warfare, and Ideology in the Greek Historians* (Cambridge, 1998).

Hunter, LW, *Aieneiou Poliorketike* (Oxford, 1927).

Huzar, EG, *Mark Antony: A Biography* (Minneapolis, 1978).

————, 'Mark Antony: Marriages vs Careers', *CJ* 81 (1985), pp. 97–111.

Hyland A, *Training the Roman Cavalry* (Stroud, 1993).

————, Equus: *The Horse in the Roman World* (London, 1990).

Irby–Massie, GL, *Military Religion in Roman Britain* (Leiden, 1999).

Ireland, S, (ed.) *Roman Britain: A Sourcebook* 3rd edition (London, 2008).

Jackson–Laufer, GM, *Women Rulers throughout the Ages: An Illustrated Guide* (New York, 1999).

Jaeger, M, *Livy's Written Rome* (Ann Arbor, 1995).

James, S, *Rome and the Sword: How Warriors and Weapons Shaped Roman History* (London, 2011).

————, 'Archaeological Evidence for Roman Incendiary Projectiles', *Saalburg Jahrbuch* 40 (1983), pp. 142–3.

James, SL, *Companion to Women in the Ancient World* (Chichester, 2012).

————, 'From Boys to Men: Rape and Developing Masculinity, in Terence's *Hecyra* and *Eunuchus*', *Helios* 25 (1998), pp. 31–48.

————, 'Slave-rape and Female Silence in Ovid's Love Poetry', *Helios* 24 (1997), pp. 60–76.

Jameson, M, 'Sacrifice Before Battle', in V Hanson (ed.), *Hoplites* (London, 1991), p. 220.

Janssen, LF, 'Some Unexplored Aspects of *devotio* Deciana,' *Mnemosyne* (1981), pp. 357–381.

Jarymowycz, R, *Cavalry: From Hoof to Track* (London, 2009).

Jed, S, *Chaste Thinking: The Rape of Lucretia and the Birth of Humanism* (Bloomington, 1989).

Jenkins, TE, *Intercepted Letters: Epistolarity and Narrative in Greek and Roman Literature* (Lanham, MD< 2006) pp. 51–59.

Jestice, PG, 'Greek Women and War in Antiquity', in Cook, *Women and War* (Santa Barbara, 2006), pp. 256–8.

Jimenez, RL, *Caesar Against the Celts* (Stroud, 1996).

Johnson, A, *Roman Forts* (London, 1983).

Johnson, WR, 'A Quean, a Great Queen? Cleopatra and the Politics of Misrepresentation', *Arion* 6 (1967), pp. 151–180.

Jones, AHM, *The Later Roman Empire*, 3 Vols. (Oxford, 1964).

Jones, BW, 'Rome's Relationship with Carthage: A Study in Aggression', *CB* 49 (1972), pp. 5–26.

Jones DE, *Women Warriors: A History* (Washington, DC, 1997).

Jones, MJ, *Roman Fort Defences to AD 117* (Oxford, 1975).

Jones, PJ, *Cleopatra: A Sourcebook* (Norman, 2006).

Kagan, D, *Men of Bronze: Hoplite Warfare in Ancient Greece* (Princeton, NJ, 2013).

Kamtekar, R, (ed.) *Virtue and Happiness: Essays in Honour of Julia Annas* (Oxford, 2012).

Keaveney, A, *Lucullus: A Life* (London, 1992).

———, *Rome and the Unification of Italy* (Liverpool, 1987).

———, 'Sulla and Italy', *Critica Storica* 19 (1982), p. 499ff.

———, 'The King and the Warlords: Romano–Parthian Relations ca. 64–53 BC', *AJPh* 103 (1982), pp. 412–418.

———, 'Roman Treaties with Parthia ca. 95 – ca. 64 BC', *AJPh* 102 (1981), pp. 195–212.

Keegan, J, *A History of Warfare* (London, 1993).

Keeley, LH, *War Before Civilisation: The Myth of the Peaceful Savage* (Oxford, 1996).

Keitel, E, 'The Art of Losing: Tacitus and the Disaster Narrative' in Kraus, (ed.), *Ancient Historiography and Its Contexts* (Oxford, 2010).

Kelly, GP, *A History of Exile in the Roman Republic* (Cambridge, 2012).

Kelly, RC, 'The Evolution of Lethal Intergroup Violence', *PNAS* 102(43) (2005), pp. 15294–15298.

Kennedy, DL, *Settlement and Soldiers in the Roman Near East* (London, 2013).

Kennell, NM, *The Gymnasium of Virtue: Education and Culture in Ancient Sparta* (Chapel Hill, NC, 1995).

Keppie, L, *The Making of the Roman Army* (London, 1984).

———, *Colonisation and Veteran Settlement in Italy 47–14 BC* (London, 1983).

Kern, PB, *Ancient Siege Warfare* (London, 1999).

King, A, (ed.) 'The Roman West in the Third Century', *British Archaeological Reports* S109, 2 Vols. (Oxford, 1981).

Kingsbury, B (ed.), *The Wars of the Romans: A Critical Edition and Translation of* De Armis Romanis (Oxford, 2011).

Kistler, JM, *War Elephants* (Westport, CT, 2006).

Klein, J, *The Royal Hymns of Shulgi, King of Ur* (Philadelphia, 1981).

Kleiner, D, *Cleopatra and Rome* (Cambridge, MA, 2005).

Knapp, BL, 'Virgil's Aeneid: Let us Sing of Arms and Women: Dido and Camilla', in BL Knapp, *Women in Myth*, Chapter 6 (New York, 1977).

Knapp, R, *The Invisible Romans* (London, 2011).

Koch, JT (ed.), *Celtic Culture: A Historical Encyclopedia* (Santa Barbara, CA, 2006).

Kochly, H, *Aineias von Vertheidigungder Stadte in Griechische Kriegschriftseller,* 1–18 (Leipzig 1853).

Kuehnemund, R, *Arminius or the Rise of National Symbol in Literature* (Chapel Hill, NC, 1953).

Kulikowski, M, *Rome's Gothic Wars: From the Third Century to Alaric* (Cambridge, 2007).

Laiou, A (ed.), *Consent and Coercion to Sex and Marriage in Ancient and Medieval Societies* (Dunbarton Oaks, 1993).

Lamb, H, *Hannibal: One Man Against Rome* (New York, 1958).

Lancel, S, *Hannibal* (Oxford, 1999).

Laqueur, W, *Guerrilla Warfare: A Historical & Critical Study* (London, 1977).

Larson, J, *Greek Heroine Cults* (Madison, WI, 1995).

Last, H, 'The Servian Reforms', *JRS* 35 (1945), pp. 30–48.

Lazenby, JF, *The Spartan Army* (Barnsley, 2011).

———, *The First Punic War: A Military History* (Stanford, 1996).

———, *The Defence of Greece 490–479 B.C.* (Warminster, 1993).

———, *Hannibal's War* (Warminster, 1978).

Le Bohec, Y, *The Imperial Roman Army* (London, 2000).

———, *Histoire Militaire des Guerres Puniques* (Monaco, 1996).

Lee, AB, 'Morale and the Roman Experience of Battle', in Lloyd (ed.), *Battle in Antiquity* (Swansea, 1996).

Lee, AG, 'Ovid's Lucretia', *G&R* 22 (1953), pp. 107–18.

Lee, J, 'For There Were Many *hetairae* in the Army: Women in Xenophon's Anabasis', *Anc. W.* 35 (2004), pp. 45–65.

Lee, WE, *Warfare and Culture in World History* (New York, 2011).

Lenski, N, '*Initium mali romano imperio*. Contemporary Reactions to the Battle of Adrianople', *TAPhA* 127 (1997a).

———, *Valens and the Fourth Century Empire*, dissertation, Princeton University (Princeton, NJ, 1995).

———, 'The Gothic Civil War and the Date of the Gothic Conversion', *GRBS* 36 (1995), pp. 51–87.

Leitao, DD, 'Sexuality in Greek and Roman Military Contexts', in Hubbard, *A Companion to Greek and Roman Sexualities* (Oxford, 2014), pp. 230–243.

Lendon, JE, 'War and Society', in Sabin, *The Cambridge History of Greek and Roman Warfare, Vol. 1* (Cambridge, 2007), pp. 498–516.

———, *Soldiers and Ghosts: A History of Battles in Classical Antiquity* (New Haven, CT, 2005).

———, 'The Rhetoric of Combat: Greek Military Theory and Roman Culture in Julius Caesar's Battle Descriptions', *Cl.Ant* 18 (1999), pp. 273–329.

Levene, DS, *Livy on the Hannibalic War* (Oxford, 2012).

———, (ed.) *Clio and the Poets: Augustan Poetry and the Traditions of Ancient Historiography* (Leiden, 2002).

Levithan, J, *Roman Siege Warfare* (Ann Arbor, 2013).

Lewis, CT, *A Latin Dictionary* (Oxford, 1969/1879).

Lewis, GC, *An Inquiry Into the Credibility of the Early Roman History* (London, 2011 reprint).

L'Hoir, FS, 'Tacitus and Women's Usurpation of Power', *CW* 88 (1994), pp. 5–25.

———, *The Rhetoric of Gender Terms: 'Man', 'Woman' and the Portrayal of Character in Latin Prose* (Leiden, 1992).

Libourel, J. (1973) 'Galley Slaves in the Second Punic War', *CPh* 68, pp. 116–19

Liddell Hart, BH, *Greater Than Napoleon: Scipio Africanus* (Edinburgh, 1930).

———, 'History's Most Glorious Failure: A Study of Hannibal', in Hammerton, *Universal History, Vol. 3* (1930), pp. 1655–66.

Lightman, M, *A to Z of Ancient Greek and Roman Women* (New York, 2008).

Lintott, AW, *The Constitution of the Roman Republic* (Oxford, 1999).

———, 'The Tradition of Violence in the Annals of the Early Roman Republic', *Historia* 19 (1970), pp. 12–29.

———, *Violence in Republican Rome* (Oxford, 1968).

Litchfield, HW, 'National Examples of *virtus* in Roman Literature', *HSCPh* 25 (1914), pp. 1–71.

Lloyd, AB (ed.), *Battle in Antiquity* (Swansea, 1996).

Loyd, A, 'The War to End All Good Wars', by Antony Loyd, review of *The Good War: Why We Couldn't Win the War or the Peace in Afghanistan*, by Jack Fairweather (London, 2014), published in *The Times*, 20 December 2014.

Lomas, HK, *Roman Italy 338 BC – AD 200: A Sourcebook* (London, 1996).

Low, P, 'War, Death and Burial in Classical Sparta', *Omnibus* 65 (2013), pp. 8–10.

Lucas, FL, 'The Battlefied of Pharsalia', *ABSA* 24 (1919–21), pp. 34–53.

———, 'The Fortune of Carthage', *Athenaeum* 28, (1921).

Luce, JV, 'Cleopatra as *Fatale Monstrum*', *CQ* 3 (1963), pp. 251–257.

Luce, TJ, 'Marius and the Mithridatic Command', *Historia*, 19 (1970), pp. 161–194.

Luckenbill, DD, *Ancient Records of Assyria and Babylonia II* (Chicago, 1926).

Luginbill, R, *Thucydides In War and National Character* (Boulder, CO, 1999).

Luttwak, EN, *The Grand Strategy of the Roman Empire: From the First Century A.D. to the Third* (Baltimore, 1979).

Lyne, ROAM, 'Virgil and the Politics of War', *CQ* 33 (1983), pp. 193–203.

Lynn, JA, *Battle: A History of Combat from Ancient Greece to Modern America* (Boulder, CO, 2003).

Macaulay, TB, *Lays of Ancient Rome* (London, 1842).

MacDonald, E, *Hannibal: A Hellenistic Life* (London, 2015).

MacDonald, S, 'Boadicea: Warrior, Mother and Myth', in S Macdonald, *Images of Women in Peace and War* (London, 1987), pp. 1–26.

MacDowall, S, *Adrianople AD 378* (Oxford, 2001).

———, *Germanic Warrior* (Oxford, 1996).

———, *Late Roman Cavalryman* (Oxford, 1995).

———, *Late Roman Infantryman* (Oxford, 1994).

MacGeorge, P, *Late Roman Warlords* (Oxford, 2003).

MacMullen, R, 'Women in Public in the Roman Empire', *Historia* 29 (1980), pp. 208–18.

———, *Soldier and Civilian in the Later Roman Empire* (Cambridge, MA, 1963).

Macurdy, GH, 'Queen Eurydice and the Evidence for Woman Power in Early Macedonia', *AJPh* 48 (1927), pp. 201–214.

Mader, D, 'Heroism and Hallucination: Cleopatra in Horace *C*. 1, 37 and Propertius 3, 11', *Grazer Beitrage* 16 (1989), pp. 183–201.

Madsen, JM, 'Mithridates VI: Rome's Perfect Enemy', *Proceedings of the Danish Institute in Athens* 6 (2010), pp. 223–237.

Maenchen-Helfen, JO, *The World of the Huns. Studies in their History and Culture* (Berkeley, 1973).

Majno, G, *The Healing Hand: Man and Wound in the Ancient World* (Cambridge, MA, 1975).

Mancini, J, *Defending the Roman Republic: Ending the 2nd Punic War* (London, 2009).

Marincola, J, *Greek and Roman Historiography* (Oxford, 2011).

Marsden, EW, *Greek and Roman Artillery* (Oxford, 1969–71).

Marshall, AJ, 'Women on Trial before the Roman Senate', *Echos du Monde Classique* 34 (1990), pp. 333–66.

———, 'Ladies in Waiting: The Role of Women in Tacitus' Histories', *Ancient Society* 15–17 (1984–6), pp. 167–84.

———, 'Roman Women and the Provinces', *Ancient Society* 6 (1975), pp. 109–129.

———, 'Tacitus and the Governor's Lady, A Note on *Annals* 3, 33–34', *G&R* 22 (1975), pp. 11–18.

Marshall, BA, *Crassus: A Political Biography* (Amsterdam, 1976).

———, 'Crassus and the Command Against Spartacus', *Athenaeum* 51 (1973), pp. 109ff.

Martin, S, 'Private Lives and Public Personae', *Mores*, online journal, accessed 14 February 2015. http://www.dl.ket.org/latin2/mores/women/womenful.htm

Marx, K and Engels, F, *Selected Correspondence 1846–1895, with commentary and notes* (New York, 1943).

Masaoki, D, 'On the Negotiations between the Roman State and the Spartacus Army', *Klio* 66 (1984), p. 170ff.

Maslen, M, 'Medical Theories on the Cause of Death in Crucifixion', *Journal of the Royal Society of Medicine* 99 (4) (2006), p.185.

Mattern, SP, *Rome and the Enemy: Imperial Strategy in the Principate* (Berkeley, 2002).

Matthews, JF, *The Roman Empire of Ammianus* (London, 1989).

Matthews, VH (ed.), *Gender and Law in the Hebrew Bible and the Ancient Near East* (London, 2004).

Matyszak, P, *Cataclysm 90 BC: The Forgotten War that almost Destroyed Rome* (Barnsely, 2014).

———, *Sertorius and the Struggle for Spain* (Barnsley, 2013).

———, *Mithridates the Great* (Barnsley, 2008).

———, *The Enemies of Rome: From Hannibal to Attila the Hun* (London, 2004).

Maxfield, V, *The Military Decorations of the Roman Army* (Berkeley, 1981).

Maxwell, G, *A Battle Lost: Romans & Caledonians at Mons Graupius* (Edinburgh, 1990).

Mayor, A, *Greek Fire, Poison Arrows and Scorpion Bombs: Biological Warfare in the Ancient World* (London, 2009).

———, *The Poison King: The Life and Legend of Mithridates, Rome's Deadliest Enemy* (Princeton, 2009).

McAuslan, I (ed.), *Women in Antiquity* (Oxford, 1996).

McCall, JB, *The Cavalry of the Roman Republic* (London, 2002).

McCartney, ES, 'The Military Indebtedness of Early Rome to Etruria', *MAAR* 1 (1915), pp. 121–67.

McDonald, AH, 'Hannibal's Passage of the Alps', *Alpine Jnl* 61 (1956), pp. 93–101.

———, 'Rome and the Italian Confederation (200–186 BC)', *JRS* 34 (1944), pp. 11–33.

McDonnell, M, *Roman Manliness:* Virtus *and the Roman Republic* (Cambridge, 2006).

McDougall, I, 'Livy and Etruscan Women', *Ancient History Bulletin* 4 (1990), pp. 24–30.

McGing, BC, 'The Foreign Policy of Mithridates VI', *Mnemosyne* 89 (Leiden, 1986).

McNally, M, *Teutoburg Forest AD 9*, (Oxford, 2011).

Meijer, F, *A History of Seafaring in the Classical World* (London, 1986).

Mellersh, HEL, *Soldiers of Rome* (London, 1964).

Messer, WS, 'Mutiny in the Roman Army: The Republic', *CPh* 15 (1920), pp. 158–75.

Miles, GB, *Livy: Reconstructing Early Rome* (New York, 1997), Chapter 5, 'The First Roman Marriage and the Theft of the Sabine Women'.

Miles, M, *Cleopatra and Egyptomania* (Berkeley, 2003).

Millar, F, *Rome, the Greek World and the East, Vol. 1: The Roman Republic and the Augustan Revolution* (Chapel Hill, NC, 2001).

Milnor, K, 'Women in Roman Historiography', in Feldherr, *Cambridge Companion to the Roman Historians* (Cambridge, 2009), pp. 276–287.

Mitchell, R, 'The Violence of Virginity in the *Aeneid*', *Arethusa* 24 (1991), pp. 219–38.

Mommsen, T, *History of Rome* (London, 2014 reprint).

Montagu, JD, *Greek and Roman Warfare: Battles, Tactics and Trickery* (London, 2006).

———, *Battles of the Greek and Roman Worlds* (London, 2000).

Morey, WC, *Outlines of Roman History* (New York, 1901).

Morgan, MG, 'The Defeat of L. Metellus Denter at Arretium', *CQ* 22 (1972), pp. 309–25.

Morkot, RG, *The A to Z of Ancient Egyptian Warfare* (Washington, DC, 2010).

———, *Historical Dictionary of Ancient Egyptian Warfare* (Washington, DC, 2003).

Morrison, JS, *Greek and Roman Oared Warships* (Oxford, 1996).

Moses, D, 'Livy's Lucretia and the Validity of Coerced Consent in Roman Law', in Laiou, *Consent and Coercion to Sex and Marriage in Ancient and Medieval Societies* (Dunbarton Oaks, 1993) p. 50.

Mueller, HF, *Roman Religion in Valerius Maximus* (London, 2002).

Murdoch, A, *Rome's Greatest Defeat: Massacre in the Teutoburg Forest* (Stroud, 2008).

———, 'Arminius', in Roberts (ed.) *Great Commanders of the Ancient World* (London, 2008).

Murgatroyd, P, '*Militia amoris* and the Roman Elegists', *Latomus* 34 (1975), pp. 59–79.

Murray, O, *Early Greece* (London, 1993).

———, *The Greek City* (Oxford, 1990).

Murray, W, *Hybrid Warfare: Fighting Complex Opponents from the Ancient World to the Present* (Cambridge, 2012).

Mustakallio, K, 'Legendary Women and Female Groups in Livy', in Setala, *Female Networks and the Public Sphere in Roman Society* (Rome, 1999), pp. 53–64.

Nakhai, BA, *The World of Women in the Ancient and Classical Near East* (Newcastle, 2008).

Nefiodkin, AK, 'On the Origin of the Scythed Chariots', *Historia: Zeitschrift für Alte Geschichte* 53 (3) (2004), pp. 369–378.

Newark, T, *Women Warlords: An Illustrated History of Female Warriors* (London, 1989).

Nicasie, MJ, *Twilight of Empire. The Roman Army from the Reign of Diocletian to the Battle of Adrianople* (1998).

Nicolet, C, *The World of the Citizen in Republican Rome* (London, 1980).

Nilsson, MP, 'The Introduction of Hoplite Tactics in Rome', *JRS* 19 (1929), pp. 1–11.

North, JA, 'The Development of Roman Imperialism', *JRS* 71 (1981), pp. 1–9.

Northwood, S, *Early Roman Armies* (London, 1995).

Nossov, KS, *War Elephants* (Oxford, 2008).

———, *Ancient and Medieval Siege Weapons: A Fully Illustrated Guide to Siege Weapons and Tactics* (London, 2006).

Oakley, SP, *A Commentary on Livy Books VI–X, Volume I, Introduction and Book VI* (Oxford, 1997).

———, *A Commentary on Livy Books VI–X, Volume II, Books VII–VII* (Oxford, 1998).

———, 'The Roman Conquest of Italy', in Rich, J (ed.), *War and Society in the Ancient World* (1993), pp. 9–37.

———, 'Single Combat and the Roman Republic', *CQ* 35 (1985), pp. 39–410.

O'Connor Morris, W, *Hannibal: Soldier, Statesman, Patriot* (London, 1927).

Ogilvie, RM, *Early Rome and the Etruscans* (Glasgow, 1976).

———, *A Commentary on Livy Books 1–5* (Oxford, 1965).

———, 'The Maid of Ardea', *Latomus* 21 (1962), pp. 477–483.

O'Gorman, E, 'Does Dido's Curse Work?' *Omnibus* 64 (2012), pp. 10–12.

Oldfather, W, *The Defeat of Varus and the German Frontier Policy of Augustus*, (Champagne, 1915).

Omitowoju, R, *Rape and the Politics of Consent in Classical Athens* (Cambridge, 2002).

O'Neill, K, 'Propertius 4, 4: Tarpeia and the Burden of Aetiology', *Hermathena* 158 (1995), pp. 53–60.

Oost, S, *Galla Placidia Augusta* (Chicago, 1968).

O'Reilly, D, *Lost Legion Rediscovered: The Mystery of the Theban Legion* (Barnsley, 2011).

———, 'The Theban Legion of St Maurice', *Vigiliae Christianae* 32.3 (1978), pp. 195–207.

Orlin, EM, *Temples, Religion, and Politics in the Roman Republic* (Leiden, 1997).

Ormerod, HA, *Piracy in the Ancient World* (Liverpool, 1924).

Osborne, R, 'Polybius on Rome v. Greece', *Omnibus* 55, (2008), pp. 26–7.

Osgood, J, *Caesar's Legacy: Civil War and the Emergence of the Roman Empire* (Cambridge, 2006).

Otis, BA, 'A Reading of the Cleopatra Ode', *Arethusa* 1 (1938), pp. 48–61.

Packman, ZM, 'Call it Rape: A Motif in Roman Comedy and Its Suppression in English–speaking Publications', *Helios* 20 (1993), pp. 42–55.

Palmer, REA, *Rome and Carthage at Peace* (Stuttgart, 1997).

Paret, P, *Makers of Modern Strategy from Machiavelli to the Nuclear Age* (Princeton, 1986).

Parker, H, *The Roman Legions* (Oxford, 1928).

Patterson, J, 'Military Organization and Social Change in the Later Roman Republic', in Rich, *War and Society in the Ancient World* (Abingdon, 1993), pp. 92–112.

Paul, GM, 'A Historical Commentary on Sallust's *Bellum Jugurthinum'*, *ARCA Classical & Medieval Texts* 13 (1984), pp. 226–7.

Payne–Gallwey, R, *The Projectile Throwing Engines of the Ancients* (London, 1907).

Peddie, J, *The Roman War Machine* (Gloucester, 1994).

Peel, M (ed.), *Rape as a Method of Torture* (London, 2004).

Pelling, CBR, 'Pharsalus', *Historia* 22 (1973), pp. 249–59.

Pembroke, S, 'Locres et Tarente, le Rôle des Femmes dans la Fondation de Deux Colonies Grecques' *Annales ESC* 25 (1970), pp. 1240–1270.

Pennington, R (ed.), *Amazons to Fighter Pilots: A Biographical Dictionary of Military Women* (London, 2003).

Penrose, A (ed.), *Rome and Her Enemies: An Empire Created and Destroyed by War* (Wellingborough, 2005).

Pitassi, MP, *The Roman Navy: Ships, Men & Warfare 350BC – AD475* (Barnsley, 2012).

Phang, SE, *Roman Military Service: Ideologies of Discipline in the Late Republic and Principate* (Cambridge, 2008).

———, 'Intimate Conquests: Roman Soldiers' Slave Women and Freedwomen', *Anc.W.* 35, 2 (2004) pp. 207–237.

———, *Marriage of Roman Soldiers (13 BC – AD 235)* (Leiden, 2001).

———, *The Navies of Rome* (London, 2012).

———, *Roman Warships* (London, 2011).

Platner, SB, 'Columna Rostrata', in C Duilii, *A Topographical Dictionary of Ancient Rome* (Oxford, 1929), p. 34.

Pollock, S, *Ancient Mesopotamia: The Eden that Never Was* (Cambridge, 1999).

Pomeroy, SB, *Women in Hellenistic Egypt* (New York, 2002).

———, *Spartan Women* (Oxford, 2002).

———, *Women's History and Ancient History* (Chapel Hill, NC, 1991), pp. 197–217.

Postgate, N, *Early Mesopotamia: Society and Economy at the Dawn of History* (London, 1994).

Potter, DS, 'The Roman Army and Navy', in Flower, *The Cambridge Companion to the Roman Republic* (Cambridge, 2004), pp. 66–88.

———, *The Roman Empire at Bay AD 180–395* (London, 2004).

———, *Literary Texts and the Roman Historian* (London, 1999).

Powell, A. (ed) (2013) *Hindsight in Greek and Roman History* (Swansea, 2013).

———, 'Julius Caesar and the Presentation of Massacre', in Welch, *Julius Caesar as Artful Reporter: The War Commentaries as Political Instruments* (London, 1998).

——— (ed.), *Roman Poetry and Propaganda in the Age of Augustus* (Bristol, 1992).

Powell, L, *Germanicus: The Magnificent Life and Mysterious Death of Rome's Most Popular General* (Barnsley, 2013).

Powers, D (ed.), *Irregular Warfare in the Ancient World* (Chicago, 2013).

Prevas, J, *Hannibal Crosses the Alps* (Cambridge, MA, 2001).

Price, JJ, *Jerusalem under Siege: The Collapse of the Jewish State 66–70 CE* (Leiden, 1992).

Pritchett, WK, *The Greek State at War* (Berkeley, 1971–1991).

Prodanovi, N, *Teuta, Queen of Illyria* (Oxford, 1973).

Pryce, FN, 'The Carthaginians and their Maritime Empire', in Hammerton, *Universal History Vol. 3* (1930), pp. 1613– 1642.

Putnam, M, *Virgil's Aeneid: Interpretation and Influence* (Chapel Hill, NC, 1995).

Quaegebeur, J, *Cleopatra VII and the Cults of the Ptolemaic Queens in Bianchi* (1988), pp. 41–54.

Quinn, K, *Virgil's Aeneid: A Critical Description* (London, 1969).

———, *Latin Explorations* (London, 1963).

Qviller, B, 'Reconstructing the Spartan Partheniai: Many Guesses and a Few Facts', *SO* 71 (1996), pp. 34–41.

Raaflaub, KA (ed.), *War and Peace in the Ancient World* (Chichester, 2007).

———, '*Searching for Peace in the Greek World*', in *War and Peace in the Ancient World* (Chichester, 2007), pp. 1–33.

——— (ed.), *War and Society in the Ancient and Medieval Worlds* (Harvard, MA, 1999).

———, 'Born to be Wolves? Origins of Roman Imperialism', in Wallace, *Transitions to Empire* (1996), pp. 273–314

———, *The Political Significance of Augustus' Military Reforms* in Hanson (1979), pp. 1005–25.

Rajak, T, *Josephus: The Historian and His Society* (London, 1983).

Raleigh, Walter, *The Works of Sir Walter Ralegh, Kt; Now First Collected: to which are Prefixed The Lives of the Author; The History of the World. Book V. Chap. 1–3* (Oxford, 1829) p. 242.

Rance, P, 'Elephants in Warfare in Late Antiquity', *Acta Antiqua* 543 (2000), pp. 355–84.

Rankin, HD, *The Celts and the Classical World* (London, 1987).

Rankov, B, 'Military Forces', in Sabin, *The Cambridge History of Greek and Roman Warfare, Vol. 2* (Cambridge, 2007), pp. 30–75.

———, Exploratio: *Military and Political Intelligence in the Roman World* (London, 1995).

Rathbone, D, 'Warfare and the State A: Military Finance and Supply', in Sabin, *The Cambridge History of Greek and Roman Warfare, Vol. 2*, pp. 158–175.

Rauh, NK, *Merchants, Sailors and Pirates in the Ancient World* (Stroud, 2003).

Rawlings, HR, 'Antiochus the Great and Rhodes, 197–191 BC', *AJAH* 1 (1976), pp. 2–28.

Rawlings, L, 'Army and Battle During the Conquest of Italy (350–264 BC)', in Erdkamp, *A Companion to the Roman Army* (Chichester, 2007).

————, 'Condottieri and Clansmen: Early Italian Warfare and the State', in Hopwood, *Organised Crime in the Ancient World* (London, 1999).

————, 'Caesar's Portrayals of Gauls as Warriors', in Welch, *Julius Caesar as Artful Reporter* (Swansea, 1998).

Rawson, E, 'The Antiquarian Tradition: Spoils and Representations of Foreign Armor', *Roman Culture & Society* (Oxford, 1991), pp. 582–98.

————, '*Crassorum funera*', *Latomus* 41 (1982), pp. 540–9.

————, 'The First Latin Annalists', *Latomus* 35 (1976), pp. 245–71.

————, 'The Literary Sources for the Pre–Marian Army', *PBSR* 39 (1971), pp. 13–31.

Ray, FE, *Greek and Macedonian Land Battles of the 4th Century BC: A History and Analysis of 187 Engagements* (New York, 2012).

Ray, J, 'Hatshepsut: the Female Pharaoh', *History Today* 44 (1994), pp. 23–9.

Redfield, J, 'The Women of Sparta', *CJ* 73 (1977), pp. 146–61.

Regan, G, 'Backfire: A History of Friendly Fire from Ancient Warfare to the 21st Century' (London, 2002).

Reinhold, M, 'The Perusine War', *CW* 26, (1933) pp.180–182.

Reiter, W, *Aemilius Paullus: Conqueror of Greece* (London, 1988).

Retief FP, 'The History and Pathology of Crucifixion', *South African Medical Journal* 93(12) (2003), pp. 938–41.

Revell, L, 'Roman Imperialism and Local Identities' (Cambridge, 2010).

Rice, JW, 'Treaties, Allies and the Roman Conquest of Italy', in de Souza, *War and Peace in Ancient and Medieval History* (Cambridge, 2008), pp. 51–75.

Rice Holmes, T, 'The War–craft of the Romans', in Hammerton, *Universal History of the World 3* (1930), pp. 1717–33.

————, *Caesar's Conquest of Gaul* (Oxford, 1911).

Rich, J (ed.), 'Warfare and Army in Early Rome', in Erdkamp, *A Companion to the Roman Army* (Chichester, 2007).

————, 'Augustus and the *Spolia Opima*', *Chiron* 26 (1996), pp. 85–127.

————, *War and Society in the Ancient World* (London, 1993).

————, 'Fear, Greed and Glory: The Causes of Roman War Making in the Middle Republic', in Rich, *War and Society in the Ancient World* (London, 1993), pp. 38–68.

————, 'The Supposed Roman Manpower Shortage of the Later Second Century BC', *Historia* 32 (1983), pp. 287–333

————, 'Declaring War in the Roman Republic in the Period of Transmarine Expansion', *Latomus* 149 (1976).

Richardson, JS, 'Hispaniae: *Spain and the Development of Roman Imperialism, 218–82 BC* (Cambridge, 2004).

————, *Appian, Wars of the Romans in Iberia* (Warminster, 2000).

————, *The Romans in Spain* (Oxford, 1996).

———, 'The Triumph, the Praetors and the Senate in the Early 2nd Century BC', *JRS* (1975), pp. 50–63.

Richmond, IA, 'Queen Cartimandua', *JRS* 44 (1954), pp. 43–52.

Ridgway, D (ed.), *Italy Before the Romans* (Edinburgh, 1979).

Ridley, FA, *Spartacus – The Leader of the Roman Slaves* (London, 1961).

Ridley, RT, 'To Be Taken with a Pinch of Salt: The Destruction of Carthage', *CP* 81 (1986).

———, 'Was Scipio Africanus at Cannae?' *Latomus* 34 (1975), pp. 161–5.

———, 'The Enigma of Servius Tullius', *Klio* 57 (1975), pp. 147–77.

Rihll, T, 'Ancient Military Technology', *Omnibus* 62 (2011), pp. 28–30.

Rivet, ALF, 'A Note on Scythed Chariots', *Antiquity* 53 (1979), pp. 130–2.

Roberts, A (ed.), *Great Commanders of the Ancient World* (London, 2008).

Robinson, V (ed.), *Morals In Wartime* (New York, 1943).

Rodgers, W, *Greek and Roman Naval Warfare* (Annapolis, 1937).

Roller, DW, *Cleopatra: A Biography* (Oxford, 2010).

Roller, MB, 'Cornelia: On Making One's Name as *mater Gracchorum*', John Hopkins University (Baltimore, MD, 2012), accessed 12 February 2015. *www.krieger.jhu.edu/classics/wpcontent/uploads/sites/20/2013/06/Mother– of–the–Gracchi*

———, 'The Consul(ar) as *exemplum*: Fabius Cunctator's Paradoxical Glory', in Beck, *Consuls and* Res Publica: *Holding High Office in the Roman Republic* (2008).

———, 'Exemplarity in Roman Culture: The Case of Horaius Cocles and Cloelia', *CPh* 99 (2004), pp. 1–56.

Rorres, C, *Death of Archimedes: Sources,* website accessed 14 February, 2015. http://www.math.nyu.edu/crorres/Archimedes/Death/Histories.html

Rosaldo, MZ, '*Women, Culture and Society*', in Rosaldo, *Women, Culture and Society* (Stanford, CT, 1974), pp. 17–42.

Rosen, K, '*Ad Glandes Perusinas (CIL* I 682 Sqq)', *Hermes* 104 (1976), pp. 123–4.

Rosenstein, N, 'Military Command, Political Political Power, and the Republican Elite', in Erdkamp, *A Companion to the Roman Army* (Chichester, 2007).

———, 'War and Peace: Fear and Reconciliation at Rome', in Raaflaub, *War and Peace in the Ancient World,* pp. 226–4.

———, *Rome at War: Farms, Families and Death in the Middle Republic* (Chapel Hill, NC, 2004).

———, '*Republican Rome*', in Raaflaub, *War and Society in the Ancient and Medieval Worlds* (1999), pp. 193–216.

———, 'Imperatores Victi: *Military Defeat and Aristocratic Competition in the Middle and Late Republic*' (Berkeley, 1990).

Roth, JP, *Roman Warfare* (Cambridge, 2009).

———, 'War', in Sabin, *The Cambridge History of Greek and Roman Warfare, Vol. 1* (2007), pp. 368–98.

————, *The Logistics of the Roman Army at War (264 BC– AD 235)* (Leiden, 1999).

Rowland, RJ, 'Rome's Earliest Imperialism', *Latomus* 42 (1983), pp. 749–62.

Roxan, MM, *Roman Military Diplomas* (London, 1978).

Runciman, S, *The Sicilian Vespers: A History of the Mediterranean World in the Later Thirteenth Century* (Cambridge, 1958).

Rusch, SM, *Sparta at War: Strategy, Tactics and Campaigns* (London, 2011).

Ryan, EA, *Rejection of Military Service by Early Christians* (Washington, DC, 1952).

Ryder, TTB, Koine Eirene: *General Peace and Local Independence in Ancient Greece* (Hull, 1965).

Sabin, P., *Lost Battles: Reconstructing the Great Clashes of the Ancient World* (2008).

———— (ed.), *The Cambridge History of Greek and Roman Warfare, Vol. 1* (Cambridge, 2007).

———— (ed.), *The Cambridge History of Greek and Roman Warfare, Vol. 2* (Cambridge, 2007).

————, 'Battle A: Land Battles' in Sabin, *The Cambridge History of Greek and Roman Warfare, Vol. 1* (Cambridge, 2007), pp. 399–343.

————, 'The Face of Roman Battle', *JRS* 90 (2000), pp. 1–17.

————, 'The Mechanics of Battle in the Second Punic War', *BICS* 41 (1996), pp. 59–79.

Saddington DB, *The Development of the Roman Auxiliary Forces from Caesar to Vespasian* (Harare, 1982).

Sage, MM, *Roman Conquests: Gaul* (Barnsley, 2008).

————, *Warfare in Ancient Greece: A Sourcebook* (London, 1996).

Saggs, HWF. *Civilisation Before Greece and Rome* (London, 1989).

Salazar, CF, *The Treatment of Wounds in Graeco–Roman Antiquity* (Leiden, 2000).

Salmon, ET, *The Making of Roman Italy* (London, 1982).

————, *Roman Colonization under the Republic* (London, 1969).

————, *Samnium and the Samnites* (Cambridge, 1967).

————, 'Notes on the Social War', *TaPha* 89 (1958), pp. 159–84.

————, 'Rome and the Latins', *Phoenix* 7 (1953), pp. 93–104, 123–55.

Salmonson, JA, *The Encyclopedia of Amazons* (London, 1991).

Salway, P, *Roman Britain* (Oxford, 1981).

Sampson, GC, *The Defeat of Rome: Crassus, Carrhae and the Invasion of the East* (Barnsley, 2014).

————, *The Collapse of Rome: Marius, Sulla and the First Civil War* (Barnsley, 2013).

————, *The Defeat of Rome in the East: Crassus, the Parthians, and the Disastrous Battle of Carrhae, 53BC* (Philadelphia, 2008).

Samuels, M, 'The Reality of Cannae', *Militargeschichlichte Miteillungen* 47 (1990), pp. 7–29.

Sancisi–Weerdenburg, H, 'Exit Atossa: Images of Women in Greek Historiography on Persia', in A Cameron, *Images of Women in Antiquity* (London, 1993), pp. 20–33.

Santosuosso, A, *Storming the Heavens: Soldiers, Emperors and Civilians in the Roman Empire* (Boulder, CO, 2001).

———, *Soldiers, Citizens, and The Symbols Of War: From Classical Greece To Republican Rome, 500–167 B.C.* (Boulder, CO, 1997).

Sartre, M, *The Middle East under Rome* (London, 2005).

Scafuro, A (ed.), 'Studies on Roman Women Part 2', *Helios* 16 (1989).

Schaff, P, *Nicene and Post–Nicene Fathers: Series II, Volume VI, The Letters of St Jerome,* (2007) Letter 127.

Schaps, D, 'The Women of Greece in Wartime', *CP* 77 (1982), pp. 193–213.

Schatzmann, I, 'The Roman General's Authority over the Distribution of Booty', *Historia* 21 (1972), pp. 17–28.

Schiff, S, *Cleopatra–A Life* (London, 2010).

Schmitz, M, *Roman Conquests: The Danubian Provinces* (Barnsley, 2103).

Schulman, AR, 'Military Organisation in Pharaonic Egypt', in Sasson, *Civilisations of the Ancient Near East, Vol. 1* (New York, 1995), pp. 289–301.

———, 'The Battle Scenes of the Middle Kingdom', *Jnl of the Society for the Study of Egyptian Antiquities* 12 (1982), pp. 165–82.

Scott–Kilvert, I, (trans.) *Polybius: The Rise of the Roman Empire* (Harmondsworth, 1979).

Scullard, HH, *Roman Politics: 220–150 BC* (Westport, CT, 1981).

———, *The Elephant in the Greek and Roman World* (London, 1970).

———, *Scipio Africanus: Soldier and Politician* (London, 1970).

———, *The Etruscan Cities and Rome* (London, 1967).

———, 'Rome's Declaration of War on Carthage in 218 BC', *RhM* (1952), pp. 209ff.

———, *Scipio Africanus in the Second Punic War* (London, 1930).

Sealey, PR, *The Boudican Revolt Against Rome* (London, 1997).

Seevers, B, *Warfare in the Old Testament: The Organization, Weapons, and Tactics of Ancient Near Eastern Armies* (Grand Rapids, MI, 2013).

Sekunda, N, *Military Forces A: Land Forces* in Sabin, *The Cambridge History of Greek and Roman Warfare, Vol. 1* (Cambridge, 2007), pp. 325–56.

———, *The Spartan Army* (London, 1998).

———, *Early Roman Armies* (Oxford, 1995).

Serrati, J, *Warfare and the State* in Sabin, *The Cambridge History of Greek and Roman Warfare, Vol. 1* (Cambridge, 2007), pp. 461–97.

Setala, P, *Female Networks and the Public Sphere in Roman Society* (Rome, 1999).

Seward, D, *Jerusalem's Traitor: Josephus, Masada and the Fall of Judea* (Cambridge, 2009).

Shapiro, HA, 'Amazons, Thracians and Scythians', *GRBS* 24 (1983), pp. 105–114.

Shatzman, I, 'The Roman General's Authority Over Booty', *Historia* 21 (1972), pp. 177–205.

Shay, J, 'Learning About Combat Stress from Homer's *Iliad*', *Jnl of Traumatic Stress* 4 (1991), pp. 561–79.

Shaw, BD, (ed.) *Spartacus and the Slave Wars* (Boston, 2001).

Shaw, I, *Egyptian Warfare and Weapons* (Oxford, 1991).

Shean, JF, 'Hannibal's Mules: The Logistical Limitations of Hannibal's Army and the Battle of Cannae', *Historia* 45 (1996), pp. 159–87.

Sheldon, RM, *Rome's Wars in Parthia: Blood in the Sand* (London, 2010).

———, *Intelligence Activities in Ancient Rome: Trust in the Gods But Verify* (London, 2007).

———, *Ambush: Surprise Attack in Ancient Greek Warfare* (London, 2001).

Sheppard, SI, *The Jewish Revolt AD 66–74* (Oxford, 2013).

Sherk, RK, *Rome and the Greek East to the Death of Augustus* (Cambridge, 1984).

Sherwin–White, AN, *Roman Foreign Policy in the East, 168 BC– AD 1* (Oklahoma, 1983).

———, 'Ariobarzanes, Mithridates, and Sulla', *CQ* 27 (1977), pp. 173–83.

———, *The Roman Citizenship 2nd edition* (Oxford, 1973).

Shutt, RHJ, 'Polybius, A Sketch', *G&R* 22 (1938), pp. 50–57.

Sicker, M, *The Pre–Islamic Middle East* (London, 2000).

Sidebottom, H, 'International Relations', in Sabin, *The Cambridge History of Greek and Roman Warfare, Vol. 2* (2007), pp. 3–29.

———, *Ancient Warfare: A Very Short Introduction* (Oxford, 2004).

Sidnell, P, *Warhorse: Cavalry in Ancient Warfare* (London, 2006).

Siefert, R, 'Rape in Wars: Analytical Approaches', *Minerva – Quarterly Report on Women and the Military* 11 (1992), pp. 17–22.

Silva, L, *Viriathus and the Lusitanian Resistance to Rome 155–139 BC* (Barnsley, 2013).

Simms, DL, *Archimedes the Engineer* (London, 1995).

Sitwell, NHH, *Outside the Empire: The World the Romans Knew* (London, 1984).

Skeat, TC, 'The Last Days of Cleopatra: A Chronological Problem', *JRS* 43 (1984), pp. 98–100.

Skutsch, O, 'The Fall of the Capitol', *JRS* 45 (1953), pp. 77–78.

Smallwood, EM, *The Jews Under Roman Rule* (Leiden, 1976).

Smethurst, SE, 'Women in Livy's History', *G&R* 19 (1950), pp. 80–87.

Smith, CJ, 'Thinking About Kings', *BICS* 54 (2011), pp. 21–42.

———, *Early Rome and Latium: Economy and Society ca. 1000 to 500 BC* (Oxford, 1996).

Smith, F, *Service in the Post–Marian Roman Army* (Manchester, 1958).

Smith, W, *A Dictionary of Greek and Roman Biography and Mythology* (London, 2007).

Snodgrass, AD, 'The Hoplite Reform and History', *JHS* 85 (1965), pp. 110–22.

Sobol, D, *The Amazons of Greek Mythology* (Cranbury, NJ, 1973).

Sorek, S, *The Jews Against Rome* (New York, 2008).

Southern, P, *Antony and Cleopatra* (Stroud, 2011).

———, *Empress Zenobia: Palmyra's Rebel Queen* (London, 2009).

———, *Beyond the Eastern Frontiers: The Roman Empire from Severus to Constantine* (London, 2001).

———, *Mark Antony* (Stroud, 1998).

Spalinger, AJ, *War In Ancient Egypt* (Chichester, 2005).

Spaulding, OA, 'The Ancient Military Writers', *CJ* 28 (1933), pp. 657–69.

Speidel, MP, *Ancient Germanic Warriors* (London, 2004).

Spencer, D, *The Roman Alexander: Reading a Cultural Myth* (Exeter, 2002).

Stadter, PA, *Plutarch's Historical Methods: An Analysis of the* Mulierum Virtutes (Cambridge, MA, 1965).

Stallibrass, S, *Feeding The Roman Army: The Archaeology of Production and Supply in NW Europe* (Oxford, 2008).

Stark, F, *Rome on the Euphrates* (London, 1966).

Starr, CG, *The Influence of Sea Power on Ancient History* (Oxford, 1989).

———, *The Roman Imperial Navy 31 BC– AD 324* (Cambridge, 1960).

Steel, C, *The End of the Roman Republic 146 to 44 BC: Conquest and Crisis* (Edinburgh, 2013).

Stehle, E, 'Venus, Cybele and the Sabine Women: The Roman Construction of Female Sexuality' *Helios* 16 (1989), pp. 143–64.

Stephensen, IP, *Roman Cavalry Equipment* (Stroud, 2003).

Stocks, C, *The Roman Hannibal: Remembering the Enemy in Silius Italicus'* Punica (Liverpool, 2014).

Stoneman, R, *Palmyra and Its Empire: Zenobia's Revolt against Rome* (Ann Arbor, 1992).

Strauss, BS, *The Anatomy of Error: Ancient Military Disasters and their Lessons for Modern Strategists* (New York, 1990).

Strickland, JM, *Rome, Regal and Republican: A Family History of Rome* (1854).

Stronk, JP, *Ctesias' Persian History: Introduction, Text and Translation* (Dusseldorf, 2010).

Sumner, GV, 'The Legion and the Centuriate Organisation', *JRS* 60 (1970), pp. 61–79.

———, 'Roman Policy in Spain Before the Hannibalic War', *HSCPh* (1968).

Suolahti, J, *The Junior Officers of the Roman Army in the Republican Period* (Helsinki, 1955).

Swartley, WM, *Slavery, Sabbath, War and Women: Case Issues in Biblical Interpretation* (Harrisonburg, VA, 1983).

Swift, LJ, *The Early Fathers on War and Military Service* (Wilmington, 1982).

Syme, R, 'The Sons of Crassus', *Latomus* 39 (1980), pp. 403–408, reprinted in *Roman Papers*, Vol. 3, edited by Anthony R Birley (Oxford, 1984).

————, *Sallust* (Berkeley, 1964).

————, *Tacitus* (Oxford, 1958).

————, *The Roman Revolution* (Oxford, 1939).

Tarn, WW, 'The Fleets of the First Punic War', *JHS* 27 (1907), pp. 48–60.

————, *Octavian, Antony and Cleopatra* (Cambridge, 1965).

————, *The Greeks in Bactria and India*, 2nd edition (Cambridge, 1951).

————, '*Parthia*', *CAH* IX (1932), pp. 605–12.

Taylor, CCW, 'The Role of Women', in Kamtekar, *Plato's Republic in Virtue and Happiness* (2012).

Taylor, MJ, *Antiochus The Great* (Barnsley, 2013).

Thapliyal, UP, *Warfare in Ancient India* (New Delhi, 2010).

Theodorakopoulos, E, *Ancient Rome at the Cinema* (Exeter, 2010).

Thiel, JH, *A History of Roman Sea Power Before the Second Punic War* (Amsterdam, 1954).

————, *Studies on the History of Roman Sea Power in Republican Times* (Amsterdam, 1946).

Thomsen, R, *King Servius Tullius: A Historical Synthesis* (Copenhagen, 1980).

Tipps, GK, 'The Battle of Ecnomus', *Historia* 34 (1985), pp. 432–465.

Toner, J, *Roman Disasters* (London, 2013).

Toynbee, AJ, *Hannibal's Legacy* (London, 1965).

Travis, H, *Roman Body Armour* (Stroud, 2012).

Trow, MJ, *Spartacus: The Myth and the Man* (Stroud, 2006).

Turner, BA, *Military Defeats, Casualties of War and the Success of Rome* (London, 2011).

Turner, J, Pallas Armata: *Military Essayes of the Ancient Grecian, Roman, and Modern Art of War* (London, 1670–1671; New York, 2011 reprint).

Turney-High, H, *Primitive War: Its Practice and Concepts* (Columbia, SC, 1949).

Turton, G, *The Syrian Princesses: The Women Who Ruled Rome AD 193–235* (London, 1974).

Tyldesley, J, *Hatchepsut: The Female Pharaoh* (New York, 1996).

Tyrrell, WB, *Amazons: A Study in Athenian Myth–Making* (Baltimore, 1984).

Urbainczyk, T. (2008) *Slave Revolts in Antiquity* (London)

————, *Spartacus* (Bristol, 2004).

Ullman, BL, 'Cleopatra's Pearls' *CJ* 52 (1957), pp. 193–201.

Usher, SF, 'Polybius and the Rise of Rome', *History Today* 13 (1957), pp. 267–74.

Van Berchem, D, *The Martyrdom of the Theban Legion* (Basel, 1956).

Van Creveld, M, *Men, Women and War: Do Women Belong on the Front Line?* (London, 2001).

Van Wees, H, 'Warfare and Society', in P Sabin (ed.), *The Cambridge History of Greek and Roman Warfare* (Cambridge, 2005).

———, 'Heroes, Knights and Nutters: Warrior Mentality in Homer', in Lloyd (ed.), *Battle in Antiquity* (Swansea, 1997), pp. 1–86.

Vaughan, AC, *Zenobia of Palmyra* (New York, 1967).

Versnel, HS, 'Two Types of Roman *devotio*', *Mnemosyne* 29 (1976), pp. 365–410.

———, *Triumphus* (Leiden, 1970).

Vikman, E, 'Ancient Origins: Sexual Violence in Warfare, Part I', *Anthropology & Medicine* 12(1) (2005), pp. 21–31.

Virlouvet, C, 'Fulvia the Woman of Passion', in Fraschetti, *Roman Women* (1993), pp. 66–81.

Vivante, B, *Daughters of Gaia: Women in the Ancient Mediterranean World* (Westport, CT, 2006).

Volkmann, H, *Cleopatra: A Study in Politics and Propaganda* (London, 1958).

Von Fritz, K, *The Theory of the Mixed Constitution in Antiquity: A Critical Analysis of Polybius's Political Ideas* (New York, 1954).

Waite, J, *Boudicca's Last Stand* (Stroud, 2007).

Walbank, FW, *A Historical Commentary on Polybius, Vol. 3* (Oxford, 1979).

———, 'Political Morality and the Friends of Scipio', *JRS* 55 (1965), p. 1ff.

———, 'Some Reflections on Hannibal's Pass', *JRS* 46 (1956), pp. 37–45.

———, *Philip V of Macedon* (Cambridge, 1940).

Walcot, P, 'On Widows and their Reputation in Antiquity', *SO* 66 (1991), pp. 5–26.

———, 'Herodotus on Rape', *Arethusa* 11 (1978), pp. 137–147.

Wallace, RW (ed.), *Transitions to Empire* (Norman, OK, 1996).

———, 'Hellenization and Roman Society in the Late 4th Century BC', in W Eder (ed.), *Staat und Staatlichkeit* (1990), pp. 278–92.

Wallbank, FW, *A Historical Commentary on Polybius* (Oxford, 1979).

Wallinga, HT, *The Boarding–bridge of the Romans* (Groningen, 1956).

Walsh, PG, *Livy* (Oxford, 1974).

———, 'Masinissa', *JRS* 55 (1965), p. 149ff.

———, *Livy: His Historical Aims and Methods* (Cambridge, 1961).

Walters, J, 'Soldiers and Whores in Pseudo–Quintilian Declamation', in Cornell, *Gender* (1997), pp. 109–14.

Ward, AM, *Marcus Crassus and the Late Roman Republic* (Missouri, 1977).

Warde Fowler, W, 'Passing Under the Yoke', *Classical Review* 27 (1913), pp. 48–51.

Warmington, EH, 'The Destruction of Carthage, A *Retratatio*', *CP* 83 (1988), pp. 308–10.

———, *Carthage* (New York, 1960).

——— (ed.), *Remains of Old Latin, 4 Vols.* (Cambridge, MA, 1940).

Warner, R (trans.), *Fall of the Roman Republic: Six Lives by Plutarch* (London, 1972).

———, *Athens at War* (London, 1970).

Warrior, VM, *The Initiation of the Second Macedonian War: An Explication of Livy, Book 31* (Stuttgart, 1996).

Warry, J, *Warfare in the Classical World* (London, 1980).

Wasinski, VM, *Women, War and Rape: The Hidden Casualties of Conflict*, dissertation, University of Leeds (Leeds, 2004).

Watson, GR, *The Roman Soldier* (London, 1969).

———, 'The Pay of the Roman Army: The Republic', *Historia* 7 (1958), pp. 113–20.

Watts, D, *Boudicca's Heirs: Women in Early Britain* (London, 2008).

Webster, G, *Boudica: The British Revolt against Rome, AD 60* (London, 1978).

Weiden Boyd, B, 'Virgil's Camilla and the Traditions of Catalogue and Ecphrasis', *AJPh* 113 (1992), pp. 213–34.

Weigall, A, *The Life and Times of Cleopatra Queen of Egypt* (London, 1914).

———, *The Life and Times of Marc Antony* (New York, 1931).

Weir, AJ, *A Study of Fulvia*, dissertation, Queen's University (Kingston, ON, 2007).

Welch, KE (ed.), *Julius Caesar as Artful Reporter* (Swansea, 1998).

———, 'Caesar and His Officers in the Gallic War Commentaries', in Welch, *Julius Caesar as Artful Reporter* (London, 1998), pp. 85–110.

Welch, T, 'Perspectives On and Of Livy's Tarpeia', *Journal on Gender Studies in Antiquity* 2 (2012).

Wellesley, K, 'Propertius' Tarpeia Poem (IV, 4)', *Acta Classica* (1969), pp. 93–103.

———, 'Tacitus as a Military Historian', in Dorey, *Tacitus* (1969), pp. 63–97.

Wells, CM, 'The Daughters of the Regiment: Sisters and Wives in the Roman Army', in Groenman-van Waateringe, *Roman Frontier Studies* 1995 (1997), pp. 571–4.

———, *The German Policy of Augustus* (Oxford, 1972).

Wells, P, *The Battle that Stopped Rome* (New York, 2004).

Wendorf, F, 'Site 117: A Nubian Final Paleolithic Graveyard near Jebel Sahaba, Sudan', in Wendorf, *The Prehistory of Nubia* (Dallas, 1968), pp. 954–87.

———, (ed.), *The Prehistory of Nubia* (Dallas, 1968).

West, GS, 'Chloreus and Camilla', *Vergilius* 31 (1985), pp. 23–25.

———, *Women in Virgil's Aeneid*, dissertation, University of California, Los Angeles (Los Angeles, CA, 1975).

Wheeler, EL, *Strategem and the Vocabulary of Military Trickery* (Leiden, 1998).

Wheelwright, J, *Amazons and Military Maids* (London, 1989).

Whitehead, D, *Aineias Tacticus: How to Survive Under Siege, 2nd edition* (Bristol, 2002).

Wicker, KO, 'Mulierum Virtutes', in HD Betz, *Plutarch's Ethical Writings and Early Christian Literature*, (Leiden, 1978), pp. 106–34.

Wiedemann, TEJ, 'Single Combat and Being Roman', *Anc Soc* 27 (1992), pp. 91–103.

————, 'Thucydides, Women and the Limits of Rational Analysis' (1983), in McAuslan, *Women in Antiquity* (Oxford, 1996), pp. 83–90.

Wilhelm, H, 'Venus, Diana, Dido and Camilla in the *Aeneid*', *Vergilius* 33 (1987), pp. 225–6.

Wilkes, JJ, *The Illyrians* (Chichester, 1992).

Williams, D, *Romans and Barbarians* (London, 1998).

————, *The Reach of Rome: A History of the Roman Imperial Frontier, 1st–5th Centuries AD* (London, 1996).

Winkler, MM, *Spartacus: Film and History* (Oxford, 2007).

Winsbury, R, *Zenobia of Palmyra: History, Myth and the Neo–Classical Imagination* (London, 2010).

Wise, T, *Hannibal's War with Rome: The Armies and Campaigns 216 BC* (Oxford, 1999).

Wiseman, TP, 'Roman Republic, Year One', *G&R* 45 (1998), pp. 19–26.

————, 'Lying Historians – Seven Types of Mendacity', in Gill, *Lies and Fiction in the Ancient World* (1993).

————, *The Credibility of the Roman Annalists in Roman Studies: Literary and Historical* (Liverpool, 1987), pp. 293–6.

————, 'The Wife and Children of Romulus', *CQ* 33 (1983), pp. 445–52.

Wistrand, E, *The So–called* Laudatio Turiae (Goteborg, 1976).

Witt, RE, *Isis in the Graeco–Roman World* (London, 1971).

Wolfram, H, *The Roman Empire and Its Germanic Peoples* (Berkeley, CA, 1997).

————, *History of the Goths* (trans. Thomas J Dunlap), (Berkeley, CA, 1988).

Woodhead, AG, *The Greeks in the West* (1962).

Woodman, AJ, *Poetry and Politics in the Age of Augustus* (Cambridge, 1984).

Woods, D, 'The Origin of the Legend of Maurice and the Theban Legion', *Journal of Ecclesiastical History* 45 (1994), pp. 385–95.

Woods, M, *Ancient Warfare: From Clubs to Catapults* (Minneapolis, 2001).

Woolley, CL, *Ur of the Chaldees*, revised edition (Ithaca, NY, 1982).

Woolliscroft, D, *Roman Military Signalling* (Barnsley, 2001).

Wyke, M, '*Meretrix Regina*: Augustan Cleopatras', in Edmondson, *Augustus* (2009), pp. 334–80.

————, 'Augustan Cleopatras: Female Power and Poetic Authority', in Powell, *Roman Poetry and Propaganda in the Age of Augustus* (1992), pp. 98–104.

———— (ed.), *Parchments of Gender: Deciphering the Bodies of Antiquity* (Oxford, 1988).

Yadin, Y, *The Art of Warfare in Biblical Lands* (Jerusalem, 1963).

Young CK, 'Archimedes's Iron Hand or Claw – A New Interpretation of an Old Mystery', *Centaurus* 46 (2004), pp. 189–207.

Zahran, Y, *Zenobia: Queen of the Desert*, 2nd edition (London, 2013).

Zetzel, JEG, 'Cicero and the Scipionic Circle', *HSCPh* 76 (1972), pp. 173–9.

Zhomodikov, A, 'Roman Republican Heavy Infantrymen in Battle', *Historia* 49 (2000).

Ziegler, K, 'Tomyris', *RE* vi, A2 (1937), pp. 1702–4.

Ziolkowski, A, '*Urbs Direpta* or How the Romans Sacked Cities', in J Rich, *War and Society in the Ancient World* (London, 1993), pp. 69–91.

———, *Credibility of Numbers of Battle Captives in Livy, Books XXI–XXV* La Parola del Passato 45 (1990), pp. 15–36.

Websites

www.perseus.org – A fathomless source of Greek and Latin texts

www.romanarmy.net – The website of the *Roman Military Research Society*

www.roman-empire.net/army/army/html

www.vindolanda.com

www@oxbowbooks.com – Booksellers/publishers specializing in classics and archaeology

www.jrmes.org.uk – Website of the *Journal of Roman Medical Equipment Studies*

www.hellenicbookservice.com

www.classicsbookshop.co.uk

www.fisher.library.utoronto.ca – Has some superb classical prints

www.jact.org – Joint Association of Classical Teachers, publishers of *Omnibus*

www.friends-classics.demon.co.uk – Publishers of *Ad Familiares*

www.yayas.org –Yorkshire Architectural and York Archaeological Society

www.scholar.lib.vt.edu/stats/ejournals/ElAnt-current.html – Website for Virginia Tech's *Electronic Antiquity*

www.womenforwomen.org.uk – Helping women survivors of war rebuild their lives

www.smithsonianmag.com/history/the-ambush-that-changed-history-72636736/yZ15hBJVWmdABgIZ.99 – Teutoburg Forest

www.bibleplaces.com

www.schillerinstitute.org

Index of Battles, Sieges and Wars

General Index